Windows NT® Scripting
Administrator's Guide

Windows NT® Scripting Administrator's Guide

William R. Stanek

M&T Books
An imprint of IDG Books Worldwide, Inc.
An International Data Group Company
Foster City, CA ◆ Chicago, IL ◆ Indianapolis, IN ◆ New York, NY

M&T BOOKS™

Windows NT® Scripting Administrator's Guide

Published by
M&T Books
An imprint of IDG Books Worldwide, Inc.
919 E. Hillsdale Blvd., Suite 400
Foster City, CA 94404
www.idgbooks.com (IDG Books Worldwide Web site)

Library of Congress Catalog Card No.: 99-66369

ISBN: 0-7645-3309-6

Printed in the United States of America

10 9 8 7 6 5 4 3 2 1

1B/QX/RQ/ZZ/FC

Distributed in the United States by IDG Books Worldwide, Inc.

Distributed by CDG Books Canada Inc. for Canada; by Transworld Publishers Limited in the United Kingdom; by IDG Norge Books for Norway; by IDG Sweden Books for Sweden; by IDG Books Australia Publishing Corporation Pty. Ltd. for Australia and New Zealand; by TransQuest Publishers Pte Ltd. for Singapore, Malaysia, Thailand, Indonesia, and Hong Kong; by Gotop Information Inc. for Taiwan; by ICG Muse, Inc. for Japan; by Norma Comunicaciones S.A. for Colombia; by Intersoft for South Africa; by Eyrolles for France; by International Thomson Publishing for Germany, Austria and Switzerland; by Distribuidora Cuspide for Argentina; by Livraria Cultura for Brazil; by Ediciones ZETA S.C.R. Ltda. for Peru; by WS Computer Publishing Corporation, Inc., for the Philippines; by Contemporanea de Ediciones for Venezuela; by Express Computer Distributors for the Caribbean and West Indies; by Micronesia Media Distributor, Inc. for Micronesia; by Grupo Editorial Norma S.A. for Guatemala; by Chips Computadoras S.A. de C.V. for Mexico; by Editorial Norma de Panama S.A. for Panama; by American Bookshops for Finland. Authorized Sales Agent: Anthony Rudkin Associates for the Middle East and North Africa.

For general information on IDG Books Worldwide's books in the U.S., please call our Consumer Customer Service department at 800-762-2974. For reseller information, including discounts and premium sales, please call our Reseller Customer Service department at 800-434-3422.

For information on where to purchase IDG Books Worldwide's books outside the U.S., please contact our International Sales department at 317-596-5530 or fax 317-596-5692.

For consumer information on foreign language translations, please contact our Customer Service department at 800-434-3422, fax 317-596-5692, or e-mail rights@idgbooks.com.

For information on licensing foreign or domestic rights, please phone +1-650-655-3109.

For sales inquiries and special prices for bulk quantities, please contact our Sales department at 650 655 3200 or write to the address above.

For information on using IDG Books Worldwide's books in the classroom or for ordering examination copies, please contact our Educational Sales department at 800-434-2086 or fax 317-596-5499.

For press review copies, author interviews, or other publicity information, please contact our Public Relations department at 650-655-3000 or fax 650-655-3299.

For authorization to photocopy items for corporate, personal, or educational use, please contact Copyright Clearance Center, 222 Rosewood Drive, Danvers, MA 01923, or fax 978-750-4470.

 is a registered trademark or trademark under exclusive license to IDG Books Worldwide, Inc. from International Data Group, Inc. in the United States and/or other countries.

 is a trademark of IDG Books Worldwide, Inc.

ABOUT IDG BOOKS WORLDWIDE

Welcome to the world of IDG Books Worldwide.

IDG Books Worldwide, Inc., is a subsidiary of International Data Group, the world's largest publisher of computer-related information and the leading global provider of information services on information technology. IDG was founded more than 30 years ago by Patrick J. McGovern and now employs more than 9,000 people worldwide. IDG publishes more than 290 computer publications in over 75 countries. More than 90 million people read one or more IDG publications each month.

Launched in 1990, IDG Books Worldwide is today the #1 publisher of best-selling computer books in the United States. We are proud to have received eight awards from the Computer Press Association in recognition of editorial excellence and three from Computer Currents' First Annual Readers' Choice Awards. Our best-selling ...*For Dummies*® series has more than 50 million copies in print with translations in 31 languages. IDG Books Worldwide, through a joint venture with IDG's Hi-Tech Beijing, became the first U.S. publisher to publish a computer book in the People's Republic of China. In record time, IDG Books Worldwide has become the first choice for millions of readers around the world who want to learn how to better manage their businesses.

Our mission is simple: Every one of our books is designed to bring extra value and skill-building instructions to the reader. Our books are written by experts who understand and care about our readers. The knowledge base of our editorial staff comes from years of experience in publishing, education, and journalism — experience we use to produce books to carry us into the new millennium. In short, we care about books, so we attract the best people. We devote special attention to details such as audience, interior design, use of icons, and illustrations. And because we use an efficient process of authoring, editing, and desktop publishing our books electronically, we can spend more time ensuring superior content and less time on the technicalities of making books.

You can count on our commitment to deliver high-quality books at competitive prices on topics you want to read about. At IDG Books Worldwide, we continue in the IDG tradition of delivering quality for more than 30 years. You'll find no better book on a subject than one from IDG Books Worldwide.

John Kilcullen
Chairman and CEO
IDG Books Worldwide, Inc.

Steven Berkowitz
President and Publisher
IDG Books Worldwide, Inc.

Eighth Annual
Computer Press
Awards ≥1992

Ninth Annual
Computer Press
Awards ≥1993

Tenth Annual
Computer Press
Awards ≥1994

Eleventh Annual
Computer Press
Awards ≥1995

Credits

ACQUISITIONS EDITOR
John Osborn

DEVELOPMENT EDITOR
Matt Lusher

TECHNICAL EDITOR
Don Murdoch

COPY EDITORS
Nicole LeClerc
Mildred Sanchez

PROJECT COORDINATORS
Linda Marousek
Tom Debolski

QUALITY CONTROL SPECIALIST
Chris Weisbart

GRAPHICS & PRODUCTION
SPECIALISTS
Mario Amador
Stephanie Hollier
Jude Levinson
Dina Quan
Ramses Ramirez

BOOK DESIGNER
Jim Donohue

COVER DESIGNER
Larry Wilson

ILLUSTRATOR
Heather Hudson

PROOFREADING AND INDEXING
York Production Services

About the Author

William R. Stanek (winscripting@tvpress.com) has a Master of Science degree in information systems and over 15 years of hands-on experience with advanced programming and development. He is a leading network technology expert and an award-winning author. Over the years, his practical advice has helped programmers, developers, and network engineers all over the world. He is also a regular contributor to leading publications like *PC Magazine*, where you'll often find his work in the "Solutions" section. He has written, co-authored, or contributed to over 20 computer books.

William has been involved in the commercial Internet community since 1991 and has been working with Windows NT since 1992. His core networking experience comes from over 11 years of military service. In 1995, he started his own consulting company, which specializes in developing medium and large-scale Web sites. William is proud to have served in the Persian Gulf War, where he was awarded the Air Force Distinguished Flying Cross. Currently, he resides in the Pacific Northwest with his wife and four children.

Preface

Thanks for picking up *Windows NT Scripting Administrator's Guide!* I'm proud of this book and I am sure it will introduce you to aspects of Windows scripting you aren't aware of, or at least give you insights into aspects of Windows scripting about which you know little.

This preface aims to clarify any cloudiness you may experience regarding whether this book is designed for you and whether it will help you solve the problems you need to solve. It also clarifies some terminology, a typographical convention or two, and it shows you what software you may need to work with this book.

Who Should Read This Book

Every book needs an audience, and you—perhaps standing in a bookstore wondering whether you should buy this book—need to know if you are someone who would benefit by reading *Windows NT Scripting Administrator's Guide*. To paraphrase the old Windows 95 installation wizard, "Everything you do will be more fun" after you read this book. Honest.

Okay, maybe not everything. But if you're like me, your trusty author, you derive happiness from having things run *right*. You know what *right* means, and you want things to run that way. It's generally possible, at least in theory, to make a computer behave in accordance with your specific vision. That's probably a big part of the reason you work with computers, rather than teach kindergarten or sell automobiles. If you take realization of vision as a measure of happiness, and you have a picture in your mind of something you want Windows to do, reading and learning from this book may well make you happier.

Windows NT Scripting Administrator's Guide appeals to administrators of Windows computers and the networks they run. But administrators are not meant to be the extent of this book's audience. The odds are very good you will like this book and benefit from the knowledge it contains if you fill one or more of these roles:

- ◆ System Administrator—System administrators who maintain Windows systems and networks for a living are those who put the operating system through its most intense paces. It stands to reason that system administrators would be among the first to realize the power of the various scripting resources that relate to Windows scripting and want to learn how to use them. *Windows NT Scripting Administrator's Guide*'s promise of ready-made solutions to problems and its in-depth explanation of the various Windows scripting techniques make the book a definite fit for system administrators.

◆ Power User – The difference between a system administrator and a power user is a paycheck. System administrators and corporate information-systems people get paid for looking after machines. Power users do many of the same things, but usually on a smaller scale and usually without getting paid for it. Like system administrators, power users often focus on getting the most utility out of their computing resources, while spending the least amount of time, money, and effort. If this is you, you'll definitely find this book useful.

◆ Curious Person Who Wants to Learn More – If you don't explicitly fall into one of the preceding two categories and you're still reading, chances are you fall into the third category of people who will like *Windows NT Scripting Administrator's Guide* – the generically curious. This book attempts to use an illustrative, hands-on approach wherever possible, which helps reveal details about the workings of Windows scripts.

What You'll Learn from This Book

Every how-to book is supposed to teach its reader how to do something, and in the process convey some body of knowledge to the reader. *Windows NT Scripting Administrator's Guide* is no exception. This book teaches you about Windows scripting and includes in-depth coverage of both command shell scripts and scripts for the Windows Script Host.

Windows NT Scripting Administrator's Guide isn't meant to be a do-everything guide to Windows scripting. Rather the book focuses on core issues and the essential details you'll want to know. Chapter by chapter you learn how to create shell scripts and scripts for the Windows Script Host. The detailed explanations provided are backed by hundreds of hands-on examples and nearly 200 complete source code listings. The book also develops extensive utility libraries that you can use to quickly and efficiently perform complex tasks.

Icons and Formatting

As you peruse these pages, you'll see that not all the text looks alike. Some text is highlighted by special icons; other text has unusual typographical characteristics. Here's a field guide to the things you'll see.

TIP

Tips inform you of little factoids that may be useful to you as you work with Windows scripting. Usually, Tip material isn't essential to getting things to work right. Rather, Tip material can be used to make things run better.

Tips look like this.

NOTE

The material contained in Notes usually is more critical than that contained in Tips. Notes say, "Note this — or you'll be sorry!" Notes often contain information about procedures you must follow or conditions that must be in place in order to get something to work properly.

Notes look like this.

CAUTION

Cautions provide a specific warning about things you should watch out for or things you shouldn't do. Be sure to pay particular attention to cautions when reading the text.

Cautions look like this.

CODE FORMAT

It's possible for code-formatted text to appear embedded in other text, as in, "The WScript.Echo method serves to write text to output when you're working with Windows scripts." It's also possible for code-formatted text to appear on separate lines, as in this example:

```
WScript.Echo "Hello World!!!"
```

Program listings are many such lines strung together. Further, it's important to note that this book uses that style for text output (to the console window) of programs, as well as for code listings and commands to be input.

ITALICS

Text formatted in *italics* means one of two things.

If the italicized text looks like normal body text, the italicization serves to call attention to a new term or some other aspect of language. For example, you might (but won't) see a sentence that says, "People who eat a double cheeseburger and a diet soda for lunch are called *numbskulls*."

If the italicized text is also in code format, the italicized text is a placeholder that should be replaced with situation-specific values. For example, in

```
copy origin destination
```

the words `origin` and `destination` stand in for path and file values. When you actually enter the command you would replace these values, such as

```
copy c:\cantaloupe\*.* n:\fruits
```

Support and Comments

Windows NT Scripting Administrator's Guide is a work in progress, just like the Windows operating system itself and the body of work that's grown up around it. It's quite likely that errors will make themselves apparent after this book has gone to press and found its way onto your desktop. I very much appreciate the efforts of readers who go through the trouble of pointing out mistakes in the text so I can fix them in future editions. Even more, I am grateful for readers who offer their own hints, tricks, code, and ideas to me for inclusion in future editions of this book.

I truly hope you find that *Windows NT Scripting Administrator's Guide* provides everything you need to perform essential scripting tasks. I'm supporting this book by e-mail and with a portion of my Web site, www.tvpress.com. Here are the details:

- ◆ E-mail – Through e-mail, you can contact me at `winscripting@tvpress.com` or `director.net@worldnet.att.net`. You're always welcome to write me with ideas, suggestions, improvements, or questions. If you provide an example that's used in a future edition of this book, I'll be especially grateful for your help and will credit you in that edition.

- ◆ Web Site – I also have a Web site, which contains support material for this book, among other things. Point your browser to `http://www.tvpress.com/winscripting/` for corrections, enhancements, news, and additional thoughts. I'll post the illustrative code from this book on the site, too.

Thank you.

Acknowledgments

Windows NT Scripting Administrator's Guide is one of the most challenging books I've written. Covering all the nitty-gritty details of the Windows command shell and Windows Script Host meant meticulous research, endless testing, and lots of programming. But I think you'll agree that the results are worth the effort. The book contains nearly 200 code examples and dozens of working scripts all designed to provide a top-notch tutorial and reference.

Yet this book wouldn't have been possible without a lot of help from others and especially the team at IDG Books. I owe a huge thank you to John Osborn, who took the book through acquisitions, and Matt Lusher, who did the development work on the book. Both are great to work with and great editors are a rare find.

I'd also like to thank Don Murdoch for the solid technical review of the book. The task of copy editing went to Nicole LeClerc and Mildred Sanchez. Together with others on the editorial staff, they did a bang-up job!

Thanks also to Studio B literary agency and my agents, David Rogelberg and Neil Salkind. Neil has a terrific knack for helping me find projects that are both fun and challenging.

Hopefully, I haven't forgotten anyone, but if I have, it was an oversight. *Honest.* ;-)

Contents at a Glance

Contents

Part I

Getting Started

CHAPTER 1
Introducing Scripting for Windows

Chapter 1

Introducing Scripting for Windows

IN THIS CHAPTER

◆ Why you should use scripting

◆ What scripts are and what they can do for you

◆ Two types of scripting: shell scripts and the Windows Script Host

◆ Shell scripting versus the Windows Script Host

WINDOWS NT SCRIPTING IS changing the face of system and network administration forever by giving everyday users and administrators the ability to automate repetitive tasks, complete activities while away from the computer, find resources that they may have misplaced, and perform many other time-saving activities. NT scripting accomplishes all of this by enabling you to create tools to automate tasks that would otherwise be handled manually, such as creating user accounts, searching files and retrieving data, or examining system information. By eliminating manual processes, you can double, triple, or even quadruple your productivity and become more effective and efficient at your job. Best of all, scripts are easy to create and you can rapidly develop prototypes of applications, procedures, and utilities, and then enhance these prototypes to provide exactly what you need or just throw them away and begin again. This ease of use gives you the flexibility to create the kinds of tools you need without a lot of fuss.

No Unix Shell Prompt Here

Often when people think of Windows scripting, they think of Unix shell scripting with the Bourne, Korn, or C shell, and indeed, there are similarities between Windows scripting and Unix scripting. Both scripting environments provide custom shells for working with scripts, both scripting environments are handled primarily through the command –line, and so on. Because of these similarities, you'll have a definite advantage if you are familiar with Unix scripting. However, Windows scripting isn't Unix scripting. It is friendlier and in many ways more powerful than its Unix counterpart – and that's why I say there's definitely no Unix shell prompt here. To see the true power of Windows scripting, let's take a brief look at what you can and can't do with the technology.

What Can You Do with Scripting?

In a world dominated by graphical user interfaces with whiz-bang point and click, you may wonder what scripting has to offer that the GUI world doesn't. The honest truth is much more than you'd imagine, especially considering that most people think of Windows scripts as glorified batch files – you know, the kind you used in MS-DOS. Well, although Windows scripts can use batch files, the scripting environment has changed considerably in Windows NT 4.0 and now includes the following:

◆ An extensible command shell environment that I'll refer to as the Windows shell or the command shell

◆ An extensible script host environment that I'll refer to as the Windows Script Host or the script host

With recent extensions, the command shell has become a full programming language. It has

◆ Variables

◆ Control flow (FOR, GOTO)

◆ Procedures

◆ Conditional statements (IF-ELSE)

◆ Basic math operations

◆ Customizable user environment

The command shell provides the tools you need to perform many tasks, especially tasks that you would normally have to type in at the keyboard. Using the command shell, you have complete access to the command line and your scripts can call any utilities that have command-line extensions. You can use

◆ AT to schedule tasks

◆ FIND to search text files

◆ KILL to stop running processes

◆ NET START and NET STOP to manage NT services

◆ NET USER to create and manage user accounts

◆ NET GROUP to create and manage group accounts

- ◆ NTBACKUP to automate backups

- ◆ And lots more!

The command shell is only one part of the scripting environment. You'll also find the Windows Script Host, a language-independent host that provides interfaces for scripting engines on 32-bit Windows systems. A *scripting engine* is an application that provides the core language functionality needed to create scripts. Microsoft provides scripting engines for VBScript and JScript — two of the most powerful scripting languages available today. Scripting engines for other languages, such as Perl and Python, are also available.

VBScript is modeled after Visual Basic and features

- ◆ Good error-handling procedures

- ◆ Powerful array-handling capabilities and multidimensional arrays

- ◆ Extensive control flow statements (`Do...Loop`, `For...Next`, `For Each...Next`, `If...Then...Else`, `Select Case`, `While...Wend`, and `With`)

- ◆ Functions, expressions, and procedures

- ◆ Good support for mathematical functions (`Atn`, `Cos`, `Sin`, `Tan`, `Exp`, `Log`, `Sqr`, `Randomize`, and `Rnd`)

- ◆ Extensive sets of ready-to-use objects with methods, properties, and events

- ◆ Routines for manipulating strings and handling regular expressions

JScript is loosely related to the Java programming language and is standards-based. The key features of JScript include

- ◆ Strong exception-handling capabilities with `try/catch`

- ◆ Good support for arrays with access to multidimensional arrays through VBScript

- ◆ Extensive control flow statements (`break`, `continue`, `for`, `for...in`, `if...else`, `return`, and `while`)

◆ Functions, procedures, and global methods

◆ Strong support for mathematical functions (`abs`, `acos`, `asin`, `atan`, `atan2`, `ceil`, `cos`, `exp`, `floor`, `log`, `max`, `min`, `pow`, `random`, `round`, `sin`, `sqrt`, and `tan`)

◆ Extensive sets of ready-to-use objects with methods, properties, and events

◆ Routines for manipulating strings and handling regular expressions

Although VBScript and JScript are normally used to create Web pages and manage Web-based applications, their environments have been extended specifically to handle workstation and server tasks. As a result, you don't have to embed the scripts in a Web page to use them, and you don't have to know anything about Web technologies, either. With the Windows Script Host, you execute scripts directly on the Windows desktop or at the Command prompt.

The core functionality of VBScript and JScript has been extended considerably for the script host. This new functionality enables you to

◆ Manage local and remote file systems and drives

◆ Work with files and directories

◆ Search files and manipulate text

◆ Create shortcuts

◆ Manage network accounts and resources

◆ Modify and maintain the registry

◆ Interact with applications, such as Microsoft Word and Excel

◆ Connect to and query databases

◆ And lots more!

Why Use Scripting

You've heard the claims about scripting and now you're thinking, so what? What's in it for me? You may be an administrator rather than a programmer/systems developer. Or maybe you're a power user who helps other users from time to time. Either way, scripting has to prove useful to your situation and needs. So in answer to the question "What's in it for me?" consider the following:

◆ Would you like to be a top performer and receive the praise you deserve? Windows scripting enables you to accomplish in hours or days what would otherwise take weeks or months with traditional techniques. You'll be more successful and more productive at work.

◆ Would you like to be able to analyze trends and be proactive rather than reactive? You can use Windows scripting to extract and manipulate huge quantities of information and turn out easy-to-use reports.

◆ Would you like to be able to seize opportunities before they disappear? Windows scripting enables you to take advantage of opportunities and be more effective. You can solve problems quickly and efficiently.

◆ Would you like to have more free time? Windows scripting frees you from mundane and repetitive tasks, enabling you to focus on more interesting and challenging tasks.

◆ Would you like to be able to integrate activities and applications? Windows scripting enables you to integrate information from existing systems and applications, allowing you to kick off a series of tasks simply by starting a script.

◆ Would you like to have fun at work? Windows scripting can be fun, challenging, and rewarding. Give it a try and you'll see!

If Windows scripting can do so much, it must be terribly complex. Right? On the contrary, it is simplicity that enables you to do so much – not complexity. Most Windows scripts are only a few lines long and you can create them in five minutes or less!

Introducing Shell Scripting

Now that you know a bit about what you can do with scripting and why you should use scripting, let's take a closer look at the command shell. The command shell is built into Windows NT and accessed through the console window. You use the command shell to create shell scripts.

To help differentiate between scripts created for the shell and scripts created for the Windows Script Host, I refer to shell scripts and Windows scripts. *Shell scripts* are scripts written for the Windows command shell. *Windows scripts* are scripts written for the Windows Script Host. In later chapters that apply specifically to one technology or the other, I'll just use *scripts* for simplicity's sake unless it's necessary to differentiate the technologies.

What Is a Shell Script?

Shell scripts are text files containing a series of commands. These are the same commands you'd normally type into a console window. However, rather than type in the commands manually each time you want to use them, you create a script to store the commands for easy execution. Once you create a script, you can execute it as if it were a program – simply double-click the script file in Windows Explorer or type the name of the script in a command prompt window.

When you execute a script, the commands in the script are executed. In the early days of shell scripting, these commands were executed one by one in a batch, which is why shell scripts were called batch files. Today, shell scripting is much more powerful, and scripts can contain procedures, conditional statements with if else, and even for loops that control execution within the script.

The easiest way to create a shell script is to use Notepad, the standard text editor in Windows. After all, shell scripts are written as standard ASCII text. When you are entering commands into the script, be sure to enter each command on a new line. This ensures proper execution of the command. When you are finished creating a shell script, save it using the .BAT extension. Yes, that's right, shell scripts still use .BAT for batch, which has its roots in the days of MS-DOS. As an alternative to .BAT, you can use the .CMD extension. Both extensions work with shell scripts in the same way.

Using the Console

Scripts often need to display output to users. The standard interface is the console window, which emulates a standard computer terminal. The most commonly used console is the command shell. Start the command shell using the Run command (click Start→Run) and then enter **cmd** in the Open field. Or, you can click Start→Programs→Command Prompt, which accesses a shortcut to the command shell.

The command shell is a 32-bit environment for working with the command line and scripts. You'll find the executable (cmd.exe) in the %SystemRoot% \System32 directory. Other windows consoles are available on NT, such as the 16-bit MS-DOS shell (command.com). When you execute commands in the MS-DOS shell, these commands are actually passed through to the command shell where they are executed. Because of this, I won't delve into the MS-DOS shell and will instead focus on the command shell. You'll use the command shell for all your scripting needs.

%SystemRoot% is an environment variable that points to the directory where you installed the operating system, such as C:\WinNT. You'll learn all about environment variables in Chapter 4.

Figure 1-1 shows a command shell. By default, the console displays 25 lines of text and is 80 characters wide. When text is displayed in the console or you enter commands, the current text is displayed in the window and prior text is scrolled up. If you want to pause the display temporarily when a script or command you've executed is writing output, press Ctrl+S. To resume execution, press Ctrl+S again.

Figure 1-1: Console windows are the standard output device for scripts.

The properties of the command shell are completely customizable. You can add buffers so that text scrolled out of the viewing area is accessible. You can resize the command shell, change its fonts, and more. I definitely recommend that you update the shell settings before you start creating scripts. To do this, click the MS-DOS icon at the top of the console window or right-click the console's display bar (where it says "Winnt\System32\cmd.exe"), and then select Properties to open the dialog box shown in Figure 1-2.

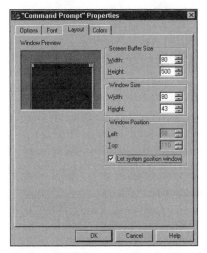

Figure 1-2: Optimize property settings for the command shell before you get started.

Click the Layout tab to set the buffer size, the window size, and the window position as follows:

◆ Size the buffer height so that you can easily scroll back through previous listings and script output. A good setting is 200 lines.

◆ Size the window height so that you can view more of the console window at one time. A good setting is 35 lines on 640×480 screens or 45 lines on 800×600 screens.

◆ Set the default window position (if desired). To do this, deselect Let system position window and then select a position for the upper-left corner of the console using Left and Top.

When you are finished updating the command shell properties, click OK. Windows NT displays a prompt asking you to specify how the settings should be applied. Either apply the changes to the current window only or save the changes for future use, which applies to all consoles you access later. You may also see an option to modify the shortcut that started the console. In this case, any time you start the console using the applicable shortcut, the console will use your settings (this applies when you choose Start→Programs→Command Prompt).

You'll learn more about the command shell in Chapter 2.

Introducing the Windows Script Host

Now that you know a bit about shell scripting, let's take a look at the Windows Script Host. In this section, you'll learn how to use the script host, scripting basics, and more.

As stated earlier, I refer to shell scripts and Windows scripts in the text for simplicity's sake. Shell scripts are scripts written for the Windows command shell. Windows scripts are scripts written for the Windows Script Host.

Getting to Know the Script Host

Unlike the command shell, which is built into Windows NT, Windows Script Host is an add-on that must be installed on the system you want to use with scripting. The script host is compatible with any 32-bit operating system, including Windows 98, Windows NT workstation and Windows NT server. You'll find the necessary software on Microsoft's MSDN site at `http://msdn.microsoft.com/scripting/`.

When you install the script host, the installation package updates your system to work with scripts. The key enhancements are the additions of:

- ◆ **WScript.exe** – A Windows executable for the script host that is used when you execute scripts from the desktop. This executable has GUI controls for displaying output in popup dialog boxes.

- ◆ **CScript.exe** – A command-line executable for the script host that is used when you execute scripts from the command line. This executable displays standard output at the command line.

- ◆ **WSH.ocx** – An ActiveX control that provides the core object model for the script host.

 As discussed earlier, the script host works in conjunction with scripting engines. Scripting engines provide the core functions, objects and methods for a particular scripting language, such as VBScript. You'll find scripting engines for VBScript and JScript on the Microsoft MSDN Web site at `http://msdn.microsoft.com/scripting/`

 To obtain updates for Windows Script Host or scripting engines, visit `http://msdn.microsoft.com/scripting/`. Note also that scripting engines are installed with other Microsoft software, including Internet Explorer. If your system has IE 5.0, the 5.0 version of the VBScript and JScript scripting engines are installed already.

What Is a Windows Script?

When you install the scripting engines, the installation package updates your system to enable the engine to work with scripts and the script host. The extension .VBS is registered for use with VBScript, and the extension .JS is registered for use with JScript. Any files that use these extensions are considered Windows scripts.

A Windows script is a text file containing a series of commands. Unlike shell scripts, Windows script commands don't resemble commands that you'd type in at the keyboard. Instead, they follow the syntax for the scripting language you are using, such as VBScript or JScript. Once you create a Windows script, you run it with WScript.exe or CScript.exe.

As with shell scripts, Windows scripts are completely text-based and can be created in Notepad. When you finish creating the script, save it with an extension appropriate for the scripting language (.VBS for VBScript and .JS for JScript).

Working with WScript and CScript

Windows scripts can be run with either WScript or CScript, and most of the time the application you use depends on your personal preference. However, you'll find that WScript works best when scripts interact with users, especially if the script displays results as standard text output. For tasks that you want to automate or run behind the scenes, you'll probably prefer CScript, as you can suppress output and prompts for batch processing.

You can use WScript and CScript with scripts in several different ways. The easiest way is to set WScript as the default application for scripts and then run scripts by double-clicking their filename in Windows Explorer. Don't worry, you don't have to do anything fancy to set WScript as the default. The first time you double-click a Windows script, you'll be asked if you'd like to associate the file extension with WScript. Click Yes. Alternatively, you may see an Open With dialog box that asks what program you would like to use to open the file. Choose WScript, and then check the Always use this program to open this file check box.

Other ways to use WScript with scripts include the following:

◆ Enter a script name at the Run command on the Start menu. Click Start→Run, and then enter the full path to the script, such as

   `D:\Working\Scripts\myscript.vbs`

◆ Run WScript from the command line. At the prompt, enter **wscript** followed by the full path to the script you want to execute. If the current directory contains the script you want to run, all you need to do is enter **wscript** and the script name. For example:

   `wscript myscript.vbs`

You can also set CScript as the default interface. When you do this, double-clicking a Windows script runs CScript instead of WScript. Or, you could run scripts from the Run prompt — just as you could when WScript was the default. To run scripts with CScript from the command line, enter **cscript** followed by the pathname of the script you want to execute. For example:

`cscript myscript.vbs`

You'll learn more about WScript and CScript in Chapter 8.

Shell Scripting versus the Windows Script Host

Shell scripting and the Windows Script Host have their good and bad points. Before moving on to more advanced topics, let's look at when you should and shouldn't use these environments.

When to Use Shell Scripting

Any time you enter commands at the command prompt, you are using the shell. To increase productivity, you can use shell scripts to execute routine tasks automatically. You can also use shell scripts with the NT scheduler to schedule tasks to run on a periodic basis, for example, every night or once a week on Sundays. Because most Windows NT tools have command-line extensions, you can use scripts to quickly and easily perform tasks that you would otherwise have to perform manually, such as account auditing or report generation.

With this in mind, shell scripting is best when you need to

- Perform a task repeatedly

- Schedule tasks to run periodically

You can also use shell scripts to automate one-time tasks that would otherwise require extensive work with command-line tools. In this case, a script can perform tasks more quickly and efficiently than you can.

You shouldn't use shell scripts when a task

- Needs to interact with a desktop application, such as Microsoft Word

- Needs to perform extensive file or data manipulation

- Is very complex, such as writing a complete enterprise-wide system

- Requires an operating system other than Windows NT

Otherwise, you'll find that shell scripts are easy to create and highly reliable.

When to Use the Windows Script Host

The Windows Script Host has many more nuances than the shell environment. You can use the technology with the scripting engine of your choice, which gives you control over what scripting language is used and allows for easy extensibility. Additionally, you'll find that Windows scripts provide the flexibility you need to perform a wide variety of tasks, such as

- Searching files or manipulating data within files
- Working with drives and directories
- Performing complex calculations
- Generating reports or print statistics

If you routinely have to manipulate data in files or create reports, Windows scripts can often perform this task better than you can. Well-programmed scripts don't make mistakes in calculations or put data in the wrong places. Unlike shell scripts, you can also use Windows scripts when you

- Need to interact with desktop applications, such as Microsoft Word
- Need to perform extensive file or data manipulation
- Require an operating system environment other than Windows NT
- Implement basic systems that interact with the user, other applications, and the operating system

Even with all their muscle, there are tasks Windows scripts aren't very good at. You shouldn't use Windows scripts when you need to run groups of commands at the command line or script Windows NT tools that have command-line extensions. You'll usually find that shell scripts are easier to use in this case. That said, the Windows Script Host does have a method for executing commands and, in some cases, you may want to run specific commands using this method.

Lastly, although the Windows Script Host doesn't have a scheduling capability, you can use the built-in scheduler, At, to schedule execution for Windows scripts. To do this, place references to Windows scripts you want to schedule in a shell script, and then run the shell script. This way, you have a single file for scheduling when scripts are run, and you can easily update this one script later.

Summary

Scripting is revolutionizing Windows administration. Tasks that previously could only be performed manually can now be automated, which frees administrators from the mundane and enables them to focus on more rewarding tasks. As you set out to learn Windows scripting techniques, you have the choice of using shell scripts at the command line or Windows scripts with the Windows Script Host. Both technologies have strong and weak points, which you'll learn more about in upcoming chapters.

Part II

Scripting the Command Shell

Chapter 2

Windows Shell Essentials

IN THIS CHAPTER

- ◆ Creating, editing, and running simple shell scripts
- ◆ Controlling shell script output
- ◆ Controlling echoing, the command prompt, and comments
- ◆ Executing shell scripts

COMMAND SHELL SCRIPTING enables you to increase productivity, be more effective, and accomplish more with fewer resources. In an increasingly complex network environment, these capabilities allow you to focus less on mundane tasks and more on interesting and challenging tasks. But before you can take advantage of the command shell, you need to learn how the command shell works, shell scripting syntax and structures, and other essential concepts, which are exactly what you'll learn in this chapter.

Creating Shell Scripts

Ever since *The C Programming Language* – Brian Kernighan and Dennis Ritchie's legendary text – first came out, it's been traditional to open a programming book with a program that writes "Hello, World!" to some output device, usually the video monitor. So let's see how you can create this program in the command shell.

Shell Scripting Basics

Start a command shell by selecting Start→Programs→Command Prompt. In the command shell window, you should see a display similar to the following:

```
Microsoft(R) Windows NT(TM)
(C) Copyright 1985-1996 Microsoft Corp.

C:\>
```

19

In the example, `C:\>` is the command prompt for the shell. Following the command prompt, you should see a blinking cursor, which indicates the shell is in interactive mode and ready to accept input. In interactive mode, you can enter scripts right at the prompt, without having to create a file. To see how, type in the following command and press Enter:

```
echo Hello, World!
```

You should see the following output:

```
Hello, World!
```

Editing and Executing Scripts

The command shell also has a batch mode, which is used when executing scripts. In batch mode, the shell starts to read the script file and executes its commands one by one. Execution of the script ends when the shell reaches the end of the file or reads an Exit command. After that, the shell returns to interactive mode.

Let's create and execute a script in batch mode. At the command prompt, enter

```
notepad
```

This should start the Notepad text editor.

 TIP If Notepad doesn't start, your command path isn't set properly and should be updated. I'll discuss the path later. For now, use Start→ Programs→Accessories→Notepad to start Notepad. Also, if you're wondering how the shell knows to run Notepad.exe, see the section of this chapter titled, "Command Execution."

In Notepad, type in the text for Listing 2-1 and save it to a file called today.bat in the current working directory. Below the script listing, you'll find the output of the script – don't enter this in the file. Run the script by entering the name of the script at the command prompt and pressing Enter. For example:

```
C:\>today
```

Listing 2-1: A very basic shell script

today.bat
```
echo Today,
echo I consider myself
```

```
echo the luckiest man
echo on the face of the earth.
echo -- Lou Gehrig
```

Output
```
C:\>echo Today,
Today,

C:\>echo I consider myself
I consider myself

C:\>echo the luckiest man
the luckiest man

C:\>echo on the face of the earth.
on the face of the earth.

C:\>echo -- Lou Gehrig
-- Lou Gehrig
```

Understanding Script Execution

The output for the script shown in Listing 2-1 probably isn't what you thought it would be. The reason for this lies in how batches of commands are executed. When executing a script, the command shell actually follows the steps shown in Figure 2-1. Following the figure, you see that command execution is sequential.

Script execution starts when you type the script name at the prompt. Afterward, the script displays the command prompt. Next, the command shell reads a line from the script, displays it, and then interprets (executes) it. If the command shell reaches end of the file, it returns to interactive mode and displays a command prompt and the blinking cursor, signaling that it is ready for input. If the line contains the exit command, the current command shell exits, which ends the shell session. Otherwise, the shell executes the command and starts back at the top of the loop, displaying the prompt and preparing to read the next line.

 To halt execution of a script, you can press Ctrl+C, and then press Y when prompted.

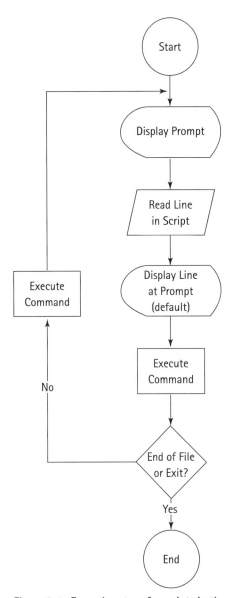

Figure 2-1: Execution steps for scripts in the command shell

As you can see, the command shell does a lot of work before it actually executes a command. While the display is useful for troubleshooting, it can be bothersome. Fortunately, you can change this default behavior, and I'll show you how later in the chapter. Look for the section titled "Controlling Script Output."

Script Arguments

As with many command line programs, arguments can be passed to scripts from the command line. You use arguments to set special parameters in a script or to pass in information needed by scripts. Each argument should follow the script name and be separated by a space. In the following example, a script named `equation` is passed the parameters `2x` and `3y`:

```
equation 2x 3y
```

In the script, you access arguments using formal parameters, where %1 represents the first argument passed in, %2 represents the second, and so on. When the command shell sees a formal parameter, the actual value is substituted for the parameter. This enables you to use parameters in a script much like you would an actual value.

To see how parameters work, use Notepad to create a script called equation.bat. The script should contain the text shown in Listing 2-2.

Note the use of the @ symbol in the example. This special command is used to turn off the display of commands on a line-by-line basis. You'll learn more about this and other special commands shortly.

Listing 2-2: Passing arguments to a script

```
@echo %1 + %2 = ?
@echo %2 - %1 = ?
@echo %1 / %2 = ?
@echo %2 * %1 = ?
```

Now type in the following command to execute the script using the arguments 2x and 3y:

```
equation 2x 3y
```

The output of the script is

```
2x + 3y = ?
3y - 2x = ?
2x / 3y = ?
3y * 2x = ?
```

To get a better understanding of arguments, try passing different values in to the script. Note what happens if you don't enter arguments or only enter one argument. You should see that the expected argument has no substitution value (meaning it is replaced with `""`). To learn more about working with arguments and parameters, see the section of Chapter 3 titled "Understanding Command Syntax."

Controlling Script Output

Now that you've worked with basic scripts, let's look at ways you can control script output as well as techniques for creating better scripts. The key commands you'll be working with in this section include the following:

- ◆ `echo` – Controls command echoing throughout a script and echoes text to the console

- ◆ `@` – Controls command echo on a line-by-line basis

- ◆ `prompt` – Controls the text used for the command prompt

- ◆ `rem` – Creates comments in scripts that aren't written to the console window

- ◆ `title` – Sets a title for the console window

- ◆ `cls` – Clears the console window

- ◆ `color` – Sets the foreground and background colors of the console window

Text Display and Command Echoing

As you've seen in previous examples, you use the `echo` command to have a script display output in the command shell. You can also use `echo` to control command echoing. Normally, when you execute commands in a script, the commands are displayed at the prompt as well as the resulting output of the command. This is called *command echoing*.

In interactive mode, you can turn off echoing by typing the following at the command prompt:

```
echo off
```

To turn echoing back on, enter this command:

```
echo on
```

To try this out, start a command shell, type the `echo off` command, and then enter other commands. You'll find that the command prompt is no longer displayed. Instead, you see only what you type into the console window and the resulting output from commands. In scripts, the `echo off` statement turns off command echoing as well as the command prompt. By adding the command `echo off` to your scripts, you keep the command shell window — or other output mechanism — from getting cluttered up with commands when all you care about is the output that those commands generate.

By the way, you can determine whether command echoing is enabled or disabled by entering the `echo` command by itself. Give it a try. If command echoing is on, you'll see

```
Echo is on.
```

Otherwise, you'll see

```
Echo is off.
```

Experiment with the `echo off` command in your scripts and you may detect a bit of a problem here. If the `echo off` command turns off command echoing, how do you prevent the `echo off` command itself from echoing? That's the subject of the next section.

Suppressing Command Echo with @

The @ command prevents commands from echoing to the output on a line-by-line basis. Because of this, you can think of @ as a line-specific `echo off` statement. The real value of the @ command comes in hiding `echo off`. In this way, you can hide all command echo in a script, meaning that the only text elements that get written to the output device are the actual output values of the various commands included in the batch file. Listing 2-3 shows how this works.

Listing 2-3: @echo off

combine.bat

```
@echo off
echo Today,
echo I consider myself
echo the luckiest man
echo on the face of the earth.
echo -- Lou Gehrig
```

Output

```
Today,
I consider myself
```

```
the luckiest man
on the face of the earth.
-- Lou Gehrig
```

The @ command only works within batch files, by the way. If you start a command shell and type @ before a command, the command shell simply ignores @. You won't get an error, though.

Echoing Blank Lines

How do you get a blank line to echo? You'd think `echo` on a line by itself would do the job, but as you learned earlier, this is not the case. Typing **echo** on a line by itself displays the status of command echoing, and that's not what you want. The `echo` command followed by a space character doesn't do the trick either. The Windows NT command shell treats spaces (in this situation) as meaningless, empty space, and so `echo` followed by one or more space characters yields the same results as `echo` followed by nothing at all.

Unfortunately, you can't really display a blank line at the command prompt. However, you can use a spacing technique to create separation between sections of text. One way to do this is to follow `echo` with some sort of unobtrusive or decorative character, such as a period or a plus sign. Depending on your situation, you might even want a whole row of these characters. The commands that you'd use to employ this solution look like this:

```
echo .
echo **********************
```

Another possible solution is to create a line of text that is wider than the character width of the console window. To do this, follow a line of text with spaces until you extend beyond the character width of the console window, and then press Enter.

Working with the Command Prompt

When echoing is turned on, the command prompt is displayed anytime you work with shell scripts at the command line. By default, the command prompt displays the current drive followed by >. You can change this default behavior using the `prompt` command. Enter **prompt** at the command line or within a script and follow it with the text of the new prompt you want to use, such as

```
prompt Hello
```

which sets the prompt to

```
Hello
```

To go back to the default prompt, enter a `prompt` command without any text following it. For example, if you enter the following command, the shell prompt is restored to its default setting:

```
prompt
```

Text you pass to the `prompt` command can contain special codes, which are replaced with additional information when the prompt is displayed. For example, `$d` in the shell prompt is replaced with the current date.

You must reference some text characters must with a special code before you can use them in a prompt. For example, you cannot use the dollar sign ($) in a prompt by itself. To get the prompt to display $, you must use the special code `$$`, which the command shell replaces with a dollar sign.

To see how special codes work, enter the following at the command line:

```
prompt $D$$
```

The prompt should now display the current time following by a $:

```
Fri 09/01/1999$
```

Here, the date displays in the format `Day MM/DD/YYYY`. Unfortunately, you cannot change the date format.

Table 2-1 provides a list of special codes you can use with the `prompt` command. Experiment with these values to learn more about their usage.

Adding Comments to a Script

It's a good idea to use comments to specify proprietary and contact information at the top of all your scripts. That way, anyone looking at your code will know who owns it (if anyone) and whom to contact with suggestions and questions. Indeed, if you look at the scripts on my Web site for this book (`http://www.tvpress.com/winscripting/`), you'll find that they all begin with a few lines about *Windows NT Scripting Administrator's Guide,* even though those lines don't appear in the chapter-by-chapter code listings.

To create comments in shell scripts, you use the `rem` statement. Essentially, comments begin with `rem` and continue to the end of the line, like this:

```
@echo off
rem This line is comment and won't be displayed as output
rem This line won't be displayed either.
rem You can even use characters like ^|&<>() in remarks.
rem Normally these characters are reserved.
```

TABLE 2-1 SPECIAL CODES USED WITH THE COMMAND PROMPT

Code	Description
$a	Ampersand character: &
$b	Pipe character: |
$c	Left parenthesis: (
$d	Displays current date, for example: Fri 09/10/1999
$e	Escape code (ASCII character code 27)
$f	Right parenthesis:)
$g	Greater-than sign: >
$h	Backspace (used to erase previous character)
$1	Less-than sign: <
$n	Current working drive, for example: C:\
$p	Current drive and path, for example: C:\ or C:*working* if you are in the working directory.
$q	Equal sign: =
$s	Inserts a space.
$t	Displays current time down to the millisecond, for example: 09:10:35.70
$v	Displays the Windows NT version, for example: Windows NT version 4.0
$_	Inserts a carriage return and linefeed.
$$	Dollar sign character: $
$+	Displays a series of plus sign (+) characters that correspond to the number of directories on the PUSHD stack. You can use PUSHD to store the current working directory before changing to a different directory.
$m	Displays the remote UNC name associated with the current drive letter in the form \\servername\share, such as \\ZETA\HOME. If the current drive is not a network drive, an empty string is displayed.

If command echoing is turned off, the command interpreter skips right over any line that begins with rem, ignoring it completely. For this reason, rem statements often find application in debugging troublesome scripts – you can "comment out" lines of code to prevent them from being run by the interpreter. Listing 2-4 shows commenting in action.

Listing 2-4: Commenting a script

rem.bat

```
@echo off
rem ***********************
rem Script: Enter a script name
rem Date: Enter today's date (and update when you modify)
rem Author: Enter your name
rem Email: Enter your email address
rem Description: Enter a short description of the script
rem ***********************

@echo This program shows how comments work.

rem The following command isn't executed:
rem dir c:\winnt

rem The next line has a comment that begins at its midpoint.
ver rem This text will not echo.
```

Output

```
This program shows how comments work.
Windows NT Version 4.0
```

As the example illustrates, there are three practical applications for the rem command in shell scripting:

◆ Inserting explanatory text into a script

◆ Preventing a command from executing

◆ Hiding part of a line from interpretation

Try to comment your code liberally, even if you think a script is simple. Odds are, you or someone else will have to make modifications to the code at some point in the future, and the person doing the modifying may be at a loss to figure out what in the world you were thinking. Code is like that — you understand it when you write it and have been thinking about it for a while, but it doesn't always stick with you.

Adding a Few Special Effects

Any good script needs a few special effects to jazz it up a bit. Basic techniques are to add a title to the console window, clear the console window before writing output, and change the text and background color.

The command shell's title bar is located at the top of the console window. Normally, this title bar displays "Command Prompt" or the file path to the command shell. You can customize the title with the `title` command, which works much like the `echo` command in that it displays whatever text follows it on the console's title bar. For example, if you want to set the title of the current console to "Working . . .", you could do this by entering the following at the command line:

```
title "Working..."
```

You can use the `title` command in your scripts to show the name of the script that is running. Another use is to show the progress of the script as it executes. As shown in Listing 2-5, progress updates are especially useful in scripts that have a long execution time.

Listing 2-5: Using titles in a script

title.bat

```
@echo off
rem ***********************
rem Script: Title
rem Date: 09/15/99
rem Author: William R. Stanek
rem Email: win32scripting@tvpress.com
rem Description: Creates titles for a long script
rem ***********************

title Setting up the environment...
rem insert environment settings here

title Reading files...
rem insert routines to read setup files

title Creating accounts...
rem insert code to create accounts
```

You clear the console window using the `cls` command. Why not try it? At the command line, type in **cls** and press Enter. The console clears and the cursor is positioned in the top left of the window. Note also that if you are using a screen buffer, all the buffered text is cleared as well. It's a good idea to use `cls` in script that writes extensively to the console. Simply enter **cls** on a line by itself in the script (see Listing 2-6).

The default console displays white text on a black background. As you learned in Chapter 1, you can modify this behavior using the Colors tab of the Command Prompt Properties dialog box. You can also set console colors using the `color` command. To do this, pass the command a color code as a 1- or 2-digit hexadecimal code. If you enter a 1-digit code, only the text color is set. With 2-digit codes, the first digit corresponds to the background color and the second digit corresponds to the text color, such as

```
color 17
```

which sets the background color to blue and the text to white.

Table 2-2 shows the color codes you can use with the `color` command. To return the console to its default colors, use `color` without any arguments, such as

```
color
```

 If you try to set the text and background to the same color, the color doesn't change.

TABLE **2-2** COLOR CODES USED WITH THE CONSOLE WINDOW

Code	Color	Code	Color
0	Black	8	Gray
1	Blue	9	Bright Blue
2	Green	A	Bright Green
3	Aqua	B	Bright Aqua
4	Red	C	Bright Red
5	Purple	D	Bright Purple
6	Yellow	E	Bright Yellow
7	White	F	Bright White

Using Script Directories and Headers

The key reason for using shell scripts is to increase efficiency and productivity. To help with this effort, you should create special directories for your scripts, and then store your scripts in these directories with names that help describe their purpose. For example, create these directories:

- ◆ scripts\shell\working – A directory to hold scripts you are developing

- ◆ scripts\shell\network – A directory for networking scripts

- ◆ scripts\shell\accounts – A directory for user, group, and computer account-related scripts

- ◆ scripts\shell\common – A directory for scripts that handle other common tasks

You should also create a standard header for your shell scripts, such as the one shown in Listing 2-6. In this example, you use comments to provide information about the script and its creator as well as to perform basic tasks that prepare the scripting environment. These tasks include

- ◆ Turning off command echoing

- ◆ Ensuring that Windows NT is the current operating system

- ◆ Setting the console title

- ◆ Clearing the console window

- ◆ Setting the text and background color of the console window

Listing 2-6: A shell script header

header.bat

```
@echo off
rem ************************
rem Script: Enter a script name
rem Date: Enter today's date (and update when you modify)
rem Author: Enter your name
rem Email: Enter your email address
rem Description: Enter a short description of the script
rem ************************

@if not "%OS%"=="Windows_NT" goto EXIT
@title "Your Script Title Here"
cls
color 07
```

```
Insert body of script here

:EXIT
```

The if statement in the example shows how you can use environment variables to control script execution. Here, if the operating system is detected as Windows_NT, the script execution continues as normal. Otherwise, the goto EXIT command is executed, which causes the script to jump ahead to the last line and stop execution. Here, :EXIT is the target label for the goto statement. You'll learn more about goto and target labels in Chapter 5.

Command Execution

By now you may be wondering how the command shell finds commands and scripts when you want to execute them. In previous examples, you've just assumed that commands you want to work with are available and that the scripts you're working with are in the current directory. But what if commands and scripts aren't where you expect them to be? Two factors play a major role in what happens in this case: command path settings and file extension associations.

Understanding the Command Path

When you execute a command in the Windows NT command shell, you start a series of events that happen mostly in the background. These events are similar to the following:

1. The shell replaces variables passed in the command with their actual values. This enables the shell to use real values rather than placeholders.

2. Multiple commands passed on a single line are broken down into individual commands and then processed. Each individual command is then separated by command name and arguments.

3. If the command name contains a file path, the shell knows you are referencing an external command and uses this path to find the command. Success means the shell found the command and then can execute it. Failure means the command cannot be found in the specified location, in which case the shell returns an error.

4. If the command name doesn't contain a file path, the shell tries to resolve the command name internally. A match means you've referenced a command built into the shell, which can execute immediately. If no match is found, the shell first looks in the current directory for the command executable, and then searches the command path for the command executable.

The details of step 4 are most important when you are working with command-line utilities or third-party tools such as those in the Windows NT Resource Kit. If the directory where your tools are located isn't in the command path, the command shell can't execute them, which can cause your scripts to fail. The command path is also used to find your scripts if they aren't in the current directory.

Setting the Command Path

The command path is set during logon using system and user environment variables, namely the %PATH% variable. To view the current path setting, you can use the related command, path. Start a command shell and type the command on a line by itself and press Enter:

```
path
```

You should see results similar to the following:

```
PATH=D:\Perl\bin;D:\WINNT\system32;D:\WINNT
```

The order in which directories are listed indicates the search order used by the command shell when looking for executables and scripts. In the previous example, the command shell searches in this order:

1. D:\Perl\bin

2. D:\WINNT\system32

3. D:\WINNT

Often, you'll find that you need to update the path information. You can do this by telling the path command to add a specific path to the existing path, such as

```
path %PATH%;d:\working\scripts
```

Here, the directory d:\working\scripts is appended to the existing command path and the sample path would be updated as follows:

```
PATH=D:\Perl\bin;D:\WINNT\system32;D:\WINNT;D:\WORKING\SCRIPTS
```

Note the use of the semicolon (;) to separate individual pathnames. In the previous example, I also used the semicolon to separate the last item in the path from the new pathname.

Updating the command path to include the location of your scripts is a good idea. It'll save you from having to type the path when you want to execute scripts.

If you want a directory to be first in the search order, specify the directory before you pass the `path` command the `%PATH%` environment variable, such as

```
path d:\working\scripts;%PATH%
```

Here, the sample path would be updated as

```
PATH=D:\WORKING\SCRIPTS;D:\Perl\bin;D:\WINNT\system32;D:\WINNT
```

 Be careful when using the PATH command, as you can easily overwrite all path information. For example, if you forget to specify the `%PATH%` environment variable, you'll accidentally delete all other path information. You can also overwrite the path information by typing the `path` command followed by semicolon. Examples of commands that can cause problems include

```
path d:\working\scripts
```
and
```
path ;
```
Both commands reset the path, deleting the other path information.

Working with File Extensions

File extensions are very important in the command shell environment. Some extensions tell the command shell that a file is executable. Other extensions tell the command shell that a particular file may be associated with an application.

FILE EXTENSIONS FOR EXECUTABLES

Executable files are defined with the `%PATHEXT%` environment variable. By default, this variable is set as follows:

```
PATHEXT=.COM;.EXE;.BAT;.CMD;
```

This setting tells the command shell that files ending in .COM, .EXE, .BAT, or .CMD can be executed. If the executable is for a command-line utility, such as

XCOPY.EXE, the utility can be executed using the parameters specified at the command line. If the executable is for a GUI application, such as NOTEPAD.EXE, the command shell starts the application.

Because the command shell knows which files are executable and which files aren't, you don't have to specify the file extension at the command line. You've seen this technique used throughout this chapter and may not have realized it – for example, when you type **today** to run a script named today.bat. Here, the command shell searches the current working directory for a file beginning with *today*. If it finds one, it uses the %PATHEXT% environment variable to determine if the file can be executed. If the shell doesn't find a match, it repeats this search in the directories specified by the command path.

If you want to create an extension for your scripts other than .BAT or .CMD, you could do this by updating the %PATHEXT% environment variable. As with the command path, you usually want to modify the current settings rather than replace them. Because of this, set the variable as follows:

```
set PATHEXT=%PATHEXT%;.NewExtension
```

such as

```
set PATHEXT=%PATHEXT%;.script
```

FILE EXTENSIONS FOR APPLICATIONS

File extensions can also be associated with specific applications. The mapping of file extensions to applications is referred to as *file associations*. File associations are what enable you to double-click on a Microsoft Word document in Windows Explorer and have it open in Microsoft Word. File associations also work in the command shell. For example, if you type the name of a text file at the command prompt, the file is opened automatically in Notepad (provided the shell can find the file in the current working directory or by searching the command path).

The reason you can open Word documents in Word and text documents in Notepad is that the extension .DOC has been associated with Microsoft Word and the extension .TXT has been associated with Notepad. To see a list of file associations, type the following command at the command line:

```
ftype | more
```

ftype is used to display a complete list of file associations and more is used to enable you to page through the results one screen at a time.

File associations are maintained in a database, which is stored in the Windows NT Registry. Settings in this database affect all users of the related workstation or server. The key elements in the file association database are

- File extension mappings, which connect a particular file extension to a particular file type

- File type mappings, which set file types to associate with launch commands

- Launch commands, which start the associated application and possibly pass in parameters

In the most basic scenario, you'd have a file extension, such as .PL, mapped to a file type, such as PERL for the Perl scripting language. The file type is then mapped to a particular launch command, such as D:\Perl\bin\Perl.exe "%1" %*. In shorthand, the mappings would look like this:

```
.PL ==> PERL
PERL ==> D:\Perl\bin\Perl.exe "%1" %*
```

You may be wondering why you should make things so complex and why you can't just map the extension directly to the launch command. Well, the reason for using the file type as an intermediary is to enable multiple file extensions to be associated with the same launch command. For example, you could associated .PL, .PL5, and .PERL with the same file type, and you would then only have one launch command entry in the database rather than three. Because you have only one command entry, you reduce the size of the database.

MORE FILE EXTENSIONS

I highly recommend exploring the file associations on your system. They can tell you a lot about how certain file types and applications work together. For example, did you know that you can start Microsoft Word, open a document, print the document, and then close the document all with a single command? You can, and the command is

```
PATH/WINWORD.EXE" &PRINT FILENAME.DOC
```

such as

```
"C:\Program Files\Microsoft Office\OFFICE\WINWORD.EXE" &PRINT
mytest.doc
```

Note that I've enclosed the command in quotation marks because it contains spaces. Any time a file path contains spaces, you'll need to use quotation marks.

To see how this works, start Windows Explorer and then select Options from the View menu. Afterward, click the File Types tab to view file associations (see Figure 2-2).

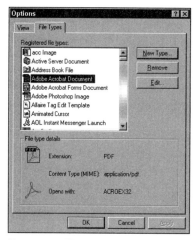

Figure 2-2: File associations viewed in Windows Explorer

Select the file type you want to examine, and then click Edit. This opens the Edit File Type dialog window shown in Figure 2-3. Use this dialog box to learn how applications and file extensions work together. The main fields of the dialog box are as follows:

◆ **Description** – Provides a description of the file type.

◆ **Content type (MIME)** – Tells you the MIME content type of files with the current extension (if any).

◆ **Default Extension for Content Type** – Shows the default extension for the file type and provides a pull-down list that displays extensions related to this file type.

◆ **Actions** – Shows the available actions that can be passed to the application when it is started. Most of the time, the actions are Open, Print, and Printto. The default action is displayed in bold and is normally Open.

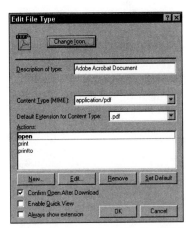

Figure 2-3: The Editor File Type dialog box can show you how to work with applications and file extensions.

Creating File Associations

To create a file association, use the `ftype` and `assoc` commands. `ftype` sets the file type and the associated launch command. `assoc` sets the file type extensions to associate with the file type. The examples that follow show how you could create a file association for Perl scripts on your system.

CREATING THE FILE TYPE MAPPING

Before you create a new file type, you should check to see if the file type exists. To do so, follow the `ftype` command with the file type you want to check, such as

```
ftype perl
```

If the Perl file type exists, you'll get a result similar to the following:

```
perl=D:\Perl\bin\Perl.exe "%1" %*
```

Otherwise, you'll get an error stating the file type doesn't exist, such as

```
File type 'perl' not found or no open command associated with it.
```

To create the Perl file type if it doesn't exist, enter the following command:

```
ftype perl=D:\Perl\bin\Perl.exe "%1" %*
```

This command maps the file type to the location of the Perl executable and specifies that arguments can be passed to the executable. The first parameter ("%1") is in quotation marks to ensure that the command is handled properly if spaces are passed in the first argument. The second argument (%*) allows one or more additional parameters to be passed in as well. These additional parameters are not configured to handle spaces, however. If they were, the application wouldn't be able to tell where one parameter ended and another began.

CREATING THE FILE EXTENSION MAPPING

Once you create the file type mapping, use assoc to create the file extension mapping. Again, before you do this, you should check to ensure that the mapping doesn't exist. Enter the following command:

```
assoc .pl
```

If the Perl file extension exists, you'll get a result similar to the following:

```
.pl=perl
```

Otherwise, you'll get an error stating the file association doesn't exist:

```
File association not found for extension .pl
```

To create the Perl file extension association if it doesn't exist, enter the following command:

```
assoc .pl=perl
```

The previous command maps the extension .pl to the Perl file type.

DELETING FILE ASSOCIATIONS

You can also use ftype and assoc to delete file types or file extension associations. To delete a file type for Perl, enter

```
ftype perl=
```

To delete the file extension for Perl, enter

```
assoc .pl=
```

AN ALTERNATIVE WAY TO CREATE ASSOCIATIONS

In the Windows NT Resource Kit, you'll find a utility called associate. Using this utility, you can associate file types and file extensions in one easy step. Simply follow the utility name with the file extension and the path to the associated application's executable, such as

```
associate .pl D:\Perl\bin\Perl.exe
```

associate then creates the file type mapping with the necessary launch command as well as the file extension mapping for you. While this utility makes the file association process easier, the utility isn't as configurable as working with ftype and assoc individually.

To delete a file association with this utility, enter the file extension followed by the /d switch, such as

```
associate .pl /d
```

Summary

The Windows command shell has many features that help you customize the shell environment. You can control echoing of commands, change the command prompt, set colors for text and backgrounds, and more. You can also use these features in shell scripts. When you execute commands at the command line and in scripts, the command path and file extensions play a key role in determining how and when commands are executed. The command shell must be able to find commands along the path. Otherwise, the commands can't be executed. Similarly, if file extensions aren't mapped properly, applications can't be started to handle various types of documents and files.

Chapter 3

Windows Shell Commands

THE COMMAND SHELL is a 32-bit environment for working with the command line and executing scripts. It has many characteristics you can take advantage of in your scripting efforts, including a strict syntax for command execution, a history that provides quick access to recently used commands, and many built-in commands. In addition, you can use command-line utilities in your scripts. To do this, you need to know how to call the utilities and how to pass in the correct parameters.

Commands, Switches, and Modifiers

In the previous chapter, I looked at commands but didn't go into detail regarding their use. Now it's time to take a closer look at commands as well as switches, modifiers, and other parameters that can be used with commands.

Internal and External Commands

Native shell commands—those built into the operating system by Microsoft—reside in two places:

◆ *Internal commands* exist internally in cmd.exe. That is, they are built into the shell itself. Examples of internal commands include `copy`, `attrib`, `ver`, and `cls`.

◆ *External commands* have their own executable files on the disk and are normally found in the WinNT\System32 folder. Look in this folder and you'll find xcopy.exe, at.exe, tree.com, and other familiar commands represented by executable files.

43

Table 3-1 lists the internal commands for the command shell (cmd.exe). The command name is followed by a brief description. For a complete listing of standard internal and external commands on Windows NT 4.0 Workstation and Server, see Appendix A.

TABLE **3-1 INTERNAL SHELL COMMANDS**

Command	Description
assoc	Displays and modifies file extension associations
call	Calls one script as a procedure in another script
cd	Displays the name of the current directory or changes the location of the current directory
chdir	Displays the name of or changes the current directory
cls	Clears the screen
color	Sets the foreground and background colors of the command shell window
copy	Copies or combines files
date	Displays or sets the date
del	Deletes one or more files
dir	Displays a list of files and subdirectories in a directory
echo	Displays messages or turns command echoing on or off
endlocal*	Ends localization of environment changes in a batch file
erase	Deletes one or more files
exit	Quits the cmd.exe program (command interpreter)
for	Runs a specified command for each file in a set of files
ftype	Displays or modifies file types used in file extension associations
goto	Directs the Windows NT command interpreter to a labeled line in a batch program
if	Performs conditional processing in batch programs
md	Creates a directory
mkdir	Creates a directory
move	Moves one or more files from one directory to another directory on the same drive

Command	Description
path	Displays or sets a search path for executable files
pause	Suspends processing of a batch file and displays a message
popd*	Restores the previous value of the current directory saved by pushd
print*	Prints a text file
prompt	Changes the Windows NT command prompt
pushd*	Saves the current directory and then changes it
rd	Removes a directory
rem	Records comments (remarks) in batch files or config.sys
ren	Renames a file or files
rename	Renames a file or files
rmdir	Removes a directory
set	Displays, sets, or removes Windows NT environment variables
setlocal	Begins localization of environment changes in a batch file
shift	Shifts the position of replaceable parameters in batch files
start	Starts a separate window to run a specified program or command
time	Displays or sets the system time
title	Sets the window title for a cmd.exe session
type	Displays the contents of a text file
ver	Displays the Windows NT version

* Indicates an internal command that is rarely used.

As far as scripting is concerned, the difference between internal and external commands isn't really important as long as you know where the external commands you want to use are located. Some resources make a distinction between the two types of commands, but they're splitting hairs. If you really want to disable an external command, you can delete its executable file, but this isn't practical.

Many utilities have command-line extensions that allow them to be passed parameters from the command line. A great resource for such utilities is the Microsoft Windows NT Resource Kit. Several versions of the Resource Kit are available, including Workstation, Server, and BackOffice. You can access utilities in the Resource Kit in your scripts as well. Lots of other sources for third-party utilities are also available.

Command Syntax

Every shell command you'll use follows the same basic syntax rule: A command consists of a command name followed by any required or optional arguments. Arguments include parameters used to pass information needed by the command and switches used to control the way the command works. In turn, switches can have modifiers that modify the behavior of the switch. Putting this all together, you see that most commands consist of the following:

◆ A *command* name that indicates the command you want to execute

◆ Zero or more *parameters* that provide the command with situation-specific information it needs to do the job you have in mind

◆ Zero or more *switches* that modify the behavior of the command

◆ Zero or more *modifiers* that further modify the behavior of switches

Command names and arguments are always separated by spaces, such as

```
dir /s d:\working
```

where dir is the command, /s is a command switch, and d:\working is a command parameter. When you work with various commands, you'll notice that some commands have only one style of use (or syntax), and others have multiple uses.

COMMANDS WITH ONE SYNTAX

An example of a command with one style of use is dir, which has the following syntax:

```
dir [/p] [/w] [/a[:attribute]] [/o[:sortorder]] [/s] [/b] [/l] [/v]
[drive:][path][filename]
```

Here, all arguments enclosed in brackets are optional, and words in italics are placeholders for actual values. If you see an argument that isn't in brackets, it is mandatory and must be typed in or set if it's a value. The following rules apply to commands with one syntax:

- Arguments in brackets are optional. These are parameters, switches, and modifiers that are used as needed.

- Words in italics are stand-ins for actual values. In the previous example, the word *drive* could represent the letter *D*, a drive designator. Note that the colon following the drive letter is not in italics. If you enter a *drive* value, you must enter a colon, too.

- Arguments not in brackets and not in italics must be typed every time the command is used.

Note that sets of brackets can have subsidiary sets of brackets — that's how switch modifiers are denoted. In the dir example, you could enter the /A switch with or without a following colon and a modifier.

Though switches and modifiers are often displayed as capital letters, the Windows NT command shell is rarely case-sensitive. In practice, dir /P is the same as dir /p.

COMMANDS WITH MORE THAN ONE SYNTAX

Sometimes, you'll see an entry in a command reference that lists two ways of using a command or involves the pipe character (|) as part of a parameter specification, such as

```
echo [ON|OFF]
echo [message]
```

This means there are two ways to use the echo command (both of which you've used previously). The first usage involves the word echo followed by one of two parameters: ON or OFF. The second usage involves following echo with a message, but no other parameters. The two uses of the command are functionally distinct and syntactically separate.

Note that in the previous example, the parameters ON and OFF are not in italics, indicating that they are to be typed literally. In contrast, *message* is in italics, indicating that it is a stand-in value that should be replaced with a real value.

Parameters

Many commands require extra pieces of information in order to perform useful work. If I said "Go" to you, you'd want extra information – such as the name of a location – in order to know what to do. In other words, you'd want situation-specific information.

Windows NT makes assumptions about many commands if no specific information is provided with them. The "Go" analogy applies here, too, because if I told you to "Go" without providing the name of a specific destination, you could reasonably assume that I was being unsociable and wanted you to "go away" or "go somewhere else" without my having to provide you with this extra information explicitly.

The ever-popular dir command makes assumptions about which directory you want to work with by listing the contents of the current working directory by default. But if you were in the C:\WinNT folder and typed

```
dir D:\working\fun
```

you would get a listing of the files in the D:\working\fun folder, even though C:\WinNT would remain the current working directory. The specific path information after the command provides a piece of information the command needs to have in order to do what you want. The path specification in this example is known generically as a *parameter.* Parameters are an important part of the shell – you'll hear a great deal about them in this book.

Switches

Shell commands are quite generic in most cases – they leave a fair amount of doubt as to what you want done specifically. While parameters can give a command information about the environment in which it's executing, it may be necessary to supplement commands with other bits of information that specify exactly how they should execute. These extra little pieces of information are called *switches,* and like parameters, they're an important part of the shell.

Every command supports a fixed set of switches – their names and functions are built into Windows NT and aren't subject to modification. In order to find out what switches a particular command supports and what those switches do, please refer to a command reference such as the one in Appendix A.

Most command-line environments support switches, though they have various ways of implementing them. In Windows NT and other Microsoft command-line environments, switches take the form of a forward slash followed by one or more characters (usually just one character, but there are exceptions).

A typical switch-enhanced command looks similar to the following:

```
dir /p
```

It's certainly possible — even common — to follow a command with more than one switch, or with a combination of switches and parameters. With the dir command, you can use the /p switch (to pause after each screen of text) and the /w switch (to display the listing in multiple columns) together, like this:

```
dir /p /w
```

 Parameters and switches are extremely important in controlling command behavior. But it does not matter in what order you put switches. In the previous example, dir /w /p would have yielded identical results.

Modifiers

Switches sometimes need to be supplemented with even more specific information that modifies the behavior of the switch. For example, the dir command supports the /o switch, which causes the directory listing to be sorted before it is written to the output. Go ahead — give it a try and see what happens. Start a command prompt and enter the following command:

```
dir /o
```

As you might have predicted, the command causes the file listing to appear with the filenames sorted alphabetically from A to Z (you might want to supplement /o with /p if the listing went by too fast). But what if you want the files listed by their filename extensions or by their size in kilobytes?

As it turns out, the /o switch has a number of modifiers that modify sorting behavior. Ascending alphabetical sorting is just the default; it's what you get if you specify /o by itself, without a modifier. However, if you use a modifier, you can get many different sort orders. The syntax for using a modifier is to follow the switch with a colon (:), and then enter the modifier. The following command sorts the contents of the current folder alphabetically by filename extension:

```
dir /o:e
```

This command sorts the current folder's contents by size, starting with the smallest file and continuing through the largest file:

```
dir /o:s
```

Negating Switches and Modifiers

What about reverse order? The command shell supports the - modifier for switches and modifiers. The - modifier negates the switch or modifier it precedes, just as the - operator does in mathematics. Here's an example again involving the dir command's sort capabilities:

```
dir /o:-n
```

This command negates the usual :n modifier. Because :n specifies an alphabetical sort of filenames from A to Z, it follows that :-n is a reverse alphabetical sort of filenames from Z to A, which is exactly the result of the previous command.

Putting Them All Together

Often, you'll want to combine commands with parameters, switches, and modifiers. This is not only legal, but it is also often necessary. For example, say you want to generate a listing of the contents of D:\working\fun, alphabetized in reverse order, with pauses after each screen of data. The command that fits this bill is as follows:

```
dir /p /o:-n D:\working\fun
```

So you see that the usual order is the command name followed by switches (the order of the switches does not make a difference) followed by parameters. In fact, you can usually put parameters before the switches without adverse effect, but Microsoft recommends that switches come first.

Getting the Most from the Command Shell

So far I've focused on basic shell techniques. Now it's time to explore the nitty-gritty details of shell usage. The sections that follow examine

- ◆ Special characters in the command shell
- ◆ Arguments for the command shell
- ◆ Command shell nesting
- ◆ Command history
- ◆ Command shell macros

Special Characters in the Command Shell

Some characters have special uses in the command shell. Whenever the command interpreter encounters one of these characters, it attempts to carry out the special procedure associated with that character, which is fine — unless that special procedure is not what you have in mind. In this situation, you have to "escape" the special characters in order for the interpreter to look at them literally, without invoking the special procedures they're associated with. Special characters include the following:

```
< > ( ) & | ^
```

These characters all have special purposes in command shell scripting and, as a result, won't work properly unless you treat them in a special way. In order to use these characters in the command shell, you have to precede them with the escape character, the caret (^). (The caret is the character above the 6 key on a standard keyboard.) To see what happens when you try to echo the special characters without escaping them, type the following at the command prompt and press Enter:

```
echo |
```

You receive an error that says The syntax of the command is incorrect. To get the reserved pipe character to display properly, type this at the command line and press Enter:

```
echo ^|
```

That works wonderfully — it echoes the | as it should. This works for all the characters, and even for the caret itself, which you can echo in the manner illustrated by Listing 3-1. Note that the escape character is required no matter where the special character appears in a line of code.

Listing 3-1: Escape characters

escape.bat

```
@echo off
echo The company saw a 10^% increase in sales last year.
echo The caret (^^) is the escape character.
```

Output

```
The company saw a 10% increase in sales last year.
The caret (^) is the escape character.
```

TIP The need to escape special characters exists only in those situations in which you want the special character to echo literally, not when it serves as part of the normal syntax of a command string.

Command Shell Arguments

When you worked with the command shell previously, you probably started it using Start→Programs→Command Prompt. Another way to start a command shell is to use the Run dialog box or type **cmd** in an open console window. These techniques enable you to pass arguments to the command shell. The arguments include switches that control how the shell works as well as parameters that execute commands, such as

```
cmd /q
```

or

```
cmd /t:01
```

Table 3-2 summarizes command shell switches. As you can see from the table, several shell parameters are set by default. Because of this, the command shell normally

◆ Uses standard ANSI character codes for command output as opposed to Unicode character codes

◆ Enables command extensions that add features to most built-in commands

TABLE 3-2 SWITCHES FOR THE COMMAND SHELL

Switch	Description
/c	Executes the command specified and then terminates the shell
/k	Executes the command specified and then remains in interactive mode
/a	Command output to files or pipes will be ANSI (default)
/u	Command output to files or pipes will be Unicode

Switch	Description
/q	Turns the echo off
/t:fg	Sets the foreground and background colors for the console window
/x	Enables command extensions (default)
/y	Disables command extensions

The syntax for the command shell is

```
cmd [/x | /y] [/a | /u] [/q] [[/c | /k] string]
```

As the syntax shows, some switches cannot be used with other switches. For example, you can't enable and disable extensions. If you use both /x and /y, the command shell remembers the last option you passed on the command line.

When you use the /c or /k switches, the command shell expects you to pass in a command or script to execute. With /c, the shell executes the referenced command/script and then exits. With /k, the shell executes the referenced command/script and then returns to interactive mode, awaiting the next command.

The /c switch is what Windows Explorer uses when you double-click a script name in its folder view. For most scripting needs, however, you'll find that the /k switch is more useful. You can use this switch to pass in commands that prep the console window, such as

```
cmd /k dir
```

This command starts a command shell and then lists the contents of the current directory.

Nesting Command Shells

Sometimes you'll want to use different environment settings or parameters for a command shell and have the ability to go back to your original settings without exiting the console window. To do this, you can use a technique called *nesting*, whereby you start a command shell within a command shell. A nested command shell inherits all the environment settings from the current command shell and then modifies the environment as necessary to meet the special needs of commands and scripts you want to execute. When you exit the nested shell and return to the previous shell, your original settings are restored and the modifications you've made aren't recorded.

To see how this works, start a command shell and enter the following commands:

```
cmd
prompt [Nested Shell]
echo Hello!
```

The text within your command shell should now look similar to this:

```
Microsoft(R) Windows NT(TM)
(C) Copyright 1985-1996 Microsoft Corp.

D:\>cmd
Microsoft(R) Windows NT(TM)
(C) Copyright 1985-1996 Microsoft Corp.

D:\>prompt [Nested Shell]

[Nested Shell]echo Hello!
Hello!

[Nested Shell]
```

Now exit the nested shell by entering the exit command. When you do this, the command prompt (which is actually stored in an environment variable) returns to its default state.

You can nest shells several levels deep if you like. To experiment with multiple levels of nesting, enter the following commands at the command line:

```
cmd
prompt [Nested Shell 1]
echo I'm 1 level deep.
cmd
prompt [Nested Shell 2]
echo I'm 2 levels deep.
cmd
prompt [Nested Shell 3]
echo I'm 3 levels deep.
```

To return to the original shell, you need to type the exit command three times, once in each nested shell. To see the results, refer to Figure 3-1.

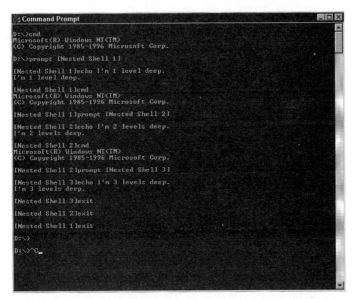

Figure 3-1: When you nest multiple levels of shells, nested shells inherit settings from higher-level shells. However, environment changes aren't passed back to higher-level shells.

Command History

The *history buffer* is a powerful feature of the command shell that remembers commands you type into the current console window. You can access entries in this buffer and execute the associated commands without having to retype them. The size of the buffer is set through the shell's Properties dialog box. Right-click a shell's title bar, select Properties, and then click the Options tab. Afterward, use the Buffer Size field to set the maximum size of the buffer.

Once commands are stored in the buffer, you can access them in several ways:

◆ **Browse the command history with the arrow keys.** Use the up-arrow and down-arrow keys to move up and down through the list of commands. When you find the command you want, simply press Enter. Or, you can press Backspace to erase options or text you don't want to use and then press Enter.

◆ **Browse the command history in a pop-up window.** Press the F7 key to display a pop-up window that contains a listing of commands in the history buffer. With the pop-up window displayed (as shown in Figure 3-2), you can select a command using the arrow keys or by pressing the corresponding number on the keyboard. You then execute the selected command by pressing Enter, or press Esc to close the pop-up window.

◆ **Search the command history.** Enter the first few letters of the command you want to execute and then press F8. The command shell searches through the history for the first command that begins with the characters you've entered. If the command you want to execute is displayed, press Enter to execute it. Otherwise, press F8 again to search the history buffer for additional matching entries.

◆ **Enter the number of a command you want to execute.** Command numbers are shown in the pop-up window when you press F7. If you know the command number, press F9, enter the command number, and then press Enter. The command corresponding to the number displays on the command-line but does not execute. Press Enter again to execute it.

 Different command shells have different command buffers. These buffers are only valid in the current command shell context.

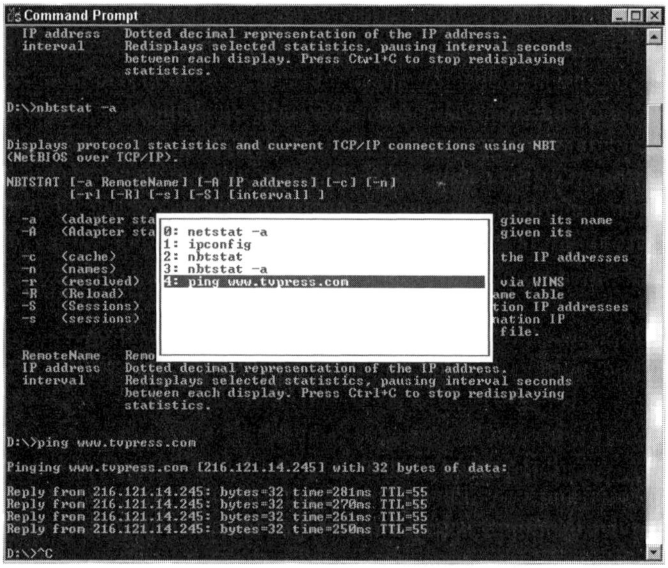

![Command Prompt screenshot showing a pop-up dialog box listing buffered commands: 0: netstat -a, 1: ipconfig, 2: nbtstat, 3: nbtstat -a, 4: ping www.tvpress.com]

Figure 3-2: Press F7 to display a pop-up dialog box that contains buffered commands.

Command Shell Macros

Command shell macros save keystrokes by enabling you to create shortcuts for long command sequences. You can also use macros to replace commands that are easily confused or hard to remember with a command that is easy to use or remember.

CREATING MACROS: THE BASICS

The command you use to create and manage macros is doskey. You can create a macro for the exit command by entering the following at the command line:

```
doskey e=exit
```

Now when you type e and press Enter, the command shell exits. Unfortunately, this macro isn't very useful in most cases. The reason is that macros normally are valid only within the current shell and are not valid when you exit the shell. However, if you set a macro in a top-level shell and then create several levels of nesting, you can use the macro in all of the nested shells.

 You can also use doskey to manage the history buffer and set the insert mode. However, you can set most of the associated options more easily in the command shell's Properties dialog box.

Anyone migrating to Windows NT from another operating system such as Unix will also find that doskey macros are helpful for transitioning to the NT command shell. For example, in Unix you use the ls command to list the contents of a directory, but in NT the related command is dir. To create a macro that enables you to type in ls for dir, enter the following command at the command line:

```
doskey ls=dir
```

Now you can type ls to get a directory listing.

PASSING ARGUMENTS THROUGH MACROS

If you've worked with the dir command before, you may know that it has switches that enable you to manipulate the directory listing. Try using a switch such as /s that lists the contents of subdirectories as well as the current directory with the ls macro created earlier. Instead of subdirectory listings, you'll get a normal directory listing. The reason for this is that the ls macro doesn't pass arguments in to the dir command. It simply executes the dir command.

To pass arguments to the command, you need to use the special code $* in the macro. This code ensures that arguments are passed to the command when it is executed. Following this, you could enhance the ls macro so it uses arguments by entering the command:

```
doskey ls=dir $*
```

You can also use macros to replace long command sequences, and this is where macros are most useful. For example, the following command provides a listing of the current directory and all its subdirectories that is sorted by file extension and placed in a text file:

```
dir /S /O:E > dirlist.txt
```

Rather than typing in this command sequence each time you want to use it, you could create the following macro:

```
doskey sdir=dir /S /O:E > dirlist.txt
```

Here, the > character redirects the output of the dir command to a text file. As a result, when you type **sdir**, you create a file containing a sorted directory listing. I'll explain more about command redirection later in the chapter.

ASSIGNING MACROS TO APPLICATIONS

By default, macros you create are associated with the command shell (CMD.EXE). Macros can also be associated with other applications that accept command-line parameters. To do this, use the /exename switch to specify the application's executable file, and then assign a macro for the application. The following example sets a macro for the built-in FTP utility:

```
doskey /exename=ftp.exe b=binary
```

Now when you type **b** in the FTP utility, you'll use binary transfer mode.

VIEWING YOUR MACROS

When you work with macros, it is often useful to be able to list available macros and to store macros for later use. To list macros for the command shell, you can use the following command:

```
doskey /macros
```

To list macros for other applications, designate the name of the application whose macros you want to view using the /exename switch:

```
doskey /macros /exename=ftp.exe
```

You can get a list of all macros for the current command shell using the `/macros:all` switch for `doskey`. When you use this switch, the macros for each application are listed under the application name:

```
[cmd.exe]
    ls=dir

[ftp.exe]
    b=binary
```

CREATING A MACRO FILE

The `doskey` command has a switch for reading macros from a file. This switch enables you to apply macros without retyping them each time you restart the command shell. The switch is `/macrofile` and it is used as follows:

```
doskey /macrofile=mymacros.txt
```

　　or

```
doskey /macrofile=c:\working\mymacros.txt
```

The format of the macro file must match the output of the `/macros:all` switch. Because the formats match up, you can use the `/macros:all` switch to create a macro file. The following example redirects the output of `/macros:all` to a file for later use:

```
doskey /macros:all > mymacros.txt
```

If you use macros regularly, you may want to modify the shortcut on the Programs menu to start the command shell and load the macros automatically. To do this, follow these steps:

1. Start a command shell and then create a directory called "macros" by entering the following command:

   ```
   mkdir c:\macros
   ```

2. Next, change to the macros directory by entering these commands:

   ```
   C:
   cd macros
   ```

3. Create the macros you want to use in the command shell and then enter the following command:

   ```
   doskey /macro:all > mymacros.txt
   ```

4. Right-click the Start button on the taskbar and select Explore All Users. This opens the Windows Explorer with the WinNT\Profiles directories ready for access.

5. In WinNT\Profiles, open the folder containing your profile (the folder with your logon name, such as wrstanek or Administrator). Afterward, access the \Start Menu\Programs folder.

6. In the Contents frame of Windows Explorer, you should see a shortcut for the Command Prompt. Right-click the shortcut and select Properties.

7. Access the Shortcut tab and then update the Target field so that it reads as follows:

```
%SystemRoot%\system32\cmd.exe /k doskey
/macrofile=c:\mymacros.txt
8. @NL:Click the Apply button and then click Close.
9. @NL:That's it, you're done. When you start a new command
prompt, your macros should be set automatically.
```

Redirecting Input and Output

Under normal circumstances, Windows NT shell commands take input from the parameters and switches specified when the commands are called and send their output to the standard console window. Sometimes, though, you want to take input from some other source, or send output to a file or other output device such as a printer. To do this, you'll use a technique called *redirection*. Redirection involves

♦ Sending the output of a command to another command

♦ Sending the output of a command to a file

♦ Sending errors that occur in executing commands

♦ Sending the output of a command to devices other than files

These key redirection techniques are summarized in Table 3-3 for quick reference and described in detail in the sections that follow.

TABLE 3-3 REDIRECTION TECHNIQUES FOR INPUT, OUTPUT, AND ERRORS

command | command	Sends the command output to the input of another command.
command < [path]filename	Takes command input from the specified file.

command > *[path]filename*	Creates the named file and sends output to it. This erases the file, without prompting, if it already exists.
command > *[path]filename*	Appends output to the named file if it exists; otherwise creates the file and writes to it.
command < *[path]filename* > *[path]filename*	Takes command input from the specified file and then sends command output to the named file.
command < *[path]filename* > *[path]filename*	Takes command input from the specified file and then appends command output to the named file.
command 2> *[path]filename*	Creates the named file and sends any error output to it. This erases the file, without prompting, if it already exists.
command 2>&1	Sends any error output to the same destination as nonerror output.

Redirecting Command Output to Another Command

Most shell commands generate output that can be redirected to another command as input. You redirect command output to the input of another command using the pipe symbol (|), which is why the technique is referred to as *piping*. (The pipe symbol appears on the key above the Enter key on a standard keyboard, along with the \ character.)

To experiment with piping, type the following command at the command line:

```
ftype| more
```

This command generates a listing of your system's file type associations and redirects the output into the `more` command, which provides added functionality for scrolling through a lengthy passage of text. Following this example, you can see the general syntax for piping is

```
cmd1 | cmd2
```

where the pipe redirects the output of *cmd1* to the input of *cmd2*. But you can also redirect output more than once:

```
ftype | sort | more
```

TIP If you experiment with the more command, you should note that this command displays output one page at a time. To see the next page of output, press the spacebar. To end the command, press Ctrl+C.

In this example, it's as if the three commands were fixtures installed on a pipeline. The ftype command serves as a source. The sort and more commands serve as "filters" that process the data stream as it progresses. Finally, the processed data spills out onto the output – the console window.

In practice, you'll rarely use piping in command shell scripting as it's usually easier to accomplish sequential processing of data by means of calls to procedures and other control structures, as covered in Chapter 5. However, piping is very useful when you type commands at the command line or when you want to create macros that use redirection.

Redirecting I/O to and from Files

By default, shell commands use switches, modifiers, and parameters as inputs and send output to the console window. But it's also possible to redirect output to files and to specify files as input sources for commands. This is a pretty powerful feature – you can use it to write files that other programs later examine in order to perform tasks or to pass a series of arguments to a command.

GETTING INPUT FROM A FILE

The < redirection symbol enables you to specify a file as an input for a command. For example, the following command sorts the contents of the file list.txt and displays the results to the console window:

```
sort < list.txt
```

You could also have specified the following command to sort the contents of the file in reverse order:

```
sort /r < list.txt
```

To see how you can use this technique in your scripts, consider the example shown in Listing 3-2. This listing shows the contents of two batch files. The first batch file, list.txt, contains a list that needs to be manipulated. The second, input.bat, contains the commands you want to execute against the list. In this case, you sort the list and get the results shown as the output.

Listing 3-2: Reading from a file

list.txt
```
yankee
bravo
delta
kilo
foxtrot
```

input.bat
```
sort < list.txt
```

Output
```
bravo
delta
foxtrot
kilo
yankee
```

SENDING OUTPUT TO A FILE

Just as you can read from a text file, you can also send output to a file. The > redirection symbol sends command output to the specified file. For example, if you want to get the OS version and store it in a file called os.txt, enter the following command at the command line:

```
ver > os.txt
```

Unfortunately, if a file with the name os.txt exists, this command overwrites the file and creates a new one. Rather than overwrite an existing file, you may want to add output to the file. To do this, you can use the > redirection symbol, which appends output to an existing file or creates a new file if necessary. For example, if you want to add the system's hostname and network status information to the os.txt file, you can enter the following commands at the command line:

```
hostname > os.txt
netstat > os.txt
```

I've used a similar technique in a script that helps track key system and network information across the enterprise (see Listing 3-3). When used on the network's servers, the script creates an important system accounting record that can be used to restore system and network settings. You can learn a lot about scripting from studying the listing. For now, don't focus on the commands; instead, focus on the syntax used. You'll learn all about these and other networking commands later in the book.

Basically, I've taken the echo statement and combined it with command redirection to create a report that is stored in a file called sysinfo.txt. Output from echo statements identifies key sections of the report. Output from networking commands is used to create the body of these key sections. After completing the report, the text of the report is listed to the console window using the `type` command.

 I think you'll agree that SysInfo is useful in the enterprise, but don't let the length of the script fool you into thinking it is complex. It isn't! Beyond the networking commands, which I cover later, you've already learned everything you need to create a similar script. The key ingredients are the script header developed in Chapter 2, the `echo` and `rem` statements also discussed in Chapter 2, and command redirection examined in this chapter.

Listing 3-3: Using redirection in a networking script

sysinfo.bat

```
@echo off
rem ************************
rem Script: SysInfo
rem Version: 0.9
rem Creation Date: 2/5/96
rem Last Modified: 9/1/99
rem Author: William R. Stanek
rem Email: win32scripting@tvpress.com
rem Description: Tracks system information and stores is it in
rem              %SystemRoot%\System32\sysinfo.txt
rem ************************

@if not "%OS%"=="Windows_NT" goto EXIT
@title "Getting system information..."
cls
color 07

rem Get system name and OS Version
rem ****************************************
echo "======================" > %SystemRoot%\System32\sysinfo.txt
echo .  > %SystemRoot%\System32\sysinfo.txt
echo . System Report  > %SystemRoot%\System32\sysinfo.txt
echo .  > %SystemRoot%\System32\sysinfo.txt
echo "======================" > %SystemRoot%\System32\sysinfo.txt
```

```
date /T > %SystemRoot%\System32\sysinfo.txt
hostname > %SystemRoot%\System32\sysinfo.txt
ver > %SystemRoot%\System32\sysinfo.txt

rem Get path and environment information
rem ****************************************
echo "=====================" > %SystemRoot%\System32\sysinfo.txt
echo .  > %SystemRoot%\System32\sysinfo.txt
echo . Path and Var Report  > %SystemRoot%\System32\sysinfo.txt
echo .  > %SystemRoot%\System32\sysinfo.txt
echo "=====================" > %SystemRoot%\System32\sysinfo.txt
path > %SystemRoot%\System32\sysinfo.txt
echo . > %SystemRoot%\System32\sysinfo.txt
echo . > %SystemRoot%\System32\sysinfo.txt
set > %SystemRoot%\System32\sysinfo.txt

rem Get NIC configuration and network status
rem ****************************************
echo "=====================" > %SystemRoot%\System32\sysinfo.txt
echo .  > %SystemRoot%\System32\sysinfo.txt
echo . Network Report  > %SystemRoot%\System32\sysinfo.txt
echo .  > %SystemRoot%\System32\sysinfo.txt
echo "=====================" > %SystemRoot%\System32\sysinfo.txt
ipconfig -all  > %SystemRoot%\System32\sysinfo.txt
echo . > %SystemRoot%\System32\sysinfo.txt
echo . > %SystemRoot%\System32\sysinfo.txt
netstat -r  > %SystemRoot%\System32\sysinfo.txt

rem Complete report
rem ****************************************
echo "=====================" > %SystemRoot%\System32\sysinfo.txt
echo . End of Report  > %SystemRoot%\System32\sysinfo.txt
echo .  > %SystemRoot%\System32\sysinfo.txt
echo "=====================" > %SystemRoot%\System32\sysinfo.txt

rem List contents of report to the shell
rem ****************************************
type %SystemRoot%\System32\sysinfo.txt

title "Report finished..."

:EXIT
```

Output (in file sysinfo.txt)

```
"====================="
```

```
.
. System Report
.
"====================="

<<system information here>

"====================="

.
. Path and Var Report
.
"====================="

<<path and variable information here>

"====================="

.
. Network Report
.
"====================="

<<network information here>

"====================="
. End of Report
.
"====================="
```

Redirecting Errors

Most program authors design command-line utilities so that normal output is directed to standard output (stdout), and important or critical output is written to standard error (stderr). This enables a command user, or a script, to ignore standard ouput text but pay attention to standard error text. While doing such things is much easier in Unix, it is difficult to tell where the output comes from under Windows NT; thus, we want to capture both standard output and standard error when scripting for Windows NT.

To redirect standard error from commands, you can use the redirection techniques discussed previously. Use the 2>&1 redirection symbol to redirect standard error to the same destination as command output. In this example, you send standard output and standard error to a file called widget.txt:

```
netstat -r > widget.txt 2>&1
```

You can also redirect only the standard error. In this example, standard output is displayed as normal and standard error is sent to the file widget.txt:

```
netstat -r 2> widget.txt
```

Listing 3-4 shows how you could use error redirection in a script.

Listing 3-4: Writing an error message to a file

sendError.bat
```
@echo off
dir netnet.ini 2> widget.txt
```
Output (in file widget.txt)
```
File Not Found
```

Naturally, this example depends upon the file netnet.ini not existing in the current folder at the time the script is run. If the file did exist, however, the error output file widget.txt would still get created; it just wouldn't have any contents.

Redirection to Devices Other Than Files

You're not limited to sending output to files. You can also send it to printers and a variety of other devices. To do this, specify a device name rather than a filename. These devices include parallel printers, serial printers, and the console window. You could send output to a parallel printer on port LPT1 as follows:

```
ftype > lpt1
```

or you could send output to a serial printer:

```
ftype > prn
```

Listing 3-5 shows how you could use an alternative output device in a script. As shown, the output of the echo statement is sent to the printer attached to port LPT1.

Listing 3-5: Writing an error message to a file

printer.bat
```
@echo off
echo This goes to the printer. > lpt1
```
Output (printed)
```
This goes to the printer.
```

Table 3-4 provides a complete list of alternative I/O devices in the command shell.

TABLE 3-4 NONFILE DEVICES AVAILABLE FOR REDIRECTION

Device Name	Input or Output?	What It Really Is
LPT*x*	Output	A parallel-port device, typically a printer connected to a parallel port.
PRN	Output	A serial printer.
CON	Both	The console, referred to generically. Depending upon context, this can refer to either the standard console input (the keyboard, usually) or the standard console output (the video monitor, in most cases).
CONIN$	Input	The standard console input (generally the keyboard).
CONOUT$	Output	The standard console output (usually the video monitor).

Common Commands Used with Redirection

Now that you've examined redirection techniques, let's take a closer look at some of the commands commonly used with redirection. These commands include `find`, `more`, and `sort`.

USING FIND

The `find` command searches for strings in files or in text passed to the command as input and then lists the text of matching lines. To create a listing of all files in the current directory starting with *S,* you could use the following command:

```
dir | find " S"
```

In the previous command, note the space within the quotation marks. The space is necessary to ensure `find` doesn't match the letter *S* that may occur in filenames (and we assume only filenames begin with space+S).

Normally, `find` searches are case sensitive, so a search for "TEST" would yield different results than a search for "test." To perform a search that isn't case-sensitive, you can use the `/i` switch, for example:

```
dir | find /i " s"
```

You can also search for input that doesn't contain the search text. Here, you use the /v switch. For example, you can search a file for all lines that do not include the word "test" as follows:

```
find /v "test" sample.txt
```

Another useful technique is to count the number of times search text occurs in a file. You can display a count of matching lines with /c. In this example, the find command tallies the number of subdirectories in the current directory:

```
dir | find /c "<DIR>"
```

USING MORE

The more command accepts output from other commands as input and then breaks this output into sections which can be viewed one screen at a time. Using this command, you could view the contents of the %SystemRoot%\system32 directory as follows:

```
dir %SystemRoot%\system32 | MORE
```

At the end of the first page, the command displays

```
--More--
```

which is a prompt waiting for input from the keyboard. Press the spacebar to see the next page of the display or Ctrl+C to stop the listing.

You can also use more to display the contents of a file, such as

```
type network_stats.txt | more
```

 The type command displays the contents of a text file to standard output, which can be redirected through other commands such as more.

USING SORT

The sort command accepts output from other commands and sorts it. By default, the sort order is alphanumerical, but you can use the /r switch to reverse the order. If a file contained a list of user accounts, you could sort the account names and put them in another file as follows:

```
sort < accounts.txt > sorted_accounts.txt
```

In the previous example, input is taken from the file accounts.txt, sent to `sort`, and then the output is redirected to the file sorted_accounts.txt.

Another way to sort is to check lines of output beginning at a specific column. For example, if the user account file had user names in columns 25–35, you could sort the file by account name as follows:

```
sort /+25 < accounts.txt > sorted_accounts.txt
```

Here, `/+25` is the switch that designates the column number at which sorting begins.

Using Multiple Commands

The Windows NT command shell provides several means of using multiple commands together. In previous sections, I've looked at piping and redirection. You can also chain commands together or have certain commands execute only if earlier commands succeeded (or failed), which is what I cover in this section. When you use multiple commands together, you create a *compound command*.

Table 3-5 summarizes the special symbols used in creating compound commands. As discussed earlier, these symbols are reserved in the command shell and must be escaped if you want to use them for other purposes.

TABLE 3-5 COMPOUND COMMAND SYMBOLS

Symbol	Syntax	Description
&	cmd1 & cmd2	Execute cmd1 and then execute cmd2. Chain additional commands by placing & between the commands.
&&	cmd1 && cmd2	Execute cmd2 if cmd1 is completed successfully. Chain additional commands by placing && between the commands.
||	cmd1 || cmd2	Execute cmd2 if cmd1 didn't complete successfully. Chain additional commands by placing || between the commands.
( )	(cmd1 & cmd2) && (cmd3) (cmd1 & cmd2) || (cmd3)	Groups sets of commands (actual syntax depends on the situation).

Executing Commands in Sequence

Let's say you want to change to the C:\temp folder, then delete all files with a .tmp filename extension. But you want to do this with one line of code rather than two. To do this, use the ampersand symbol (&). The & symbol enables you to chain as many commands together as you like. Listing 3-6 shows how this works.

Listing 3-6: Chaining commands together

cleanup.bat

```
@echo off
cd c:\temp & del *.tmp
```

Output

```
<None, other than the fact that a folder-load of .tmp files are
obliterated.>
```

 This is a good script to run regularly, because it cleans out resource-hogging temporary files left over after application crashes (applications that close normally delete their own temporary files). When you run the script, though, make sure there aren't any applications open that might have legitimate temporary files in the folder. You might set this to run at startup or shutdown time. To learn how you can schedule automated jobs, see the section of Chapter 6 titled "Scheduling Local and Remote Jobs."

Conditional Chaining

It makes more sense to chain commands when the execution of later commands depends upon how earlier commands worked. This enables you to check conditions and then do something (or not do something) in response to those conditions.

PRECEDING COMMAND SUCCESS

Sometimes you want a command to execute only if a prior command worked properly. Let's say you installed a program that maintains an error log in a file called error.log. The error log file only appears if an error has in fact occurred, and as an administrator, you want to monitor the contents of any error logs that have appeared.

　　Listing 3-7 shows a batch file that uses the dir command to check for the existence of error.log. Then, if the file is found, the command shell moves the file to a central folder on a network drive that you can monitor. (The && symbol is a sort of quick and dirty `if` statement. You'll learn more about full-fledged `if` statements in Chapter 5.)

Listing 3-7: Preceding success

succeed.bat

```
dir c:\working\error.log && move error.log r:\errorlogs
```

Output

```
<None, except for a relocated file if your system is appropriately
configured.>
```

PRECEDING FAILURE

Sometimes, you may want to do something only if a preceding command failed. For example, you may be involved in distributing files to a series of workstations, some of which run Windows 9*x* and some of which run Windows NT Workstation. Windows 9*x* machines have folders called Windows on their boot disks. Windows NT Workstation machines typically have folders called WinNT on their boot disks. Let's say you want to copy files from the N:\install path to whichever of those folders exists on the local machine. You can make this happen with the || command, as shown in Listing 3-8.

Listing 3-8 guarantees that you're in the C:\WinNT folder, if it exists, and that you're in the c:\windows folder otherwise. The only risk is that you've run the batch file on a machine with a nonstandard OS installation, such as one in which the user has chosen to install Windows 98 in a folder called C:\windows98.

Listing 3-8: Preceding failure

fail.bat

```
cd C:\winnt || cd C:\windows
xcopy n:\install\*.*
```

Output

```
<None, except for a relocated file if your system is appropriately
configured.>
```

Grouping Commands

Often when you combine multiple commands, you'll need a way to group commands together to prevent conflicts or to ensure an exact order is followed. You group commands with the () symbols. To understand why grouping may be needed, consider the following example. You want to write the hostname and OS version to a file using a compound command, so you use this statement:

```
hostname & ver > system.txt
```

When you examine the system.txt file, you find that it contains only the OS version and not the hostname and OS version. The reason for this is that the command shell executes the commands in sequence as follows:

```
1. hostname
2. ver > system.txt
```

Because the commands are executed in sequence, the system hostname is written to the console window and the OS version is written to the file. To get both commands to output to the file, you would need to use the following compound command:

```
hostname > system.txt & ver > system.txt
```

Or you could group the commands together with (and) as follows:

```
(hostname & ver) > system.txt
```

Here, the output of both commands is collected and then redirected to the file. I think you'll agree that an added benefit of grouping – besides preventing inadvertent conflicts – is that compound commands are easier to read.

You can also use grouping with conditional success and failure. In the following example, both *cmd1* and *cmd2* must be successful in order for *cmd3* to execute:

```
(cmd1 & cmd2) && (cmd3)
```

In this example, both *cmd1* and *cmd2* must fail in order for *cmd3* to execute:

```
(cmd1 & cmd2) || (cmd3)
```

Command grouping is used extensively with if and if...else constructs. Another grouping technique you'll use extensively with these constructs is the multiline command. A *multiline command* is a set of commands that execute in a series, such as the commands specified within an if statement.

You use the open parenthesis to specify where the multiline command begins and the close parenthesis to specify where the multiline command ends. Upon reading the end of the multiline command, the shell executes the command series and writes standard output and standard error.

To try out multiline commands in interactive mode, start a command prompt and enter the following:

```
(
```

When you press Enter, you should see that the command prompt changes to "More?". Now enter these additional commands:

```
echo 1...
echo 2...
echo 3...
echo Blast off!
```

Although the shell reads the commands, they aren't actually executed. To tell the shell to execute them, complete the multiline command by typing the close parenthesis at the command prompt:

```
)
```

Now when you press Enter, the command shell displays the output of the commands:

```
1...
2...
3...
Blast off!
```

You'll learn more about multiline commands and if statements in Chapter 5.

Summary

The command shell provides a powerful environment for working with shell scripts. You can run many different types of commands at the command line. You can use the built-in commands or you can use command-line utilities, which are available in the Windows NT Resource Kits and from third-party vendors. Regardless of source, most commands have parameters, modifiers, and switches you can use to control their behavior. To get the most out of commands, you need to master the available command options (or at least have handy references such as Appendixes A and B). Commands can also be grouped together, and when you do this, you need to use the pipe symbol or compound command symbols to chain the commands together.

Chapter 4

Working with Variables and the Environment

IN THIS CHAPTER

◆ Getting acquainted with variables

◆ Using variables

◆ Using mathematical expressions

THE BASIC SCRIPTS YOU'VE worked with so far won't cut it in the real world. To tap into the true power of Windows NT scripting, you need to learn about variables, among other things. But first things first. In a computer programming language, variables are places in memory into which you can put values. Some computer languages let you fool around with actual memory addresses, but you don't have to worry about the actual allocation of memory in the Windows NT shell scripting environment. You can (indeed, you have to) let Windows NT take care of that for you. Simply assign names and values to variables, and then use those names and values to write adaptable procedures.

Getting Acquainted with Variables

In Windows NT, things that execute – programs, services, and so on – are called *processes*. Logically enough, processes are entities that occupy the central processing unit (*CPU* or *processor)*. A basic tenet of Windows NT architecture is that processes are generally independent of one another. This contributes to the operating system's relative stability. One process can crash or otherwise terminate without causing the other processes on the same CPU to end.

The result of this architecture is that Windows NT processes are much like living beings. Processes are born, they live, and then they die. In this part of the book, we'll concern ourselves with only one kind of process: processes running cmd.exe. These are the kinds of processes that run shell scripts. Between the time cmd.exe is instantiated (by running cmd.exe) and the time cmd.exe is killed (with the exit command or a window-closing procedure, such as a click on the X button in the top-right corner of the cmd.exe window), instances of cmd.exe are independent processes.

What we commonly call *variables* are more properly called *environment variables* in the Windows NT command shell. This is the case because shell commands – including those contained in shell scripts – execute within instances of cmd.exe. The instance of cmd.exe in which your commands run forms their environment – the surroundings in which they go about their business. The characteristics of this environment are environment variables.

System and User Environment Variables

Environment variables come from many different sources. Just as you could look around and describe your personal surroundings, Windows NT looks around and describes what it sees in terms of processors, users, paths, and so on. Some variables are built into the operating system or derived from the system hardware during startup. These variables are called built-in system variables and are available to all Windows NT processes regardless of whether anyone is logged in interactively. System variables can also come from the Windows NT Registry. These variables are stored in the Registry's HKEY_LOCAL_MACHINE hive and are set as the system boots.

Other variables are set during logon and are called *built-in user variables*. The built-in user variables available are the same no matter who is logged on the computer. As you might expect, they are only valid during an actual logon session. Because of this, shell scripts executed with the AT command cannot rely on user variables to be available. User variables can also come from the Windows NT Registry. Here, the variables are stored in the Registry's HKEY_CURRENT_USER hive and are set during user login. These user variables are valid only for the current user and may not be available for other users.

Table 4-1 lists the key built-in system and user variables you may want to work with in shell scripts. You can create additional variables with set commands in AUTOEXEC.BAT and Windows NT logon scripts.

TABLE 4-1 BUILT-IN SYSTEM AND USER VARIABLES

Variable Name	Description	Sample Value
COMPUTERNAME	Name of the system on which the command is being executed.	ZETA
COMSPEC	Complete path to the current instance of cmd.exe.	D:\WinNT\system32\cmd.exe
HOMEDRIVE	Drive name on which the current user's profile resides.	D:

Variable Name	Description	Sample Value
HOMEPATH	Location of the root directory on the home drive.	\
LOGONSERVER	UNC name of the domain controller that handled the current user's logon procedure.	\\ZETAMAIN
NUMBER_OF_PROCESSORS	Number of CPUs present in the machine on which the command is being executed.	1
OS	Name of the operating system. All versions of Windows NT put Windows_NT in this variable.	Windows_NT
PATH	List of directories in which Windows NT looks for executables when they're requested.	Path=D:\Perl\ bin;D:\WinNT\ system32;
PATHEXT	Filename extensions the operating system recognizes as belonging to executable files.	.com;.exe;.bat;. cmd;.vbs;.js;.pl
PROCESSOR_ARCHITECTURE	Architecture of the processors. This is x86 on standard Intel systems and alpha on DEC Alpha systems.	x86
PROMPT	Command prompt settings on the current machine.	pg
SYSTEMDRIVE	Drive name (letter plus colon) on which the current, local instance of Windows NT resides.	D:
SYSTEMROOT	Path to the current, local instance of Windows NT.	D:\WinNT
USERDOMAIN	Name of the domain the current user is logged on to. This is the same as COMPUTERNAME if the user is not logged into a domain.	ZETA_D
USERNAME	Username of the current user.	wstanek
USERPROFILE	Path to the current user's user profile.	D:\WINNT\ Profiles\ wstanek

Managing Environment Variables in the Registry

Windows NT stores all system configuration information in the Registry. Indeed, if you look hard enough, it's likely you'll find all your missing ballpoint pens and the mates to your single socks in the Registry's depths. But more central to this book is the fact that the Registry holds environment variable names and values. Windows NT looks at the variable values in the Registry every time it starts.

Rather than edit the variables directly in the Registry, you'll usually want to use the System applet's Environment tab, which is accessed as follows:

1. Open the Control Panel.

2. Start the System applet. The System Properties dialog box appears.

3. Select the Environment tab, as shown in Figure 4-1.

4. You can now create, edit, and delete environment variables.

Figure 4–1: The Environment tab of the System Properties dialog box is the easiest way to set the environment variables stored in the Registry.

The Environment tab consists of two parts. The upper section (labeled System Variables) lists system variables. The lower section (labeled User Variables for *UserName*) lists user variables. You can create a new variable as follows:

1. Highlight one of the existing variables in the System Variables or User Variables section, depending upon which kind of variable you want to create.

2. In the Name box, enter the name of the variable you want to create, typing over the name of the variable you clicked.

3. In the Value box, enter the value of the variable you want to create, typing over the value of the variable you clicked.

4. Click the Set button.

To edit the value of a variable

1. Highlight the variable whose value you want to modify.

2. In the Value box, replace the variable's existing value with the value you want the variable to have.

3. Click the Set button.

To delete a variable

1. Highlight the variable you want to delete.

2. Click the Delete button.

Variable changes are made directly in the Registry and aren't normally applied to the OS environment. If you want to apply the changes to the environment, you must click Apply. Now when you start a new command shell, the command shell will inherit the changes. Existing command shells, however, will not inherit the changes. For system variables, you must reboot to apply the changes throughout the environment. For user variables, the user must log out and then log back in.

Viewing Environment Variables at the Command Line

You can see a listing of all the variables known in the current instance of the command shell by typing set at the prompt:

```
set
```

Listing 4-1 shows what set yielded on my system.

Listing 4–1: Output from the set command

```
COMPUTERNAME=ZETA
ComSpec=D:\WINNT\system32\cmd.exe
```

```
HOMEDRIVE=D:
HOMEPATH=\
INCLUDE=e:\devstudio\vc\include;D:\Program Files\Mts\Include
LIB=e:\devstudio\vc\lib;D:\Program Files\Mts\Lib
LOGONSERVER=\\ZETAMAIN
MSDevDir=E:\DevStudio\SharedIDE
NUMBER_OF_PROCESSORS=1
OS=Windows_NT
Os2LibPath=D:\WINNT\system32\os2\dll;
Path=D:\Perl\bin;D:\WINNT\system32;D:\WINNT;C:\MSSQL7\BINN;
e:\devstudio\sharedide\bin;e:\devstudio\vc\bin
PATHEXT=.COM;.EXE;.BAT;.CMD;.VBS;.JS;.PL
PROCESSOR_ARCHITECTURE=x86
PROCESSOR_IDENTIFIER=x86 Family 6 Model 3 Stepping 3
PROCESSOR_LEVEL=6
PROCESSOR_REVISION=0303
PROMPT=$P$G
SystemDrive=D:
SystemRoot=D:\WINNT
TEMP=D:\TEMP
TMP=D:\TEMP
USERDOMAIN=ZETA_D
USERNAME=administrator
USERPROFILE=D:\WINNT\Profiles\Administrator
windir=D:\WINNT
```

If you don't want to see names and values for every existing variable, and you know the name of the variable whose value you want to examine, just type set followed by the variable name, as shown in the following example:

```
set variablename
```

where `variablename` is the name of a specific variable, such as

```
set COMPUTERNAME
```

If you use set to request a name-and-value pair for a variable that does not exist, the command shell will give you an error stating that the environment variable is not defined.

When you follow `set` with all or part of a variable name, the command shell returns name-and-value pairs for all variables whose names begin that way. To try this out, type the following at the command prompt:

```
set USER
```

The resulting output on an NT server system should be similar to the following:

```
USERDOMAIN=ZETA_D
USERNAME=administrator
USERPROFILE=D:\WINNT\Profiles\Administrator
```

Working with Variables

In addition to the normal system and user variables, you can create variables anytime while Windows NT is running, which is exactly what you'll do when you program in the command shell. As an experiment, let's see what happens when we ask to see the value of a variable we know does not exist. At a command prompt, type

```
set mypants
```

The command shell replies

```
Environment variable mypants not defined
```

So let's define and set that variable. At the command prompt, type this:

```
set mypants=c:\onfire
```

Nothing happens visibly as a result of that command. It does something under the surface, as you'll soon see. To reveal the change, type this:

```
set mypants
```

That command yields the following:

```
mypants=c:\onfire
```

This experiment demonstrates that the environment has been changed to include a variable called `mypants`. You know what they say about your impact on the environment, right? Be careful about what variables you strew around—don't create more than you need, lest you crowd your machine's memory or confuse yourself.

Special Variables

Some variables have special meaning in the command shell. In previous chapters, you learned about special-purpose variables such as PATH, PATHEXT, and PROMPT. Other special-purpose variables you may want to work with include

- ◆ COMSPEC – Specifies the exact path to the Windows NT command shell executable

- ◆ CMDCMDLINE – References the exact command line used to start the current command shell executable

- ◆ DIRCMD – Tracks additional switches for the DIR command

- ◆ ERRORLEVEL – Tracks the exit code of the most recently used command

USING COMSPEC AND CMDCMDLINE

When you invoke a command shell from within a script, you should use the COM-SPEC variable to ensure you invoke the command shell in the %SYSTEMROOT%\System32 directory. If you don't use COMSPEC, the command shell started is the first one found in the current path.

Using COMSPEC is easy. Instead of using the following code in a script

```
cmd /C start.bat
```

you use

```
%COMSPEC% /C start.bat
```

The CMDCMDLINE variable references the exact command line used to start the current command shell, including all switches and arguments. This variable cannot be changed with the set command and does not appear in the list of normal environment variables.

You use CMDCMDLINE as follows:

```
echo %CMDCMDLINE%
```

If the command shell was started with cmd /Q the output would be

```
cmd /Q
```

USING DIRCMD

The DIRCMD variable stores default options for the dir command. For example, if you set DIRCMD as follows:

```
set DIRCMD=/p /o:s
```

Every time you execute `dir` in the current command shell, the directory listing is displayed by page and sorted by size. Further, if these default options are set in the Windows NT Registry (or through the System applet) as a user variable, they are permanent and used for all sessions of the current user.

To override the default switches for `dir`, you must unset the `DIRCMD` variable or negate the switches. At the command line, you could negate the switches set in the previous example as follows:

```
dir /-p /o:-s
```

Unfortunately, in your scripts, you won't always know what specific switches the user has applied and there's no easy way to negate all the values in `DIRCMD`. Because of this, I recommend that you unset `DIRCMD` before you use `dir` in your scripts as shown in Listing 4-2. Once you unset `DIRCMD`, you know (and can set) the exact behavior for `dir`.

Listing 4-2: Overriding DIRCMD options

directory.bat
```
@echo off
rem unset DIRCMD to ensure DIR works as expected
set DIRCMD=

rem start working with DIR as normal
dir /o > test.txt
```
Output
```
Output is sent to the file test.txt.
```

USING ERRORLEVEL

The `ERRORLEVEL` variable tracks the exit code of the last command you executed. While a nonzero exit code generally indicates an error, the type and severity of the error varies. An exit code of 2 indicates an execution error (the command failed to execute properly). An exit code of –2 indicates a math error, such as happens when you create a number that is too large for the command shell to handle. An exit code of 1 usually indicates a general error.

Windows NT provides two ways to work with the `ERRORLEVEL` variable. You can test for a specific error condition:

```
if "%ERRORLEVEL%"=="2" echo "You have an error!"
```

Or, you can use the following special syntax and test for a condition equal to or greater than the specified exit code:

```
if errorlevel 2 echo "You have an error!"
```

A more complete example of working with errors and exit codes is shown in Listing 4-3. This example demonstrates how you could handle errors using GOTO routines. Note that if the ERROR1 subroutine didn't have the goto EXIT statement, the script would proceed right on to the ERROR2 subroutine and echo the error statement in that subroutine.

Listing 4–3: Handling errors in shell scripts

errors.bat
```
@echo off
set DIRCMD=

dir dud > test.txt
if "%ERRORLEVEL%"=="2" goto ERROR1

dir doodle > test.txt
if errorlevel 2 goto ERROR2

:ERROR1
echo "Error1 for listing of dddd"
goto EXIT

:ERROR2
echo "Error2 for listing of dddd"
goto EXIT

:EXIT
```

Output
```
Output depends on whether the named directories exist. Normally,
you'll see:

File Not Found
"Error1 for listing of dddd"
```

Using Variables

Variables do more than just tell you about Windows NT and the hardware and software environment it lives in. You'll use variables to store values as you perform operations in the command shell. Unlike most programming languages, you cannot declare a variable in the Windows NT command shell without simultaneously assigning it a value. This makes a certain amount of sense, since from a practical point of view there's no reason to have a variable that contains nothing. If *Seinfeld* was a television show about nothing, there are no *Seinfeld* variables in the Windows NT command shell.

Variable Names

In Windows NT, variable names aren't case-sensitive but are case-aware. This means the command shell tracks variable names in the case you used but doesn't care about the case when you are working with the variable. Beyond this, very few restrictions apply to variable names. In fact, all of the following variable names are technically valid:

```
1variable
5
.
\
```

The last three names in the list above are horrendous, even if they do actually yield variables called 5, ., and \. How, then, should you name your variables? Well, the most important thing is to use descriptive names, such as the following:

```
sum
subtotal
earnings
```

Descriptive variable names are especially helpful when you — or someone else — needs to modify the code in the future. Though it's tempting to use single-letter variable names to save typing, try not to unless you're writing a program in which single-letter variables would be readily understood. For example, if you were writing a program that calculated the area of a circle, it would be fine to use r as the variable that held the radius, because everyone remembers that convention from geometry.

What if you need to have multiple-word variable names? You can do that, as long as your words aren't separated by spaces. Here are some examples of acceptably formatted multiword variable names:

```
novemberTotal
lizzy_borden
She-Of-Whom-We-Do-Not-Speak
```

These variables are all technically okay, and you're free to use whichever style you like best. Generally, though, most programmers format multiword variable names like `novemberTotal`; that is, a variable name with a lowercase initial letter on the first word and uppercase initial letters on each subsequent word. Why is this? It's a standard convention, and you may want to get used to naming things this way if you aspire to program in C, Java, or other languages.

 As you set out to work with variables, keep in mind that variable names are case-aware but they're not case-sensitive. This means that you could refer to the `novemberTotal` variable as `novembertotal`, `NOVEMBERTOTAL`, or even `noVEMberTOTal`.

To define a new variable, use this syntax:

```
set variablename=value
```

where `variablename` is the variable name and `value` is its related value. Because spaces are valid in both names and values, don't use spaces around the equal sign (=) unless you want the name and/or value to include these spaces.

 Don't worry about making your variable names too long. Names can be more than 80 characters in length — longer than you'd ever want to try to manage in a real script.

Variable Values

Though many programming languages make a great production of data types and other concessions to the fact that, for instance, the numerical value 5 is different from the word `five`, the Windows NT command shell does not. Variables store sequences of characters as strings. This is true even when the string happens to consist solely of one or more numerals.

When you create variables, everything following the equal sign (=) is assigned as the variable value, including spaces and punctuation marks. All of the following may be assigned to variables, and all of the following are strings:

```
spamSpamSpamSpamSpam
R
56
34.21
```

```
Oh, Lucy! I'm home!
"Wow!"
```

Before you use special characters, be sure to escape them with the caret symbol (^) as discussed in Chapter 2. Following this, you could use the ampersand symbol (&) in a value as follows:

```
set myTest=Yes ^& No
```

Now if you display the value of myTest, you get

```
Yes & No
```

Variables values can be lengthy — 1,000 characters or more. As is the case with the maximum length of variable names, you will never want to try to manage variable values anywhere close to that long. It's also true that variable values are limited by the amount of memory available on the system on which they exist. It is possible that an intermittently overloaded server could cause unpredictable behavior in a script, and it wouldn't be detectable under test conditions unless the load were duplicated. The reason for this is that as the server load increases, the amount of free memory normally decreases. If the system gets low on memory or runs out of memory, a script may not have the resources it needs to execute commands or carry out operations.

Variable Substitution

If the only way you could access variable values was with the set command, variables wouldn't be very useful. Fortunately, you can access variable values in other ways. One of these ways is to use a process called *substitution* to compare a variable name with its actual value. You saw this type of substitution at work in the following line from Chapter 3's header script:

```
if not "%OS%"=="Windows_NT" goto EXIT
```

Here, you are determining whether the value of the OS environment variable is equal to Windows_NT and, if it is, you goto the EXIT label. The percent signs surrounding the variable name tell the command shell you are referencing a variable. Without these percent signs, Windows NT would perform a literal comparison of "OS" and "Windows_NT".

Note also the use of quotation marks in the example. Using quotation marks ensures an exact comparison of string values.

You can also use variable substitution to replace a variable name with its actual value. In this example, a reference to the SYSTEMROOT environment variable is replaced by its actual value:

```
net user > %SYSTEMROOT%\System32\users.txt
```

Here, if SYSTEMROOT is set to D:\WinNT, the net user command would write output to the file D:\WinNT\System32\users.txt.

You can also use variable substitution when you are assigning values to other variables, such as

```
filePath=%SystemRoot%\System32\users.txt
```

Here, filePath is assigned the following value (on my system):

```
C:\WinNT\System32\users.txt
```

But watch out, substituting variables within other variables can get you into trouble. To see how, try Listing 4-4.

Listing 4-4: Using variable substitution

subst.bat
```
@echo off
set text1=Home run king at bat...
set text2=%text1%
echo %text2%

set score=%Runs%
set Runs=5
echo %score%
```
Output
```
Home run king at bat...
Echo is off.
```

In the first example, you create a variable, reference it later, and then get the expected result from echo. In the second example, you substitute a variable that hasn't been declared yet, create the necessary variable, and then try to echo text2's value. Instead of getting the number of runs, you get the same result as if you had entered **echo** on a line by itself. The reason for this is that NULL was substituted for %RUNS% — the variable didn't exist when you referenced it.

Understanding Variable Scope

It's fair to think of an instance of cmd.exe as a system process in which command shell activities can be carried out. Unless you take specific steps to make it otherwise, anything the command shell does to alter the process environment applies only within the confines of the current system process. What does this mean?

Well, once an instance of cmd.exe is running, it can execute commands that cause variables to be instantiated, set, or eliminated. However, changes made within one instance of cmd.exe are not "visible" to other cmd.exe processes or to explorer.exe. To see what I'm talking about, start a command shell window and type this:

```
set testVariable=A
```

This creates a variable called testVariable and sets it equal to A. To verify that the command shell knows about testVariable, **type**

```
set testVariable
```

You should see this output:

```
testVariable=A
```

Next, start another command shell window by running the same shortcut you used to start the first. In the second window, type

```
set testVariable
```

You get this result:

```
Environment variable testVariable not defined
```

The reason for this is that the second cmd.exe process doesn't know about testVariable. You set this variable in a different process.

 The other thing worth observing is that variables die with their processes. Create an instance of cmd.exe, create a variable in it, close the cmd.exe window, open another one, and use `set` to inquire of your variable's value. You'll get a "not defined" error.

Localizing Variables

Sometimes you may want to limit the scope of variables even further than their current command shell process. To do this, you can create a local scope within a script and in this way ensure that changes are localized to specific areas within the script. Later, you can end the local scope and restore the environment to its original settings.

You start a local scope within a script using SETLOCAL and then end the scope with ENDLOCAL. Several events take place when you use these commands. The call to SETLOCAL creates a snapshot of the environment. Any changes you make within the scope are then localized and discarded when you call ENDLOCAL.

Listing 4-5 shows an example of local scopes. In the local scope, you create working variables, which you can then use within the scope. Once you exit the scope, however, the original environment is restored and the variable values reflect this.

Listing 4-5: Creating local scopes within scripts

localscope.bat
```
@echo off
set numStrikes=0
set numBalls=0

rem Create a local scope
setlocal
set numStrikes=2
set numBalls=2
echo %numStrikes% Strikes ^& %numBalls% Balls
endlocal

echo %numStrikes% Strikes ^& %numBalls% Balls
```
Output
```
2 Strikes & 2 Balls
0 Strikes & 0 Balls
```

Local scopes behave much like nested command shells. As with the nested command shells discussed in Chapter 3, you can nest several layers of localization. While each layer inherits the environment of its parent, any changes in the nested layer are not reflected in the parent environment.

Variable Destruction

It's good form to dispose of variables when you're done working with them. Doing this has several advantages:

- ◆ It frees up memory for other uses.
- ◆ It prevents you from getting unexpected results when you accidentally refer to a zombie variable in the future.
- ◆ It keeps your scripting environment neat and orderly.

There's no magic word you use to kill a variable. Rather, there is a special way of using the set command. Effectively, you set an existing variable equal to nothing. Listing 4-6 shows this effect in practice.

Listing 4–6: Destroying a variable

destroy.bat
```
set hotelName=Empress
set hotelName
set hotelName=
set hotelName
```

Output
```
hotelName=Empress
Environment variable hotelName not defined
```

The set command in the first line defines and assigns a value to hotelName. The next line yields hotelName=Empress, since the variable exists and has a value. Line three sets hotelName equal to nothing, eliminating it. For that reason, the last line generates an error message as a result of inquiring after a nonexistent variable.

As you can see, the syntax for deleting a variable is

```
set variablename=
```

such as

```
set totalsales=
```

It's no big deal if you use this method to destroy a variable that does not exist. Try it if you want. Nothing will change, and no errors will appear. This is why it's critical to supply the correct variable name when performing this procedure. If you were to accidentally misspell the variable name and didn't verify the deletion manually, you'd have no idea that the expected deletion hadn't taken place.

Using Mathematical Expressions

Often you'll want to perform some kind of mathematical operation and assign the results to a variable. As with other assignment operations, `set` applies in this case. You have to do something special, though, before assigning the resulting value to a variable. Here's the syntax you need to use:

```
set /a sum=4+5
```

The big trick is the /a switch. This switch tells the Windows NT script interpreter to resolve the equation and then assign that value to the variable `sum`.

Expressions are evaluated using 32-bit signed integer arithmetic, allowing for values -2^{32} to $2^{32}-1$. If you exceed this range, you'll get an error code (–2) instead of the intended value.

Operators

Even if you've never programmed a computer before, you're probably familiar with operators such as the plus (+) and minus (–) signs. Operators are simply the characters you use to perform mathematical and logical operations on numerical values. Key operators you'll use in the command shell are as follows:

- ◆ **Arithmetic operators.** These operators perform familiar mathematical operations on numerical values.

- ◆ **Assignment operators.** These operators combine an assignment operation (symbolized by the equal sign) with an arithmetic operation.

- ◆ **Comparison operators.** These operators compare values and are usually used with `if` statements. You'll find a complete discussion of these operators in Chapter 5.

- ◆ **Bitwise operators.** You can use these operators to manipulate the sequences of binary bits that represent numbers.

ARITHMETIC OPERATORS

Arithmetic operators tell Windows NT to perform math operations on numerical values. The numerical values can be expressed literally with a number, such as 5, or as a variable that contains a numerical value, such as %INTEREST%.

Arithmetic operators available in the Windows NT command shell are listed in Table 4-2. Most of these operators are fairly basic. You use * in multiplication, / in division, + in addition, and - in subtraction. You use the equal sign (=) to assign values to variables, as you've already done several times. You use % (modulus) to obtain the remainder from division.

Several examples of using arithmetic operators follow:

```
set /a numUser=5+3
set /a numUser=%NUSER% + %XUSER%
set /a numUser=%NUSER% - 1
```

TABLE 4-2 ARITHMETIC OPERATORS

Operator	Operation
*	Multiplication
/	Division
+	Addition
-	Subtraction
%	Modulus
=	Assignment

TIP   If you ever get the urge to evaluate arithmetic expressions at the command line without generating a script file, you can. You use set in a special way. Here's the trick:

```
set /a expression
```

Try it. Type this:

```
set /a 5*5*8
```

When you press Enter, you get

```
200
```

Note that this doesn't assign the result of the operation to any variable — it just figures out the product of the three numbers and outputs the result to the command shell.

What's Modulus?

What's modulus? It's a special operation that results on the remainder of a division operation. The best way to explain it is with some examples. These aren't code — they're just math expressions:

10 % 3 = 1

10 % 8 = 2

10 % 5 = 0

10 % 12 = 10

See? You divide the number on the right into the number on the left, and then take the remainder and give that as the result of the modulus operation. A modulus operation yields 0 if the right operand divides evenly into the left operand. If the right operand is greater than the left operand, the result is the same as the left operand.

ASSIGNMENT OPERATORS

As a convenience, the command shell supports five operators that combine arithmetic and assignment. The += operator, for instance, combines the effects of the + operator and the = operator. The following two expressions are equivalent – they give identical results when entered at the command line:

```
set /a sum=sum+1
set /a sum+= 1
```

Table 4-3 provides a complete list of the combined operators.

TABLE 4-3 ASSIGNMENT OPERATORS

Operator	Operation
+=	Increment (add and assign)
-=	Decrement (subtract and assign)
*=	Scale up (multiply and assign)
/=	Scale down (divide and assign)

%=	Modulus and assign

Listing 4-7 illustrates how the combined operators work in real life.

Listing 4-7: Combined operators

combined.bat
```
@echo off
set demo=5
echo %demo%
set /a demo+=1
echo %demo%
set /a demo-=1
echo %demo%
set /a demo*=2
echo %demo%
set /a demo/=2
echo %demo%
set /a demo%=4
echo %demo%
```

Output
```
5
6
5
10
5
4
```

There's a bug in the %= operator when it's used in a script, and it's revealed in Listing 4-7. You'll note that the result of

```
@set /a demo%=4
```

should be 1, but it's given as 4. This is an error.

The problem doesn't appear in interactive mode. If you open a command shell window and type the following:

```
set demo=5
set /a demo%=4
```

you get the correct answer: 1. Don't forget this problem when you're using the %= operator in a script.

BITWISE OPERATORS

Bitwise operators have to do with modifying and comparing binary numbers. Table 4-4 lists the bitwise operators.

TABLE 4-4 BITWISE OPERATORS

Operator	Operation
<<	Left shift
>	Right shift
&	Logical AND
|	Logical OR
^	Logical Exclusive OR (XOR)

Here's a quick rundown of how bitwise operators work:

◆ << adds zeros (bits) to the right end of a binary number. 0b10 << 1 yields 0b100, which is decimal 8.

◆ > chops bits from the right end of a binary number. For example, 0b101011 > 2 yields 0b1010, the equivalent of decimal 18.

◆ & compares two binary numbers, comparing each bit in each and yielding a 1 where both numbers being compared have a 1. If the two values being compared are not the same length, the operator treats the shorter number as if it has leading zeroes. For example, 0b10011011 & 0b110101010 results in 0b10001, which is 17 in decimal notation.

◆ | compares two binary numbers, comparing each bit in each and yielding a 1 where one or both of the numbers being compared have a 1. If the two values being compared are not the same length, the operator treats the shorter number as if it has leading zeroes. For example, 0b1010 | 0b1000 results in 0b1010, which is 20 in decimal notation.

◆ ^ compares two binary numbers, comparing each bit in each and yielding a 1 where one – and only one – of the numbers being compared has a 1. If the two values being compared are not the same length, the operator treats the shorter number as if it has leading zeroes. For example, 0b1010 ^ 0b1000 results in 0b1000, which is 16 in decimal notation.

Often, the easiest way to understand logical operations is to use truth tables. In a truth table, rows correspond to all possible combinations of values for the arguments. There is a column for each argument and a column for the result. The following truth table gives a visual depiction of how logical AND works:

p	q	p AND q
0	0	0
0	1	0
1	0	0
1	1	1

The following truth table gives a visual depiction of how logical OR works:

p	q	p OR q
0	0	0
0	1	1
1	0	1
1	1	1

The following truth table gives a visual depiction of how logical XOR works:

p	q	p XOR q
0	0	0
0	1	1
1	0	1
1	1	0

All of the bitwise operators use characters that are reserved in shell for other purposes. Because of this, you'll need to escape each character in bitwise operators before using them, such as

```
set /a value = 0x56^<^<3
```

or

```
set /a value = 0x56^|3
```

Operator Precedence

What happens when the command shell has to evaluate an expression that involves more than one operator? For example:

```
6+5*5
```

If evaluated from left to right, this expression equals 55 (6+5=11, 11*5=55). But that's not how Windows NT approaches the expression. Rather, the command shell evaluates the expression as 31 (5*5=25, 6+25=31). It gets that result because it evaluates multioperator expressions according to a strict sequence called the *precedence of operations*. The sequence is as follows:

1. Modulus

2. Multiplication and division

3. Addition and subtraction

SIMULATING PARENTHESES

It's important to note that you can't override the precedence of operations with parenthetical grouping the way you can in most programming languages. As a practical matter, this means that for the sake of clarity you'll do most multistep mathematical operations on more than one line, assigning intermediate values to variables as you proceed from step to step.

For example, let's say you want to evaluate

```
((4+5)*(10+3-1))+1
```

The best way to evaluate this expression in a batch file would be with a series of intermediate steps that eventually were combined to yield the final answer. Listing 4-8 shows a solution to the problem.

Listing 4-8: Simulating parentheses

parens.bat

```
set /a innerLeft=4+5
set /a innerRight=10+3-1
set /a outer=%innerLeft% * %innerRight%
set /a final=%outer% + 1
echo The result is %final%.
```

Output

```
The result is 109.
```

If you were to figure out ((4+5)*(10+3-1))+1 on paper, you'd evaluate the stuff in the innermost parentheses first (4+5 and 10+3-1), then figure out the expression in the next set of parentheses up in the hierarchy (9*12), and finally add 1 to the value (108+1). All you did here was use a variable to hold the value of each parenthetical expression temporarily.

True enough, that third variable, outer, isn't necessary. You would have gotten the same result if you'd skipped that line and replaced the next-to-last line with this:

```
set /a final=%innerLeft% * %innerRight% + 1
```

I opted to go with the extra line for the sake of clarity.

SIMULATING EXPONENTS

No operator, keyword, or other ready-made tool exists to help you raise values to exponents in the command shell. There are, however, less convenient ways to get the interpreter to give you values for things such as 5^2 or 13^4.

For example, the easiest way to get a value for 5^2 is to enter

```
set /a 5*5
```

That yields 25.

We get 13^4 by following the same pattern:

```
set /a 13*13*13*13
```

That results in 28561.

Will Hunting wouldn't be impressed, but this is how things get done in the Windows NT command shell. It's a limited environment, and we often have to use inelegant workarounds to get things done there.

This method really only works in two situations—those in which the following conditions are true:

◆ **The exponent is known at the time the script is written.** If you're going to hard-code a specific number of multiplication operations into a script, that number of multiplication operations had better be appropriate to any conditions the script is executed under. There's no way to gauge and react to circumstances at execution time when you use this method.

◆ **The exponent isn't too large.** You can see that this method wouldn't work well if you had to enter all the multiplication operations that represent, say, 2^{24}.

In situations that don't satisfy those two conditions, you can use for loops to simulate exponents. Loops, which you'll learn about in Chapter 5, can be used to perform a variable number of multiplication operations, based on conditions. They're compact and don't require you to write a lot of code.

Variable Substitution with Arithmetical Expressions

It's true that everything stored in a variable is a string, but the truth is that the command shell has some limited ability to figure out when the string happens to comprise only numerals.

The command shell provides you with some latitude in substituting variables containing numerical values – but this works *only in interactive mode*. It doesn't work in batch files. Here's how to demonstrate this phenomenon:

```
set test=5
set /a test*5
```

That yields 25, and note how there was no need to put percent signs around test in the second line.

When in scripting mode, variable substitution works the same with numbers as with string values. You have to surround the variable name with percent signs. Listing 4-9 shows how this works.

Listing 4-9: Variable substitution with arithmetical expressions

mathsub.bat

```
@set radius=5
@set pi=3
@set /a area = %pi%*%radius%*%radius%
@echo The area of a circle with radius %radius% is %area%.
```

Output

```
The area of a circle with radius 5 is 75.
```

Number Systems

The Windows NT command shell supports calculations on numbers of four different bases:

◆ **Hexadecimal.** Base 16; precede numbers with 0x

◆ **Decimal.** Base 10; normal number values and the default number base

◆ **Octal.** Base 8; precede numbers with 0

◆ **Binary.** Base 2; precede numbers with 0b

Be cautious with all command shell mathematics. If you have complex or nondecimal calculations to perform, do them with a spreadsheet or a more powerful programming language (such as one of the Windows Script Host languages, discussed in detail later in this book). The Windows NT command shell isn't what you need.

HEXADECIMAL NUMBERS

Hexadecimal numbers are used to represent values in a number system of base 16. The digits used in hexadecimal (or *hex)* numbers are the numerals 0 through 9, plus the letters A through F (or a through f), which are used as digits to represent the values 10 through 15. Hex numbers frequently find use as a relatively convenient way to represent large binary values, and have applications in computer memory addressing schemes, for example.

The Windows NT command shell identifies any value that begins with 0x as a hexadecimal number, and will evaluate mathematical expressions containing such numbers accordingly. Listing 4-10 shows a script that illustrates how the command shell works with hexadecimal values.

Listing 4-10: Hexadecimal arithmetic

hex.bat

```
@set addend1=0x12b
@set addend2=0x19f4
@set /a hexResult=addend1+addend2
@echo %hexResult%
```

Output

```
6943
```

It's worth noting that the result is given as a decimal number. This is how the command shell works with all bases — no matter what bases go in, a decimal number always comes out.

DECIMAL NUMBERS

The command shell loves whole decimal numbers. Odds are, so do you. Most of the arithmetic you'll encounter in this book will be performed on decimal numbers. There are some things to keep in mind, though, when you work with base 10 numbers.

The command shell is designed to work with round numbers. It doesn't have any capacity to work with noninteger numbers – that is, numbers with a decimal point and something to the right of it.

The Windows NT command shell can't do math with noninteger numbers. You can assign noninteger numbers (numbers with a decimal point and some nonzero numbers to the right of it) to variables, but if you try to operate on them with set /a, you'll get errors. This is a pretty serious limitation from a theoretical point of view, but as a practical matter it doesn't come up much. You just don't do much complicated calculating at the command line.

Listing 4-11 shows a script that illustrates what happens when you attempt to work with noninteger numbers.

Listing 4-11: Working with noninteger numbers

real.bat
```
@echo Let's try to add with a noninteger number: 2+5.6
@set /a 2+5.6
@echo Let's try a division expression with a noninteger result: 10/4
@set /a result=10/4
@echo %result%
@echo No stomach for reals.
```

Output
```
Let's try to add with a noninteger number: 2+5.6
Missing operator.
Let's try a division expression with a noninteger result: 10/4
2
No stomach for reals.
```

This experiment revealed two things:

♦ Attempting to perform math with a noninteger will cause an error.

◆ Any noninteger result of an arithmetic operation will have its fractional component (the decimal point and everything to its right) summarily chopped off. The command shell doesn't even do any rounding.

OCTAL NUMBERS

Octal numbers represent values in a number system of base 8. Like hex, the octal system has applications as a shorthand for binary and is most often seen in association with computer-related calculations. In the Windows NT command shell, octal numbers begin with leading zeroes. Listing 4-12 provides an example using octal numbers.

 Note that octal numbers in the command shell begin with leading zeroes. This can cause problems, because those of us in the decimal world are used to leading zeroes being meaningless. That's not the case in the command shell. For example, 013, an octal number, is equal to decimal 11. Be sure to strip any leading zeroes from decimal values to prevent them from being treated as octal numbers.

Listing 4-12: Octal arithmetic

octal.bat
```
@set firstOctalNumber=04523
@set secondOctalNumber=07012
@set /a octalResult=firstOctalNumber+secondOctalNumber
@echo %octalResult%
```

Output
```
5981
```

 Again, the output is a decimal number. The fact is, any arithmetic result that gets stored in a variable is stored as a decimal number.

BINARY NUMBERS

The command shell can work with base 2 numbers, which consist only of ones and zeroes. You can distinguish binary numbers by their leading 0b sequence (that's zero-b). However, because there are extensive problems evaluating binary numbers in the command shell, you should use hexadecimal or octal rather than binary.

MIXING BASES

What happens when you add an octal value to a decimal value, or multiply a binary value by a hex number? You get a decimal number. To see this, try running Listing 4-13.

Listing 4-13: Mixing bases

bases.bat

```
@set octalNumber=09
@set hexNumbcr=0x8h
@set decimalNumber=49
@set /a intermediate=decimalNumber * octalNumber
@set /a finalResult=intermediate - hexNumber
@echo %finalResult%
```

Output

```
-8
```

Regardless of the number base you use in calculations, the output is always a decimal value.

Summary

Variables have an important role in scripts. You use them to hold values, to read system configuration information, and to help you perform many other tasks. Variables are defined and set in several ways. Built-in system and user environment variables are set during system startup or when users log in. Other variables are set in the Windows Registry by applications or through shell commands.

When you perform calculations, you'll use variables to hold the result of the mathematical operation you are performing. The command shell supports four different types of mathematical operators. Use arithmetic operators to perform standard math functions, such as adding and subtracting values. Use assignment operators to increment, decrement, and scale values. Use comparison operators to compare values. Use binary operators to work with binary values.

Chapter 5

Programming the Windows Shell

IN THIS CHAPTER

◆ Manipulating strings and parameter values

◆ Creating subroutines and procedures

◆ Conditional executing for `if` statements

◆ Controlling flow with `for` loops

THE WINDOWS NT COMMAND shell is a lot more powerful than most people realize, especially when it comes to helping you quickly create solutions. Core shell programming involves string manipulation, procedures, conditional execution, and looping. To manipulate the values of strings and parameters passed in to scripts, you'll use substitution, indexing, and more. Beyond strings, you'll find programming constructs, such as `goto`, `call`, `if`, and `for`. You'll use `goto` and `call` to create procedures, `if` statements to conditionally execute commands, and `for` to repeatedly execute commands.

Manipulating String and Parameter Values

With string manipulation techniques, you can search and replace string values in variables, extract substrings from variables, and manipulate parameter values. There's even a special syntax for replacing values in parameters.

Searching and Replacing Values in Strings

The Windows NT command shell supports two formats for searching and replacing string values in variables. You can temporarily substitute strings values for display or use in another command (without actually modifying the value of the variable). Or, you can permanently replace values in the variable through an assignment.

To see how temporary substitution works, enter Listing 5-1. Here, you create a variable called Now and set its value. Afterward, you temporarily replace "great" with "good" and display the result. Because the replacement isn't permanent, you can then display the variable as originally set.

Listing 5-1: Temporary substitution

tempsub.bat
```
@echo off
set Now=Today is a great day!
echo %Now:great=good%
echo %Now%
```
Output
```
Today is a good day!
Today is a great day!
```

From Listing 5-1, you can see that temporary substitution follows this syntax:

```
%varName:oString=tString%
```

where *varName* is the name of the variable you are working with, *oString* is the original value to replace, and *tString* is the temporary replacement string. Be careful though, all occurrences of the original string are replaced — not just the first occurrence.

You can permanently replace values within the string as well. To do this, you need to use an assignment operator, as you see in Listing 5-2. Here, all occurrences of D: in the command path are replaced with C:, and the .bat extension in the execution path is replaced with .scr.

Listing 5-2: Permanent substitution

permsub.bat
```
@echo off
echo Original file and ext path:
echo %PATH%
echo %PATHEXT%
echo =========
set PATH=%PATH:d:=c:%
set PATHEXT=%PATHEXT:.BAT=.SCR%
echo New file and ext path:
echo %PATH%
echo %PATHEXT%
```
Output
```
Original file and ext path:
D:\Perl\bin;D:\WinNT\system32;D:\WinNT;D:\Program Files\Mts;
.COM;.EXE;.BAT;.CMD;.VBS;.JS
```

```
=========
New file and ext path:
c:\Perl\bin;c:\WinNT\system32;c:\WinNT;c:\Program Files\Mts;
.COM;.EXE;.SCR;.CMD;.VBS;.JS
```

From Listing 5-2, you can see that permanent substitution follows this syntax:

varName=%varName:oString=pString%

where *varName* is the name of the variable you are working with, *oString* is the original value to replace, and *pString* is the replacement string.

Working with Substrings and Indexing

The Windows NT command shell also supports syntax for extracting substrings from variables. A substring is a section of a string that you can use with other commands or reassign to the variable to set a new value. The syntax for obtaining substrings from a variable is

%varName:~startChar,numChars%

where *varName* is the name of the variable you are examining, *startChar* is the index position to start at, and *numChars* sets the number of characters to read *after* the starting position. The index position of the first character is 0. For the second character, the index position is 1, and so on.

You could extract and display characters 6–12 from a variable as follows:

```
echo %USERPROFILE:~5,7%
```

You could also display all characters after a certain position to the end of the variable text. Here, all characters after the fifth character are displayed:

```
echo %USERPROFILE:~5%
```

TIP   Don't worry about setting *numChars* too high. The command shell won't generate an error. Instead, you'll simply get a substring containing all the characters after a certain position to the end of the variable text.

Substrings don't have to be echoed back at the command line; you can substitute the values into other commands. You could also assign a new value for the variable using the substring, such as

```
set USERPROFILE=%USERPROFILE:~2,8%
```

A more detailed example of working with substrings is shown in Listing 5-3. Enter the example to get a better understanding of substrings.

Listing 5-3: Using substrings

substrings.bat
```
@echo off
rem create a localized environment
setlocal
set USERPROFILE=C:\WinNT\PROFILES\Administrator

rem display a substring containing characters 10-18
echo %USERPROFILE:~9,8%

rem display characters 3 to the end
echo %USERPROFILE:~2%

rem display the first 9 characters
echo %USERPROFILE:~0,9%

rem set variable to substring value
set USERPROFILE=%USERPROFILE:~0,3%
echo %USERPROFILE%

endlocal
```
Output
```
PROFILES
\WinNT\PROFILES\Administrator
C:\WinNT\
C:\
```

Manipulating Parameter Values

The section of Chapter 2 titled "Script Arguments" took a brief look at working with values passed to scripts on the command line. This section takes a closer look at formal parameters and also shows you how to work with parameter qualifiers.

USING PARAMETER VALUES

Each value passed in to a script can be examined with formal parameters. The script name itself is represented by the parameter %0. The parameter %1 represents the first argument passed in to the script, %2 the second, and so on until %9 for the ninth argument. For example, if you create a script called param and then used the following command to call the script:

```
param No Yes Stanek
```

You'd find that the related parameter values are

- %0 – param
- %1 – No
- %2 – Yes
- %3 – Stanek

Additional parameters beyond the ninth are not lost. Instead, they are stored in a special parameter: %* (percent + asterisk). The %* parameter represents all arguments passed to the script. To examine additional parameters, you can use the `shift` command. If you call `shift` without arguments, all parameters are shifted by 1. This means %0 is discarded and replaced with %1, %2 becomes %1, and so on. You can also specify where shifting begins so you can retain previous parameters if necessary. For example, if you use

```
SHIFT /3
```

%4 becomes %3, %5 becomes %4, and so on, but %0, %1, and %2 are unaffected.

Formal parameters cannot be manipulated like environment variables. You can't search and replace values as discussed previously, and you can't examine substrings, either. Thankfully, there is a workaround. Just assign the parameter to a variable and then manipulate the variable:

```
set theParam=%1
echo %theParam:~0,5%
```

USING PARAMETER QUALIFIERS

The Windows NT command shell also provides parameter qualifiers that extract file path components from arguments passed in to a script, such as the filename, file path, or drive designator. For example, if you passed in the following argument to a script:

```
d:\winnt\system32\cmd.exe
```

you could use the d qualifier to extract the drive designator:

```
echo %~d1
```

Here, you tell echo to display the drive designator that is a part of the first parameter. If the parameter contains a file path, you get a valid result, such as D:. If the parameter doesn't contain a file path, you get a NULL value. You could also let the command shell infer the path information based on the current working directory. For example, if the current working directory is D:\working and you started a script called param, the following command on %0:

```
echo %~f0
```

would show this as the path:

```
D:\working\param.bat
```

Table 5-1 shows a complete listing of parameter qualifiers and their uses. What previous examples don't show is that you can combine qualifiers. For example, to obtain the drive and path information, you could use d and p together, such as

```
echo %~dp0
```

 The Windows NT command shell isn't case-sensitive in most instances. Although I've shown the qualifiers in lowercase, they could be used in up-percase as well.

TABLE **5-1 PARAMETER QUALIFIERS**

Qualifier	Description
d	Obtain drive designator (drive letter and the colon character), such as D:
f	Obtain the fully qualified path name, such as D:\working\param.bat
p	Obtain path name only, such as \working\
n	Obtain filename only (without the file extension), such as param
x	Obtain file extension, such as .bat
s	Used with n or x to display the short (MS-DOS) filename or extension

Listing 5-4 shows parameter qualifiers at work in a script. To obtain the same display results, enter the following argument as the script's first parameter:

```
C:\winnt\system32\cmd.exe
```

Listing 5–4: Using parameter qualifiers

qualifiers.bat Parameter for Arg1

```
C:\winnt\system32\cmd.exe
```

qualifiers.bat

```
@echo off
echo %~f1
echo %~d1
echo %~p1
echo %~dp1
echo %~n1
echo %~x1
echo %~nx1
```

Output

```
c:\WinNT\system32\CMD.EXE
c:
\WinNT\system32\
c:\WinNT\system32\
CMD
.EXE
CMD.EXE
```

Just when you thought you'd learned everything there was to know about qualifiers, you discover there's one more thing: a special qualifier used to search paths and find a filename that matches the specified parameter. For example, if you entered **cmd.exe** as the first argument, the following command would search the command path for it and return the first match:

```
%~$PATH:1
```

such as

```
C:\WinNT\system32\CMD.EXE
```

You could also search the LIB or INCLUDE paths, such as

```
%~$LIB:2
```

or

```
%~$INCLUDE:1
```

Creating Subroutines and Procedures

Normally, the Windows NT command interpreter executes scripts line by line starting from the beginning of the file. To change the order of execution, you can use subroutines and procedures. To create subroutines, you use `goto`. To create procedures, you use `call`. The difference between a subroutine and a procedure is primarily in command shell behavior.

With subroutines, execution of the script continues at the designated label and proceeds to the end of the file. With procedures, execution of the script continues at the designated label, proceeds to the end of the file, and then returns to the line following the `call` statement. Additionally, while arguments passed in to the script are available in a subroutine, they are not available within a procedure. Because of this, you'll have to use special techniques to access arguments within a procedure.

Using Labels and goto

I've used labels and `goto` in lots of previous examples, and you probably have a fair understanding of how they work already. Still, you can learn a few new tricks by taking a closer look.

A label identifies a location in your script. To create a label, enter a keyword on a line by itself, beginning with a colon:

```
:SUB1
```

While labels can contain just about any valid type of character, you'll usually want to use alphanumeric characters as this makes the labels easy to read when you are going through the code.

When you use `goto`, execution of the script continues at the line following the target label. If the label is before the script, you can go back to an earlier part of the script. This can create an endless loop (unless there is a control to bypass the `goto` statement). Here's an example of an endless loop:

```
:THE_BEGINNING
.
.
.
goto THE_BEGINNING
```

If the label is after the `goto` statement, you can skip commands and jump ahead to a new section of the script, such as

```
goto SUB1
.
.
```

```
:SUB1
```

Here, execution of the script continues to the end of the file and you cannot go back to the unexecuted commands unless you use another goto statement. However, sometimes you may not want to execute the rest of the script and instead will want to halt execution. To do this, create an exit label like the one you learned about in Chapter 2 and then goto the exit at the end of the routine.

 Watch out! If the label you call doesn't exist, you get an error when the end of file is reached and the script exits without executing other commands.

A detailed example of working with goto and labels is shown in Listing 5-5. In this example, the value of the script's first parameter determines what subroutine is executed. For this example, use 1 as the first parameter. Note that the first if statement handles the case when no parameter is passed in by displaying an error message and exiting. The goto statement following the if statements handles the case when an invalid parameter is passed in. Here, the script simply goes to the :EXIT label.

 In this example, I use a colon (:) to identify the label after the goto and in the label designator itself. With goto, this is a good style technique, but it isn't required. Later, when you use call, however, the colon is required and you'll get an error if you don't use it.

Listing 5-5: Working with goto

gototest.bat Parameter for Arg1

```
1
```

gototest.bat

```
@echo off
if "%1"=="" (echo Error: Arg1 missing) & (goto :EXIT)
if "%1"=="1" goto :SUB1
if "%1"=="2" goto :SUB2
if "%1"=="3" goto :SUB3
goto :EXIT

:SUB1
```

```
echo In subroutine 1
goto :EXIT

:SUB2
echo In subroutine 2
goto :EXIT

:SUB3
echo In subroutine 3
goto :EXIT

:EXIT
echo Exiting...
```

Output

```
In subroutine 1
Exiting...
```

Using call

While `goto` is useful, you'll often need more precise control over the way a script is executed, and this is where `call` comes into the picture. With `call`, you can create controlled procedures and even call other scripts without ending execution of the current script.

CREATING PROCEDURES WITH CALL

When you use `call` to access a procedure, the script goes to the specified label, executes its commands, and then continues execution until the end of the file. When the end of the file is reached, control returns to the first line following `call`. This behavior can lead to some unpredictable results, especially if you don't end the procedure with an `EXIT` or `EOF` label.

To see how, enter Listing 5-6 exactly as shown, and then execute the script with 1 as the first parameter. In this example, I've omitted the `goto :EOF` statement from procedure 1, and as a result

1. Commands in procedure 1 and 2 are executed.

2. The end of file is reached and control returns to the line following `call`.

3. Commands in procedure 1 and 2 are executed a second time.

4. The end of file is reached and the script exits.

Listing 5-6: Testing call with improper syntax

calltest.bat

```
@echo off
if "%1"=="1" call :PRO1
if "%1"=="2" call :PRO2

:PRO1
echo In procedure 1

:PRO2
echo In procedure 2
goto :EOF

:EOF
```

Output

```
In procedure 1
In procedure 2
In procedure 1
In procedure 2
```

To correct the problem, you should place a `goto` statement at the end of each procedure. You should also insert statements that handle the case when no parameter is passed in and when an invalid parameter is passed in. The updated script should look like Listing 5-7. If you don't enter any parameters, the output is as shown.

Listing 5-7: Proper use of call with error checking

calltest.bat

```
@echo off
if "%1"=="" (echo Error: Arg1 missing) & (goto :EOF)
if "%1"=="1" call :PRO1
if "%1"=="2" call :PRO2
goto :EOF

:PRO1
echo In procedure 1
goto :EOF

:PRO2
echo In procedure 2
goto :EOF
```

```
:EOF
```

Output

```
Error: Arg1 missing
```

You can also use `call` to execute another script. When you do this, the behavior is almost exactly like a procedure. The script executes normally. When the command shell reaches the end of the script file, control returns to the calling script and the first line following the `call` is executed. If you don't use `call` and reference a script name within a script, the second script executes, but control isn't returned to the caller.

ACCESSING ARGUMENTS IN PROCEDURES

Within procedures, you can't access arguments passed to the script. The reason for this is that the command shell passes arguments into the procedure (whether you set them or not). In a procedure, %0 refers to the procedure name, %1 refers to the first argument passed in, %2 refers to the second, and so on. These procedure-specific arguments remain in effect until the end of the file is reached and control returns to the first line following the `call`. Can you see why it's a good idea to end procedures with `goto :EOF`?

Any arguments you want to pass in to a procedure follow the `call` label, such as

```
Arg1=Simpsons
Arg2=Star Trek
Arg3=None
call :PRO1 Arg1 Arg2 Arg3
```

Now within the procedure, you'll have these arguments available:

```
%0=:PRO1
%1=Simpsons
%2=Star Trek
%3=None
```

If you want to access7 arguments passed in to the script from within a procedure, you could assign arguments to variables, such as

```
Arg1=%1
Arg2=%2
call :PRO1 Arg1 Arg2
```

Or you could simply assign all the script arguments to the procedure using %*, such as

```
call :PRO1 %*
```

Because you've passed in all script arguments — including %0 — the procedure now sees %0 as the script name, %1 as the first argument passed in to the script, and so on.

LOCALIZING CHANGES WITHIN PROCEDURES

When you work with `call`, you need to remember that any variable changes you make within a procedure or another script are reflected in the current command shell environment. To localize changes, you should use `setlocal` and `endlocal`:

```
:PRO1
setlocal
.
.
.
endlocal
goto :EXIT
```

If you change control to another procedure before exiting the current procedure with `goto :EXIT`, you should ensure that you end the localization if necessary. To do this, you can insert the `endlocal` statement into the statement that changes control, such as you see in this example:

```
:PRO1
setlocal
rem working
.
.
.
rem need to call other sub in case of error
if "%ERRORLEVEL%"=="2" (endlocal) & (goto :EXIT)
.
.
.
endlocal
goto :EXIT

:EXIT
```

Conditional Execution with if

When you want to conditionally execute commands, you'll use the `if`, `if not`, and `if ... else` statements. While previous examples have worked with `if` statements, you haven't explored `if not`, `if ... else`, `if defined`, or the associated comparison operators, such as `equ`.

Using if

You've seen if in many previous examples. Its basic syntax is

```
if condition command
```

The if statement evaluates the condition and if it is true, it executes the command:

```
if "%1"=="1" call :PRO1
```

When the condition is false, the command doesn't execute and the command shell proceeds to the next statement. As you've seen, you can also use if statements with compound commands, such as

```
if "%ERRORLEVEL%"=="2" (endlocal) & (goto :EXIT)
```

Here, both the endlocal and goto statements are executed when the condition is true.

Using if not

When you want to execute a statement only if it is false, you can use if not. The basic syntax is

```
if not condition command
```

The if not statement evaluates the condition and if it is false, it executes the command. Otherwise, the command doesn't execute and the command shell proceeds to the next statement. You could use if not to test for error conditions other than zero as follows:

```
if not errorlevel 0 (echo Error!!!) & (goto :EXIT)
```

Using if ... else

Another useful if structure is if ... else. You use if ... else to specify actions for true and false conditions, such as

```
if condition (true-command) else (false-command)
```

The if statement evaluates the condition and if it is true, it executes the true command. Otherwise, the false command is executed. Because if ... else is a compound statement, you must use parentheses to separate the commands as shown previously and in the following example:

```
if errorlevel 0 (echo No error.) else (echo Error!!!)
```

To complicate things a bit, you can use not to reverse the logic of if ... else. Here, the syntax would be

```
if not condition (false-command) else (true-command)
```

Using if defined and if not defined

The if defined and the if not defined statements are designed to help you test for the existence of variables and their respective syntax:

```
if defined variableName command
```

and

```
if not defined variableName command
```

Both statements are useful in your shell scripts. In the first case, you execute a command if the specified variable exists. In the second case, you execute a command if the specified variable doesn't exist.

Listing 5-8 shows how you could use these statements in an if ... else construct. The example tests for the existence of a variable called subTOTAL and if it exists, procedure 1 is executed. Otherwise, procedure 2 is executed. However, because I've unset subTOTAL (to ensure it doesn't exist), procedure 2 is always executed.

Listing 5-8: Checking for defined variables

definedtest.bat

```
@echo off
set subTOTAL=
if defined subTOTAL (call :PRO1) ELSE (call :PRO2)
goto :EOF

:PRO1
echo In procedure 1
goto :EOF

:PRO2
echo In procedure 2
goto :EOF

:EOF
```

Output
```
In procedure 2
```

String Comparisons with if

By now you should be fairly familiar with string comparisons using if statements, but you probably don't know the how's and why's of string comparisons. The most basic type of string comparison is when you compare two strings using the equality operator (==), such as

```
if stringA==stringB command
```

Here, you are performing a literal comparison of the strings and if they are exactly identical, the command is executed. This syntax is fine for literal strings but not very practical in shell scripts. When you work with parameters and arguments, values may contain spaces or there may be no value at all for a variable. Because of this, you may get errors if you perform comparisons without double quotation marks. Thus, to prevent errors, use the following syntax:

```
if "%varA%"=="%varB%" command
```

   or

```
if "%varA%"=="string" command
```

String comparisons are always case-sensitive unless you specify otherwise with the /i switch. This switch tells the command shell to ignore the case in the comparison, and you can use it as shown in Listing 5-9.

Listing 5-9: Ignoring case in string comparisons

ignorecase.bat
```
@echo off
set GRADES=BACB
if /I "%GRADES:~0,1%"=="a" (echo Grade 1 is: %GRADES:~0,1%
Excellent!)
if /I "%GRADES:~0,1%"=="b" (echo Grade 1 is: %GRADES:~0,1% Great
Job!)
IF /I "%GRADES:~0,1%"=="c" (echo Grade 1 is: %GRADES:~0,1% Good!)
IF /I "%GRADES:~0,1%"=="d" (echo Grade 1 is: %GRADES:~0,1% Try
harder!)
```

Output
```
Grade 1 is: B Great Job!
```

To perform more advanced equality tests, you'll need to use the comparison operators shown in Table 5-2. These operators are used in place of the standard equality operator and use the following syntax:

```
if "value1" COMPOP "value2" command
```

such as

```
if "%GRADES:~0,1%" EQU "A" (echo Excellent!)
```

TABLE 5-2 COMPARISON OPERATORS

Operator	Description
equ	Equality — evaluates to true if the values are equal
neq	Inequality — evaluates to true if the values are not equal
lss	Less than — evaluates to true if value1 is less than value2
leq	Less than or equal to — evaluates to true if value1 is less than or equal to value2
gtr	Greater than — evaluates to true if value1 is greater than value2
geq	Greater than or equal to — evaluates to true if value1 is greater than or equal to value2

for Looping

The for command enables you to repeatedly execute a command or a series of commands. Because the for command is designed specifically to work with the command shell environment, it is different from any other for command you may have worked with in other programming languages.

for Looping Fundamentals

for loops have a different syntax when you are working interactively at the command line than when you are working in a script. When you work interactively with looping, you use the following for structures:

```
for %variable in (fileSet) do command
for /D %variable in (directorySet) do command
```

```
for /R [path] %variable in (fileSet) do command
for /l %variable in (stepRange) do command
for /f ["options"] %variable in (source) do command
```

But in a script, you use these `for` structures:

```
for %%variable in (fileSet) do command
for /D %%variable in (directorySet) do command
for /R [path] %%variable in (fileSet) do command
for /l %%variable in (stepRange) do command
for /f ["options"] %%variable in (source) do command
```

If you examine these `for` structures, you'll see that the fundamental difference is that `%variable` is used interactively and that `%%variable` is used within scripts. Here, `%variable` and `%%variable` represent replaceable iteration variables, which you'll learn more about in a moment. Beyond this difference, `for` loops at the command line and within scripts are handled in the exact same way. The various structures used with `for` loops have specific purposes, which include the following:

♦ Iterating through groups of files

♦ Iterating through directories

♦ Stepping through a series of values

♦ Parsing text files, strings, and command output line by line

Still, at their core, the `for` structures all follow this basic syntax:

```
for iterator do command
```

The iterator is used to control the execution of the `for` loop. For each step or element in the iterator, the specified command is executed. To execute multiple commands, you can use a compound command or a procedure call.

The iterator usually contains an iterator variable (either `%variable` or `%%variable`) and a set of elements to execute against (`fileSet`, `directorySet`, `stepRange`, or `source`). Essentially, iterator variables are just placeholders for values you want to work with. While similar to standard variables, iterator variables have several unique qualities:

♦ Iterator variables only exist within the `for` loop.

♦ Iterator variable names must be in the range from `%A` to `%Z`, such as `%A`, `%B`, or `%C`.

♦ Iterator variables are case-sensitive, meaning `%%I` is different from `%%i`.

When the `for` loop's command executes, iterator variables are replaced with their actual values. These values come from the element set specified in the `for` loop and could consist of a list of files, a list of directories, and so on.

Iterating through Groups of Files

When you want to perform repetitive tasks on groups of files and directories, the command shell beats most other options — even the Windows Script Host — and one of the reasons is the file iterator syntax shown here:

```
for %%variable in (fileSet) do command
```

With file iterator looping, you use fileSet to define a set of files that you want to work with. A file set can be

♦ A single file as specified by a filename, such as myFile.txt

♦ A group of files specified with wild cards, such as *.bat

♦ Multiple groups of files with spaces separating filenames, such as

```
*.bat *.cmd *.exe
```

Once you know the basic rules, using `for` loops to work with files is easy. If you wanted to list all the executable files in the %SYSTEMROOT%\system32 directory, you could use the following command in a script:

```
@echo off
for %%I in (%SystemRoot%\system32\*.exe) do echo %%I
```

The result would be a long listing of .exe files that started something like this:

```
C:\WinNT\system32\addusrw.exe
C:\WinNT\system32\AUTOCHK.EXE
C:\WinNT\system32\charmap.exe
C:\WinNT\system32\PENTNT.EXE
C:\WinNT\system32\os2ss.exe
C:\WinNT\system32\OS2.EXE
C:\WinNT\system32\clipbrd.exe
```

Right about now you may be thinking that you could've gotten the same list using

```
dir %SYSTEMROOT%\system32\*.exe
```

and you'd be right. The difference, however, is that the for loop searches the file path and iterates the echo command separately for each matching file. The one-by-one iteration process enables you to manipulate the matching values as you see fit. You could even call a procedure to execute a series of commands using the results, such as you see in Listing 5-10.

Listing 5-10: Working with for loops

forloop.bat
```
@echo off
for %%I in (%SYSTEMROOT%\system32\*.exe) do call :PRO1 %%I

:PRO1
rem Work with the individual file passes as %1
echo %1

rem Work with the file some more
goto :EOF

:EOF
```

Here, the matching file entries are passed to procedure 1 and the procedure is executed. When the end of the file is reached, control returns to the for statement and the loop continues until there are no more entries to work with.

Because the iterator variable is treated as a special parameter, you can use any of the qualifiers listed in Table 5-1 as well. This enables you to extract filenames, paths, directories, and more. In this example, you extract the filename and extension:

```
for %%I in (%SYSTEMROOT%\system32\*.exe) do call :TEST %%~nxI
```

Iterating through Directories

Sometimes you'll want to work with directories rather than files and you can use

```
for /d %%variable in (directorySet) do command
```

The for /d loop iterates through the specified directory set but doesn't include subdirectories. To access subdirectories (and indeed the whole directory tree structure), you can use for /r loops, which I'll discuss in a moment.

Iterating directories works exactly like iterating files with one exception. You specify directory paths rather than files. If you wanted to list all the directories in %SYSTEMROOT%, you would do the following:

```
@echo off
for /d %%I in (%SystemRoot%\*) do echo %%I
```

A partial result list would be similar to

```
C:\WinNT\system32
C:\WinNT\system
C:\WinNT\repair
C:\WinNT\Help
C:\WinNT\Fonts
C:\WinNT\Config
C:\WinNT\Cursors
```

You can combine the file and directory looping techniques to perform actions against all files in a directory set, such as

```
@echo off
for /d %%I in (%SYSTEMROOT% %SYSTEMROOT%\*) do (
@for %%J in ("%%I\*.ini") do echo %%J)
```

The first `for` loop returns a list of top-level directories under the `%SYSTEMROOT%`, which also includes `%SYSTEMROOT%` itself. The second for loop iterates all .ini files in each of these directories. The @ symbol preceding the second `for` statement is necessary to ensure that the second loop executes properly. The double quotations with the file set (`"%%I\*.ini"`) ensure directory names containing spaces are handled properly.

Because you'll often want to work with subdirectories as well as directories, the command shell provides `for /r` loops. Using this loop structure, you can examine an entire directory tree from a starting point specified with `path`:

```
for /r [path] %%variable in (fileSet) do command
```

Here's how you could extend the previous example to list all .ini files on the C: drive without needing a double `for` loop:

```
@echo off
for /R C:\ %%I in (*.inI) do echo %%I
```

A partial result list on my computer looks like this:

```
C:\boot.ini
C:\MSSQL7\sqlsunin.ini
C:\MSSQL7\Binn\sqlctr.ini
C:\MSSQL7\Binn\cnfgsvr.ini
```

```
C:\WinNT\fpexplor.ini
C:\WinNT\frontpg.ini
C:\WinNT\win.ini
```

As you can see, `for /r` loops are simpler than double loops and more powerful. You can even combine `/r` and `/d` without needing a double loop. In this example, you obtain a listing of all directories and subdirectories under `%SYSTEMROOT%`:

```
for /R %SYSTEMROOT% /D %%I in (*) do echo %%I
```

 If `/r` is not followed by a path, the current working directory is assumed.

Stepping through a Series of Values

With `for` loops, you can also step through a range of values and perform tasks using these values. The syntax for this type of `for` loop is

```
for /l %%variable in (start,step,end) do command
```

The whole idea with *start*, *step*, and *end* is to enable you to create a range of values and then move through this range by the designated step value. The iterator variable is initialized with *start* and then incremented by *step* until the value of the variable is greater than *end*. The command executes for each value of the iterator variable.

The following example shows how you could count from 0 to 10 by 2s:

```
@echo off
for /l %%I in (0,2,10) do echo %%I
```

The output is

```
0
2
4
6
8
10
```

As you can see from the previous example, the command shell behaves as follows:

1. It initializes the iterator variable to 0 and checks to see if it is greater than the *end* value. If it is, the shell exits the loop. Otherwise, the shell executes the specified command.

2. The next time through the loop, the command shell increases the iterator variable's value by *step* and checks to see if it is greater than the *end* value. If it is, the shell exits the loop. Otherwise, the shell executes the specified command and repeats this step.

You can also use a negative *step* value to move through a range in decreasing values. You could count from 10 to 5 by 1s as follows:

```
@echo off
for /l %%I in (10,-1,5) do echo %%I
```

The output is

```
10
9
8
7
6
5
```

Parsing Text Files, Strings, and Command Output

Just as you can work with file and directory names, you can also work with the contents of files and the output of commands. To do this, you'll use the following for loop structure:

```
for /f ["options"] %%variable in (source) do command
```

Here, "options" specifies the options for matching text, and source specifies where the text comes from, which could be one or more text files, a string, or the output from a command such as dir.

PROCESSING TEXT FILES

With for /f loops, each line of text is handled much like a record in a flat-file database where each token field in the record is delimitated by a specific character, such as a tab or a space (which are the default delimiters). Listing 5-11 contains three line records, and each line contains three token fields. Following the line record is a comment separated from the fields by a # symbol.

Listing 5-11: Sample flat-file database

data.txt
```
Name Department Extension
==== ========== =========


wstanek Engineering x5590 # William Stanek
mtwain Marketing x3354 # Mark Twain
sadams Shipping x2545 # Samuel Adams
```

Listing 5-12 shows how you could examine the records in the file using a `for` loop. As you see, fields in the file are identified by iterator variables, starting with the first variable, %%A. If the script had used %%I as the first iterator variable, the variables representing the first three fields would be %%I, %%J, and %%K.

Listing 5-12: Using a for loop to examine the database

datatest1.bat
```
@echo off
for /f %%A in (data.txt) do (
echo User Name: %%A Department: %%B Extension: %%C)
```

Output
```
User Name: Name Department: %B Extension: %C
User Name: ==== Department: %B Extension: %C
User Name: wstanek Department: %B Extension: %C
User Name: mtwain Department: %B Extension: %C
User Name: sadams Department: %B Extension: %C
```

TIP   A bug in the Windows NT command shell prevents you from using filenames that contain spaces. This is true even if you enclose the filename in double quotation marks, such as

```
for /F %%A in ("User Data.txt") do (
echo User Name: %%A Department: %%B Extension: %%C)
```

The workaround is to make the command shell display the contents of the file using the `type` command, such as

```
for /F %%A in ('type "User Data.txt"') do (
echo User Name: %%A Department: %%B Extension: %%C)
```

In the previous example, note the use of single and double quotation marks. You must use this exact syntax.

Unfortunately, the output of Listing 5-12 is less than optimal. By default, `for` loops only examine the first token field and you need to override this setting with options. Options determine how token fields are examined and when they are used. Available option flags include the following:

- `eol` – Sets the end-of-line comment character, such as `eol=#`. Everything after this character is considered to be a comment.

- `skip` – Sets the number of lines to skip at the beginning of files, such as `skip=5`.

- `delims` – Sets delimiters to use instead space and tab, such as `delims=,:`.

- `tokens` – Sets which token fields from each line are to be placed in iterator variables, such as `tokens=1,3` or `tokens=2-5`. You can specify up to 26 tokens provided you start with A as the first iterator variable. By default, only the first token is examined.

To clean up the output of the script, you could modify the script as shown in Listing 5-13. Here, three options are used. The `skip` option is used to skip the first two lines of text. The `eol` option is used to specify the end-of-line comment character as #. Finally, the `tokens` option specifies that tokens 1 to 3 should be placed in iterator variables.

Listing 5-13: Modifying the for loop

datatest2.bat

```
@echo off
for /f "skip=2 eol=# tokens=1-3" %%A in (data.txt) do (
echo User Name: %%A Department: %%B Extension: %%C)
```

Output

```
User Name: wstanek Department: Engineering Extension: x5590
User Name: mtwain Department: Marketing Extension: x3354
User Name: sadams Department: Shipping Extension: x2545
```

When you work with text files, you should note that all blank lines in text files are skipped and that multiple source files can be specified with wild cards or by entering the filenames in a space-separated list, such as

```
for /f %%A in (data1.txt data2.txt) do (echo User Name: %%A)
```

With tokens, you can specify which fields you want to work with in many different ways. Here are some examples:

- `tokens=1,4,6` – Use tokens 1, 4, and 6.

◆ tokens=2-3 — Use tokens 2 and 3.

◆ tokens=* — Examine each line in its entirety and do not break into fields.

Now that you know some additional details about working with files, you could create a more useful user creation script, such as that in Listing 5-14. In this example, the flat-file database is modified to contain more detailed records. Each line contains five token fields that are separated by commas, and the comments have been removed. The second section of the listing shows the actual script that creates the user accounts. Note the technique used to pass arguments to the procedure. You'll learn more about user management scripts in Chapter 6.

 You'll need Administrator privileges to create accounts. Further, if you use this example data file and script, make sure you delete the sample accounts later.

Listing 5-14: Enhanced database file

userdata.txt

```
First Last UserName Department Extension
===== ==== ======== ========== ==========
William,Stanek,wstanek,Engineering,x5590
Mark,Twain,mtwain,Marketing,x3354
Samuel,Adams,sadams,HR,x2545
```

createusers.bat

```
@echo off
rem examine contents of userdata.txt.
for /f "delims=, skip=2 eol=# tokens=1-5" %%A in (userdata.txt)@@1b
    do (call :CREATE_USER %%A %%B %%C %%D %%E)
goto :EOF


:CREATE_USER
rem Create accounts.
echo Creating Account for: %1 %2
    net user %3 "changeme" /ADD /FULLNAME:"%1 %2"@@1b
            /COMMENT:"Dept: %4 Ext: %5" /doMAin


goto :EOF


:EOF
```

Output
```
Creating Account for: William Stanek
The command completed successfully.

Creating Account for: Mark Twain
The command completed successfully.

Creating Account for: Samuel Adams
The command completed successfully.
```

PROCESSING STRINGS AND COMMAND OUTPUT

Loops can also be used to process strings and command output. When you process the output of strings, you enclose the string or variable name you want to work with in double quotation marks. This ensures the string or variable can be evaluated properly.

You could parse a string as follows:

```
set test=Start;Middle;Finish
for /f "delims=; tokens=1,3" %%A in ("%TEST%") do (echo %%A %%B)
```

The output is

```
Start Finish
```

You can also use loops to process the output of commands. When you do this, you enclose the command name and its parameters in single quotes. Single quotes tell the command shell to execute the command and then process the results. In Listing 5-15, you use this technique to reformat the output of netstat -a so that only active network connections and their status are displayed. Note that it may take a few seconds to get a response, so be patient.

Listing 5-15: Modifying command output

net-test.bat
```
@echo off
for /f "tokens=2,4" %%A in ('netstat -a') do (call :PRO1 %%A %%B)
goto :EOF

:PRO1

set PORT=%1
echo %PORT:~5% Status: %2
goto :EOF

:EOF
```

Output

```
135 Status: LISTENING
135 Status: LISTENING
1027 Status: LISTENING
1028 Status: LISTENING
1030 Status: LISTENING
1433 Status: LISTENING
137 Status: LISTENING
138 Status: LISTENING
```

The example uses substrings to display only the port number and assumes that the local computer name is four characters in length (which it is on my system). Normally, the output of nestat -a looks like this:

```
TCP    zeta:135               0.0.0.0:0              LISTENING
```

Here, zeta is the computer name. In the script, the substring statement (%PORT:~5% Status: %2) is used to delete the zeta: part of the string.

Summary

As you've seen in this chapter, the command shell really is a lot more powerful than most people realize. With variables and arguments, you can search and replace values, obtain substrings, and extract command paths. Through subroutines and procedures, you can control execution within scripts and call other scripts. To conditionally execute statements, you can use if and if ... else statements. You can even repeatedly execute statements with for loops. for loops also let you work with directories and files.

Chapter 6

Managing the Enterprise

IN THIS CHAPTER

◆ Remote scheduling in the enterprise

◆ Automated job scheduling

◆ Automated services management

◆ Automated systems management

◆ Automated security, application, and error management

WHEN SERVICES STOP WORKING or systems malfunction, e-mail messages don't get delivered, the corporate Web site goes down, or something else equally important breaks. To prevent this, system administrators either spend a lot of their time monitoring services and systems or they opt to install costly monitoring and reporting software that watches services and systems for them. Instead of spending countless hours babysitting systems or shelling out a few thousands dollars for software you don't need, put the power of shell scripting to work and implement the automated solutions covered in this chapter.

Using shell scripts, you can monitor, manage, and troubleshoot network resources anywhere in the enterprise. The chapter starts with a look at how you can remotely schedule updates and maintenance of network resources and then explores specific administration tasks, such as monitoring services, managing system resources, and event log tracking. Appendixes A and B contain detailed references for many of the commands used in this chapter. Use the appendixes to learn more about specific commands.

Remote Scheduling in the Enterprise

Often when you work with remote administration, you'll want to perform after-hours tasks on various network computers, such as your file server or print server. By performing updates and maintenance during nonbusiness hours, you don't impact productivity and the workflow essential to smooth-running operations. But who wants to come in at 12 midnight on a Wednesday evening?

Fortunately, using the command shell, you can schedule tasks to run on remote systems and thus automatically run jobs or perform administrative tasks without having to be in the office. To remotely schedule tasks, you'll use the NT scheduling services (either Schedule or Task Scheduler) and the AT command to schedule recurring or one-time tasks. An added benefit of remotely scheduling tasks is that you don't have to waste time traveling to computers to perform maintenance tasks. This saves you time whether the computers are located in the next room, the next building, or a completely different country.

Local and Remote Scheduling Services

Schedule and Task Scheduler are services that handle scheduling in NT. Schedule is installed on systems using a standard NT installation up to and including NT Service Pack 3. Task Scheduler is installed on systems with an enhanced NT installation that is using NT Service Pack 4 or later, or Internet Explorer 4.0 or later with IE Service Pack 1. If a scheduling service isn't running, tasks you've scheduled with AT won't run either. You can start, stop, and manage the schedule services in several different ways. On a local system, use the Services applet in the Control Panel. On a remote system, use shell commands and command-line utilities. When you work with the schedule service, keep the following in mind:

◆ NT scheduling services log on as the LocalSystem account by default, which usually doesn't have adequate permissions to perform most administrative tasks. Instead, you should configure the scheduling service to run with a specific user account that can log on to a given system. This service account may need to have the specific user privileges and access rights. You should configure these permissions and then test the accuracy of these settings during development of your scripts.

◆ Domain user settings, such as drive mappings, aren't always available when you use scheduling services. Further, these types of settings should not be counted on – a script should configure whatever user settings are necessary. This ensures that everything the script does is under its control.

Because of these limitations, you will need to reconfigure your scheduling service. Two schools of thought apply here:

◆ You can configure the service for remote management from a central computer, scheduling tasks on the central computer and then creating scripts that manage remote resources as necessary.

◆ You can configure the service on each individual workstation and server, scheduling tasks on each computer separately.

The sections that follow examine tasks that relate to these techniques.

REMOTE MANAGEMENT FROM A CENTRAL COMPUTER

Remotely managing systems from a central computer is often the best solution in a complex environment. Here, you run the scheduling service on a single administration system and configure this system to connect to network resources as necessary. I'll call this system the Schedule Server.

The first step is to configure the scheduling service to use an NT domain account with sufficient privileges. The easiest way to do this is to create a special account and then assign whatever privileges, access rights, and group memberships are necessary to perform scheduled tasks. Name the account something that is identified easily as being used for scheduling, such as NetScheduler.

 TIP If you use Workgroups rather than NT domains, use the Individual Configuration. Also, if you are working with multiple domains, you'll need to ensure that proper permissions are granted for each domain.

Next, on the Schedule Server update the scheduling service settings so that it uses the new account and ensures that the service is configured to start automatically. To do this, start the Services applet in the Control Panel, and then double-click the entry for the scheduling service used on your system — either Schedule or Task Scheduler. You should now

1. Select the Startup type as Automatic and then select the This Account radio button in the Log On as area. See Figure 6-1.

2. Enter the name of the scheduling account in the field provided.

3. Enter the password for the account and then confirm it.

4. Click the OK button.

Figure 6-1: Configure the scheduling service to start automatically, and then configure the service to use the account you've set up.

Now that you've configured the scheduling service, schedule tasks on your system using the AT command.

Okay, so you hate the manual configuration process and you're thinking that surely there must be a way to automate this (just in case you have to perform these processes a few more times). Well, there is a way to automate both procedures and you can do so using the script shown in Listing 6-1. If you forget to enter the proper parameters, the output for the script is as shown. Listing 6-1 makes use of several NT command-line utilities including

- net user — To create the necessary scheduling account

- net localgroup — To add the scheduling account to the local Administrators group

- net group — To add the scheduling account to the Domain Users group

- ntrights.exe — To add user logon for the scheduling account

- instsrv.exe — To install and configure the Schedule service

- regedit.exe — To modify the registry and configure the service to start automatically

 Ntrights.exe and instsrv.exe are utilities from the Windows NT Server 4.0 Resource Kit Supplement 2 or later. Also, a temporary file is created on the system at C:\temp\sched.reg. You'll need to ensure that the directory C:\temp is available and you have proper access permissions in this directory. Otherwise, set a new directory path for the script to use.

Listing 6-1: Configuring the scheduling account and service

schedconfig.bat

```
@echo off
@if not "%OS%"=="Windows_NT" goto :EXIT
@if "%1"=="" (set INFO=echo && set SEXIT=1) else (set INFO=rem &&
@@1b
set SEXIT=0)

%INFO% ***********************
%INFO% Script: SchedulerConfig
%INFO% Version: 0.9.5
```

```
%INFO% Creation Date: 12/5/97
%INFO% Last Modified: 9/1/99
%INFO% Author: William R. Stanek
%INFO% Email: win32scripting@tvpress.com
%INFO% ************************
%INFO% Description: Configures the scheduling service
%INFO%              and related account on Windows NT.
%INFO% ************************
%INFO% Args: Pass in a password for the scheduling account to
%INFO%       bypass info screen. Use at least 8 characters.
%INFO% ************************

@if "%SEXIT%"=="1" goto :EXIT

@title "Configure Scheduling..."
cls
color 07

rem Set working directory
cd C:\temp

rem Create user and assign to groups
net user NetScheduling %1 /add /expires:never /passwordreq:yes
      /comment:"NT Scheduling Account"
      /profilepath:%SystemRoot%\profiles\NetScheduling
net localgroup Administrators /add NetScheduling
net group "Domain Users" /add NetScheduling

rem Assign logon right
ntrights +r SeServiceLogonRight -u NetScheduling

rem Configure and start Schedule service
net stop schedule
instsrv Schedule remove
instsrv Schedule %SystemRoot%\system32\atsvc.exe -a
%ComputerName%\scheduler -p %1
net start Schedule

rem create registry modification file
echo regedit4 > c:\temp\sched.reg
echo [HKEY_LOCAL_MACHINE\SYSTEM\CurrentControlSet\Services\Schedule]
@@lb
```

```
> c:\temp\sched.reg
echo "Start"^=dword:00000002 > c:\temp\sched.reg

rem update registry using the mod file
REGEDIT /s c:\temp\schedule.reg

del c:\temp\sched.reg /Q
:EXIT
```

Output

```
************************
 Script: SchedulerConfig
 Version: 0.9.5
 Creation Date: 12/5/97
 Last Modified: 9/1/99
 Author: William R. Stanek
 Email: win32scripting@tvpress.com
 ************************
 Description: Configures the scheduling service
             and account on Windows NT.
 ************************
 Args: Pass in a password for the scheduling account to
       bypass info screen. Use at least 8 characters.
 ************************
```

In the beginning of the script, I show you a modified header format, and you
may be wondering what is going on here:

```
@if "%1"=="" (set INFO=echo && set SEXIT=1) else (set INFO=rem &&
@@1b
set SEXIT=0)
%INFO% ************************
```

What I've done is to implement a simple (yet powerful) technique for automatically creating descriptions from comment lines, giving the lines dual purpose.
When no parameters are passed in to the script, lines that would not ordinarily be
displayed are echoed to the command line. Yet when proper parameters are passed
in to the script, the lines are interpreted as comments and not displayed. The switch
that handles this process is a variable called INFO. If INFO is set to echo, lines beginning with %INFO% echo to the screen. If INFO is set to rem, lines beginning with
%INFO% are interpreted as comments. Further, to ensure that the script exits when
you display comments, you can set an exit flag:

```
@if "%SEXIT%"=="1" goto :EXIT
```

You'll see the modified header format used throughout this chapter. The next major section of the script

♦ Configures the necessary scheduling account

♦ Sets group membership and permissions

♦ Assigns logon rights

The `net user` utility is used to create an account called `NetScheduling` using the password you entered as argument 1. The password for the account is set so it doesn't expire, and the account is assigned a profile as well. The profile is used by the scheduling account each time it logs on and prevents a problem where you may end up with multiple profile folders for this account.

The `net localgroup` utility adds the scheduling account to the local Administrators group and then the `net group` utility adds the account to the Domain Users group (which is normally the default anyway). After that, ntrights.exe is used to allow the account to log on as a service.

Next, instsvr.exe is used to remove the old Schedule service and reinstall it using the new password. The `net start` command starts the Schedule service so that it is active and then you create a .reg file needed to modify the service Registry settings in the `C:\temp` folder. The Registry Editor (regedit.exe) uses the file to set the Schedule service startup value to Automatic rather than Manual. Finally, you clean up temporary files by deleting the registry file from `C:\temp`.

INDIVIDUAL CONFIGURATIONS

Sometimes you'll want to schedule tasks to run on a specific computer and you won't want to manage these tasks remotely from a Schedule server. In this case, you can configure the scheduling service on individual workstations and servers as necessary and then schedule tasks on these computers separately.

For workgroup computers (that are not part of a domain), you'll need to do the following:

1. Create a special account for scheduling on each computer that you use.

2. Configure the scheduling service on each computer.

For computers that are part of a single domain, you'll need to do the following:

1. Create one NT domain account that can be used for scheduling. If one already exists, you don't need another one.

2. Configure the scheduling service on each computer.

On the other hand, if you plan to work with multiple domains, follow these steps:

1. Create an NT account in the master domain that can be used for scheduling. Then configure the account so that it can access additional resource domains as necessary.

2. Configure the scheduling service on each computer.

Regardless of which technique you choose, the process of creating accounts and configuring the scheduling service is the same as discussed in "Remote Management from a Central Computer." You'll just need to go through the process several times (rather than once).

Scheduling Local and Remote Jobs

The Windows NT Schedule service is implemented in atsvc.exe and controlled with the at.exe (AT) utility. Using AT, you can schedule jobs on local and remote systems. Jobs can be set to run once or regularly at specified times.

SCHEDULING JOBS WITH AT

When you work with AT, you must follow several rules. Jobs are scheduled using a 24-hour clock where 00:00 is midnight and 12:00 is 12 noon. To schedule jobs, you must be a member of the local Administrators group. Because AT does not automatically load the command interpreter before running commands, you must explicitly load cmd.exe at the beginning of a command, as shown in the following example where all files are removed from the temp directory daily at midnight:

```
AT 00:00 /every:M,T,W,Th,F,S,Su "cmd /c del /Q c:\temp\*.*"
```

However, when you work with executables – files with extensions as defined in the PATHEXT variable – you don't have to start an instance of the command interpreter and you can work with the executable directly. Still, the executable must be in a directory accessible along the command path (PATH).

 The command path is covered in Chapter 2. To learn how to set the command path see the section of that chapter titled "Setting the Command Path."

In the following example, the shell script is scheduled to run on the first and fifteenth of the month at 3 a.m.:

```
AT 03:00 /every:1,15 cleanup.bat
```

> **TIP**
>
> To capture the output of a shell script and any errors that may occur, redirect the output to a file. Because you want to manipulate output from the script, you will need to start the script via the command shell. For example:
>
> ```
> AT 03:00 /every:1,15 cmd /c "h.bat" > error.txt 2>&1
> ```
>
> The double quotation marks around the script name are necessary to ensure that the redirection isn't improperly interpreted as script arguments.

When you use numeric dates, you can use any value in the range 1–31. In this example, you set the same batch file to run every five days:

```
AT 03:00 /every:5,10,15,20,25,30 cleanup.bat
```

You schedule jobs to run relative to the current date simply by not specifying a run date. In this example, you start a system update at 5 a.m.:

```
AT 05:00 update.bat
```

Another way to schedule jobs is to specify that the job should run on the next occurrence of a date. For example, if today is Monday and you want the job to run next Monday, you can use the following command:

```
AT 00:30 /next:M start_move.bat
```

By default, all jobs run as background processes. You can, however, set jobs to run interactively, and you do this using the /interactive switch as follows:

```
AT 09:30 /interactive /every:M,W,F backup.bat
```

SCHEDULING JOBS ON REMOTE SYSTEMS

If you're like me and don't want to leave your desk to schedule jobs, don't worry. The AT command enables you to schedule jobs to run on remote systems (and you can do this without ever having to log in to the remote system). All you need to do is enter the UNC name of the computer before you specify other parameters. For example, if you want to schedule a job to run on a computer called OMEGA, you could type the following command at the command line on your system:

```
AT \\OMEGA 02:30 /every:T,Th cleanup.bat
```

You can also use the IP address of the computer such as

```
AT \\209.62.12.11 02:30 /every:T,Th cleanup.bat
```

In order to successfully schedule the task and run it at the scheduled time, the example assumes that

◆ You've configured OMEGA properly as outlined previously in "Individual Configurations."

◆ The cleanup.bat script is located in an appropriate directory.

◆ The remote system is running the Server service (which is necessary to remotely schedule tasks).

As you can see, several conditions apply when you work with remote systems. To remove some of these dependencies, you can run scheduled tasks from your system and use network shares to perform tasks and execute shell scripts. Network shares should be referenced with the UNC path, such as \\ZETA\CORP_DATA, rather than a network drive letter, such as H:. As stated previously, you can't depend on user variables and environment settings when working with scheduled tasks. While the H: drive may be mapped for you during an interactive logon session, it may not be mapped when the scheduled task executes. Following this example, you can schedule a script to copy files on a network share as follows:

```
AT 01:30 /every:T,Th,S backup.bat
```

And then in the script, use the UNC path to reference the network share:

```
copy \\zeta\corp_data\*.doc \\omega\back\docs
copy \\zeta\corp_data\*.xls \\omega\back\xls
copy \\zeta\corp_data\*.ppt \\omega\back\ppt
```

Any time a command requires path information, you should use the full path or the complete UNC path.

Another way to work with network shares is to map shares to network drives temporarily. Listing 6-2 shows how you could map the corp_data and back shares to network drives and then release the drives when finished with them.

Listing 6-2: Mapping network shares to network drives

netdrive.bat
```
@echo off
rem map network drives
```

```
net use y: \\zeta\corp_data /persistent:no
net use z: \\omega\back /persistent:no

rem work with drives
copy y:\*.doc z:\docs
copy y:\*.doc z:\docs
copy y:\*.xls z:\xls
copy y:\*.ppt z:\ppt

rem delete drive mapping
net use y: /delete
net use z: /delete
```

VIEWING SCHEDULED TASKS

You can view scheduled tasks on local and remote systems. On a local system, enter AT on a line by itself and press Enter:

```
at
```

On a remote system, enter AT followed by the UNC name of the system you want to examine:

```
at \\omega
```

When you view tasks, the output you get is similar to the following:

```
Status ID Day                      Time      Command Line
--------------------------------------------------------------
       1   Each M                  12:15 AM  update.bat
       2   Each T                  12:15 AM  backup.bat
       3   Each W                  12:15 AM  maint.bat
       4   Each M T W Th F S Su    12:00 AM  systemtest.bat
       5   Each M T Su             12:15 AM  del /Q c:\temp\*.*
       6   Next 8                   5:00 AM  mods.bat
```

The fields of the output tell you a lot about the scheduled jobs:

Status	Provides a status for each job and is normally blank, which indicates a status of OK. If there is a problem, the status shows an error message, such as :ERROR.
ID	Provides a unique identifier for each job.

Day   Tells you when the job is scheduled to run. Recurring jobs
                        begin with the keyword Each, such as Each M for every
                        Monday. One-time jobs begin with the keyword Next, such as
                        Next 8 for the next time it is the eighth day of the month.

Time   Tells you when the command is scheduled to run. Note that
                        the time is displayed with an AM or PM indicator rather than
                        the 24-hour clock used for scheduling jobs.

Command Line   Tells you what command or executable is run at the scheduled
                        time.

You can use the ID to view individual jobs such as

```
at 3
```

   or

```
at \\zeta 3
```

When you view individual jobs, you get output for the specific job such as

```
Task ID:       3
Status:        OK
Schedule:      Each W
Time of day:   12:15 AM
Interactive:   No
Command:       maint.bat
```

DELETING SCHEDULED TASKS

With the AT command, you can delete scheduled tasks by ID number or you can
cancel all scheduled tasks. You can delete a specific task as follows:

```
at 3 /delete
```

   or

```
at \\zeta 3 /delete
```

To cancel all tasks, enter the /delete switch without a task ID:

```
at /delete
```

   or

```
at \\zeta /delete
```

Scheduling Local Jobs with Task Scheduler

Task Scheduler is a new feature for NT. Task Scheduler runs as a service and allows you to configure jobs through the Scheduled Task wizard. You can only schedule tasks for the local computer, not for remote systems.

SCHEDULING AND VIEWING TASKS

The Scheduled Task wizard and currently scheduled tasks are accessed through the %SYSTEMROOT%\Tasks folder. For example, if you installed Windows NT in D:\Winnt, the Tasks folder is located at D:\Winnt\Tasks. As Figure 6-2 shows, the Tasks folder provides a summary listing of scheduled tasks.

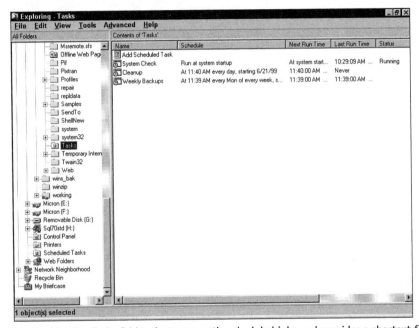

Figure 6-2: The Tasks folder shows currently scheduled jobs and provides a shortcut for starting the Scheduled Task wizard.

You can work with the entries in the Tasks folder as follows:

♦ Double-click Add Scheduled Task to start the Scheduled Task wizard.

♦ Double-click an existing task entry to view or change its properties. Advanced options can be set through the Settings tab.

♦ Select a task entry and press Delete to delete the task.

CREATING TASKS WITH THE SCHEDULED TASK WIZARD

The Scheduled Task wizard makes scheduling tasks easy through its point and click interface. You can think of this wizard as a graphical version of AT with extensions that let you customize task scheduling to the Nth degree.

To schedule a task, run the Scheduled Task wizard by double-clicking on Add Scheduled Task in the Tasks folder and then follow these steps:

1. After starting the Scheduled Task wizard, you'll see a welcome dialog box that tells you a bit about the wizard. Click the Next button to continue.

2. As Figure 6-3 shows, the next dialog box lets you select a program to schedule. Unfortunately, the dialog doesn't show available scripts. Click the Browse button to open the Select Program to Schedule dialog. This is really a standard Open File dialog with a different label. Use the dialog to find the script you want to run. For example, if you want to run a script called cleanup.bat in the D:\scripts folder, you would use the dialog to access the D:\scripts folder and then enter **cleanup.bat** as the filename.

Figure 6-3: Click the Browse button to select a script to schedule.

3. Next enter a name for the task as shown in Figure 6-4. The name should be short but descriptive so you can tell at a glance what the task does.

Figure 6-4: Enter a descriptive name for the task and then determine when the task should be run.

4. Select a run schedule for the task. Tasks can be scheduled to run on a periodic basis, such as daily, weekly or monthly, or when a specific event occurs, such as when the computer starts or when the task's user logs in. Being able to easily run scripts during startup or login is a significant enhancement for Task Scheduler and it makes your job as an administrator easier.

TIP You can use Task Scheduler to create jobs that run when a particular user logs in. To do this, log in as the user and then create the necessary tasks. Be sure to select the When I Log On option.

5. Continue by clicking the Next button and then select a date and time to run the scheduled task. The next dialog you see depends on when the task is scheduled to run.

6. If you've selected a daily running task, the date and time dialog appears as shown in Figure 6-5. Set a start time and date. Daily scheduled tasks can be configured to run

- Every Day – 7 days a week.

- Weekdays – Monday to Friday only.

- Every Nth Day – Every second, third, ... Nth day.

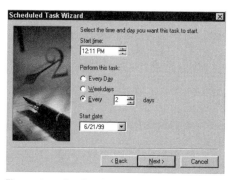

Figure 6-5: Configuring a daily scheduled task

7. If you've selected a weekly running task, the date and time dialog appears as shown in Figure 6-6. Configure the task using these fields:

- Start Time – Sets the start time of the task.

- Every Nth Week – Allows you to run the task every week, every other week , or every Nth week.

- Day of Week – Sets the day(s) of the week when the task runs, such as every Monday or every Monday and Friday.

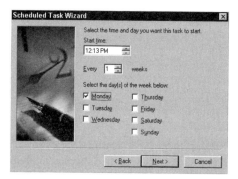

Figure 6-6: Configuring a weekly scheduled task

8. If you've selected a monthly running task, the date and time dialog appears as shown in Figure 6-7. Configure the task using these fields:

- Start Time – Sets the start time of the task.

- Day – Sets the day of the month the task runs. For example, if you select 5, the task runs on the fifth day of the month.

- The Nth Day – Sets task to run on the Nth occurrence of a day in a month, such as the second Monday or the third Tuesday of every month.

- Of the Months – These check boxes let you select which months the task runs.

Figure 6-7: Configuring a monthly scheduled task

9. If you've selected One Time Only for running the task, the date and time dialog appears as shown in Figure 6-8. Set the start time and start date.

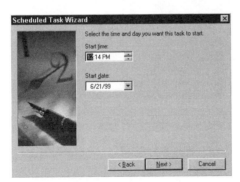

Figure 6-8: Configuring a one time only task

10. With tasks that run when the computer starts or when the task's user logs on, you don't have to set the start date and time. The task runs automatically when the related event occurs.

11. After you've configured a start date and time, click the Next button to continue. As shown in Figure 6-9, enter a user name and password that can be used when running the scheduled task. Then click the Next button.

Figure 6-9: Enter a username and password to use when running the task.

12. The final wizard dialog box provides a summary of the task you are scheduling (see Figure 6-10). Click Finish to complete the scheduling process.

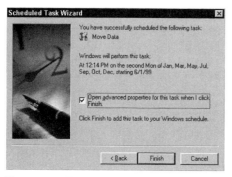

Figure 6-10: The final dialog provides a task summary. If it looks good, click Finish.

TIP   If an error occurs when creating the task, you'll see an error prompt. Click OK. The task should still be created. Afterward, in Windows Explorer, access the task's properties dialog and correct the problem.

Automated Job Scheduling Across the Enterprise

When you work in a large network environment, you'll often want the same series of jobs to run on multiple systems. For example, if you have a server farm, you may want to clean up directories, run backups, and perform other administrative tasks automatically. Because the systems in the farm are set up identically, you can create a script to help you manage jobs on each system without having to configure all the necessary jobs by hand.

Listing 6-3 provides a script for managing scheduled tasks on local and remote systems. The first argument sets the type of task you want to perform. You can use the script to

◆ View jobs on a group of servers; enter **V**

◆ Check for job errors; enter **C**

◆ Replicate sets of jobs across the enterprise; enter **R**

◆ Delete jobs on multiple systems; enter **D**

 The R and D options may affect multiple systems. Be sure that you've configured the sched-svr.txt and sched-repl.txt files appropriately before running these commands. Additionally, schedmgr.bat doesn't check to see if the target systems are available. You may want to add error-checking code to handle this situation.

Listing 6-3: Managing Job Scheduling across the enterprise

sched–svr.txt
```
\\OMEGA
\\GAMMA
\\ZETA
\\THETA
\\EPSILON
```

sched–repl.txt
```
00:00 /every:1,5,10,15,20,25,30 cleanup.bat
00:20 /every:M,W,F backup.bat
00:40 /every:Su "cmd /c del /Q c:\temp\*.*"
```

schedmgr.bat
```
@echo off
@if not "%OS%"=="Windows_NT" goto :EOF
@if "%1"=="" (set INFO=echo && set SEXIT=1) else (set INFO=rem &&
@@lb
set SEXIT=0)
```

```
%INFO% ************************
%INFO% Script: Schedule Manager
%INFO% Version: 0.9.7
%INFO% Creation Date: 5/7/99
%INFO% Last Modified: 9/1/99
%INFO% Author: William R. Stanek
%INFO% Email: win32scripting@tvpress.com
%INFO% ************************
%INFO% Description: Manages scheduled tasks on local and
%INFO%             remote systems.
%INFO% ************************
%INFO% Args: View jobs on a group of servers:
%INFO% Enter V at first parameter
%INFO% *
%INFO% Check for job errors on a group of servers
%INFO% Enter C at first parameter
%INFO% *
%INFO% Replicate jobs to multiple systems
%INFO% Enter R at first parameter
%INFO% *
%INFO% Delete jobs on a group of servers
%INFO% Enter D at first parameter
%INFO% *
%INFO% Server list comes from sched-svr.txt in current dir
%INFO% Enter UNC server names on separate lines, such as:
%INFO% \\OMEGA
%INFO% \\ZETA
%INFO% Add any necessary comments by preceding with # character
%INFO% *
%INFO% Scheduled jobs are entered in sched-repl.txt in
%INFO% current directory. Enter the job information without
%INFO% the at or system name, such as:
%INFO% 00:00 /every:M,T,W,Th,F,S,Su "cmd /c del /Q c:\temp\*.*"
%INFO% 00:15 /next:1,15 "cmd /c del /Q c:\temp\*.*"
%INFO% Add any necessary comments by preceding with # character
%INFO% ************************

@if "%SEXIT%"=="1" goto :EOF

@title "Schedule Manager"
cls
color 07

if /i "%1"=="V" goto :VIEW
```

```
if /i "%1"=="C" goto :CHECK
if /i "%1"=="R" goto :REPL
if /i "%1"=="D" goto :DELETE
goto :EOF

:VIEW
rem view jobs scheduled on remote systems
@title "Schedule Manager...View"
for /f "eol=#" %%A in (sched-svr.txt) do (call :VIEWMAIN %%A)
goto :EOF

:CHECK
rem check for job errors
@title "Schedule Manager...Check Errors"
for /f "eol=#" %%A in (sched-svr.txt) do (call :CHECKMAIN %%A)
goto :EOF

:REPL
rem replicate jobs to multiple systems
@title "Schedule Manager...View"
for /f "eol=#" %%A in (sched-svr.txt) do (call :REPLMAIN %%A)
goto :EOF

:DELETE
rem view jobs scheduled on remote systems
@title "Schedule Manager...Delete"
for /f "eol=#" %%A in (sched-svr.txt) do (call :DELMAIN %%A)
goto :EOF

:VIEWMAIN
rem Lists jobs on systems across enterprise
echo ********************
echo System: %1
echo ********************
at %1
pause
cls
goto :EOF

:CHECKMAIN
rem Checks for job errors across enterprise
echo ********************
echo System: %1
echo ********************
```

```
at %1 | find /i "error"
pause
goto :EOF

:REPLMAIN
rem Replicates jobs to multiple systems
echo ********************
echo System: %1
echo ********************
for /f "eol=# tokens=*" %%B in (sched-repl.txt) do (at %1 %%B)
goto :EOF

:DELMAIN
rem Deletes jobs on systems across enterprise
echo ********************
echo System: %1
echo ********************
at %1 /delete
goto :EOF

:EOF
```

The main section of the script is driven by `if` statements, which check to see which type of task you want to perform and jump to the appropriate sections of the script. For example, if you enter **V**, the command shell jumps to the `:VIEW` label. Each task is performed in two steps. In the first step, a `for` loop parses the contents of sched-svr.txt and then calls a task-related procedure, such as

```
:VIEW
rem view jobs scheduled on remote systems
@title "Schedule Manager...View"
for /f "eol=#" %%A in (sched-svr.txt) do (call :VIEWMAIN %%A)
goto :EOF
```

In the second step, the screen output is set up and the data is manipulated as necessary to perform the desired tasks such as

```
:VIEWMAIN
rem Lists jobs on systems across enterprise
echo ********************
echo System: %1
echo ********************
at %1
pause
```

```
cls
goto :EOF
```

The script obtains needed information from two files: sched-svr.txt and sched-repl.txt. The sched-svr.txt file contains the list of systems you want to work with. In this file, enter UNC server names on separate lines and enter comment lines with #:

```
#Backup domain controller
\\GAMMA
#Primary domain controller
\\DELTA
```

The sched-repl.txt file contains the jobs you want to schedule on multiple systems. Enter the job information without the AT command or the system name, such as

```
00:00 /every:1,5,10,15,20,25,30 cleanup.bat
00:20 /every:M,W,F backup.bat
```

You can also add comments to the file by preceding them with the # character, such as

```
#Performs cleanup of temporary directories
00:00 /every:1,5,10,15,20,25,30 cleanup.bat
#Backs up primary data directories
00:20 /every:M,W,F backup.bat
```

Another interesting feature is the use of pause to wait for a key press before continuing. pause is used to ensure that information doesn't flash by too quickly. When you use pause in a script, users see the following statement:

```
Press a key to continue ...
```

Automated Services Management

When you automate the management of essential services, you save time and money, freeing up resources and personnel to focus on more important issues. As you might expect, there are many different ways to automate the management of services, so let's explore the basics first and then move on to an actual management script.

Services Available on NT Servers and Workstations

Windows NT workstations and servers run many different services and many more can be installed with applications, such as Microsoft IIS or Microsoft SQL Server. Standard Windows NT services include

Alerter	Protected Storage
Client Service for Netware	Remote Access AutoDial Manager
Clipbook Server	Remote Access Connection Manager
Computer Browser	Remote Access ISNSAP Service
DHCP Client	Remote Access Server
Directory Replicator	Remote Procedure Call (RPC) Locator
Eventlog	Remote Procedure Call (RPC) Service
File Server for Macintosh	Remoteboot
FTP Server	Schedule
Gateway Service For Netware	Server
License Logging Service	Simple TCP/IP Services
LPDSVC	SNMP
Messenger	Spooler
Microsoft DHCP Server	System Event Notification
Net Logon	Task Scheduler
Network DDE	TCP/IP NetBIOS Helper
Network DDE DSDM	Telephony
Network Monitoring Agent	Ups
NT LM Security Support Provider	Windows Installer
Plug and Play	Windows Internet Name Service
Print Server for Macintosh	Workstation

Services that are installed by other Microsoft products, such as IIS, and which may be available to you include

Content Index

FTP Publishing Service

IIS Admin Service

Microsoft NNTP Service

Microsoft Search

Microsoft SMTP Service

MSDTC

MSSQLServer

Site Server Authentication Service

Site Server LDAP Service

Site Server Message Builder Service

SQLServerAgent

World Wide Web Publishing Service

Managing Services

You can control services at the command line regardless of their source. In shell scripting, you'll use four utilities to manage services:

- ◆ `net continue` – Used to resume a paused service
- ◆ `net pause` – Used to temporarily stop service
- ◆ `net start` – Used to view running services and start services
- ◆ `net stop` – Used to stop services

To view services running on a system, enter **net start** on a line by itself as follows:

```
net start
```

If you know the name of a service, you can use `net start` to start it as well. For example, here is how you can start the World Wide Web Publishing Service:

```
net start "World Wide Web Publishing Service"
```

Note the use of double quotation marks with service names that have spaces. To stop a service, enter the `net stop` command followed by the service name such as

```
net stop "FTP Publishing Service"
```

If you want to temporarily stop and then restart a service, you can use `net pause` and `net continue` respectively. First, pause the service as follows:

```
net pause MSSQLServer
```

You can then work with system resources without affecting the service. When you are finished making modifications, you can resume the service as follows:

```
net continue MSSQLServer
```

As you've seen, working with system services is fairly easy, yet you can use these simple facilities to create powerful management tools.

Automated Services Manager Script

Listing 6-4 provides a dynamic script for automating the management of services. What makes this script so powerful is that you can use it to manage many different services. You can start a dozen different services with a single command and then stop those services by issuing another command. You can track services and ensure that they are running properly. If the services aren't running properly, you can restart them and if they still don't start, you can take other precautions, such as trying to kill a hung service and then restarting it. You can also restart the server in an extreme case.

As is convention for most management scripts you'll find in this chapter, the first argument sets the type of task you want to perform. Available tasks include

- ◆ Enter V to view services running on the system

- ◆ Enter S to start a group of services

- ◆ Enter E to end (stop) a group of services

- ◆ Enter T to track and automatically restart services if they stop

---

TIP Add tasks for pausing and resuming services if you'd like. Also, you can use Telnet to remotely log in to a server and run the script on remote systems. Or you may want to extract the tracking section and use this as a regularly scheduled job.

Listing 6-4: Managing services in the enterprise

serv-mgr.txt
```
FTP Publishing Service
IIS Admin Service
Microsoft NNTP Service
Microsoft SMTP Service
World Wide Web Publishing Service
Site Server Authentication Service
```

Site Server LDAP Service
Site Server Message Builder Service

services-mgr.bat

```
@echo off
@if not "%OS%"=="Windows_NT" goto :EOF
@if "%1"=="" (set INFO=echo && set SEXIT=1) else (set INFO=rem &&
@@lb
set SEXIT=0)

%INFO% ************************
%INFO% Script: Service Manager
%INFO% Version: 0.9.5
%INFO% Creation Date: 4/20/99
%INFO% Last Modified: 9/1/99
%INFO% Author: William R. Stanek
%INFO% Email: win32scripting@tvpress.com
%INFO% ************************
%INFO% Description: Manages services on local
%INFO%                and remote systems.
%INFO% ************************
%INFO% Args: View current services running on the system:
%INFO% Enter V at first parameter
%INFO% *
%INFO% Start a service
%INFO% Enter S at first parameter
%INFO% *
%INFO% End a service running on the computer
%INFO% Enter E at first parameter
%INFO% *
%INFO% Track and restart a service running on the computer
%INFO% Enter T at first parameter
%INFO% *
%INFO% When starting, stopping or tracking services,
%INFO% the service list comes from serv-mgr.txt
%INFO% in current directory.
%INFO% Enter the exact service name, such as:
%INFO% World Wide Web Publishing Service
%INFO% *
%INFO% Add any necessary comments by preceding with # character
%INFO% ************************

@if "%SEXIT%"=="1" goto :EOF

@title "Service Manager"
```

```
cls
color 07

if /I "%1"=="V" goto :View
if /I "%1"=="S" goto :Start
if /I "%1"=="E" goto :End
if /I "%1"=="T" goto :Track
goto :EOF

:VIEW
rem view services running on a system
@title "Service Manager...View"
net start
goto :EOF

:START
rem start services on system
@title "Service Manager...Start"
for /f "eol=# tokens=*" %%A in (serv-mgr.txt) do (call :STARTMAIN
@@lb
"%%A")
goto :EOF

:END
rem stop services on system
@title "Service Manager...Stop"
for /f "eol=# tokens=*" %%A in (serv-mgr.txt) do (call :STOPMAIN
@@lb
"%%A")
goto :EOF

:TRACK
rem track services on system
@title "Service Manager...Tracking"
for /f "eol=# tokens=*" %%A in (serv-mgr.txt) do (call :STARTTRACK
@@lb
"%%A")

rem pause for 5 minutes before repeating the service check
rem sleep.exe is in the Windows NT Resource Kit
sleep.exe 300
rem if you don't have the resource kit, comment out the sleep
rem command and uncomment the pause statement below:
rem PAUSE
```

```
goto :TRACK

:STARTMAIN
echo *********************
echo Starting Service %1
echo *********************
echo ******************** >%SystemRoot%\service-mgr.log
echo Service Started Admin: %1 >%SystemRoot%\service-mgr.log
echo. | date | find /i "current">%SystemRoot%\service-mgr.log
echo. | time | find /i "current">%SystemRoot%\service-mgr.log
echo *********************** >%SystemRoot%\service-mgr.log
net start %1
if errorlevel==1 goto :STARTERROR
goto :EOF

:STOPMAIN
echo *********************
echo Stopping Service %1
echo *********************
echo ******************** >%SystemRoot%\service-mgr.log
echo Service Stopped Admin: %1 >%SystemRoot%\service-mgr.log
echo. | date | find /i "current">%SystemRoot%\service-mgr.log
echo. | time | find /i "current">%SystemRoot%\service-mgr.log
echo ******************** >%SystemRoot%\service-mgr.log
echo Stopping %1 Service...  >%SystemRoot%\service-mgr.log
net stop %1
if errorlevel==1 goto :STOPERROR
goto :EOF

:STARTTRACK
net start | find /i %1
if errorlevel==1 goto :RESTART
goto :EOF

:RESTART
echo ******************** >%SystemRoot%\service-mgr.log
echo Error Service Stopped: %1 >%SystemRoot%\service-mgr.log
echo. | date | find /i "current">%SystemRoot%\service-mgr.log
echo. | time | find /i "current">%SystemRoot%\service-mgr.log
echo ******************** >%SystemRoot%\service-mgr.log
echo Trying to Restart: %1 >%SystemRoot%\service-mgr.log
echo ******************** >%SystemRoot%\service-mgr.log
echo Trying to Restart: %1
net start %1
```

```
if errorlevel==1 goto :ERROR
echo ******************** >%SystemRoot%\service-mgr.log
echo Successful Restart: %1 >%SystemRoot%\service-mgr.log
echo Successful Restart: %1
echo ******************** >%SystemRoot%\service-mgr.log

goto :EOF

:ERROR
rem Configure what you would like to happen in case of error.
rem At this point, you can use kill to unhang the service
rem or simply restart the server.
echo ******************** >%SystemRoot%\service-mgr.log
echo Error Starting Service: %1 >%SystemRoot%\service-mgr.log
echo. | date | find /i "current">%SystemRoot%\service-mgr.log
echo. | time | find /i "current">%SystemRoot%\service-mgr.log
echo ******************** >%SystemRoot%\service-mgr.log
echo ******************** >%SystemRoot%\service-mgr.log
echo Trying to kill: %1 >%SystemRoot%\service-mgr.log
echo ******************** >%SystemRoot%\service-mgr.log
echo Trying to kill: %1
KILL.EXE %1
rem echo Restarting the system
rem echo ******************** >%SystemRoot%\service-mgr.log
rem echo ******************** >%SystemRoot%\service-mgr.log
rem echo !!!Error Starting Service: %1
rem echo !!!Restarting the system in 2 minutes
rem SHUTDOWN.EXE /L /R /T:120 /Y
goto :EOF

:EOF
```

You'll find that the service manager script is organized much like the schedule manager script. The main section of the script is driven by if statements, which check the type of task you want to perform and jump to the appropriate section of the script. For example, if you enter S, the command shell jumps to the :START label. As compared to the schedule manager script, tasks in the service manager script are performed as a series of steps as well. However, when you reach the second step, the scripts differ. In addition to setting up the screen output, the script also writes to a log file.

To write date entries in the log, you have to trick the command shell into accepting a dot (.) as an invalid date. The command used is

```
echo . | date
```

which results in output similar to the following:

```
The current date is: Fri 05/07/1999
Enter the new date: (mm-dd-yy) .
The system cannot accept the date entered.
Enter the new date: (mm-dd-yy)
```

Because you don't want to put all that unnecessary information into the log file, use find to extract only the line containing the current date as follows:

```
echo. | date | find /i "current"
```

The resulting output is then

```
The current date is: Fri 05/07/1999
```

You can use the same procedure to get the current time. In the script, the date and time commands are

```
echo. | date | find /i "current">%SystemRoot%\service-mgr.log
echo. | time | find /i "current">%SystemRoot%\service-mgr.log
```

The service tracking mechanism also has some interesting code that you should examine. In the first step of tracking, you can put the script in a continuous loop by having the subroutine call its own label. You can then use a for loop to examine each individual service you want to watch, calling STARTTRACK for each service. When control returns from STARTTRACK, use sleep.exe, a Windows NT Resource Kit utility, to pause before checking the list of services again. The main argument for sleep is the number of seconds to pause. These steps come together as

```
:TRACK
for /f "eol=# tokens=*" %%A in (serv-mgr.txt) do (call :STARTTRACK
@@1b
"%%A")
SLEEP.EXE 300
goto :TRACK
```

The job of the STARTTRACK procedure is to determine if a service is running. To do this, you can view a list of all services running on the system and send the output to the find command, which searches for the currently referenced service. If the output from net start contains an entry for the service, find returns the service name, no error occurs, and the script goes back to the for loop in the TRACK subroutine. On the other hand, if the find search doesn't return the service name, an error occurs and an `if` statement is used to jump to the `:RESTART` subroutine as shown here:

```
:STARTTRACK
net start | find /i %1
if errorlevel==1 goto :RESTART
goto :EOF
```

Restart writes output to an error log and attempts to start the failed service. If the service starts, control returns to the `for` loop in the `STARTTRACK` subroutine. If the service fails to start, an error occurs and the `:ERROR` subroutine is used to handle it. At this point, the service is probably hung, which is why it won't restart. If you have the Windows NT Resource Kit, you can use kill.exe to cure this problem in most instances. After stopping the hung service, let control return to the `START-TRACK` subroutine and in approximately 5 minutes, the script will automatically start the service (and repeat this process if necessary).

To customize the error handling, you can add commands to the `:ERROR` subroutine. For example, I've commented out commands that'll restart the system in case of a hung service. You can also add counters that track repeated attempts to restart services and then restart the system when a predefined threshold is reached.

The script obtains the list of services needed from the file serv-mgr.txt. This file should be in the current working directory. If it isn't, you'll need to modify the script and insert the necessary file path. To help track when services are started, stopped, and restarted, the script writes entries in a log file called `service-mgr.log`. This file is created in the `%SYSTEMROOT%` directory. Sample entries from the log follow:

```
*********************
Service Stopped Admin: "world wide web publishing service"
The current date is: Fri 05/07/1999
The current time is: 22:06:38.23
*********************
Stopping "world wide web publishing service" Service...
*********************

*********************
Error Service Stopped: "world wide web publishing service"
The current date is: Fri 05/07/1999
The current time is: 22:06:50.23
*********************
Trying to Restart: "world wide web publishing service"
*********************

*********************
Successful Restart: "world wide web publishing service"
*********************
```

Automated Systems Management

Systems management is something administrators do every day. It shouldn't be difficult — it should be easy. Many command-line utilities can be used to make the day-to-day management of systems easier. These utilities include

- ◆ `shutdown` — A Windows NT Resource Kit utility that halts or restarts computers anywhere on the network
- ◆ `net print` — Displays print jobs and manages shared print queues
- ◆ `net session` — Displays and manages connections to network servers
- ◆ `net share` — Displays and manages shared network resources

Each of these command-line utilities can be used to automate key administration tasks. The sections that follow examine these utilities and then show how these utilities could be used in a system management script.

Shutting Down Systems Remotely

The Windows NT Resource Kit provides several different utilities for shutting down and rebooting Windows NT systems. The GUI tool is called shutgui.exe. The command-line tool is shutdown.exe. To use these tools, you must have the user rights to "Shut down the system" and to "Force Shutdown from a remote system." These rights are set in User Manager in workgroups and User Manager for Domains in NT Domains. Further, if you schedule system shutdown or reboot using AT, the scheduling account must have these rights.

Key switches you'll want to use with the `shutdown` utility are

- ◆ `/l` — Shuts down the local computer
- ◆ `/a` — Aborts a shutdown (if still within the specified delay)
- ◆ `/r` — Reboots computer after shutdown
- ◆ `/t:nn` — Sets delay before shutdown
- ◆ `/y` — Answers any command confirmation queries with Yes
- ◆ `/c` — Forces applications to close

To shutdown and reboot the local computer, use the `/l` and `/r` switches as follows:

```
shutdown /l /r
```

To shutdown and reboot a remote computer, enter the computer name before the necessary switches:

```
shutdown \\OMEGA /r
```

You can set a timeout delay in seconds for shutdown using /t. The following command sets a 60-second delay on the reboot of Omega:

```
shutdown \\OMEGA /r /t:60
```

Be careful when you use the /c switch. The /c switch forces applications to close regardless of their state and as a result, applications close without saving data first. This can cause data loss.

You can also set a message to display prior to shutdown. This message is enclosed in double quotation marks and should follow any switches you use. For example:

```
shutdown \\OMEGA /r /t:120 "System will reboot in 2 minutes!"
```

Examining Printer Queues

You can use net print to view and manage network print queues. When you want to view print jobs in a queue, enter **net print** and the UNC path to the queue, such as

```
net print \\PRINTSERVER\CORPPRINTER
```

Print queues show you current print jobs by ID and status. If a print job has an error printing, you can delete it using its ID, such as

```
net print \\PRINTSERVER 0036 /delete
```

You can also pause jobs temporarily. To do this, use the /hold switch:

```
net print \\PRINTSERVER 0010 /hold
```

When you are ready to resume printing, use the /release switch:

```
net print \\PRINTSERVER 0010 /release
```

Examining Network Connections to Servers

The net session command provides information on connections to a server system. You can view all connections to a server by entering the command on a line by itself or you can view a connection from a particular server, such as

```
net session \\zeta
```

You can disconnect computers using the /delete switch. The following command disconnects all open sessions, causing the affected systems to close the related resources:

```
net session /delete
```

To disconnect sessions from a particular system, enter its UNC name, such as

```
net session \\omega /delete
```

Examining Network Shares

The net share utility is used to manage shared printers and directories. To view a list of currently shared resources, enter **net share** on a line by itself as follows:

```
net share
```

You can create a shared directory by specifying the share name and assigning a directory path, such as

```
net share work=d:\working
```

You can control how the share is used with the /unlimited switch and the /users switch. The /unlimited switch specifies that an unlimited number of users can connect to the share. The /users switch sets a specified number of concurrent connections. In this example, the number of concurrent connections is limited to 256:

```
net share work=d:\working /users:256
```

To delete a shared resource, enter the share name and the /delete switch:

```
net share work /delete
```

You can view the results of these exercises in the Windows Explorer Network Neighborhood or by typing the command **net share** on a line by itself.

Automated Systems Management Script

Listing 6-5 provides a starting point for a comprehensive systems management script. You can use this script to manage server connections, shared resources, and network print queues. Add procedures to handle tasks that you perform routinely and then incorporate this script into your shell-scripting library. Because there are many options, the script uses letter combinations to determine which tasks to perform. These letter combinations are

◆ **VS** to view shared resources

◆ **CS** to create shared resources

◆ **DS** to delete shared resources

◆ **VC** to view server connections

◆ **DC** to delete server connections

◆ **VP** to view network printer queues

Listing 6-5: Managing Systems

system-mgr.bat

```
@echo off
@if not "%OS%"=="Windows_NT" goto :EOF
@if "%1"=="" (set INFO=echo && set SEXIT=1) else (set INFO=rem &&
@@lb
set SEXIT=0)


%INFO% ************************
%INFO% Script: Systems Manager
%INFO% Version: 0.9.2
%INFO% Creation Date: 4/01/99
%INFO% Last Modified: 9/1/99
%INFO% Author: William R. Stanek
%INFO% Email: win32scripting@tvpress.com
%INFO% ************************
%INFO% Description: Manages system resources.
%INFO% ************************
%INFO% Args: View current shares:
%INFO% Enter VS at first parameter
%INFO% *
%INFO% Delete a shared resource
%INFO% Enter DS at first parameter
%INFO% *
%INFO% Create a shared resource
%INFO% Enter CS at first parameter
%INFO% *
%INFO% View server connections:
%INFO% Enter VC at first parameter
%INFO% *
```

```
%INFO% Delete server connections:
%INFO% Enter DC at first parameter
%INFO% *
%INFO% View printer jobs on a network queue:
%INFO% Enter VP at first parameter
%INFO% *
%INFO% The file outfile28.txt is created in the current directory
%INFO% This file is used to temporarily store information typed in
%INFO% at the console.
%INFO% ************************

@if "%SEXIT%"=="1" goto :EOF

@title "Systems Manager"
cls
color 07

rem set temporary output file
set ofile="outfile28.txt"

if /I "%1"=="VS" goto :View
if /I "%1"=="DS" goto :Delete
if /I "%1"=="CS" goto :Create
if /I "%1"=="VC" goto :VConn
if /I "%1"=="DC" goto :DConn
if /I "%1"=="VP" goto :VPrin


goto :EOF

:View
@title "Systems Manager...View Shares"
echo ************************
echo Current Shares on %computername%
echo ************************
net share
goto :EOF

:Delete
@title "Systems Manager...Delete Shares"
echo ************************
echo Current Shares on %computername%
echo ************************
net share
echo ************************
```

```
echo Enter the name of the share to delete
echo Then press Ctrl+Z and Enter
echo ************************

rem get choice and read file
copy con %ofile% >nul
for /f "tokens=*" %%A in ('type "%ofile%"') do (call :DELMAIN "%%A")
goto :EOF

:Create
@title "Systems Manager...Create Shares"
echo ************************
echo Current Shares on %computername%
echo ************************
net share
echo ************************
echo Enter the name of the share to create
echo and the drive to map, such as:
echo work=d:\working
echo Then press Ctrl+Z and Enter
echo ************************

rem get choice and read file
copy con %ofile% >nul
for /f "tokens=*" %%A in ('type "%ofile%"') do (call :CREMAIN "%%A")
goto :EOF

:DELMAIN
echo ********************
echo Deleting: %1
echo ********************
net share %1 /delete
if errorlevel==1 goto :DERROR
goto :EOF

:CREMAIN
echo ********************
echo Creating: %1
echo ********************
net share "%1" /UNLIMITED
if errorlevel==1 goto :CRERROR
goto :EOF

:DERROR
```

```
echo *************************
echo Error deleting share!
echo Please re-enter.
echo *************************
copy con %ofile% >nul
for /f "tokens=*" %%A in ('type "%ofile%"') do (call :DELMAIN "%%A")
goto :EOF

:CRERROR
echo *************************
echo Error creating share!
echo Please re-enter.
echo *************************
copy con %ofile% >nul
for /f "tokens=*" %%A in ('type "%ofile%"') do (call :CREMAIN "%%A")
goto :EOF

:VConn
@title "Systems Manager...View Connections"
echo *************************
echo Current Connections to %computername%
echo *************************
net session
goto :EOF

:DConn
@title "Systems Manager...Disconnect"
echo *************************
echo Current Connections to %computername%
echo *************************
net session
echo *************************
echo Enter the name of the computer to disconnect
echo such as:
echo \\ZETA
echo Then press Ctrl+Z and Enter
echo *************************
copy con %ofile% >nul
for /f "tokens=*" %%A in ('type "%ofile%"') do (call :DCONMAIN @@lb
"%%A")

:DCONMAIN
echo *******************
echo Disconnecting: %1
```

```
echo *********************
net session "%1" /DELETE
if errorlevel==1 goto :DCONERROR
goto :EOF

:DCONERROR
echo ************************
echo Error disconnecting: %1
echo Please re-enter name.
echo ************************
copy con %ofile% >nul
for /f "tokens=*" %%A in ('type "%ofile%"') do (call :DCONMAIN @@1b
"%%A")
goto :EOF

:VPrin
@title "Systems Manager...View Print Queues"
echo ************************
echo View Print Jobs
echo ************************
echo Enter the name of the shared printer queue to examine
echo such as:
echo \\ZETA\CORPRINTER
echo Then press Ctrl+Z and Enter
echo ************************
copy con %ofile% >nul
for /f "tokens=*" %%A in ('type "%ofile%"') do (call :VPRINMAIN @@1b
"%%A")
goto :EOF

:VPRINMAIN
echo ************************
echo Viewing Print Jobs on: %1
echo ************************
net print %1
if errorlevel==1 goto PERROR
goto :EOF

:PERROR
echo ************************
echo Error, please re-enter.
echo ************************
copy con %ofile% >nul
for /f "tokens=*" %%A in ('type "%ofile%"') do (call :DELMAIN "%%A")
```

```
goto :EOF

:EOF
```

Output

```
*************************
Current Shares on ZETA
*************************


Share name    Resource                           Remark


-------------------------------------------------------------------
D$            D:\                                Default share
ADMIN$        D:\WINNT                           Remote Admin
IPC$                                             Remote IPC
C$            C:\                                Default share
E$            E:\                                Default share
print$        D:\WINNT\System32\spool\DRIVERS Printer Drivers
NETLOGON      D:\WINNT\System32\repl\import\s Logon server share
work          d:\working
HP            LPT1:                              Spooled 12th Floor


*************************
Enter the name of the share to create
and the drive to map, such as:
work=d:\working
Then press Ctrl+Z and Enter
*************************
test=d:\working
*********************
Creating: "test=d:\working"
*********************
test was shared successfully.
```

As the sample output for the script shows, Systems Manager has a new feature not found in previous scripts – the ability to accept input from the command line. Normally, command-line scripts don't accept input, unless you use a Windows NT Resource Kit utility such as choice.exe. Using choice, you specify the available choices by entering the /c switch and then a prompt as follows:

```
choice /c:1234 Enter a choice
```

When a script containing this line is run, choice displays

```
Enter a choice [1,2,3,4]
```

You can also use letters, such as

```
choice /c:YN Do you want to continue?
```

Here, the output would be

```
Do you want to continue? [Y,N]
```

To determine which key the user pressed, use the error code returned by `choice`. An error code of 1 indicates that the first choice was chosen. An error code of 2 indicates that the second choice was chosen and so on. In a script, you can use the error codes as shown:

```
choice /c:1234 Enter a choice
if errorlevel==1 goto :SUB1
if errorlevel==2 goto :SUB2
if errorlevel==3 goto :SUB3
if errorlevel==4 goto :SUB4

choice /c:YN Enter a choice
if errorlevel==1 goto :YES
if errorlevel==2 goto :NO
```

Although choice is a fairly handy utility, it doesn't allow you to enter parameters, such as directory or share names. To obtain this type of information, you need to get input directly from the command line. You can do this by copying input from the console (your keyboard) to a named file and then examining the contents of the file. In this example, input is copied from the console to the file keyboard.txt:

```
copy con keyboard.txt
```

To end the keyboard input and continue script execution, press Ctrl+Z followed by Enter. This command creates the file and returns control to the script. Because you usually don't want to see the output from the console, you should redirect output into `NUL` as follows:

```
copy con keyboard.txt >NUL
```

Once you obtain the necessary input for the file, you can use a `for` loop to examine each line in the file:

```
for /f "tokens=*" %%A in ('type "%ofile%"') do (call :MAIN "%%A")
```

Using `tokens=*`, each line of data is passed in its entirety to the procedure called `MAIN`. The iterator variable `%%A` is passed to `MAIN` enclosed in double quotes, which ensures that the entire line is treated as a whole even if it contains spaces. If you want to pass multiple parameters, you can do this as well. Here, you would enter them on the same line and delimit them with spaces or commas:

```
arg1 arg2 arg3
```

Afterward, you can then modify the `for` loop to work with the additional fields. In this example, fields 1–3 are passed to the procedures and are delimited with commas:

```
for /F "tokens=1-3 delims=," %%A in ('type "%ofile%"') do (call @@lb
:MAIN "%%A" "%%B" "%%C")
```

Automated Security, Application, and Error Management

System event logs provide the essential details for everything that is happening on a system. You can use event logs to look for security attacks on a system, to check the status of applications and more. Unfortunately, on a busy network, you often don't have time to slog through the logs every few minutes to watch for problems — even for critical systems. A solution is to create shell scripts that watch the logs for you and to do this, you'll usually want to use `dumpel`.

Examining Event Logs

The `dumpel` utility provides many different ways to examine information in event logs. You can dump entire event logs on specific systems and write the logs to files, search the event logs for specific events by ID, or even search event logs for events logged by a specific user.

The event log you want to examine is specified with the `/l` switch as system, application, or security. If you use the `/l` switch without specifying any other switches, the utility dumps the specified log on the current system to the command line. To dump logs to a file, use the `/f` switch and specify a log file. The following example dumps the system log to a file on the `\\ZETA\DATA\LOG` share:

```
dumpel /l system /f \\ZETA\DATA\LOG\%computername%.log
```

The `dumpel` utility works with the local system by default but you can access event logs on remote systems as well. Use the `/s` switch to specify the system name:

```
dumpel /l system /f omega.log /s omega
```

Event logs are created by writing one event per line to a log file or the command line. Fields in the event entry are normally separated by spaces, but you can use /t to specify tabs or /c to specify commas as delimiters. You can also use the /format switch to determine which fields to store in the event entries and their exact order. To do this, follow the /format switch with any combination of the modifiers shown in Table 6-1. The following example dumps the security log on the local system and restricts output to the date, time, event ID, and event type fields:

```
dumpel /l security /format dtIT
```

 The dumpel format modifiers are case sensitive. You must use the case shown.

TABLE 6-1 FORMATTING MODIFIERS FOR DUMPEL

Modifier	Description
C	Event category
c	Computer name
d	Date
I	Event ID
s	Event comment string
S	Event source
t	Time of day
T	Event type
u	User name

To search the event logs for specified events by ID, use the /e switch and then enter an event identifier, such as 528. You can use up to 10 /e switches. The good thing about this switch is that only entries containing the specified event are returned. The following example shows how you can track multiple events in the security log:

```
dumpel /l security /f zetasec.log /e 528 /e 529 /e 576 /e 578
```

Events logged include

- ◆ 528 – Successful logon
- ◆ 529 – Failed logon attempt
- ◆ 576 – Privilege use for special privileges
- ◆ 578 – Privilege use on security object

 TIP The easiest way to determine the types of identifiers you want to track is to go through system event logs and write down the IDs of events you'd normally be interested in.

Using the /m switch, you can search for events logged by specified users, such as system or Administrator. Unfortunately, you cannot specify multiple users, but you can use the /r switch with the /m switch to specify that you want to see all events except those for the specified user. In the following example, you search for events logged by the system account:

```
dumpel /l application /f zetasec.log /m system
```

In this example, you search for all events except those logged by system:

```
dumpel /l application /f zetasec.log /m system /r
```

You'll often have existing log files and may not need to create new ones. In this case, use the /b switch to search the existing log file specified with /l. In the following example, you search the zetasec.log:

```
dumpel /b /l zetasec.log /e 529
```

In this example, you search the zetasec.log and write the results to a file:

```
dumpel /b /l zetasec.log /e 529 /f failedlogins.log
```

Automated Event Checking and Tracking

Listing 6-6 provides a script for checking and tracking event logs on systems throughout the enterprise. The script obtains the list of systems to monitor from the file event-sys.txt. This file should be in the current working directory. If it isn't, you'll need to modify the script and insert the necessary file path. Additionally, the file should not use UNC names. The dumpel utility used to obtain events creates the UNC name for you.

The script uses letter combinations to determine which tasks to perform. These letter combinations are

- ◆ VA to view application logs for the systems specified in event-sys.txt

- ◆ VC to view system computer logs for the systems specified in event-sys.txt

- ◆ VS to view security logs for the systems specified in event-sys.txt

- ◆ C to create log files for each system, which can be later searched or browsed

Listing 6-6: Managing event logs

event-sys.txt

```
RAZOR
SHARKTOOTH
GREATWHITE
PIRANNA
```

event-mgr.bat

```
@echo off
@if not "%OS%"=="Windows_NT" goto :EOF
@if "%1"=="" (set INFO=echo && set SEXIT=1) else (set INFO=rem &&
@@lb
set SEXIT=0)

%INFO% ***********************
%INFO% Script: Event Manager
%INFO% Version: 0.9.4
%INFO% Creation Date: 3/15/99
%INFO% Last Modified: 9/1/99
%INFO% Author: William R. Stanek
%INFO% Email: win32scripting@tvpress.com
%INFO% ***********************
%INFO% Description: Tracks events on local
%INFO%             and remote systems.
%INFO% ***********************
%INFO% Args: View application logs:
%INFO% Enter VA at first parameter
%INFO% *
```

```
%INFO% View computer system logs
%INFO% Enter VC at first parameter
%INFO% *
%INFO% View security logs
%INFO% Enter VS at first parameter
%INFO% *
%INFO% Create log files
%INFO% Enter C at first parameter
%INFO% *
%INFO% When working with logs, the list of systems
%INFO% comes from event-sys.txt  in current directory.
%INFO% Enter the exact computer name, such as:
%INFO% OMEGA
%INFO% GAMMA
%INFO% BETA
%INFO% *
%INFO% Add any necessary comments by preceding with # character
%INFO% ************************

@if "%SEXIT%"=="1" goto :EOF

@title "Service Manager"
cls
color 07

if /i "%1"=="VA" goto :VApp
if /i "%1"=="VC" goto :VSys
if /i "%1"=="VS" goto :VSec
if /i "%1"=="C" goto :Create
goto :EOF

:VAPP
rem view application logs
@title "Event Manager...View Apps"
for /f "eol=# tokens=*" %%A in (event-sys.txt) do (call :APPMAIN
@@lb
"%%A")
goto :EOF

:VSYS
rem view system logs
@title "Event Manager...View System"
for /f "eol=# tokens=*" %%A in (event-sys.txt) do (call :SYSMAIN
@@lb
```

```
    "%%A")
    goto :EOF

    :VSEC
    rem view system logs
    @title "Event Manager...View Security"
    for /f "eol=# tokens=*" %%A in (event-sys.txt) do (call :SECMAIN
    @@lb
    "%%A")
    goto :EOF

    :CREATE
    rem get list of computers to monitor
    @title "Event Manager...Create Logs"
    for /f "eol=# tokens=*" %%A in (event-sys.txt) do (call :CREATEMAIN
    @@lb
    "%%A")
    goto :EOF

    :CREATEMAIN
    set sys=%1
    echo ********************
    echo Creating logs for: %1
    echo ********************
    dumpel /l application /f "%sys%app.log" /S %1
    dumpel /l system /f "%sys%sys.log" /S %1
    dumpel /l security /f "%sys%sec.log" /S %1
    echo ********************
    echo Finished creating logs for: %1
    echo ********************
    goto :EOF

    :APPMAIN
    echo ********************
    echo Application log for: %1
    echo ********************
    dumpel /l application /S %1 | more
    echo ********************
    echo End of Application log for: %1
    echo ********************
    goto :EOF

    :SYSMAIN
    echo ********************
```

```
echo System log for: %1
echo ********************
dumpel /l system /S %1 | more
echo ********************
echo End of System log for: %1
echo ********************
goto :EOF

:SECMAIN
echo ********************
echo Security log for: %1
echo ********************
dumpel /l security /S %1 | more
echo ********************
echo End of Security log for: %1
echo ********************
goto :EOF

:EOF
```

When the script creates logs, log files are written to the current working directory. These files are named as follows:

```
%computername%app.log
%computername%sys.log
%computername%sec.log
```

such as

```
razorapp.log
```

You can add procedures to the script to search the log files and report key events using the /b, /m, and /e switches, such as

```
dumpel /b /l razorapp.log /e 529
```

or

```
dumpel /b /l razorapp.log /M system
```

The types of events you will want to track depend primarily on your network configuration and the applications you use. Go through the events logs on key systems in the enterprise and note the IDs of important events, especially those for errors. Make separate lists for the application, system, and security logs. Then modify the script to report on these events.

Another feature you may want to implement is to create the log files on a network share that can be accessed by all administrators. Here, you simply need to modify the script to use the correct path, such as

```
dumpel /l application /f \\OMEGA\DATA\"%sys%app.log" /s %1
dumpel /l system /f \\OMEGA\DATA\"%sys%sys.log" /s %1
dumpel /l security /f \\OMEGA\DATA\"%sys%sec.log" /s %1
```

You can take this idea a step further and publish the logs for easy access over the corporate intranet or a secure Web server. Here, you would reformat the log files using HTML and then copy them to a directory on your Web server. Now you can access log files quickly and easily using a standard Web browser.

Summary

The Windows command shell provides an extremely robust environment for managing local and remote resources. As you've seen in this chapter, you can use shell scripts to monitor, manage, and troubleshoot network resources. These techniques can save the company thousands of dollars as compared to expensive monitoring and management software. Don't forget that the scripts provided in this chapter are meant to serve as starting points. Customize the scripts for your environment by adding new procedures, error checking, and more.

Part III

Windows Scripting Host

Chapter 7

Exploring Windows Script Host

WINDOWS SCRIPT HOST ENABLES you to script many operating system features using VBScript, Jscript, and other scripting languages. The key advantages to working with standard scripting languages are features and extensibility. Unlike the command shell, which is built-into the operating system and infrequently updated, the Windows Script Host and its individual components can be updated and installed separately from the operating system. You'll find that Windows Script Host is especially useful when you want to script the latest features of the Windows operating system and when you want to interact with desktop applications, such as Microsoft Word, Excel, or Access. The core lessons you learn in this chapter form the foundation of everything you do with Windows Script Host.

Windows Script Host Architecture

Windows Script Host (WSH) is a standard feature of Windows 98 and Windows 2000 and is available as an add-on for Windows NT 4.0. Windows Script Host provides architecture for building dynamic scripts that consists of a core object model, script hosts, and scripting engines, – each of which is discussed in the sections that follow.

Core Object Model

The core object model and script hosts are packaged with WSH for Windows. Although the Windows Script Host is fairly new, several versions have already shipped, including WSH 1 and WSH 2. WSH 1 is standard on most versions of

Windows 98, and if you install WSH through Service Pack 4 or 5 for Windows NT 4.0. WSH 2 ships with Windows 2000 and is available for Windows 98 and Windows NT 4.0. You can download the latest version online at the MSDN Web site (`http://msdn.microsoft.com/scripting/`).

Whether you install WSH on Windows NT 4.0 or work with WSH on Windows 98/2000, the core object model is implemented in the WSH.ocx ActiveX control. WSH.ocx provides the key functionality necessary for scripts to interact with the operating system. In WSH, objects are simply named containers that you'll use to interact with operating system components. For example, you'll use the `WshNetwork` object to access and configure network resources, like printers and drives.

Each object has properties and methods that are used to perform certain types of tasks. Properties are attributes of an object that you can access. Methods are procedures that you'll use to perform operations. As with other object-based programming languages, you can work with objects in a variety of ways. You can use built-in objects, create new objects based on the built-in objects, or you can define your own objects using unique methods and properties.

Table 7-1 provides a summary of the WSH object model. The WSH object hierarchy can be broken down into two broad categories: exposed objects and non-exposed objects. Exposed objects, like `WScript`, are the ones you'll work with in your scripts. Non-exposed objects, like `WshCollection`, are accessed through the methods or properties of other objects. These objects do the behind-the-scenes work.

TABLE 7-1 CORE WSH OBJECTS

Object Type	Object	Description
Exposed Object	`WScript`	Top-level object that provides access to core objects and other functionality such as object creation.
	`WScript.WshNetwork`	Automation object used to access and configure network resources, like printers and drives. Also provides user, domain, and computer information.
	`WScript.WshShell`	Automation object that provides access to the environment and file folders.
Non-exposed Object	`WshArguments`	Accessed through `WScript.Arguments`. Obtains command-line arguments.

Object Type	Object	Description
	`WshCollection`	Accessed through `WshNetwork.EnumNetworkDrives` or `WshNetwork.EnumPrinterCollection`. Used for iteration through a group of items, such as printers or drives.
	`WshEnvironment`	Accessed through `WshShell.Environment`. Allows you to work with environment variables.
	`WshShortcut`	Accessed through `WshShell.CreateShortcut`. Used to create and manage file shortcuts.
	`WshSpecialFolders`	Accessed through `WshShell.Folder`. Used to work with file folders.
	`WshUrlShortcut`	Accessed through `WshShell.CreateShortcut` method. Used to create and manage URL shortcuts.

 Most of the Microsoft technical documentation refers to some objects using the wrong letter case. For example, WScript is referred to as Wscript for both VBScript and JScript. Unfortunately, the JScript scripting engine (through version 5.1) doesn't recognize this object unless you reference it as WScript, and since VBScript really doesn't care about letter case, either Wscript or WScript works just fine. For consistency's sake, I refer to WScript in both VBScript and JScript. If this conflict is resolved and the object name is corrected to be Wscript in future versions of the JScript scripting engine, you may need to change WScript references to Wscript.

Script Hosts

To execute Windows scripts, you'll use one of the two script hosts available, either WScript or CScript. WScript has GUI controls for displaying output in pop-up dialog boxes and is used primarily when you execute scripts from the desktop. CScript is the command-line executable for the script host that is used when you execute scripts from the command line. Although you can work with both of these hosts in much the same way, there are some features specific to each and I'll discuss these features later in the section titled "Running Scripts with the Script Hosts." For now, let's focus on how the script hosts work.

When you install WSH and the Microsoft scripting engines, several file extensions are mapped for use with the script hosts. These files extensions are:

- ◆ .js – Designates scripts written in JScript.

- ◆ .vbs – Designates scripts written in VBScript.

- ◆ .ws – Designates a Windows script file.

- ◆ .wsh – Designates a WSH properties file.

As discussed in Chapter 1, the .js and .vbs extensions are reserved for use with Windows scripts. You don't need to use any special elements in .js or .vbs files. These files are also completely text-based and can be created in any text editor – even the Windows Notepad.

A limitation of .js and .vbs files is that they can only contain JScript or VBScript statements and you cannot mix and match as it were. This is where .ws files come into the picture. You can use .ws files to create WSH jobs or what I call *batch* scripts. These batch scripts can combine multiple types of scripts and can also include type libraries containing constants.

Batch scripts contain markup tags that identify elements within the batch, such as individual jobs and the scripting language being used. These markup tags are defined as XML (Extensible Markup Language) elements. XML is structured much like HTML and uses plain text characters. You can use any text editor to create batch scripts and because batch scripts contain XML, you can also use an XML editor.

 Markup languages often are used on the Web, and the most commonly used markup language is HTML (HyperText Markup Language). Markup tags are formatted using plain-old ASCII text. For example, the XML identifier for a batch script job is `<job> </job>`, and you'll find step-by-step instructions on how to use this identifier later in the chapter.

Windows scripts can also use .wsh files. These files contain default settings for scripts, such as timeout values and script paths. Because of the introduction of .ws files and direct in-script support for most script properties, .wsh files are rarely needed.

Scripting Engines

Scripting engines provide the core language functionality for Windows scripts and are packaged separately from the Windows Script Host itself. You can obtain scripting engines for JScript, VBScript, Perl, TCL, Python, and more. JScript and VBScript are the most widely used scripting languages and are the focus of the discussion in this book.

The official Microsoft scripting engines for VBScript and JScript are standard components on Windows 98 and Windows 2000. Most versions of Windows 98 have the version 4 scripting engines. Windows 2000 ships with the version 5 scripting engines. On Windows NT 4.0, you'll need to install the scripting engines. You'll find that the latest versions are available on the Internet (http://msdn.microsoft.com/scripting/).

With Windows Scripting, many of the features available for scripting with Internet Explorer and the Web aren't available. Functions needed for Web scripting simply aren't needed for Windows Scripting and vice versa. For example, in JScript, none of the window-related objects are available in WSH. The reason is that you normally don't need to access documents, forms, frames, applets, plug-ins, or any of those other browser-related features. The exception to this is if you create a script that starts a browser session; within the browser session, you can use the browser-related objects all you want.

Right now you may be wondering what exactly is and isn't supported by Windows scripts. In a nutshell, the scripting engines support core language and language run-time environments. The core language includes operators, statements, built-in objects, and built-in functions. Operators are used to perform arithmetic, comparisons, and more. Statements are used to make assignments, to conditionally execute code, and to control the flow within a script. For example, you can use `for` looping to execute a section of code for a specific count. These types of statements are all defined in the core language. Beyond this, the core language also defines the core functions and objects that perform common operations such as evaluating expressions, manipulating strings, and managing data.

The run-time environment adds objects to the core object model. These objects are used to work with the operating system and are available only with Windows Script. Table 7-2 provides a complete list of the available VBScript objects. The list is organized according to where the objects originate, either in the runtime or the core object model.

For a detailed look at these objects and their associated methods and properties, see the JScript and VBScript documentation, available from the MSDN scripting Web site: http://msdn.microsoft.com/scripting/

TABLE 7-2 VBSCRIPT OBJECTS FOR WINDOWS SCRIPTING

Run-time Objects	Core Objects
Dictionary Object	Class Object
Drive Object	Dictionary Object
Drives Collection	Err Object
File Object	FileSystemObject Object
Files Collection	Match Object
FileSystemObject Object	Matches Collection
Folder Object	RegExp Object
Folders Collection	
TextStream Object	

Table 7-3 provides a complete list of available JScript objects. Again, the list is organized according to where the objects originate.

TABLE 7-3 JSCRIPT OBJECTS FOR WINDOWS SCRIPTING

Run-time Objects	Core Objects
Drive Object	Array Object
Drives Collection	Boolean Object
File Object	Date Object
Files Collection	Dictionary Object
FileSystemObject Object	Enumerator Object
Folder Object	Error Object
Folders Collection	FileSystemObject Object
TextStream Object	Function Object
	Global Object
	Math Object

Run-time Objects	Core Objects
	Number **Object**
	Object **Object**
	RegExp **Object**
	Regular Expression **Object**
	String **Object**
	VBArray **Object**

Running Windows Scripts

Now that you learned a bit about the WSH architecture, let's look at key concepts you should know about when running Windows scripts, including:

◆ How to create Windows script files

◆ How to run scripts with WScript and CScript

Creating Windows Script Files

WSH provides several different ways to work with Windows scripts. The easiest technique is to create scripts using only a single scripting language and then save the script using the appropriate extension for the scripting engine. For example, if you use VBScript, you save the script with the .vbs extension. The script file doesn't need to contain any special markup or instructions of any kind. You can also combine multiple types of scripts in a batch script.

With batch scripts, you can use a single file and save it with the .ws file extension. Because batch scripts can use scripts written in multiple scripting languages, you must somehow identify the type of scripts you are using and other important aspects of these scripts. To do this, you use the XML markup tags supported by the Windows Script Host. These tags include:

◆ <?job ?> – Sets special instructions for all scripts in the batch

◆ <?XML ?> – Sets special instructions for parsing file as XML

◆ <package> – Encloses multiple job definitions

◆ <job> – Identifies the job (or script name)

- ◆ `<object>` — Exposes objects for use in scripts
- ◆ `<reference>` — References an external type library
- ◆ `<script>` — Identifies the scripting language and source

 Discussions on XML can (and have) filled entire books, so I won't try to teach XML. Instead, I will focus only on what you need to know to create batch scripts. For more detailed instruction on XML, I highly recommend three titles published by IDG Books: *XML in Plain English,* by Sandra Eddy; *XML Bible* by Elliotte Rusty Harold; and *XML: A Primer,* by Simon St. Laurent. I've read all three books and found them to be quite good.

The sections that follow examine each of these elements in turn. If you've never worked with markup tags before, don't worry; you don't have to know anything about XML or HTML. I promise.

IDENTIFYING THE JOB NAME

Batch scripts are really designed to help administrators create scripting libraries with functions that can be easily accessed. Because you can potentially have dozens of scripts in a single library, you need a container to be able to reference the script you want to run and you do this with the `job` element. As with most elements, the `job` element has a pair of markup tags associated with it. The `<job>` tag marks the beginning of the `job` element and the `</job>` tag marks the end of the `job` element, such as:

```
<job>
 Insert body of job here
</job>
```

To identify the name of the job, you use the `id` *attribute.* An attribute is simply a property of an element that can be used to set values. Using the `id` attribute, you set the job name as follows:

```
<job id="CreateFolders">
</job>
```

The `job` element is a top-level element that can contain zero or more occurrences of these other elements: `object`, `reference`, and `script`. The `job` element itself also can be used more than once in a .ws file, provided that you enclose the file within a `package` element. Enclosing multiple jobs is the only purpose of the `package` element and its use is mandatory when you have two or more jobs in a .ws file.

When you use multiple jobs, you shouldn't nest `job` elements within `job` elements. Instead, you should start one job, end it, and then start another, such as:

```
<package>
<job id="CreateFolders">
 Insert body of job here
</job>
<job id="DeleteFolders">
 Insert body of job here
</job>
<job id="ViewFolders">
 Insert body of job here
</job>
</package>
```

ADDING SCRIPTS AND SETTING THE SCRIPTING LANGUAGE

When you add scripts to the batch, you need to tell the script hosts about the script you are using. You do this with the `script` element. The `<script>` tag marks the beginning of a script and the `</script>` tag marks the end of a script. You always use the `script` element within a `job` element, such as:

```
<job id="CreateFolders">
<script>
 Insert script here
</script>
</job>
```

The script host also needs to know what language you are using. You specify the scripting language with the `language` attribute. Valid values for the `language` attribute include: `VBScript`, `JScript`, `JavaScript`, and `PerlScript`. You could set the scripting language to `VBScript` as follows:

```
<script language="VBScript">
 'Insert VBScript here
</script>
```

WSH jobs can contain multiple scripts. When they do, you need to insert additional `script` elements. In the following example, the job uses scripts written in VBScript and JScript:

```
<job id="CreateFolders">
<script language="VBScript">
 'Insert VBScript here
</script>
```

```
<script language="JScript">
'Insert JScript here
</script>
</job>
```

SETTING THE SCRIPT SOURCE

The source code for scripts doesn't have to be in the batch file. You can store the source in separate .js, .vbs, and .pl files and then reference the source file from within the batch. Source files that aren't located in the batch are referred to as external scripts, and their location is set with the src attribute.

The src attribute expects you to reference source locations using URLs (Universal Resource Locators). URLs are what you use when you browse the Web. However, while a typical Web URL looks like this: http://www.centraldrive. com/index.html, a typical file URL looks like this: file://c:\working\ myscript.vbs. Here, http: identifies the HyperText Transfer Protocol used on the Web, and file: identifies the File protocol used with file systems.

Source files can be referenced with relative file paths or absolute file paths. You access local files – files on your local system – using a relative file path. URLs with relative file paths generally do not name a protocol. When you use a relative path to locate a file, you locate the file in relation to the current batch script. You can use relative file paths in three key ways:

To access a file in the current directory, such as:

```
<script language="JScript" src="test.js" />
```

To access a file in a parent directory of the current directory, such as:

```
<script language="JScript" src="../test.js" />
```

To access a file in a subdirectory of the current directory, such as:

```
<script language="JScript" src="scripts/test.js" />
```

Another way to access files is directly. You do this by specifying the complete path to the file you want to access, such as:

```
<script language="JScript" src="file://c:\scripts/test.js" />
```

As shown in the previous examples, you don't use an end script tag when you specify a script source. Instead, you tell the script host to end the element with the /> designator. A more complete example of using external scripts is shown in Listing 7-1.

Listing 7-1: Working with multiple jobs and source files

multijobs.ws

```
<package>
<job id="CreateFolders">
  <script language="VBScript" src="fget.vbs" />
  <script language="JScript" src="fcreate.js" />
</job>
<job id="DeleteFolders">
  <script LANGUAGE="VBScript" src="testfolder.vbs" />
  <script LANGUAGE="VBScript" src="delcreate.vbs" />
</job>
<job id="ViewFolders">
<Script LANGUAGE="VBScript">
 'Insert VBScript here
</script>
<script language="JScript">
 'Insert JScript here
</script>
</job>
</package>
```

One of the primary reasons for placing multiple scripts in the same file is the ability to take advantage of the strengths of a particular scripting language. For example, VBScript features extensive support for arrays and JScript doesn't. You can create a script that makes use of VBScript's arrays and then pass this information back to JScript where you can then take advantage of JScript's extensive mathematical functions to manipulate the data in the arrays.

You'll find specific examples of combining scripting languages in Chapters 9-12. For specific pointers and helpful tips, see the section in Chapter 9 titled "Combining JScript and VBScript."

REFERENCING EXTERNAL OBJECTS AND TYPE LIBRARIES

External objects and type libraries allow you to extend the functionality of Windows scripts. With external objects, you can gain additional features. With type libraries, you can define sets of constants to use with scripts.

Windows scripts can use external objects and type libraries as long as those objects and libraries are defined appropriately for use with WSH. External objects must be defined as ActiveX objects and installed on the system running the script. Type libraries must be accessible for external calls and saved as .tlb, .olb, or .dll files.

When you use external objects in scripts, you need a way to tell your system about an object. You do this with the `classid` attribute of the `object` element. The `classid` attribute is a reference to the globally unique identifier (GUID) for the ActiveX object you want to use. Each ActiveX object has a GUID, and when the object is installed on a system, this value is stored in the Windows Registry. An ActiveX object has the same GUID on your system as it does on any other system.

The value `{0002DF01-0000-0000-C000-000000000046}` is the GUID for Internet Explorer. This value is also referred to as the CLSID or class ID for Internet Explorer. Your system accesses the appropriate object by looking up the class ID in the Windows Registry. Using the `classid` attribute, you reference controls by their CLSID value, such as:

```
<object classid="clsid:0002DF01-0000-0000-C000-000000000046" />
```

In the example, the curly braces are removed from the CLSID. You must remove the curly braces from all CLSIDs before referencing them as well.

Right now you are probably wondering how to obtain the monstrous CLSID value. The easiest way to obtain the CLSID value is through the Registry Editor. You can run the Registry Editor by starting regedit.exe (or regedt32.exe).

As shown in Figure 7-1, the Registry Editor files entries by category into directories. For OLE and ActiveX objects, the directory you want to examine is the `HKEY_CLASSES_ROOT` directory. Although the Registry Editor features a Find function under the Edit menu, this feature is only useful if you know the exact name of the object you are searching for. Therefore, you will probably want to browse for the object you are looking for. To do this, select `HKEY_CLASSES_ROOT` on local machine from the Window menu. With the `HKEY_CLASSES_ROOT` folder open, you will see folders for each registered item. Entries are listed by file extension, name, and GUID. The named entries are what you are looking for. Many ActiveX objects are filed beginning with the keyword Internet.

When you find the entry you are looking for, click in its folder to view subfolders associated with the entry. The CLSID subfolder is the one you want to examine, so click on the CLSID subfolder associated with the entry. Now, in the right pane of the Registry Editor, you should see the CLSID associated with the entry.

Double-click the CLSID entry in the right pane to display the Edit String dialog box. With the CLSID highlighted, you can press Ctrl + C to copy the CLSID to the clipboard. Now when you are ready to use the CLSID, paste the value from the clipboard using Ctrl + V.

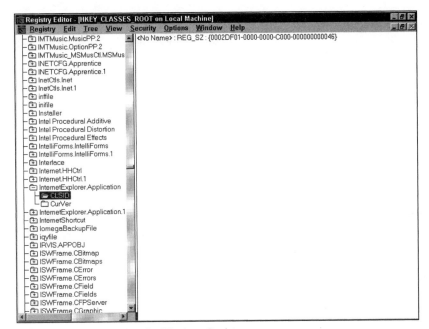

Figure 7-1: Working with the Windows Registry

Before you can use the object, you need to create a reference to the object. You do this by giving the object an identifier, such as IE for Internet Explorer. This identifier is assigned with the id attribute, such as:

```
<job id="WorkwithIE">
  <object ID="ie"
  classid="clsid:0002DF01-0000-0000-C000-000000000046" />
  <script language="VBScript" src="useie.vbs" />
</job>
```

Once you create an object reference, you can work with the object's methods and properties as you would any other object. The object is also available to multiple scripts associated with the current job.

The Reference element can also use CLSIDs to reference type libraries containing constants that you want to use in your scripts. With Reference, you set the CLSID with the `guid` attribute and should also specify the library version with the `version` attribute. If you do not specify a version, version 1.0 is assumed. Because you are referencing a GUID directly, you do not need the `CLSID:` prefix and can use these attributes as follows:

```
<job id="WorkwithTypeLib">
  <object guid="0002DF01-0000-0000-C000-000000000046"
          version=1.2/>
  <script language="VBScript" src="uselib.vbs" />
</job>
```

Rather than specifying `guid` and `version`, you can specify a file location for the type library using the `url` attribute. When you do this, you set the relative or absolute location of the library file. In the source code, you must then create instances of the object class or classes the library contains.

 If having to work with CLSIDs and the Registry seems like a lot of work, that's because it is. In practice, you'll probably want to create instances of objects within scripts rather than reference external objects. To do this, you'll use the `CreateObject()` method of the WScript object. You'll learn more about `CreateObject()` in Chapter 9.

SETTING JOB PROPERTIES

Another element you may want to work with in a batch script is `<?job ?>`. This element sets error-handling instructions for the script host on a per job basis. Each job in a .ws file can have a separate `<?job ?>` element. The basic syntax for `<?job ?>` is:

```
<?job error="flag"
      debug="flag" ?>
```

where *flag* is a Boolean value, such as true or false. By default, scripts don't have a timeout and most of the flags are set to false. A complete description of the attributes is provided as Table 7-4.

TABLE 7-4 PROCESSING ATTRIBUTES FOR USE WITH BATCH SCRIPTS

Attributes	Description
error	Set to true to allow error messages for syntax or run-time errors. Default is false.
debug	Set to true to enable debugging. When enable, you can start the script debugger. Default is false. (This assumes a debugger is configured.)

Listing 7-2 shows an example of using error-handling in a script. Note that each job has a separate instruction.

Listing 7-2: Setting special instructions in a batch script

instruct.ws

```
<package>
<job id="Backup">
<?job error="true" ?>
  <reference URL="file:c:\components\comp.lib">
  <script language="VBScript" src="backupset1.vbs" />
  <script language="VBScript" src="backupset2.vbs" />
  <script language="VBScript" src="backupset3.vbs" />
</job>
<job id="Restore">
<?job error="true" ?>
  <reference url="file:c:\components\comp.lib">
  <script language="VBScript" src="restore.vbs" />
</job>
</package>
```

SETTING SCRIPT PROPERTIES

The <?job ?> element provides the easiest way to set script properties but you can also use separate .wsh files to set script properties. The primary reason to use .wsh files is when you want to set separate properties for individual scripts that aren't part of a batch script. In practice, however, it is usually easier to add the script to a batch file and then set the properties using the <?job ?> element. This ensures that all the property settings are centrally located and easier to manage than separate property settings that you may forget about (and then wonder why your script is behaving strangely).

You can also set script properties in Windows Explorer or when you run scripts at the command-line. Both of these options are preferable to .wsh files. If you want to set properties for scripts in Windows Explorer, follow these steps:

1. Right-click a script file in Windows Explorer.

2. Select Properties on the shortcut menu.

3. Choose the Script tab as shown in Figure 7-2.

4. You can now set the default timeout value and determine whether the CScript logo is displayed. Use the timeout value to stop execution of a script that has been running too long and possibly prevent a runaway process from using up precious CPU time.

5. Choose OK or Apply.

6. These properties are used with WScript.

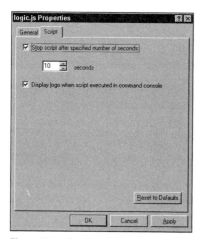

Figure 7-2: Setting Script properties through the Script tab in Windows Explorer

As I stated, you can also set script properties at the command-line. You can do this only when you execute a script using CScript and I'll show you how to do this in the next section.

SETTING PARSING INSTRUCTIONS

The <?XML ?> element allows you to set parsing instructions for the .ws file. If you use this element, the batch script is parsed as XML. The element has two attributes: version and standalone.

You use the version attribute to set the version of the XML specification to which the file conforms, such as 1.0. You use the standalone attribute to specify whether the file includes a reference to an external Document Type Definition (DTD). Normally, you want to set the value of standalone to Yes, which indicates that the batch script is a standalone document that does not use an external DTD.

If used, parsing instructions are set on the first line of the .ws file, such as:

```
<?XML version="1.0" standalone="yes" ?>
<package>
<job id="job1">
</job>
<job id="job2">
</job>
</package>
```

Running Scripts with the Script Hosts

Two script hosts are provided for running scripts: WScript and CScript. WScript is a script host with GUI controls for displaying output in pop-up dialog boxes and is used primarily when you execute scripts from the desktop. The related executable is WScript.exe and it isn't related to the WScript object that is a part of the core object model.

CScript is the command-line version of the script host. All output from CScript is displayed at the Windows command prompt unless you specify otherwise by using a pop-up or dialog box. The related executable for CScript is CScript.exe.

STARTING A SCRIPT

When you install WSH and the scripting engines on a system, several file types are mapped for use with the script hosts. These mappings allow you to run scripts like any other executable program. You can run scripts using any of the following techniques:

♦ Start Windows Explorer, and then browse until you find a script. Double-click on the script.

♦ Double-click on a desktop shortcut to a script.

♦ Enter a script name at the Run command on the Start Menu. Be sure to enter the full file extension and path if necessary, such as C:\scripts\myscript.vbs.

♦ At the command-line prompt, enter wscript followed by a script name, such as:

```
wscript myscript.vbs
```

♦ At the command-line prompt, enter cscript followed by a script name, such as:

```
cscript myscript.js
```

ASSOCIATING FILE EXTENSIONS FOR SCRIPTS

Running scripts from the desktop or Windows Explorer is a bit different from running a script at the command line, and the first time you use a script with a particular file extension, you may need to associate the extension with the script host. To associate the extension with the script host of your choice, follow these steps:

1. The Open With dialog box appears, prompting you to click the program you want to use to open the file.

2. Select either CScript or WScript.

3. Be sure to check the Always Use This Program To Open This File check box.

4. Click OK or Apply.

5. Now the select script host is the default for all files with this extension.

COMMAND-LINE OPTIONS FOR SCRIPTS

When you run scripts from the desktop or Windows Explorer property settings, scripts can be applied as outlined under "Setting Script Properties." These settings are for WScript. CScript, on the other hand, is a command-line executable and like most command-line programs, can be configured using switches and modifiers.

The command-line syntax for cscript is:

```
cscript [host_options] [script_name] [script_args]
```

where script name is the name of the script, *host_options* are options to set for CScript, *script_name* is the name of the script, and *script_args* are arguments to pass in to the script. The script name must include the file extension and any necessary path information, such as:

```
cscript startup.vbs
cscript c:\scripts\startup.vbs
cscript c:\"my scripts"\startup.vbs
```

Table 7-5 shows the available options for CScript. As you can see, options and arguments are differentiated using slashes. Host options are preceded with two slashes (//) and script arguments don't use slashes. For example, you can set a timeout for a script and pass in the script parameter "debug" as follows:

```
cscript //t:30 logon.vbs debug
```

TABLE 7-5 OPTIONS FOR CSCRIPT

Option	Description
//?	Shows command usage.
//b	Sets Batch Mode, which suppresses command-line display of user prompts and script errors. (Opposite of //i)
//d	Turns on the debugger.
//e:*engine*	Run the script with the specified scripting engine.
//h:Cscript	Registers Cscript.exe as the default application for running scripts.
//h:Wscript	Registers Wscript.exe as the default application for running scripts. If not specified, Wscript.exe is assumed as the default.
//i	Sets Interactive Mode for scripts, which allows display of user prompts and script errors. Interactive mode is the default.
//Job:"Job Name"	Runs the specified Job from a WSC file.
//logo	Displays CScript logo at run time. This is the default setting.
//nologo	Turns off display of the CScript logo at run time.
//s	Saves the current command-line options for the user logged on to the system.
//t:*nn*	Sets a timeout for the script, which is the maximum number of seconds (*nn*) the script can run. By default, scripts have no limit.
//x	Executes the program in the debugger.

As you can see from the table, scripts can be run in interactive mode or batch mode. In batch mode, scripts don't display prompts or errors, and this behavior is very useful when you want to schedule scripts to run with the At scheduler. For example, if you want to run a Windows script every day at midnight, you would probably want to run in batch mode, such as:

```
AT 00:00 /every:M,T,W,Th,F,S,Su "cscript //b cleanup.vbs"
```

Whether you run scripts from the command-line or via the At scheduler, you'll often want to set more than one option. Having to retype scripting options each time you use a script isn't fun, which is why the //s option is provided. Using this option, you can set default options to use each time you run CScript. For example, if you enter the following command:

```
cscript //b //nologo //t:30 //d //s
```

CScript is set to use batch mode, no logo, a timeout of 30 seconds, and debugging whenever you run scripts. The only way to override the default options is to save a different set of options, such as:

```
cscript //i //s
```

Keep in mind, however, that the default options are only valid for the user currently logged in to the system. When you schedule commands to run with AT, or log in using a different login ID, the default options won't be available. Rather than depending on default options and //s, you may want to try a different approach and that is to set the options you want to execute via a shell script. Listing 7-3 shows an example of how you can do this. You can then schedule the script to run once a week on Sundays using the following AT command:

```
AT 02:00 /every: Su "c:\scripts\backups.bat"
```

Listing 7-3: Executing a Windows script from a shell script

backups.bat
```
cscript //b //Job:"WSBackup" //t:6000 backup1.ws
cscript //b //Job:"SVRBackup" //t:6000 backup2.ws
```

backup1.vbs
```
'Start Workstation backups
<job id="WSBackup">
  <script language="VBScript" src="wsbackupset1.vbs" />
  <script language="VBScript" src="wsbackupset2.vbs" />
  <script language="VBScript" src="wsbackupset3.vbs" />
</job>
```

backup2.vbs
```
'Start Server backups
<job id="SVRBackup">
  <script language="VBScript" src="svrbackupset1.vbs" />
  <script language="VBScript" src="svrbackupset2.vbs" />
  <script language="VBScript" src="svrbackupset3.vbs" />
</job>
```

As you work with WScript and CScript, you may find that you prefer one to the other. Don't worry, you can switch the default script host at any time. To use CScript as the default, enter the following command:

```
cscript //h:CScript
```

To use WScript as the default enter:

```
cscript //h:WScript
```

USING DRAG AND DROP WITH SCRIPTS

Windows Script Host 2.0 and later supports the drag and drop features of Windows 98 and Windows 2000. This feature allows you to drag one or more files onto a script file and then run the script with the files as arguments.

When you drag files onto a WSH script, the file names are translated into arguments on the command line. These file names can be managed just like any other script arguments. The number of files you can drag onto a script is limited by the maximum command-line length your computer allows. If the total number of characters in all filenames (including the spaces added between filenames) exceeds this limit, the drag and drop operation will fail.

To give drag and drop a test run, use the script shown in Listing 7-4. The script echoes the filenames you drag onto the script. For now don't worry about the how's and why's of the code. You'll learn more about scripting and VBScript in Chapter 8.

Listing 7-4: Using drag and drop

dragndrop.vbs
```
Set objArgs = WScript.Arguments
For I = 0 to objArgs.Count - 1
  WScript.Echo "File " + I + ": " + objArgs(I)
Next
```

Summary

Windows Script Host provides a fairly advanced architecture for working with scripts. The architecture includes a core object model, script hosts, and scripting engines – all of which have been specially tailored for use in administration. As you set out to learn more about Windows Scripting, don't forget the lessons you've already learned for shell scripting. Many of the techniques you've learned can be applied directly to Windows Scripting. In the next chapter, you learn how to work with VBScript and JScript, the primary scripting languages you'll use with Windows scripts.

Chapter 8

Core Scripting

IN THIS CHAPTER

- ◆ VBScript variables and arrays
- ◆ VBScript Operators and control flow
- ◆ VBScript functions and subroutines
- ◆ JScript variables and data types
- ◆ JScript strings and arrays
- ◆ JScript Operators and control flow
- ◆ JScript functions

IF YOU WANT TO CREATE Windows scripts, the two primary scripting languages you will use are VBScript and JScript. VBScript is a streamlined version of Microsoft's popular Visual Basic programming language that retains the ease of use and many of the powerful features that made Visual Basic so popular. JScript, on the other hand, has a syntax that is similar to the Web darling, Java, offering its own unique twist on object-based programming.

Both VBScript and JScript have their strengths and weaknesses, which makes choosing the right scripting language for your project a challenge. As you set out to learn these scripting languages, don't forget that you can create batch scripts that combine scripts written in both VBScript and JScript. This allows you to draw on the strengths of each scripting language and to use your favorite scripting techniques regardless of whether they are from VBScript or JScript. Throughout the chapter, I'll try to point out specific differences between VBScript and JScript whenever possible.

 Earlier chapters introduced many of the core scripting techniques that I'll explore in this chapter. Don't worry, I won't waste your time re-introducing concepts I've already discussed. Instead, I'll focus on what's different — primarily syntax and structure. So strap on your seat belt and get ready to dive in.

VBScript Essentials

Working with VBScript is like slipping into a comfortable easy chair. The syntax is easy to understand; the structures are easy to learn; and you'll soon feel right at home – even if you don't have time to explore every nook and cranny.

Working with Variables

Variables are a part of most scripting languages, and VBScript is no exception. A variable is simply a placeholder for a value you want to work with.

VARIABLE NAMING IN VBSCRIPT

You can create a variable by assigning the variable a name, which you can refer to in your code later. Variable names, like other VBScript structures, follow standard naming conventions. These naming rules are

- Names must begin with an alphabetic character.

- Names cannot contain periods.

- Names must be less than 256 characters in length.

Variable names also have an additional property that isn't true of other structures in VBScript. They are case sensitive, meaning `testa`, `testA`, and `TESTA` are all different variables. However, method, function, and object references in VBScript are not case sensitive. For example, you can echo to the screen using any of the following commands:

```
wscript.echo "Case Test!"
Wscript.echo "Case Test!"
WScript.Echo "Case Test!"
```

But in reality the correct capitalization for this reference is `WScript.Echo`.

DECLARING VARIABLES IN VBSCRIPT

In VBScript, variables are declared either explicitly or implicitly. To declare a variable explicitly, use the keyword `Dim` to tell VBScript that you are creating a variable and then specify the variable name, such as

```
Dim wereSmoking
```

You can then assign a value to the variable, such as

```
wereSmoking = "Oh Yeah, Baby!"
```

You can also declare multiple variables at the same time. You do this by separating the variable names with commas:

```
Dim wereSmoking, letsGo, testRun
```

To declare a variable implicitly, use the variable name without first declaring it; you don't need to use the Dim keyword. Here, VBScript creates the variable for you.

The problem with implicit variables is that any name is assumed to be valid, so you can mistakenly assign values to the wrong variable and you won't know it. Consider the following example, where you assign a value to numEmployees and later assign a value to a variable called numEmployee:

```
numEmployees = mGroup + bGroup + iGroup

'working with the variable

'now you need to increase the number of employees
numEmployee = numEmployees + 1
```

 Everything following a single quotation mark is interpreted as a comment. You can use comments anywhere in a line of code.

Here, you meant to increase numEmployees, but increased numEmployee instead. To avoid situations like this, you can set Option Explicit, which requires that all variables be declared explicitly with the Dim keyword and also ensures the validity of your variables. This option should be placed at the beginning of your script as shown in Listing 8-1.

Listing 8-1: Using variables

variable.vbs
```
Option Explicit
'Setting variables
Dim mGroup, bGroup, iGroup
Dim numEmployees

mGroup = 5
bGroup = 8
iGroup = 12

'Total number of employees
```

```
numEmployees = mGroup + bGroup + iGroup

'write total to command-line using WScript.Echo
```

WScript.Echo "Total employees: ", numEmployees

Output

```
25
```

VARIABLE TYPES IN VBSCRIPT

VBScript assigns all variables to the `variant` data type. Variants can hold numeric or string data and each is handled differently. The key way VBScript determines if something is a number or a string is the use of double quotation marks. In the previous code sample, `mGroup`, `bGroup`, and `iGroup` are all handled as numbers. If you add double quotation marks to the values, they would be treated as strings, such as

```
mGroup = "5"
bGroup = "8"
iGroup = "12"
```

The use of strings yields very different results when you add the values together and as a result, the value of `numEmployees` is

```
5812
```

The reason for this is that while numbers are summed, strings are concatenated so you get the literal sum of all characters in the string. To complicate things a bit more, VBScript also uses *variable subtypes*. Variable subtypes are summarized in Table 8-1. Subtypes allow you to put certain types of information into categories so they can be handled better as dates, floating-point numbers, integers, or whatever. For example, if you are working with dates and you need to add two dates together, you wouldn't want the result to be an integer. Instead, you'd want the dates to be handled as dates and the result of any operations to be dates, which is exactly what subtypes offer.

TABLE 8-1 VARIABLE SUBTYPES IN VBSCRIPT

Subtype	Description
Boolean	A Boolean value that contains either True or False.
Byte	An integer byte value in the range 0 to 255.
Currency	A floating-point number in the range –922,337,203,685,477.5808 to 922,337,203,685,477.5807. Note the use of up to 4 decimal places.

Subtype	Description
Date (Time)	A number that represents a date between January 1, 100 to December 31, 9999.
Double	A double-precision, floating-point number in the range −1.79769313486232E308 to −4.94065645841247E−324 for negative values; 4.94065645841247E−324 to 1.79769313486232E308 for positive values.
Empty	An uninitialized variant. Value is 0 for numeric variables or an empty string ("") for string variables.
Error	An error number used with run-time errors
Integer	An integer in the range −32,768 to 32,767.
Long	An integer in the range −2,147,483,648 to 2,147,483,647.
Null	A variant set to NULL that contains no valid data.
Object	An object reference.
Single	A single-precision, floating-point number in the range −3.402823E38 to −1.401298E−45 for negative values; 1.401298E−45 to 3.402823E38 for positive values.
String	A variable-length string.

Generally, if you use whole numbers, such as 2 or 6, with a variable, VBScript creates the variable as an Integer. Variables with values that use decimal points, such as 1.25 or 2.2, are generally assigned as Doubles, double-precision floating-point values. Variables entered with a mixture of alphabetical and numeric characters, such as Ouch and W-4, are created as Strings.

CONVERTING VARIABLE TYPES

VBScript can automatically convert between some variable types, and this eliminates most variable conflict. However, if you try to add a string variable to a numeric variable type, you will get an error. Because of this, do not try to perform numeric calculations with alphanumeric data.

That said, VBScript includes many different functions for converting data from one subtype to another. These functions are summarized in Table 8-2.

TABLE 8-2 FUNCTIONS FOR CONVERTING VARIABLE SUBTYPES

Function	Description
CBool(*expression*)	Converts any valid expression to a Boolean value. Returns either True or False.
CByte(*expression*)	Converts any valid expression to a Byte value.
CCur(*expression*)	Converts any valid expression to a Currency value.
CDate(*date*)	Converts any valid date string to a Date value. Returns a date value that can be used when adding dates and times.
CDbl(*expression*)	Converts any valid expression to a Double value.
CInt(*expression*)	Converts any valid expression to an Integer value.
CLng(*expression*)	Converts any valid expression to a Long value.
CSng(*expression*)	Converts any valid expression to a Single value.
CStr(*expression*)	Converts any valid expression to a String value.

Working with conversion functions is a lot easier than you may think. To convert a value, just pass the value to the conversion function, as follows:

```
mGroupString = "5"
bGroupString = "8"

mGroupInt = CInt(mGroupString) 'Set to integer value 5
bGroupInt = CInt(bGroupString) 'Set to integer value 8
```

The CBool(), CDate() and CString() functions deserve a special note because they return output that is a bit different from what you may be used to. To learn more about these functions, examine Listing 8-2.

Listing 8-2: Working with conversion functions

convert.vbs
```
aGroup = 24: bGroup = 12      'Initialize variables

Test = CBool(aGroup = bGroup) 'Test contains false

bGroup= bGroup * 2            'Double value of bGroup
Test = CBool(aGroup = bGroup) 'Test contains true
```

```
dateStr = "January 15, 2000"    'Define a date as a string
aDate = CDate(dateStr)          'Convert to Date data type

timeStr = "6:21:30 PM"          'Define a time as a string
aTime = CDate(timeStr)          'Convert to Date data type

aDouble = 812.125               'Define a numeric value
aString = CStr(aDouble)         'Convert to a string
```

Working with Arrays

Using arrays, you can group related sets of data together. The most common type of array you'll use is one-dimensional, but you can create arrays with up to 60 dimensions if you want to. While a one-dimensional array is like a column of tabular data, a two-dimensional array is like a spreadsheet with rows and columns, and a three-dimensional array is like a 3-D grid.

INITIALIZING ARRAYS

Arrays are declared much like regular variables except you follow the variable name with information describing size and dimensions of the array. You can initialize an array with ten data elements as follows:

```
Dim myArray(9)
```

Values in an array always begin at 0 and end at the number of data points in the array minus 1. This is why an array with ten data points is initialized as myArray(9). To access elements in an array, reference the element's index position within the array. For example, myArray(0) references the first element, myArray(1) references the second element and so on. Use the index position to set values for the array as well, such as

```
myArray(0) = "Mark Twain"
myArray(1) = "Robert Louis Stevenson"
```

USING ARRAYS WITH MULTIPLE DIMENSIONS

Multiple dimensions are created by separating the size of each dimension with commas, such as alphaArray(3,3,3) or betaArray(2,5,5,4). You can create a two-dimensional array with four columns each with four rows of data points as follows:

```
Dim myArray(3,3)
```

Next, if you want to obtain the value of a specific cell in the spreadsheet, you can use the following:

```
theValue = arrayName(columns -1, rows -1)
```

where `columns` is the column position of the cell and `rows` is the row position of the cell. Following this, you can get the value of the cell in column 2, row 1 with this statement:

```
myValue = myArray(1,0)
```

DYNAMICALLY SIZING ARRAYS

Sizing arrays on the fly enables you to use input from users to drive the size of an array. You can declare a dynamic array without specifying its dimensions, as follows:

```
Dim variableArray()
```

and then size the array later using the `ReDim` function

```
ReDim variableArray(inputA - 1)
```

or

```
ReDim variableArray(numColumns - 1, numRows - 1)
```

You can also use `ReDim` to change the size of an existing array. For example, you can increase the size of an array from 10 elements to 20 elements. However, when you change the size of an existing array, the array's data contents are destroyed. To prevent this, use the `Preserve` keyword, as follows:

```
ReDim Preserve variableArray(numColumns - 1, numRows - 1)Operators
in VBScript
```

Operators are used to perform mathematical operations, to make assignments, and to compare values. The two key types of operators you'll use in VBScript are arithmetic operators and comparison operators. As you'll see, VBScript supports fewer operators than the command line. While this may seem limiting, VBScript makes up for this by enabling you to use floating-point values and integers with high precision.

VBScript also uses logical operators such as AND, NOT OR, and XOR. With the exception of NOT, these operators are rarely used and when you do use them, they are used much like the command shell's bitwise operators.

ARITHMETIC OPERATORS

VBScript supports a standard set of arithmetic operators. These operators are summarized in Table 8-3.

TABLE 8-3 ARITHMETIC OPERATORS IN VBSCRIPT

Operator	Operation
+	Addition
=	Assignment
/	Division
^	Exponent
Mod	Modulus
*	Multiplication
-	Subtraction/Negation

As you can see from Table 8-3, there are few surprises when it comes to VBScript operators. Still, a few standouts are worth mentioning. In VBScript, you determine remainders using the Mod function versus the % for the command-line. But the syntax is essentially the same. With the expression

```
Answer = 6 Mod 2
```

Answer is set to 0. With the expression

```
Answer = 5 Mod 2
```

Answer is set to 1.

You can multiply by an exponent with the ^ operator. To achieve the same result as 4 *4 * 4 * 4*4, you would use

```
Answer = 4^5
```

You can negate a value using the - operator, such as

```
Answer = -2 * 3
```

If you mix operators, VBScript performs calculations using the same precedence order you learned in school. For example, multiplication and division in equations are carried out before subtraction and addition, which means

5 + 3 * 3 = 14

And

3 / 3 + 2 = 3

Table 8-4 shows the complete precedence order for operators. As the table shows, exponents have the highest precedence order and are always calculated first.

TABLE 8-4 OPERATOR PRECEDENCE IN VBSCRIPT

Order	Operation
1	Exponents (^)
2	Negation (-)
3	Multiplication (*) and Division (/)
4	Remainders (Mod)
5	Addition (+) and Subtraction (-)

COMPARISON OPERATORS

When you perform comparisons, you check for certain conditions, such as, is A greater than B or is A equal to C. VBScript supports a set of comparison operators that aren't much different from the comparison operators used with command shell scripting. The key difference is that you use standard mathematical symbols rather than abbreviations like neq. As with command shell scripting, you primarily use comparison operators with conditional statements, such as if then and if then else. The available operators are summarized in Table 8-5.

TABLE 8-5 COMPARISON OPERATORS IN VBSCRIPT

Operator	Description
=	Equality; evaluates to true if the values are equal.
<>	Inequality; evaluates to true if the values are not equal.
<	Less than; evaluates to true if value1 is less than value2.

Operator	Description
<=	Less than or equal to; evaluates to true if value1 is less than or equal to value2.
>	Greater than; evaluates to true if value1 is greater than value2.
>=	Greater than or equal to; evaluates to true if value1 is greater than or equal to value2.

Listing 8-3 shows how you can use comparison operators in a script. Note that you can use these operators to compare numbers as well as strings. This is different from command shell scripting where you have different operators for assigning values (=) and testing equality (==). Note also that there is no set precedence order for comparisons. Comparisons are always performed from left to right.

Listing 8-3: Working with comparison operators

compare.vbs

```
theSum = 5
testVar = 3
if theSum = 0 Then
  WScript.Echo "The sum is zero."
End If
if theSum = testVar Then
  WScript.Echo "The values are equal."
End If
if theSum <>0 Then
  WScript.Echo "The sum does NOT equal zero."
End If
if theSum <>testVar Then
  WScript.Echo "The values are NOT equal."
End If
if theSum < 0 Then
  WScript.Echo "The value is less than zero."
End If
if theSum > 0 Then
  WScript.Echo "The value is greater than zero."
End If
if theSum <= testVar Then
  WScript.Echo "theSum is less than or equal to testVar."
End If
```

```
if theSum >= 0 Then
    WScript.Echo "The value is greater than or equal to zero."
End If
```

Output

```
The sum does NOT equal zero.
The values are NOT equal.
The value is greater than zero.
The value is greater than or equal to zero.
```

One other comparison operator you should learn about is the special operator Is. You use Is to compare objects, such as buttons. If the objects are equivalent, the result of the comparison is True. If the objects are not equivalent, the result of the comparison is False. You can test to see if the object aButton references the VBScript object Button as follows:

```
Answer = aButton Is Button
If Answer = True Then
    WScript.Echo "aButton is equivalent to Button."
Else
    WScript.Echo "aButton is NOT equivalent to Button."
End If
```

You can also perform the comparison directly in an If statement:

```
If aButton Is Button Then
    WScript.Echo "aButton is equivalent to Button."
Else
    WScript.Echo "aButton is NOT equivalent to Button."
End If
```

PERFORMING OPERATIONS ON STRINGS

The most common string operations you'll want to perform are assignment and concatenation. You assign values to strings using the equal sign, ensuring that the value is enclosed in double quotation marks, such as

```
theString = "This is a String."
```

Concatenation is the technical term for adding strings together. Although you can use the + operator to concatenate strings, the normal operator for string concatenation is the & operator. Using the & operator, you can add strings together as follows:

```
custAddress = streetAdd & " " & cityState & " " & zipCode
```

Sometimes you may also want to display the value of a string in a message box. Here, you will use the & operator as well. For example

```
theString = "Ouch!"
WScript.Echo "The string value is: " & theString
```

would display a dialog box with the message:

```
The string value is: Ouch!
```

Conditional Controls in VBScript

Traffic lights control the flow of traffic on the street. Conditional instructions control the flow of instructions in your code.

USING IF ... THEN

You use If statements to execute a set of instructions only when certain conditions are met. In VBScript, If...Then structures follow this syntax:

```
If condition = True Then
   'Handle the condition
End If
```

or

```
If condition Then
    'Handle the condition
End If
```

Note the use of the End If statement. This is what makes it possible to execute multiple commands when a condition exists, such as

```
If sum > 9 Then
   WScript.Echo "The sum exceeds the expected Result"
   'Reset sum to zero
   sum = 0
End If
```

You can control the execution of instructions based on a false condition as follows:

```
If condition = False Then
   'The condition is false
End If
```

or

```
If Not condition  Then
  'The condition is false
End If
```

USING ELSE AND ELSEIF

You can extend the `If Then` condition with `Else` statements. The `Else` statement provides an alternative when a condition that you specified is not met. The structure of an `If Then Else` statement is as follows:

```
If roadTest = "Yes" Then
    WScript.Echo "The condition has been met."
Else
    WScript.Echo "The condition has not been met."
End If
```

To add more conditions, you can use `ElseIf` statements. Each additional condition you add to the code is then checked for validity. An example using `ElseIf` is shown in Listing 8-4.

Listing 8-4: Working with ElseIf

conditionals.vbs

```
If theValue < 0 Then
  WScript.Echo "The value is less than zero."
ElseIf theValue = 0 Then
  WScript.Echo "The value is equal to zero."
ElseIf theValue = 1 Then
  WScript.Echo "The value is equal to one."
ElseIf theValue = 2 Then
  WScript.Echo "The value is equal to two."
ElseIf theValue = 3 Then
  WScript.Echo "The value is equal to three."
ElseIf theValue = 4 Then
  WScript.Echo "The value is equal to four."
ElseIf theValue = 5 Then
  WScript.Echo "The value is equal to five."
Else
  WScript.Echo "Value doesn't match expected parameters."
End If
```

SELECT CASE

Checking for multiple conditions using `ElseIf` is a lot of work for you and for the VB interpreter. To make things easier, use `Select Case` anytime you want to check more than three conditions. Using `Select Case`, you can rewrite Listing 8-4 in a way that is clearer and easier to understand, which is exactly what Listing 8-5 shows.

Listing 8-5: Working with Select Case

multicond.vbs

```
theValue = 3
Select Case theValue
   Case < 0
     WScript.Echo "The value is less than zero."
   Case 0
     WScript.Echo "The value is equal to zero."
   Case 1
     WScript.Echo "The value is equal to one."
   Case 2
     WScript.Echo "The value is equal to two."
   Case 3
     WScript.Echo "The value is equal to three."
   Case 4
     WScript.Echo "The value is equal to four."
   Case 5
     WScript.Echo "The value is equal to five."
   Case Else
     WScript.Echo "Value doesn't match expected parameters."
End Select
```

Output

```
The value is equal to three.
```

If you compare the `ElseIf` example and the `Select Case` example, you will see that the `Select Case` example requires less code and has a simpler structure. You can apply this same structure anytime you want to check for multiple conditions. Start the structure with the name of the variable whose value you want to check. In the following example, you compare the value of `userInput`:

```
Select Case userInput
```

Afterward, you can check for specific conditions, such as

```
Case < 0
 'less than zero
Case > 0
 'greater than zero
Case = 0
 'equal zero
```

or

```
Case "Yes"
 'value is yes
Case "No"
 'value is no
```

Use `Case Else` to specify statements that should be executed if no match is found in the specified `Case` statements, such as

```
Case Else
    WScript.Echo "Value doesn't match expected parameters."
    WScript.Echo "Please check your input again."
```

CONDITIONAL CONTROLS AND STRINGS

When you perform string comparisons with conditional controls, pay particular attention to the letter case. VBScript automatically performs case-sensitive comparisons and doesn't support a flag similar to the `/i` flag used in command shell scripting. Because of this, a comparison of "Yes" and "YES" returns False.

To avoid potential problems you should convert the string to upper- or lowercase for the comparison. Use `lcase()` to convert strings to lowercase. Use `ucase()` to convert strings to uppercase. Listing 8-6 shows how these functions can be used with `If...Then`. You can also use these functions with `Select Case`.

Listing 8-6: Changing the case of a string

stringcase.vbs

```
'Setting variables
m = "Yes"
n = "YES"
If m = n Then
  WScript.Echo "Anything? Nope, I didn't think so."
End If
If lcase(m) = lcase(n) Then
  WScript.Echo "Values are equal when converted to lower case"
End If
if ucase(m) = ucase(n) Then
  WScript.Echo "Values are equal when converted to upper case"
End If
```

Output

```
Values are equal when converted to lower case
Values are equal when converted to upper case
```

Control Flow with Looping

Sometimes you want to repeatedly execute a section of code. In VBScript, there are several ways to do this including

◆ For Next looping

◆ For Each looping

◆ Do While looping

◆ Do Until looping

◆ While looping

USING FOR NEXT LOOPS

Compared to the command shell, VBScript For loops are very basic. In VBScript, you can use For loops to execute a code segment for a specific count. The structure of For loops is as follows:

```
For Counter = startNum to endNum
   'add the code to repeat
Next
```

The following example uses a For loop to initialize an array of 10 elements:

```
For i = 0 to 9
   testArray(i) = "Placeholder"
Next
```

After the For loop is executed, all ten elements in the array are initialized to the value Placeholder. Using the Step keyword, you can step through the counter at specific intervals. You can step by 2's as follows:

```
For i = 0 to 20 Step 2
   testArray(i) = "Even"
Next
```

When you use a negative step value, you should reverse the normal order of the counter. So instead of going in ascending order, go in descending order, such as

```
For i = 20 to 0 Step -1
   testArray(i) = "Unknown"
Next
```

USING FOR EACH LOOPS

With For Each loops, you iterate through each element in an object or array. For Each loops are very similar to standard For loops. The key difference is that the number of elements in an object or array determines the number of times you go through the loop. In Listing 8-7, you initialize an array using a regular For loop and then display its values using a For Each loop.

Listing 8-7: Using For Each loops

foreach.vbs

```
'initialize array
Dim testArray(10)

'set array values
For i = 0 to 9
   testArray(i) = "Placeholder" & i
Next

'display array values
For Each i IN testArray
  WScript.Echo i
Next
```

Output

```
Placeholder0
Placeholder1
Placeholder2
Placeholder3
Placeholder4
Placeholder5
Placeholder6
Placeholder7
Placeholder8
Placeholder9
```

As you can see, the basic syntax of For Each loops is

```
For Each element IN objArray
'add code to repeat
Next
```

where *element* is the counter for the loop and *objArray* is the object or array you want to examine.

USING EXIT FOR LOOPS

With `For` and `For Each` loops, you'll sometimes want to exit the loop before iterating through all the possible values. To exit a `For` loop ahead of schedule, you can use the `Exit For` statement. The best place for this statement is within an `If Then` or `If Then Else` condition test, such as

```
For Each i IN testArray
  WScript.Echo i

  If i = "Unknown" Then
    Exit For
  EndIf


Next
```

USING DO WHILE LOOPS

Sometimes you'll want to execute a code segment while a condition is met. To do this, you will use `Do While` looping. The structure of this loop is as follows:

```
Do While condition
    'add the code to repeat
Loop
```

With `Do While`, the loop is executed as long as the condition is met. This means to break out of the loop, you must change the condition at some point within the loop. The following example shows a `Do While` loop that changes the status of the condition:

```
Do While continue = True
    y = y + 1
    If y < 10 Then
       WScript.Echo "Y is less than 10."
    ElseIf Y = 10 Then
      WScript.Echo "Y equals 10."
    Else
      WScript.Echo "Exiting the loop."
      continue = False
    EndIf
Loop
```

By placing the condition at the top of the loop, you ensure that the loop is only executed if the condition is met. In the previous example, the loop wouldn't be executed at all if continue is set to False beforehand. However, you may want to execute the loop at least once before you check the condition. To do this, you can place the condition test at the bottom of the loop, such as

```
Do
    y = y + 1
    If y < 10 Then
       WScript.Echo "Y is less than 10."
    ElseIf Y = 10 Then
      WScript.Echo "Y equals 10."
    Else
      WScript.Echo "Exiting the loop."
      continue = False
    EndIf


Loop While continue = True
```

USING DO UNTIL LOOPS

Another form of control loop is a Do Until loop. With Do Until, you execute a loop *until* a condition is met instead of *while* a condition is met. As with Do While, you can place the condition test at the beginning or end of the loop. The following loop is executed zero or more times until the condition is met:

```
Do Until Answer = "No"
    'Add code to execute
    'Be sure allow the condition to be changed
Loop
```

To ensure that the loop is executed at least once, use the following structure:

```
Do
    'Add code to execute
    'Be sure to allow the condition to be changed
Loop Until Answer = "No"
```

USING EXIT DO LOOPS

Using Exit Do, you can exit a Do While and Do Until before a condition occurs. As with Exit For, the best place for an Exit Do statement is within a If Then or If Then Else condition test, such as

```
Do Until Answer = "No"
    'Add code to get answer
    'check to see if user wants to quit
    If Answer = "Quit" Then
```

```
        Exit Do
    End If
Loop
```

USING WHILE ... WEND LOOPS

The final type of control loop available in VBScript is a `While ... WEnd` loop. With this type of loop, you can execute a loop while a condition is met, such as

```
While x < 10
  'Execute this code
  x = x+1
  WScript.Echo x
WEnd
```

The condition can only be placed at the beginning of the `While ... WEnd` loop.

Using Procedures in VBScript

VBScript procedures aren't much different from command shell procedures. They are structured similarly. You can pass in arguments and return values. You can even use `Call` to call a procedure if you want to. VBScript supports two types of procedures:

- ◆ **Functions** — Procedures that return a value to the caller
- ◆ **Subroutines** — Procedures that do not return a value to the caller

VBScript also supports a special type of subroutine called an event. Events occur when a certain condition exists, such as when a key is pressed, and can also be simulated in the code with method calls. I don't discuss events in this chapter. You just don't use them much with Windows scripting.

WORKING WITH FUNCTIONS

Many different built-in functions are available in VBScript. In earlier examples, you've seen `lcase()`, `ucase()`, and more. You can also create your own functions. These functions can perform many different types of tasks. Yet all functions have one thing in common: They are designed to return a value.

The basic structure of a function declaration is

```
Function functionName(arg1, arg2, ..., argN)
    'Add your function code here.
End Function
```

As you can see, you declare the function, specify a name, and then set arguments that you want to pass to the function. Afterward, you add statements the function should execute and then end the function. When the function finishes executing, control returns to the caller and execution of the script continues from there.

You can call a function using several different techniques. You can use the Call statement, such as

```
Call summary()
```

You can call a function directly in an assignment, such as

```
value = test()
```

You can also call a function within a statement:

```
WScript.Echo "The name you entered is: " & getID()
```

When there are no parameters to pass to the function, the parentheses are optional. This means you can use

```
userID = getID
```

To return a value from a function, assign a value to a variable with the same name as the function. For example, if you create a function called test, you can return a value from the function as follows:

```
Call test(3,4,2)
Function test(varA, varB, varC)
   total = varA * varB * varC
   test = total / 2
End Function
```

Normally, all variables initialized within functions are temporary and exist only within the scope of the function. Thus, you can think of these variables as having a local scope. However, if you use a variable that is initialized outside the function, that variable has global scope. In the following example, you use a global variable in the function:

```
sample = "Placeholder"
WScript.Echo test
Function test()
   test = sample
End Function
```

The output is

```
Placeholder
```

Listing 8-8 creates a function called getID(). The function accepts no parameters and so none are defined. A temporary variable called testName is used to store input, and the function InputBox is used to display an input prompt to users. Once the user enters a name, the Do While loop is exited and the value the user entered is assigned to the function, allowing the value to be returned to the calling statement. The result is that the user input is echoed after the text "You entered:".

Listing 8-8: Using functions in a script

functions.vbs
```
WScript.Echo "You entered: " & getID()

Function getID()
   Dim testName
   testName = ""
   Do While testName = ""
      testName = InputBox("Enter your full name:")
   Loop
   getID = testName
End Function
```
Output
```
You entered: William Stanek
```

InputBox is a built-in function for getting user input. VBScript also supports message boxes with graphical buttons that can be selected. You'll learn about both of these features later in the chapter.

You can break out of a function and return to the caller using the Exit Function statement. This statement is useful when a condition has been met and you want to return to the calling statement without finishing the execution of the function.

WORKING WITH SUBROUTINES

A *subroutine* is a procedure that does not return a value to the caller. Other than this, subroutines behave almost exactly like functions. Variables initialized within subroutines have local scope. You can call subroutines and pass in arguments. You can even exit the subroutine when a condition has been met, and you do this with `Exit Sub`.

Following this procedure, the basic structure of a subroutine is

```
Sub subroutineName(argument1, argument2, ..., argumentN)
    'Add subroutine code here.
End Sub
```

You can use a subroutine in your code as follows:

```
Sub displayError(errMessage,title)
   MsgBox "Error: " & errMessage,, title
End Sub
```

 MsgBox is listed as a function in most documentation, but it is actually a built-in subroutine for displaying messages. Also, the double comma used in the example isn't a mistake. This is how you enter a null value for a parameter that you don't want to use.

In the example, `displayError` is the name of the subroutine. The subroutine expects one parameter to be passed in. and this parameter holds an error message to display to the user. You can call this subroutine in several different ways. You can use a `Call` statement, such as

```
Call displayError "Input is invalid.","Error"
```

or you can call the subroutine directly:

```
displayError "Input is invalid.","Error"
```

 When you call subroutines, you shouldn't use parentheses to enclose parameters. Parentheses are only used with functions.

When there are no parameters to pass to the subroutine, the parentheses are optional as well, such as

```
Call mySub
```

However, subroutines cannot be used in expressions. For example, the following call causes an error:

```
test = displayError()
Sub displayError(errMessage)
   MsgBox "Error: " & errMessage
End Sub
```

JScript Essentials

JScript is Microsoft's version of JavaScript. If you are familiar with Java or JavaScript, you'll be able to jump right in with JScript. Many advanced programmers prefer JScript to VBScript. JScript offers more features and more control over many elements of your scripts. More features and controls also means that in some ways JScript is more complex than VBScript.

 TIP If you're not a programmer and don't want to go into advanced scripting, I recommend using VBScript. VBScript's syntax is easier to work with.

Variables and Data Types

As with VBScript, JScript allows you to work with constants and variables. Constants are distinguished from variables because their values do not change within the program.

VARIABLES AND NAMING CONVENTIONS

JScript variable names are case-sensitive, which means varA, VARA, and VarA all refer to different variables. Variable names can include alphabetic and numeric characters as well as the underscore (_) character, but must begin with an alphabetic character or the underscore character. Further, variable names cannot include spaces or punctuation characters. Using these variable-naming rules, the following are all valid names for variables:

```
test
test_var
_testA
userAnswer
```

Unlike VBScript, the case-sensitivity rule applies to all structures in JScript. This means you can't call WScript.Echo using anything but WScript.Echo and that all of these statements result in errors:

```
wscript.echo("Case Test!")
Wscript.echo("Case Test!")
WScript.echo("Case Test!")
```

As with VBScript, variables can have a global or local scope. By default, all variables have a global scope, meaning they can be accessed anywhere in the script. Variables declared within a function, however, cannot be accessed outside the function. This means the variables have a local scope.

In JScript, variables are generally initialized with the var keyword, such as

```
var userAnswer = "Unknown"
```

But you don't have to use the var keyword all the time. The var keyword is optional for global variables but mandatory for local variables. I'll talk more about functions in the section titled "Using Functions in JScript."

WORKING WITH DATA TYPES

Much like VBScript, JScript assigns a data type to variables based on their contents. This means you don't have to worry about assigning a specific data type. That said, you should learn how to use the basic data types shown in Table 8-6.

TABLE 8-6 DATA TYPES IN JSCRIPT

Data Type	Description	Example
Undefined	No value assigned; a variable that has been initialized but doesn't have a value has this data type	Var qResult
Boolean	A logical value; either true or false	BoolVar = false
Number	An integer or floating-point value	ANum = 305.333
String	Characters within single or double quotation marks	AString = "Wow!"
Null	The value of an undefined variable	Test = null

JScript automatically converts between data types whenever possible, which eliminates most variable conflicts. However, if you try to add a string variable to a numeric variable type, you will usually have problems. You will also have problems if JScript expects a string and you reference a numeric value. You'll find solutions for these problems in the section titled "Using Strings."

With numerical data, JScript supports base 8, base 10, and base 16 and uses the same techniques you learned for the command shell to determine what base a number is in. Numbers with a leading zero are considered to be octal — base 8. Numbers with the 0x prefix are considered to be hexadecimal — base 16. All other number formats are considered to be standard decimal numbers — base 10. Examples of numbers in these formats include

- Decimal — 18, 65, 32

- Octal — 025, 031, 011

- Hexadecimal — 0x2C, 0xCC, 0xFF

JScript does not support base 2 (binary) but does support bitwise operators and functions that can perform binary operations.

Using Strings

Because JScript automatically types variables, you do not need to declare a variable as a string. Yet in order for JScript to recognize a variable as a string, you must use single or double quotation marks to enclose the value associated with the variable, such as

```
aString = "This is a String."
```

When you work with strings, the two most common operations you'll perform are concatenation and conversion. These topics are examined in the sections that follow.

CONCATENATING STRINGS
In your scripts, you will often need to add strings together. For example, if a user enters their full name as three separate variables representing their first, middle, and last name, you may want to add these strings together. To do this, you will use the + operator to concatenate the strings, such as

```
userName = first + " " + middle + " " + last
```

Keep in mind that if you enclose numeric values within quotation marks, JScript still interprets the value as a string. This can lead to strange results when you try to add values together. As shown in the following example, if you add variables together that contain strings, you will not get the intended results:

```
varA = "25"
varB = "32"
varC = 8
test1 = varA + varB //the result is "2532" not 57.
test2 = varB + varC //the result is "328" not 40.
```

Now that you know not to enclose numeric values in quotation marks, you probably will not have problems with strings and variables in your code. However, this problem also can occur when you accept user input and try to perform calculations based on user input. This is because user input is interpreted as a string unless you tell JScript otherwise by converting the string to a number.

CONVERTING TO AND FROM STRINGS

As with VBScript, JScript supports built-in functionality for converting data types, but this functionality isn't implemented in the same way. In JScript, you use method calls more often than function calls. You can think of a method as a predefined function that is related to an object. Normally, to call a method, you reference the object by name followed by a period, and then the name of the method you are invoking. For example, to convert a number to a string, use the `toString()` method of a variable or object, as follows:

```
varA = 15
varB = varA.toString() // varB is set to a string value of "15"
```

However, some built-in methods don't require an object reference. For example, to convert string values to numbers, you will use one of two built-in methods: `parseInt()` or `parseFloat()`. The `parseInt()` method converts a string to an integer. The `parseFloat()` method converts a string to a floating-point number. These methods can be used without referencing an object, such as

```
varA = "35.5"
varB = "27"
test1 = parseFloat(varA) //test1 is set to 35.5
test2 = parseInt(varB) //test2 is set to 27
```

Using Comments

JScript supports two types of comments:

♦ Single-line comments that begin with a double slash (//), such as

```
//This is a comment
```

◆ Multiple-line comments that begin with the /* delimiter and end with the */ delimiter, such as

```
/* This is a comment */
```

If you have a begin comment delimiter, you must have a matching end comment delimiter. JScript interprets everything between the begin and end comment tag as a comment.

Using Arrays

Compared to VBScript, JScript arrays are very simple. JScript arrays can only be a single dimension and are initialized with the new Array() statement. As with VBScript, arrays always begin at 0 and end at the number of data points in the array minus 1. Following this, an array with 6 data points can be initialized as follows:

```
cities = new Array(5)
```

If the size of your array is determined by user input or otherwise subject to change, you can initialize the array without specifying its size, such as

```
myArray = new Array()
```

Unlike VBScript, however, you don't have to set the size of the array before using it. You simply assign values to the array.

After you initialize an array, you can insert values for elements in the array. The most basic way to do this is with individual statements that reference the array element by its index. Listing 8-9 shows an example of setting values for the cities array.

Listing 8-9: Assigning values to array elements

arrayvalues.js
```
cities = new Array(5)
cities[0] = "New York"
cities[1] = "Chicago"
cities[2] = "Seattle"
cities[3] = "Los Angeles"
cities[4] = "Miami"
cities[5] = "Boston"
```

After you set values for array elements, you access those values by referencing the element's index, such as

```
theValue = cities[2]
```

Here, theValue is set to Seattle.

Another way to populate an array with values is to set the values directly in the array declaration. Here is how you would do this for the cities array:

```
cities = new Array("New York","Chicago","Seattle","Los
Angeles","Miami","Boston")
```

Operators in JScript

JScript supports all of the operators available with the Windows command shell. You'll find arithmetic operators, comparison operators, assignment operators, and bitwise operators. You'll also find logical operators, such as && and ||, which are also available with Windows command shell scripting.

USING ARITHMETIC OPERATORS

JScript's arithmetic operators are summarized in Table 8-7. The syntax is nearly identical in every case to the command-shell operators and to VBScript, so there are few surprises.

TABLE 8-7 ARITHMETIC OPERATORS

Operator	Operation
*	Multiplication
/	Division
+	Addition
-	Subtraction
%	Modulus
=	Assignment
++	Increment
--	Decrement

Two operators you must pay special attention to are ++ and --, which are called unary operators. Typically, if you want to increment a value by one, you can write out the statement as follows:

```
A = A + 1
```

Alternately, you can use the increment operator (++), as follows:

```
++A
```

The result of the previous statement is that A is incremented by one. Similarly, you could decrease the value of A using the decrement operator (--), such as

```
--A
```

When using the increment or decrement operator in a statement, the placement of the operator is extremely important. The result of this statement is that A and B are set to 6:

```
B = 5
A = ++B
```

The JScript interpreter reads the statement as "add 1 to B and store the result in A." If you change the position of the increment operator as follows:

```
A = B++
```

the JScript interpreter reads the statement as "set A equal to B then add 1 to B." The result is that A is set to 5 and B is incremented to 6.

Table 8-8 shows the precedence order for operators in JScript. As the table shows, negation operators have the highest precedence order and are always calculated first.

TABLE 8-8 PRECEDENCE OF ARITHMETIC OPERATORS

Order	Operation
1	Negation (-)
2	Multiplication (*) and Division (/)
3	Modulus (%)
4	Addition (+) and Subtraction (-)

USING COMPARISON OPERATORS

Comparison operators are used to check for certain conditions, such as, is A equal to B. Generally, you will use a control flow, such as conditional looping, in conjunction with your comparison. For example, if A is equal to B, then you will perform a specific task. If A is not equal to B then you will perform a different task.

When performing comparisons, you are often comparing objects as well as numeric and textual data. To see if a variable is equal to another variable, you will use the comparison operator (==). The operator returns a result that is true if the objects are equivalent or false if they are not equivalent. The following example checks for equality:

```
if (aValue == varA) {
    //The variables are equal
}
```

To see if variables are not equal, use the inequality operator. The following example checks for inequality:

```
if (aValue != varA) {
    //The variables are not equal
}
```

To see if one variable is less than or greater than another variable, use the less than and greater than operators. You can check for values greater than or less than a variable as follows:

```
if (aValue < varA) {
    //aValue is less than varA
}
if (aValue > varA) {
    //aValue is greater than varA
}
```

Another type of comparison you can perform is to see whether a variable is less than or equal to a value. Likewise, you can see whether a variable is greater than or equal to a value. An example of this type of comparison follows:

```
if (aValue <= varA) {
    //aValue is less than or equal to varA
}
if (aValue >= 0) {
    //aValue is greater than or equal to varA
}
```

Table 8-9 summarizes the comparison operators available in JScript. As you've seen from the examples in this section, JScript and VBScript support a slightly different set of comparison operators. JScript uses a separate equality operator (==) and also has a different inequality operator (!=).

TABLE 8-9 COMPARISON OPERATORS IN JSCRIPT

Operator	Description
==	Equality; evaluates to true if the values or objects are equal.
!=	Inequality; evaluates to true if the values or objects are not equal.
<	Less than; evaluates to true if value1 is less than value2.
<=	Less than or equal to; evaluates to true if value1 is less than or equal to value2.
>	Greater than; evaluates to true if value1 is greater than value2.
>=	Greater than or equal to; evaluates to true if value1 is greater than or equal to value2.

USING ASSIGNMENT OPERATORS

Assignment operators are useful for assigning a value to a named variable. Some assignment operators, such as the equal sign (=), are used in just about every statement you will write. Other assignment operators, such as divide by value, are used rarely — if at all.

Like the increment and decrement operators, you can use assignment operators to save some typing. Instead of typing

a = a +7

you can type

a += 7

Although both statements perform the same operation, the second statement does so with less typing. Saving a few keystrokes becomes increasingly important in long scripts and in a series of repetitive statements. Assignment operators are summarized in Table 8-10. As you can see, these are the exact same operators available for Windows command shell scripting.

TABLE 8-10 ASSIGNMENT OPERATORS

Operator	Descriptions
+=	Increments (adds and assigns value)
-=	Decrements (subtracts and assigns value)
*=	Multiply and assign value
/=	Divide and assign value
%=	Modulus and assign value

USING LOGICAL OPERATORS

Logical operators are great for performing several comparisons within a control flow. For example, if you want to check whether A is greater than B, and C is less than B before you perform a calculation, you can use a logical operator.

Like comparison operators, logical operators return either true or false. Generally, if the operation returns true, you can perform a set of statements. Otherwise, you can skip the statements or perform other statements.

The most commonly used logical operators are logical And (&&) and logical Or (||). These operators compare two Boolean expressions, the results of comparison operators, or other logical expressions to produce a Boolean value, which can be true or false. The logical And returns a true value only when both expressions being compared return a true value. The logical Or returns a true value when either or both expressions return a true value.

Another logical operator available in JScript is called Not (!). You will use the Not operator just as you do the keyword Not in VBScript and the command shell. Listing 8-10 shows how logical operators could be used in your scripts.

Listing 8-10: Working with logical operators

logic.js

```
varA = 3
varB = 2
varC = 5
varD = 1

if (varA > varC && varB < varD) {
   //evaluates when the results of both tests are true
   WScript.Echo("Both tests are true.")
}
if (varA > varB || varC < varB) {
```

```
    //evaluates when at least one side is true
    WScript.Echo("At least one side is true.")
}
if (!(varA <= varB)) {
    //evaluates when varB is less than varA
    WScript.Echo("Less than.")
}
```

Output

```
At least one side is true.
Less than.
```

Table 8-11 summarizes the available logical operators. As you can see, these operators are very similar to those available for the Windows command shell.

TABLE 8-11 LOGICAL OPERATORS

Operator	Operation
&&	Logical And
||	Logical Or
!	Logical Not

USING BITWISE OPERATORS

Bitwise operators are used to perform binary math. There is little use for binary math in JScript and you will probably never need to use JScript's bitwise operators. Just in case though, the bitwise operators are summarized in Table 8-12. Most of these operators are the same operators available with Windows command shell scripting.

TABLE 8-12 BITWISE OPERATORS

Operator	Description
&	Bitwise And; returns 1 if both bits compared are 1.
|	Bitwise Or; returns 1 if either bit compared is 1.

Continued

TABLE 8-12 BITWISE OPERATORS (*Continued*)

Operator	Description
^	Bitwise Or; returns 1 only if one bit is a 1.
~	Bitwise Not; turns zeros to ones and ones to zeros.
<<	Shift Left; shifts the values left the number of positions specified by the operand on the right.
>	Shift Right; shifts the values right the number of positions specified by the operand on the right.
>>	Zero Fill Shift Right; fills with zeros when shifts right.

Control Flow with Conditionals

When you want to execute a set of instructions only if a certain condition is met, you can use if or if...else structures. Unlike VBScript, JScript does not support elseif statements.

USING IF

You can use if statements to control execution based on a true or false condition. The syntax for JScript if statements is a bit different than you are used to. Note the use of parentheses and curly brackets in the following example that tests for a true condition:

```
if (choice = "Y") {
    //then condition is true and choice equals Y
    //execute these statements
}
```

You can also control the execution of instructions based on a false condition. To do this, you use the ! operator and add an extra set of parentheses, such as

```
if (!(choice = "Y")) {
    //then condition is false and choice doesn't equal Y
    //execute these statements
}
```

USING IF...ELSE

You can extend `if` statements with the `else` statement. The `else` statement provides an alternative when a condition you specified is not met. The structure of an `if...else` condition is as follows:

```
if (choice="Y") {
   //condition is true and choice equals Y
  //execute these statements
}
else {
   //condition is false and choice doesn't equal Y
   //execute these statements
}
```

Control Flow with Looping

Sometimes you want to repeatedly execute a section of code. You can do this several ways in JScript. You can use

- ◆ `for` **and** `for in`
- ◆ `while` **and** `do while`
- ◆ `switch case`

USING FOR LOOPS

Using `for` loops in your code is easy. The following example uses this structure to initialize an array of 10 elements:

```
for (x = 0; x < 10; x++) {
   anArray(x) = "Test"
}
```

This `for` loop initializes a counter to zero, then sets a condition that the loop should continue as long as x is less than 10. During each iteration of the loop, the counter is incremented by 1. When the loop finishes, all 10 elements in the array are initialized to the value `Placeholder`. As you can see, the structure of a `for` loop in JScript is as follows:

```
for (initialize counter; condition; update counter) {
  code to repeat
}
```

USING FOR IN LOOPS

JScript's `for in` loops work much like VBScript's `For Each` loops. Both looping techniques are designed to iterate through each element in an object or array. They differ only in the syntax used.

Listing 8-11 shows how you can examine the elements in an array using a `for in` loop. Note that with JScript, you have to index into the array even when you are in the `for in` loop.

Listing 8-11: Examining values in an array

values.js

```
anArray = new Array()

for (x = 0; x < 10; x++) {
   anArray[x] = "Test"
}

counter = 0
for (i in anArray) {
  WScript.Echo("Value " + counter + " equals: " + anArray[i])
  counter++

}
```

USING WHILE AND DO WHILE LOOPS

JScript's `while` loops are used much like the `While` loops in VBScript. To execute a code segment while a condition is met, you will use `while` looping. The structure of a loop that checks for a true condition is as follows:

```
while (condition) {
   //add code to repeat
}
```

The structure of a loop that checks for a false condition is as follows:

```
while (!condition) {
   /add code to repeat
}
```

As long as the condition is met, the loop is executed. This means to break out of the loop, you must change the condition at some point within the loop.

You can put the condition check at the bottom of the loop using a `do while` construct, such as

```
do {
   //add code to repeat
} while (condition)
```

USING CONTINUE AND BREAK STATEMENTS

When you are working with conditional looping, you will often want to break out of a loop or continue with the next iteration of the loop. In JScript, the break statement allows you to end the execution of a loop and the continue statement allows you to begin the next iteration of a loop without executing subsequent statements. Whenever your script begins the next iteration of the loop, the condition is checked and in for loops, the counter is updated as necessary.

USING SWITCH CASE

JScript's switch case is the functional equivalent of VBScript's Select Case. To see how similar the structures are compare Listing 8-12 with Listing 8-5. As you'll see, these listings check for the similar information. However, JScript doesn't support the less than operation used with VBScript, so I omitted this from the example. JScript doesn't support any other case either, such as VBScript's Case Else. Instead, JScript supports a default case.

Listing 8-12: Working with switch case

switchcase1.js
```
theValue = 5
switch (theValue) {
   case 0 :
     WScript.Echo("The value is equal to zero.")
   case 1 :
     WScript.Echo("The value is equal to one.")
   case 2 :
     WScript.Echo("The value is equal to two.")
   case 3 :
     WScript.Echo("The value is equal to three.")
   case 4 :
     WScript.Echo("The value is equal to four.")
   case 5 :
     WScript.Echo("The value is equal to five.")
   default :
     WScript.Echo("Value doesn't match expected parameters.")
}
```

If you run Listing 8-11, you learn another interesting fact concerning switch case–JScript can execute multiple case statements. In this case, the script executes case 5 and the default. To prevent JScript from executing multiple case statements, you need to exit the switch case using the break keyword as shown in Listing 8-12.

Listing 8-13: Revised switch case example

switchcase2.js

```
theValue = 5
switch (theValue) {
   case 0 :
     WScript.Echo("The value is equal to zero.")
     break
   case 1 :
     WScript.Echo("The value is equal to one.")
     break
   case 2 :
     WScript.Echo("The value is equal to two.")
     break
   case 3 :
     WScript.Echo("The value is equal to three.")
     break
   case 4 :
     WScript.Echo("The value is equal to four.")
     break
   case 5 :
     WScript.Echo("The value is equal to five.")
     break
   default :
     WScript.Echo("Value doesn't match expected parameters.")
}
```

Using Functions in JScript

In JScript, functions are the key structure you use to create customizable procedures. JScript doesn't support subroutines or GOTO. As you will quickly discover, JScript functions work much like VBScript functions and again, the main difference is syntax.

FUNCTION STRUCTURE

In JScript, the basic structure of a function is

```
function functionName(parameter1, parameter2, ..., parameterN) {
   //Insert function code here.
}
```

You can use functions in your code as follows:

```
function getInput() {
   var userInput
   var timeOut = 10;    // set wait time
   var title = "Getting Input"; // set title
   var button = 4;      // Yes/No
   // create object
   var wshell = WScript.CreateObject("WScript.Shell");
   userInput = wshell.Popup ("Do you want to continue?",
               timeOut,title,button)

   return userInput
}
```

Note the use of Popup() in the example. Unlike VBScript, none of the standard JScript dialog or input boxes are available in Windows Script Host and as a result, Popup() is the only way to display messages and get user input. For more information on Popup()s, see Chapter 9.

In the example, getInput is the name of the function. Because the function accepts no parameters, none are defined after the function name. A temporary local variable called userInput is created to store the user's input. Once the user enters a value, the while loop is exited. This value is then returned to the calling statement. Generally, all functions return one or more values using the return statement.

CALLING FUNCTIONS

Calling a function in JScript is just like calling a function in VBScript. You can call a function as follows:

```
getInput()
```

   or

```
Input = getInput()
```

When you call a function, you can pass in parameters as well. To better understand how parameters are used, I'll create a function that converts a time entry to seconds. This function called numseconds() accepts 4 parameters: xYears, xDays, xHours, and xMinutes. Because these parameters are passed directly to the function, you do not need to create temporary variables to hold their values within the function. The code for the function numSeconds() is as follows:

```
function numSeconds(xYears, xDays, xHours, xMinutes) {
   var count
   tempSeconds = ((365 * xYears + xDays) * 24 + xHours) * 3600 +
60@@1b
      * xMinutes
   return count
}
```

When you call this function, the parameters are expected and must be entered in the order defined. Here is a statement that calls the numSeconds() function:

```
theSeconds = numSeconds(5,25,10,30)
```

Summary

Both VBScript and JScript have a place in your Windows scripts. VBScript provides an easy to use syntax and good control over many aspects of the code. JScript provides a more advanced syntax and a more extensive object set that lets you go farther and do more. The next chapter builds on everything discussed in this chapter. You learn how to work with objects, how to display dialogs and get user input, and how to perform other essential tasks as well.

Chapter 9

Dialogs, Logon Scripts and More

IN THIS CHAPTER

◆ Working with input boxes

◆ Using message boxes and pop-up dialogs

◆ Examining script information

◆ Combining JScript and VBScript

◆ Using logon scripts

WINDOWS SCRIPTS PROVIDE the best mechanisms for interacting with users and customizing user logons. You'll find input boxes, message dialogs, pop-up dialogs, and other graphical interfaces that make it easy to get input and display output whenever necessary. You'll also find extensive features for creating logon scripts that customize the user environment, launch applications, provide users with guided tours, and more. These features beat the offerings in the command shell hands-down, and to learn more, read on.

Getting Input and Displaying Messages

With logon scripts and other scripts designed for users, you'll often need to get input or display output. Windows Script Host provides many different ways to do this. The key techniques you'll want to use are

◆ WSH echo with either JScript or VBScript

◆ VBScript input boxes

◆ VBScript message boxes

◆ WSH pop-up dialogs with either JScript or VBScript

Each of these techniques is examined in the sections that follow.

Using WSH Echo with VBScript and JScript

Remember the command shell `echo` statement used to display lines of text? Well, a similar function is available for Windows scripts as well. You call `Echo` as a function of the WScript object. If you are using CScript and are in interactive mode, output from `echo` is written to the command line. If you are using WScript and are in interactive mode, output from `Echo` is displayed in a pop-up dialog box.

You can use `Echo` in VBScript and JScript as shown in Listing 9-1. Note the difference in syntax. With VBScript, you pass `Echo` strings and can use the standard concatenation rules to add strings together. In JScript, you must use parentheses and pass strings individually in a comma-separated list, which is then concatenated for you.

Listing 9-1: Using Echo in VBScript and JScript

VBScript	JScript
techo.vbs	**techo.js**
WScript.Echo "Go for it!"	WScript.Echo("Go for it!")
WScript.Echo "1: " + iResults	WScript.Echo("1: ", iResults)

Using VBScript Input Boxes

Think of input boxes as customizable dialogs that you can use to get input from users. This input can be any kind of text, such as the user's login name or a response to a question. To create input boxes, use the `InputBox()` function and add a prompt and title as necessary. In the example shown in Figure 9-1, `InputBox()` sets a display prompt and a title for the input box using the following statement:

```
Input = InputBox("Please enter your login name:",
                 "Setup Script")
```

Here, the `Input` variable holds the value of the user's response and can be used later in the script to test the validity of the input. As shown, the prompt and title you want to use are strings enclosed in double quotation marks and separated with a comma.

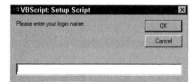

Figure 9-1: Input boxes can have titles and display prompts.

The order of elements in an input box must be exact. You cannot enter a title without entering a prompt – even if the prompt used is just an empty string, such as

```
Input = InputBox("","Setup Script")
```

If necessary, you can follow the prompt and the title with a default value for the input. This value is then used when the user clicks OK without entering a value. For example, with the login example, you might want to set the default user to anony-mous, such as

```
Input = InputBox("Please enter your login name:",
                 "Setup Script",
                 "anonymous")
```

The quotes around the default value aren't necessary when you use numeric val-ues. As stated before though, the order of input parameters is important. If you don't use a prompt or title, you must insert placeholder values, such as

```
Input = InputBox("Please enter your login name:",
                 "","anonymous")
```

By default, input boxes are centered on the screen but you can specify where the input box should be displayed as well. You do this by specifying the *x/y coordinate* for the upper-left corner of the input box. The *x* coordinate sets the horizontal dis-tance in pixels from the left edge of the screen. The *y* coordinate sets the vertical distance in pixels from the top of the screen. The *x* and *y* coordinates follow the prompt and title in sequence. For example:

```
Input = InputBox("Please enter your login name:","Setup
Script",,150,100)
```

If you position an input box, you must always set both coordinates as shown. In the examples for this section, the basic syntax for input boxes is

```
varA = InputBox("prompt","title",defaultValue,X,Y)
```

TIP   All values entered into input boxes are considered to be strings, even if the user enters numerical values. To convert the input to an integer, use the CInt() function.

Using VBScript Message Boxes

Message boxes are only available in VBScript. You'll use message boxes to display information to users and to allow users to make selections. Because message boxes can have labeled buttons, such as Yes and No, they are a bit more complex than input boxes. Message boxes can also be customized with special icons, such as a question mark for informational message boxes.

MESSAGE BOX BASICS

The most basic type of message box is one that calls the Msgbox function and displays a message, such as

```
Msgbox "Starting cleanup now..."
```

When you use a basic message box, you get a plain dialog box with an OK button. To add pizzazz to message boxes, you can customize the dialog with titles, icons, and multiple button styles. To add these elements to message boxes, use the following syntax:

```
Msgbox "Message to display", buttonType + iconType,
    "Message box title"
```

As with input boxes, message box parameters must be used in the order specified and you can't skip parameters. For example, if you want to add a title to a message box without specifying a button or icon type, you can use the following command:

```
Msgbox "Starting cleanup now...",,"Admin Script"
```

ADDING BUTTONS TO MESSAGE BOXES

As stated previously, the OK button is the default button for all message boxes. But you can use many different buttons including Yes, No, Cancel, Retry, Ignore, and Abort. Here is how you can add Yes, No, and Cancel buttons to a message box:

```
dim vbYesNoCancel
vbYesNoCancel = 3
Msgbox "Do you want to continue installation?", vbYesNoCancel
```

where vbYesNoCancel represents the button types you want to add and 3 is the parameter value for this type of button. A message box with the Yes, No, and Cancel buttons is shown in Figure 9-2.

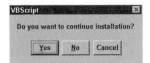

Figure 9-2: Message boxes can use many different types of buttons.

If you want to, you can use other types of buttons as well, such as vbOkCancel or vbAbortRetryIgnore. These button types are constants, which are variables whose value doesn't change. Because the script engine knows these values, you actually don't have to use the constant and can refer to the value directly in the call to Msgbox. However, if you do this, you lose the advantage of being able to tell at a glance what types of buttons are used with a particular message box.

Table 9-1 provides a complete list of constants you can use to set button types and their corresponding values. These constants represent all of the available button combinations.

TABLE 9-1 BUTTONS FOR MESSAGES BOXES

Constant	Description	Value
VbOkOnly	Displays the OK button	0
VbOkCancel	Displays OK and Cancel buttons	1
VbAbortRetryIgnore	Displays Abort, Retry, and Ignore buttons	2
VbYesNoCancel	Displays Yes, No, and Cancel buttons	3
VbYesNo	Displays Yes and No buttons	4
VbRetryCancel	Displays Retry and Cancel buttons	5

ADDING ICONS TO MESSAGE BOXES

By default, message boxes use an information icon, but you can change this icon if you want to. Adding a unique icon to a message box is easy. Just keep in mind that buttons and icons are part of the same parameter, which is why you use the plus sign to separate the button types from the icon type. An example message box with an icon follows:

```
Dim vbRetryCancel: vbRetryCancel=5
Dim vbCritical: vbCritical=16
Msgbox "Error writing to disk", vbRetryCancel + vbCritical
```

In this example, I've combined the initialization of the value with the actual declaration that sets the value. You can rewrite these statements on separate lines as follows:

```
Dim vbRetryCancel
vbRetryCancel=5
Dim vbCritical
vbCritical=16
Msgbox "Error writing to disk", vbRetryCancel + vbCritical
```

If you don't want to use constants to represent the numerical values you want to use, you can rewrite these statements as follows:

```
Msgbox "Error writing to disk", 21
```

where 21 is the sum of 5 + 16.

Table 9-2 shows a complete list of icons you can add to message boxes. As with buttons, the use of a constant is optional but makes it easier to work with the script.

TABLE 9-2 ICONS FOR MESSAGES BOXES

Constant	Description	Value
VbCritical	Displays an icon with an X, used for critical errors.	16
VbQuestion	Displays an icon with a question mark, used for questions.	32
VbExclamation	Displays an icon with an exclamation point, used for minor errors, cautions, and warnings	48
VbInformation	Displays an icon with an I, used for informational messages (default).	64

EVALUATING BUTTON CLICKS IN MESSAGE BOXES

When you present users with multiple options, such as Yes/No or Retry/Cancel, you need to know what button was selected. Because you are using a procedure call to make the evaluation, the syntax for the message box changes slightly. The new syntax is

```
returnValue = Msgbox ("Message to display", buttonType + iconType,
"Message box title.")
```

Here, the syntax change is that you must use parentheses and assign the return value to a variable.

Table 9-3 provides a summary of the status codes returned when message box buttons are pressed. Once you assign a variable to store the returned status code, you can use an If Then or Select Case structure to perform actions in response to the button click.

TABLE 9-3 BUTTON STATUS CODES

Button	Constant	Return Value
Ok	VbOk	1
Cancel	VbCancel	2
Abort	VbAbort	3
Retry	VbRetry	4
Ignore	VbIgnore	5
Yes	VbYes	6
No	VbNo	7

A script that evaluates button clicks in message boxes and then handles the result is shown in Listing 9-2. While the example uses an If Then loop to evaluate the button click, you could easily use a Select Case structure as well.

Listing 9-2: Evaluating button selection in a script

evalbuttons.vbs

```
Dim vbYesNoCancel: vbYesNoCancel=3
Dim vbQuestion: vbQuestion=32
Dim vbYes: vbYes=6
Dim vbNo: vbNo=7
Dim vbCancel: vbCancel=2

retry = Msgbox ("Write to disk failed. Try again?",
               vbYesNoCancel + VBQuestion)

If retry = vbYes Then
    WScript.Echo "You selected Yes."
ElseIf retry = vbNo Then
```

```
    WScript.Echo "You selected No."
Else
    WScript.Echo "You selected Cancel."
End If
```

WSH Pop-up Dialogs with VBScript and JScript

JScript doesn't support `InputBox()` or `Msgbox()`. In the browser implementation of JScript, dialog boxes and inputs are associated with the `window` object. Unfortunately, the `window` object is not available in WSH (unless you start a browser instance as I'll point out later). To work around this problem, the developers of WSH created the `Popup()` function. `Popup()` is essentially an implementation of the VBScript `Msgbox()` function that is available in both JScript and VBScript.

Everything you've learned about VBScript message boxes applies to pop-up dialogs. The only real difference is that these dialog boxes are accessed through the `Popup()` method of the `Shell` object and the addition of a timeout mechanism. The basic syntax for `Popup()` follows:

VBScript	JScript

`answ = object.Popup("msg",`
            `["title"],`
            `[wait],`
            `[type])`
	`answ = object.Popup(msg,`
	            `[wait],`
	            `["title"],`
	            `[type])`

These options are used as follows:

♦ *msg* – the message you want to display

♦ *wait* – the number of seconds to wait before closing the pop-up

♦ *title* – the title for the pop-up

♦ *type* – the value representing the button and icon types to use. These values are the same as listed previously in Table 9-1 and Table 9-2.

Because the `Popup()` method is accessed through the `Shell` object, you must create an instance of `Shell` and then reference the `Popup()` method of this object. You create instances of objects using the `CreateObject` method of the `WScript` object. Creating an object instance is a bit different in VBScript and JScript. In VBScript, you create an object reference using the `Set` keyword. In JScript, you create an object reference using the `var` keyword. The object reference is then used in the code to access methods and properties of the object you instantiated.

The following example creates an object instance in both VBScript and JScript:

VBScript	JScript
| ```
Set w =
  WScript.CreateObject("WScript.Shell")
WScript.CreateObject("WScript.Shell");
``` | ```
var w =
``` |

Listing 9-3 shows how you can use CreateObject() and Popup() in a script. As discussed, you create an instance of Shell and then reference its Popup() method. Note that the value for the buttons (4) comes from Table 9-1. You can also set icons for the popup using values in Table 9-2. When you use both icons and buttons, you add the values together and then assign this value in the type property.

Listing 9-3: Using CreateObject and Popup

VBScript	JScript
popup.vbs	**popup.js**
| ```
answer = getInput()
function getInput()
Dim answ
timeOut = 10
title = "Select Y/N"
button = 4
'create object
Set w =
  WScript.CreateObject("WScript.Shell")
getInput = w.Popup ("Do you want to
    continue?",timeOut,title,button)

End Function
``` | ```
answer = getInput()
function getInput() {
  var answ
  var timeOut = 10;
  var title = "Select Y/N"
  var button = 4
  //create object
  var w =
WScript.CreateObject("WScript.Shell");
  answ = w.Popup ("Do you want to
    continue?", timeOut, title, button)
  return answ
}
``` |

The return value from Popup tells you which button the user selected. Return values are the same as those listed previously in Table 9-3 with one important addition. Because pop-ups have a timeout value, users may not press any button and in this case, the method returns −1.

Listing 9-4 shows how you can handle user selections and errors in both VBScript and JScript. Note that the primary difference is syntax.

Listing 9-4: Handling errors and user selection

VBScript	JScript
usersel.vbs	**usersel.js**
| ```
function getInput()
Dim answ
``` | ```
function getInput() {
  var answ;
``` |

Continued

Listing 9-4: Handling errors and user selection *(Continued)*

VBScript	JScript

```
timeOut = 30
title = "Write Failure!"
btype = 18
'create object
Set w =
WScript.CreateObject("WScript.Shell")
getInput = w.Popup ("Error writing to
   the drive. Try
   again?",timeOut,title,btype)


End Function
answer = getInput()
Select Case answer
  Case 3
    WScript.Echo "You selected Abort."


  Case 4
    WScript.Echo "You selected Retry."


  Case 5
    WScript.Echo "You selected Ignore."


  Case Else
    WScript.Echo "No selection in the
      time allowed. "


End Select
```

```
var timeOut = 30;
var title = "Write Failure!";
var type = 18;
//create object
var w =
WScript.CreateObject("WScript.Shell");
  answ = w.Popup ("Error writing to
    the drive. Try
    again?",timeOut,title,type);
  return answ;
}
answer = getInput()
switch (answer) {
 case 3 :
   WScript.Echo("You selected
     Abort.")
   break
 case 4 :
   WScript.Echo("You selected
     Retry.")
   break
 case 5 :
   WScript.Echo("You selected
     Ignore.")

   break
 default :
 WScript.Echo("No selection in the time
   allowed.")
   break
 }
```

Examining Script Information

To accommodate a variety of user environments, your scripts will often need to test for version information before running. For example, if the user system is running the version 4 script engines, you don't want to try to run a version 5 script on the system as doing so could have unpredictable results. To prevent problems, you should check the script host version and the script engine version at a minimum. Other scripting information you may want to check includes the location of the script hosts on the user's system, arguments passed in to the script at startup, and environment variables set on the system.

Last, with user scripts, you may also want to run other applications from within a script. For example, you may want to create a logon script that provides a menu for selecting the type of applications the user may want to start, such as Development Tools or Productivity Tools. Then based on the response, you would start the related set of applications.

Checking Script Host Information

When you want to examine information related to the script hosts (WScript or CScript), you'll use these properties of the WScript object:

- ◆ WScript.Fullname — Returns the full path to the current script host, such as

    C:\WINNT\System32\cscript.exe

- ◆ WScript.Path — Returns the path to the script host, such as

    C:\WINNT\System32

- ◆ WScript.Version — Returns the script host version, such as

    5.1

You can use these properties in VBScript and JScript as shown in Listing 9-5.

Listing 9-5: Checking script host information

VBScript	JScript
wsprops.vbs	wsprops.js
v = WScript.Version	v = WScript.Version
If v >= 5 Then	if (v >= 5) {
main()	main()
Else	}
error()	else {
End If	error()
Function main	}
WScript.Echo "Running..."	function main() {
End Function	WScript.Echo("Running...")
Function error	}
WScript.Echo "Error!"	function error() {
End Function	WScript.Echo("Error!")
	}

Checking Scripting Information

Just as you can examine information related to the script host, you can also examine information related to the script engine and the current script. To examine properties of the script engine you'll use built-in functions available in VBScript and JScript. To examine script properties, you'll use properties of the WScript object. These functions and properties are

- ScriptEngine() – A built-in function that returns the script engine language, such as VBScript or JScript

- ScriptEngineMajorVersion() – A built-in function that returns the script engine version, such as 5 or 6

- ScriptEngineMinorVersion() – A built-in function that returns the revision number of the script engine, such as 1 or 2

- ScriptEngineBuildVersion() – A built-in function that returns the build version of the script engine, such as 3715

- ScriptFullName – A property of WScript that returns the full path to the current script, such as c:\scripts\userlog.vbs

- ScriptName – A property of WScript that returns the file name of the current script, such as userlog.vbs

Listing 9-6 shows an example of how you can use these functions and properties in a script.

Listing 9-6: Checking script engine and scripting information

VBScript	JScript
seprops.vbs	**seprops.js**

```
WScript.Echo GetSEInfo()

WScript.Echo GetScript()

Function GetSEInfo
  Dim info
  info = ""
  info = ScriptEngine & " Version "
  info = info &
    ScriptEngineMajorVersion & "."
  info = info &
    ScriptEngineMinorVersion & "."
  info = info &
```

```
se = GetSEInfo()
WScript.Echo(se)

sc = GetScript()
WScript.Echo(sc)

function GetSEInfo()
{
  var info;
  info = "";
  info += ScriptEngine() + " Version
    ";
  info += ScriptEngineMajorVersion()
    + ".";
```

VBScript	JScript

```
   ScriptEngineBuildVersion          info += ScriptEngineMinorVersion()
  GetSEInfo = info                     + ".";
End Function                         info += ScriptEngineBuildVersion();
Function GetScript                   return(info);
  Dim info
  scr = "Name: "                    }
  scr = WScript.ScriptName & " Full function GetScript()
    path: "
  scr = scr & WScript.ScriptFullName {
  GetScript =  scr                    var scr;
End Function                          scr = "Name: ";
                                      scr += WScript.ScriptName + " Full
                                          path: ";
                                      scr += WScript.ScriptFullName;
                                      return(scr);

                                    }
```

Checking Script Arguments

Arguments set information needed by the script at runtime and are often needed with Windows scripts. Unlike the command shell, WSH doesn't feature an extensive set of variables for working with arguments, and as a result you can't use %1, %2, and so on in Windows scripts. Instead, script arguments are placed in a container object called `WScript.Arguments`. You can think of container objects as arrays with properties that are used to work with elements in the array.

As with other objects, you need to create an instance of `WScript.Arguments` before you can work with it. For example

VBScript	JScript
`Set theArgs = WScript.Arguments`	`var theArgs = WScript.Arguments`

After you create the object instance, you can use the Item property to access arguments passed in to a script according to their index position in the `WScript.Arguments` object. The first script argument is at index position 0, the second at 1, and so on. You can assign argument 1 to a variable as follows:

VBScript	JScript
`arg1 = theArgs.Item(0)`	`arg1 = theArgs.Item(0)`

In the command shell argument zero refers to the script name. As you've seen, this is not the case in WSH.

Both VBScript and JScript support a property for determining how many arguments were passed in as well. In VBScript, you use the `Count` property. In JScript, you use the Length property. If two arguments were passed in to a script, these statements would return 2:

VBScript	JScript
`numArgs = theArgs.Count`	`numArgs = theArgs.Length`

As shown in Listing 9-7, you can also use For loops to examine each argument in turn.

Listing 9-7: Examining arguments using a For loop

VBScript	JScript

argloop.vbs

```
Set theArgs = WScript.Arguments
For I = 0 to theArgs.Count - 1
  WScript.Echo theArgs(I)
Next
For Each i IN theArgs
  WScript.Echo i
Next
```

argloop.js

```
var theArgs = WScript.Arguments
for (x = 0; x < theArgs.Length; x++)
{
  WScript.Echo(theArgs.Item(x))
}
```

Working with Environment Variables

As with the command shell, environment variables play an important role in Windows scripting. In Windows scripts, you can access environment variables is several different ways. In this section, I examine a technique that you can rely on time and again, rather than the additional techniques that may cause problems in your scripts.

Environment variables are accessed via the `WScript.Shell` object, so you need to create an instance of `WScript.Shell` before you can work with environment variables. For example

VBScript	JScript
`Set ws = WScript.CreateObject("WScript.Shell")`	`var ws = WScript.CreateObject("WScript.Shell");`

Next, as shown in Listing 9-8, use the `ExpandEnvironmentStrings()` method of `WScript.Shell` to specify the environment variable you want to work with. All the environment variables described previously in Table 4-1 from Chapter 4 are available. You can use the paths returned by `ExpandEvironmentStrings()` to set file and directory locations.

Listing 9-8: Working with system environment variables

VBScript	JScript

```
sysenv.vbs
Set WshShell = WScript.CreateObject
  ("WScript.Shell")
WScript.Echo
  WshShell.ExpandEnvironmentStrings
  ("%PATH%")
WScript.Echo
  WshShell.ExpandEnvironmentStrings
  ("%WINDIR%")
WScript.Echo
  WshShell.ExpandEnvironmentStrings
  ("%COMPUTERNAME%")
WScript.Echo
  WshShell.ExpandEnvironmentStrings
  ("%ComSpec%")
WScript.Echo
  WshShell.ExpandEnvironmentStrings
  ("%DIRCMD%")
WScript.Echo
  WshShell.ExpandEnvironmentStrings
  ("%PATH%")
WScript.Echo
  WshShell.ExpandEnvironmentStrings
  ("%HOMEDRIVE%")
WScript.Echo
  WshShell.ExpandEnvironmentStrings
  ("%HOMEPATH%")
WScript.Echo
  WshShell.ExpandEnvironmentStrings
  ("%INCLUDE%")
WScript.Echo
  WshShell.ExpandEnvironmentStrings
  ("%LIB%")
WScript.Echo
  WshShell.ExpandEnvironmentStrings
  ("%LOGONSERVER%")
WScript.Echo
  WshShell.ExpandEnvironmentStrings
  ("%MSDEVDIR%")
```

```
sysenv.js
var WshShell = WScript.CreateObject
  ("WScript.Shell")
WScript.Echo
  (WshShell.ExpandEnvironmentStrings
  ("%PATH%"))
WScript.Echo
  (WshShell.ExpandEnvironmentStrings
  ("%WINDIR%"))
WScript.Echo
  (WshShell.ExpandEnvironmentStrings
  ("%COMPUTERNAME%"))
WScript.Echo
  (WshShell.ExpandEnvironmentStrings
  ("%ComSpec%"))
WScript.Echo
  (WshShell.ExpandEnvironmentStrings
  ("%DIRCMD%"))
WScript.Echo
  (WshShell.ExpandEnvironmentStrings
  ("%PATH%"))
WScript.Echo
  (WshShell.ExpandEnvironmentStrings
  ("%HOMEDRIVE%"))
WScript.Echo
  (WshShell.ExpandEnvironmentStrings
  ("%HOMEPATH%"))
WScript.Echo
  (WshShell.ExpandEnvironmentStrings
  ("%INCLUDE%"))
WScript.Echo
  (WshShell.ExpandEnvironmentStrings
  ("%LIB%"))
WScript.Echo
  (WshShell.ExpandEnvironmentStrings
  ("%LOGONSERVER%"))
WScript.Echo
  (WshShell.ExpandEnvironmentStrings
  ("%MSDEVDIR%"))
```

Continued

Listing 9-8: Working with system environment variables *(Continued)*

VBScript	JScript
| ```
WScript.Echo
  WshShell.ExpandEnvironmentStrings
  ("%OS%")
WScript.Echo
  WshShell.ExpandEnvironmentStrings
  ("%PATHEXT%")
WScript.Echo
  WshShell.ExpandEnvironmentStrings
  ("%SystemDrive%")
WScript.Echo
  WshShell.ExpandEnvironmentStrings
  ("%SystemRoot%")
WScript.Echo
  WshShell.ExpandEnvironmentStrings
  ("%TEMP%")
WScript.Echo
  WshShell.ExpandEnvironmentStrings
  ("%TMP%")
WScript.Echo
  WshShell.ExpandEnvironmentStrings
  ("%USERDOMAIN%")
WScript.Echo
  WshShell.ExpandEnvironmentStrings
  ("%USERNAME%")
WScript.Echo
  WshShell.ExpandEnvironmentStrings
  ("%USERPROFILE%")
``` | ```
WScript.Echo
  (WshShell.ExpandEnvironmentStrings
  ("%OS%"))
WScript.Echo
  (WshShell.ExpandEnvironmentStrings
  ("%PATHEXT%"))
WScript.Echo
  (WshShell.ExpandEnvironmentStrings
  ("%SystemDrive%"))
WScript.Echo
  (WshShell.ExpandEnvironmentStrings
  ("%SystemRoot%"))
WScript.Echo
  (WshShell.ExpandEnvironmentStrings
  ("%TEMP%"))
WScript.Echo
  (WshShell.ExpandEnvironmentStrings
  ("%TMP%"))
WScript.Echo
  (WshShell.ExpandEnvironmentStrings
  ("%USERDOMAIN%"))
WScript.Echo
  (WshShell.ExpandEnvironmentStrings
  ("%USERNAME%"))
WScript.Echo
  (WshShell.ExpandEnvironmentStrings
  ("%USERPROFILE%"))
``` |

Running Programs from within Scripts

The Run() method of the WScript.Shell object lets you run programs. You can

◆ Start Windows applications, such as Microsoft Word, Excel or PowerPoint

◆ Run command-line programs, such as shutdown.exe or regedt32.exe

◆ Run command shell scripts

To use the Run() method, you create an instance of WScript.Shell and then access Run(). This example starts the Windows Notepad in VBScript and JScript:

VBScript	JScript
| ```
Set ws =
  WScript.CreateObject("WScript.Shell")

ws.Run("notepad")
``` | ```
var ws =
  WScript.CreateObject("WScript.
  Shell");

ws.Run("notepad")
``` |

The file path you pass to Run() is parsed by WSH. This allows you to use any available environment variable in the file path (including those that may not be available through WshShell.Environment). You can use %SystemRoot% for the SystemRoot environment variable as follows:

VBScript	JScript
| ```
Set ws =
WScript.CreateObject("WScript.Shell")
ws.Run
  ("%SystemRoot%\system32\notepad")
``` | ```
var ws =
WScript.CreateObject("WScript.Shell");
ws.Run
  ("%SystemRoot%\\system32\\notepad")
``` |

TIP As you can see in the example, JScript file paths are referenced in a slightly different way than in VBScript. The reason for this is that JScript treats the slash character as a special character and as a result, you must escape it with another slash character.

You can also pass in arguments to command-shell programs and to Windows applications that support command-line parameters. Simply follow the application name with the parameters you want to use. Be sure to add a space between the application name and the parameters. The following example starts Notepad with the active script accessed for editing:

VBScript	JScript
| ```
Set ws =
  WScript.CreateObject
  ("WScript.Shell")
ws.Run("notepad " &
  WScript.ScriptFullName)
``` | ```
var ws =
  WScript.CreateObject("WScript.Shell");

ws.Run("notepad " +
  WScript.ScriptFullName)
``` |

The Run() method has more features than you'll probably ever use but just in case, you can set additional features using the following syntax:

```
object.Run ("command", [winStyle], ["waitOnReturn"])
```

where *command* is the program or shell script you want to run, *winStyle* is the window style, and *waitOnReturn* specifies whether the script should wait or continue execution. If *waitOnReturn* is not specified or set to False, the script continues execution without waiting on process termination. If *waitOnReturn* is set to True, script execution pauses until the application stops running or is exited – at which time, the Run() method returns any error code returned by the application and script execution resumes.

If you want to track error codes, assign Run() to a variable and then check the error code returned by the application. Generally, a non-zero error code indicates an error of some kind. Listing 9-9 shows how you can run a shell script and check the error code the script returned. In this example, note that VBScript allows you to evaluate the error code as a number, but JScript treats the error code as a string.

Listing 9-9: Examining arguments using a For loop

VBScript	JScript

runerrors.vbs

```
Set ws =
  WScript.CreateObject
  ("WScript.Shell")
ret = ws.Run("log.bat",0,"TRUE")
If ret = 0 Then
  WScript.Echo "No error"
Else
  WScript.Echo "Error"
End If
```

runerrors.js

```
var ws =
  WScript.CreateObject
  ("WScript.Shell");
ret = ws.Run("log.bat",0,"TRUE")
if (ret="0") {
  WScript.Echo("No error")
} else {
  WScript.Echo("Error")
}
```

If you specify an invalid program or script name, WSH won't report an error and an error code won't be set. In this case, ret would be a null string.

Table 9-4 shows options you can use for window style. The most useful styles are 0 for running programs and scripts in the background, and 1 for displaying the window normally. You can then use other options to minimize or maximize the application.

TABLE 9-4 WINDOW STYLE OPTIONS

Option	Description
0	Runs a program or script in the background.

Option	Description
1	Runs a program or script normally and displays a window if necessary. Generally, use this option before options 2–10.
2	Activates a program and displays it as a minimized window.
3	Activates a program and displays it as a maximized window.
4	Activates a program and displays it in most recent size and position.
5	Activates a program and displays it in its current size and position.
6	Minimizes the specified window and activates the next top-level window in the Z order.
7	Minimizes the program window without activating it.
8	Displays the program window in its current state but doesn't activate it.
9	Activates and restores the window. If the window is minimized or maximized, the system restores it to its original size and position.
10	Sets the display state based on the state of the Windows script.

Combining JScript and VBScript

You'll often encounter situations where you implement a script in one scripting language and then wish you could use features of another scripting language in the same script. Well, using batch scripts (.WS files), you can combine scripts written in JScript and scripts written in VBScript in the same file. You can then call functions in one script from another script and return values to the caller.

In VBScript, you can

◆ Call JScript functions and return values

In JScript, you can

◆ Call VBScript subroutines to execute a section of code

◆ Call VBScript functions and return values

When the function or subroutine you've called finishes executing, control returns to the caller and execution of the original script continues from there. Listing 9-10 provides a detailed example of calling VBScript and JScript functions. You can use this technique in your own scripts as well.

Listing 9-10: Calling functions of other scripting languages

combo.ws

```
<!-- Author: William R. Stanek -->
<!-- Descr: Combined example for JScript and VBScript -->

<Job ID="Job1">
<Script LANGUAGE="JScript">
function GetInfoJS()
{
    var info;
    info = "";
    info += ScriptEngine() + " Version ";
    info += ScriptEngineMajorVersion() + ".";
    info += ScriptEngineMinorVersion() + ".";
    info += ScriptEngineBuildVersion();
    return(info);
}

</Script>
<Script LANGUAGE="VBScript">
Function GetInfoVB
  Dim info
  info = ""
  info = ScriptEngine & " Version "
  info = info & ScriptEngineMajorVersion & "."
  info = info & ScriptEngineMinorVersion & "."
  info = info & ScriptEngineBuildVersion
  GetInfoVB =  info
End Function
</Script>

<Script LANGUAGE="VBScript">
WScript.Echo "VB2VB: " + GetInfoVB()
WScript.Echo "VB2JS: " + GetInfoJS()
</Script>

<Script LANGUAGE="JScript">
versionVB = GetInfoVB()
WScript.Echo("JS2VB: ", versionVB)

versionJS = GetInfoJS()
WScript.Echo("JS2JS: ", versionJS)
</Script>
</Job>
```

Output

VB2VB: VBScript Version 5.0.3715

VB2JS: JScript Version 5.0.3715

JS2VB: VBScript Version 5.0.3715

JS2JS: JScript Version 5.0.3715

Using Logon Scripts

Logon scripts set commands that should be executed each time a user logs in. You can use logon scripts to set system time, map network drive paths, make printer connections, and more. The steps you should follow to configure accounts for use with logon scripts as well as to distribute and create logon scripts are covered next.

Placing and Distributing Logon Scripts

As the name implies, logon scripts are executed when users logon to the network accounts. One user or many users can use a single logon script. As the administrator, you control what commands, scripts, and programs are executed when a user logs on and you also control which users use which scripts.

In a Windows NT domain, the location of logon scripts is relative to the server authenticating the logon. On the authenticating server, the default location of logon scripts is %SYSTEMROOT%\System32\repl\import\scripts. Any directory path information associated with the logon script name is relative to the default path for logon scripts, and you can set the logon script name as follows:

- ◆ Set the file name only, such as eng.bat. Here, the complete path to the logon script is assumed to be

  `%SystemRoot%\System32\repl\import\scripts\eng.bat`

- ◆ Set a relative path and file name, such as eng\regusers.bat. Here the complete path to the logon script is assumed to be

  `%SystemRoot%\System32\repl\import\scripts\eng\regusers.bat`

In a Windows NT domain, domain controllers are responsible for authenticating logon and are also the source for logon scripts. Each domain controller on the network – primary and backups – need to have a copy of the logon scripts you are using in the appropriate directory (%SYSTEMROOT%\System32\repl\import\scripts\).

You don't have to manually copy scripts to backup domain controllers. Logon scripts can also be automatically distributed. Start by placing your logon scripts in the export directory of the primary domain controller. The full path to this directory is

`%SystemRoot%\System32\repl\export\scripts\`

Next, configure the directory Replicator service to replicate the scripts directory to the backup domain controllers. In this way, logon scripts should be available throughout the domain and are updated automatically whenever you update the scripts in the primary domain controllers export directory.

 A complete discussion of replication and the Replicator service are beyond the scope of this book. For more information, see *Microsoft Windows NT 4.0 Server Administrator's Pocket Consultant.*

Creating Logon Scripts

The limits for logon scripts are the limits of your imagination. Logon scripts can run any Windows shell command; they can work with VBScript, JScript, and the Windows Script Host. You just have to know how to code the script correctly for the user's environment. The keys to creating a good logon script are to assume that only the core environment variables are available on the user's system and to use full file paths whenever possible.

The most common tasks you'll want logon scripts to handle are to configure network, printer, and file-related resources. You may want to

◆ Display a message of the day

◆ Display a network usage policy or disclaimer in a browser

◆ Configure default printers and set up other printers

◆ Map network drives and set default drive paths

◆ Start applications or run commands

◆ Set the system time

On Windows 95, Windows 98, and Windows NT systems, you can only use shell scripts as logon scripts. These scripts must end with the .bat or .cmd extension. Although there is a way to hack the Windows registry and force the system to allow you to use Windows scripts, I don't recommend this. It is just as easy to use a shell script to call a Windows script containing your logon commands.

Listing 9-10 shows a basic logon script that I'll use to demonstrate some key concepts. In this example, I use a shell script to start two Windows scripts: st.vbs and st.js. These Windows scripts in turn execute my logon commands.

Listing 9-10: A basic logon script

startup.bat

```
net time \\ZETA
net use X: \\DELTA\RESOURCES
net use Y: \\OMEGA\DATA\FILES

cscript \\zeta\NETLOGON\st.vbs
cscript \\zeta\NETLOGON\st.js
```

st.vbs

```
Set ws = WScript.CreateObject("WScript.Shell")
ws.Run "notepad " & WScript.ScriptFullName
```

st.js

```
var ws = WScript.CreateObject("WScript.Shell");
ws.Run("notepad " + WScript.ScriptFullName)
```

Though very basic, this logon script shows the key concepts you'll need to develop first-class logon scripts. As the example shows, in a logon script, the following rules apply:

◆ Shell commands often provide the easiest mechanisms for configuring the basics. In the example, I use `net time` to synchronize the system time with the network time server (or primary domain controller) and `net use` to map default drives. Of course, I could have used Windows script commands, but it is so easy to use shell commands.

◆ CScript and WScript use the user's default working directory, and all paths must be set relative to this directory or you should use a full file path. This example accesses the NETLOGON share on the primary domain controller (ZETA). On a Windows NT Server, NETLOGON is a shared directory that points to %SYSTEMROOT%\System32\repl\import\scripts.

◆ Programs may not behave as you expect them to. In the example, I had to modify the VBScript `Run` command to get it to work properly. For some reason, VBScript version 5 treated `Run` as a subroutine rather than an object method and as a result, I had to remove the parentheses.

◆ Everything you've learned (or will learn) in this book can be used in a logon script. You just have to create scripts to perform the logon routines needed in your environment.

Configuring Accounts to User Logon Scripts

Logon scripts aren't run automatically. You need to configure accounts to use them and you do this by setting the Logon Script Name property for each account that should use a particular logon script. In Windows NT, the steps you follow to configure an account to use a logon script are as follows:

1. Choose Start → Programs → Administrative Tools (common) and then select User Manager for Domains.

2. In User Manager for Domains, double-click on the name of the account you want to configure. You can also select multiple accounts in the User Name list and then choose the Properties option of the User menu. This opens the User Properties dialog shown in Figure 9-3.

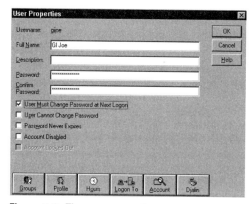

Figure 9-3: The user account or accounts you are working with is configured with the properties dialog.

3. In the User Properties dialog, click on the Profile button. This opens the dialog shown in Figure 9-4.

4. Enter the name of the logon script in the Logon Script Name field and then click OK. Be sure to use the full filename, such as logon.bat or startup.cmd.

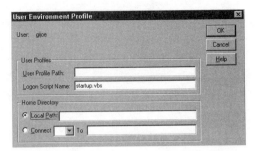

Figure 9-4: Enter the name of the logon script.

Summary

Windows Script Host provides many different ways to present information to users and to get user input. You can use plain old `echo`, VBScript message boxes, VBScript input boxes, and WSH pop-ups. After you get user input, you need to determine the user's response and handle any errors that occur. WSH also provides many mechanisms for obtaining environment information, and you can examine properties of the script host as easily as you can examine script arguments. The key to success is in knowing how to use the available objects, methods, and properties. All of these techniques can be used in logon scripts to configure the user's system and perform common tasks. In the next chapter, you learn how to manage network resources with Windows Script Host.

Chapter 10

Managing File Systems

IN THIS CHAPTER

♦ Understanding the FileSystemObject

♦ Creating folders and examining folder properties

♦ Copying, moving, and deleting folders

♦ Creating files and examining file properties

♦ Copying, moving, and deleting files

♦ Creating the file system administrator script

WHILE SHELL SCRIPTS ALLOW you to work with files and directories at the command-line level, the command shell doesn't really let you work with these file system features at the desktop level. To work with the file system at the desktop level, you need to use Windows scripts. With Windows scripts, you have complete access to files, folders, drives, and shortcuts at the desktop level. You can examine just about any file system property and can create and manipulate these elements as well. In this chapter, you learn essential file and folder administration techniques.

Understanding the FileSystemObject

The top-level object for working with the Windows desktop and file systems is the FileSystemObject (FSO). It is through FSO that you access most of the other file system related objects. Because this object is so complex, lets take a step-by-step look at its components including related objects, methods, and properties.

FSO Objects and Collections

The FileSystemObject is implemented in the scripting run-time library (Scrrun.dll) and as such, it is an extension of the JScript and VBScript scripting engines rather than a part of the Windows Script Host object model. This distinction is important if you plan to use Windows Script Host with other scripting engines. For example, if you plan to use the PerlScript scripting engine, you will use

PerlScript's file system objects or you can define file system functions in VBScript and JScript and access them as part of a batch script job.

Many different objects and collections are accessed through the FileSystem Object. These elements are summarized in Table 10-1. As you know already, objects are containers for related sets of methods and properties. Collections, on the other hand, may be new to you. Collections are containers for groups of related items, such as the Drives collection that contains references for all the drives on a particular system. Normally, collections are accessed through the properties and methods of other objects. For example, to examine drives on a system, you'll use the Drives property of the FileSystemObject.

TABLE 10-1 OBJECTS AND COLLECTIONS ACCESSED THROUGH FILESYSTEMOBJECT

Object/Collection	Description
Drive Object	Used to examine drive information. Here, a drive is any type of storage device, including disk drives, CD-ROM drives, RAM disks, and network drives.
Drives Collection	Provides a list of physical and logical drives on the system.
File Object	Used to examine and manipulate files.
Files Collection	Provides a list of files in a folder.
Folder Object	Used to examine and manipulate folders.
Folders Collection	Provides a list of subfolders in a Folder.
TextStream Object	Used to read and write text files.

FSO Methods and Properties

As shown in Table 10-2, the FileSystemObject provides many different methods for working with file systems. These methods sometimes provide the same functionality as methods of lower-level objects. For example, the FileSystemObject's CopyFile method is identical to the File object's Copy method. They both expect the same arguments and have the same syntax.

TABLE 10-2 METHODS OF FILESYSTEMOBJECT

Method	Description
BuildPath	Appends file path information to an existing file path.
CopyFile	Copies files from one location to another.
CopyFolder	Copies folders from one location to another.
CreateFolder	Creates a folder.
CreateTextFile	Creates a text file and returns a TextStream object.
DeleteFile	Deletes a file.
DeleteFolder	Deletes a folder and all its contents.
DriveExists	Determines if a drive exists.
FileExists	Determines if a file exists.
FolderExists	Determines if a folder exists.
GetAbsolutePathName	Returns the full path to a file or folder.
GetBaseName	Returns the base name of a file or folder.
GetDrive	Returns a Drive object.
GetDriveName	Returns a drive name.
GetExtensionName	Returns a file extension from a path.
GetFile	Returns a File object.
GetFileName	Returns a filename from a path.
GetFolder	Returns a Folder object.
GetParentFolderName	Returns the parent folder name from a path.
GetSpecialFolder	Returns an object pointer to a special folder.
GetTempName	Returns a randomly generated file or folder name that can be used with CreateTextFile.
MoveFile	Moves files from one location to another.
MoveFolder	Moves folders from one location to another.
OpenTextFile	Opens an existing text file and returns a TextStream object.

The only property of the `FileSystemObject` is `Drives`. You use this property to return a `Drives` collection that contains a list of all physical and logical drives on the system.

Using the FileSystemObject

As stated earlier, the `FileSystemObject` isn't a part of the Windows Script Host object model and is instead a part of the Scripting type library. Because of this, you access the `FileSystemObject` via the `Scripting` object, such as

VBScript	JScript
`Set fs = WScript.CreateObject` `("Scripting.FileSystemObject ")`	`fs = new ActiveXObject` `("Scripting.FileSystemObject");`

In the previous examples, note that you create the `FileSystemObject` in JScript using the `ActiveXObject` method rather than the `CreateObject` method. `ActiveXObject` is a JScript method designed to return references to ActiveX Automation objects.

Once you create an instance of the `FileSystemObject` you can use its objects, methods, and properties. You only need one instance of the `FileSystemObject` in a script and when you are finished using it, you may want to destroy the object instance and free up the memory it uses. To do this, you can set the reference variable to null, such as

VBScript	JScript
`Set fs = Nothing`	`fs = ""`

Nothing is a reserved keyword in VBScript. You use Nothing in an assignment to null the object (free the memory associated with the object).

Folder Administration

Folders are an important part of the file system and whether you want to access existing folders or create new folders you can use Windows scripts to get the job done. Often, the way you work with folders depends on the tasks you want to perform. For example, if you want to examine folder properties, you will first need to create a `Folder` object and then you can work with the `Folder` object. The sections that follow examine key folder administration tasks, including

◆ Viewing folder contents

◆ Examining and working with folder properties

◆ Checking for and creating folders

◆ Deleting, copying, and moving folders

◆ Working with special folders

Viewing Folder Contents

Before you can view the contents of a folder, you must create a reference to the folder you want to work with. You do this with the `GetFolder` method of the `FileSystemObject`. The `GetFolder` method expects to be passed the path of the folder you want to work with and returns a `Folder` object that you can use in your scripts. The following example shows how you can call `GetFolder`:

VBScript	JScript

`Set fs = CreateObject`
`   ("Scripting.FileSystemObject")`
`Set f = fs.GetFolder("C:\WinNT")`
	`fs = new ActiveXObject`
	`   ("Scripting.FileSystemObject");`
	`var f = fs.GetFolder("C:\\WinNT")`

 TIP Don't forget that you must use escape directory paths in JScript. If you forget to use double slashes, your scripts may not work.

After calling `GetFolder`, you can use the `Subfolders` and `Files` properties of the `File` object to examine the elements contained in the specified folder. These properties return `Folder` and `File` collections respectively, which you can iterate through with a `For` loop.

Listing 10-1 shows an example using `GetFolder`. The example displays a pop-up dialog containing a list of all subfolders under the C:\WinNT directory.

Listing 10-1: Examining collections of subfolders and files

VBScript	JScript
showfolder.vbs	**showfolder.js**

```vbscript
Set w = WScript.CreateObject
  ("WScript.Shell")
w.Popup ShowFolders("C:\WinNT")
Function ShowFolders(folderName)

Dim fs, f, f1, fc, s
s = ""
Set fs = CreateObject
  ("Scripting.FileSystemObject")
Set f = fs.GetFolder(folderName)
Set fc = f.SubFolders
For Each f1 in fc

s = s & f1.name
s = s & (Chr(13) & Chr(10))
Next
  ShowFolders = s
End Function
```

```jscript
var w = WScript.CreateObject
  ("WScript.Shell");
w.Popup (ShowFolders("C:\\WinNT"))
function ShowFolders(folderName)
{
var fs, f, fc, s;
s = ""
fs = new ActiveXObject
  ("Scripting.FileSystemObject");
f = fs.GetFolder(folderName);
fc = new Enumerator(f.SubFolders);
for (; !fc.atEnd(); fc.moveNext())
{
  s += fc.item();
  s += "\r\n"
}
return(s);
}
```

As Listing 10-1 shows, the techniques you use to examine collections in VBScript and Jscript differ. In VBScript, you can use a simple For Each structure to examine the contents of the collection. The structure of the For Each loop isn't really any different from structures I've used in past examples. You start out by obtaining a Folder object:

```vbscript
Set fs = CreateObject("Scripting.FileSystemObject")
Set f = fs.GetFolder(folderName)
```

Next, you obtain the SubFolders collection within the folder:

```vbscript
Set fc = f.SubFolders
```

Then you examine each item in the collection using a For Each loop:

```vbscript
For Each f1 in fc
s = s & f1.name
s = s & (Chr(13) & Chr(10))
Next
```

You use the s variable to hold the list of folder names, placing the names on separate lines by combining Chr(13) and Chr(10). Chr(13) is a carriage return and Chr(10) is a line feed.

With JScript, on the other hand, accessing collections requires some new techniques. You start out by obtaining a pointer to a Folder object:

```
fs = new ActiveXObject("Scripting.FileSystemObject");
f = fs.GetFolder(folderName);
```

Next, because the items in a collection aren't directly accessible in JScript, you use the Enumerator() method to obtain the SubFolders collection within the specified folder:

```
fc = new Enumerator(f.SubFolders);
```

Enumerator provides access to special methods for working with collections. These methods are

- atEnd — Returns True if the current item is the last in the collection. Otherwise, returns False.

- item — Returns an item in a collection.

- moveFirst — Resets the collection pointer to the beginning of the collection. Returns undefined if there is no first item.

- moveNext — Advances to the next item in the collection. Returns undefined if the enumerator is at the end of the collection.

In the example, these methods are used to move through the collection. The following For loop states that while not at the end of the collection iterate through the available items:

```
for (; !fc.atEnd(); fc.moveNext())
  {
    s += fc.item();
    s += "\r\n"
  }
```

You use the s variable to hold the list of folder names, placing the names on separate lines by combining \r and \n. The special character \r is a carriage return, and \n is a line feed.

Examining and Working with Folder Properties

When you work with folders, you often want to examine their properties, such as the creation date or the date last modified. You can use these properties to view folder attributes, to display folder information to users, and more. Before you can examine folder properties, you must reference the folder through its `Folder` object. You can then work with any of the folder properties available. The following example shows how you can examine the creation date of a specified folder, such as

VBScript	JScript

```
Set fs = CreateObject
  ("Scripting.FileSystemObject")
Set f = fs.GetFolder("C:\WinNT")
creDate = f.DateCreated
```

```
fs = new ActiveXObject
  ("Scripting.FileSystemObject");
var f = fs.GetFolder("C:\\WinNT")
creDate = f.DateCreated
```

A complete list of folder properties is shown in Table 10-3. All folder properties are read-only, except for the `Attributes` property. This means you can read the properties but you can't change their values.

TABLE 10-3 PROPERTIES OF THE FOLDER OBJECT

Property	Description	Sample Return Value
Attributes	Sets or returns folder properties. See "Examining and Working with File Properties" for complete details.	16
DateCreated	Returns the folder creation date and time.	11/01/99 5:12:11 PM
DateLastAccessed	Returns the date the folder was last accessed.	11/21/99
DateLastModified	Returns the date and time the folder was last modified.	11/21/99 7:27:24 PM
Drive	Returns the drive letter on which the folder resides.	C:
Files	Returns a `Files` collection.	-
IsRootFolder	Returns 1 (True) if the folder is the root folder, such as C:\ or D:\. Otherwise returns zero.	0
Name	Returns the folder name.	WinNT

Property	Description	Sample Return Value
ParentFolder	Returns the Folder object of the parent folder.	C:\
Path	Returns the path to the folder.	C:\WinNT
ShortName	Returns the MS-DOS-compliant name of the folder.	WinNT
ShortPath	Returns the MS-DOS-compliant path to the folder.	C:\WinNT
Size	Returns the byte size of all files and subfolders in the folder.	299847634
SubFolders	Returns a SubFolders collection.	-
Type	Returns the folder type.	File Folder

Most of the folder properties have fairly obvious uses. For example, you use the CreationDate property when you want to display the folder's creation date to a user or perform a calculation based on the creation date.

Some properties are more useful than you might imagine. For example, you can use IsRootFolder and ParentFolder to move through directory structures. Here, you create an instance of a folder and set it to a path, such as C:\WinNT\System32\LogFiles. Then use the ParentFolder property to move through each of the parent folders, stopping when you reach the root folder C:\. An example using this technique is shown as Listing 10-2.

Listing 10-2: Using IsRootFolder and ParentFolder

VBScript	JScript
checkfolder.vbs	**checkfolder.js**

```
folderP = CheckFolders
  ("C:\WinNT\System32\LogFiles")
Set w = WScript.CreateObject
  ("WScript.Shell")
w.Popup folderP
Function CheckFolders(folderPath)

Dim fs, f, n, s
```

```
folderP = CheckFolders
  ("C:\\WinNT\\System32\\LogFiles")
var w = WScript.CreateObject
  ("WScript.Shell");
w.Popup (folderP)
function CheckFolders(folderPath)
{
 var fs, f, n, s;
```

Continued

Listing 10-2: Using IsRootFolder and ParentFolder *(Continued)*

VBScript	JScript

```
s = ""
n = 0
Set fs = CreateObject
("Scripting.FileSystemObject")
Set f = fs.GetFolder(folderPath)
If f.IsRootFolder Then
  s = "This is the root folder."
Else
  Do Until f.IsRootFolder
f = f.ParentFolder;
    n = n + 1
  Loop
End If
'Work with folder
s = "Folder is nested " & n & "
  levels deep."

CheckFolders = s
End Function
```

```
s = "";
n = 0;
fs = new ActiveXObject
("Scripting.FileSystemObject");
f = fs.GetFolder(folderPath);
if (f.IsRootFolder)
  s = "Root folder."
 else {
   do {     Set f = f.ParentFolder

    n++;
  }
while (!f.IsRootFolder)
//Work with folder
s = "Folder is nested " + n + "
  levels deep."
}
return(s);
}
```

Output

Folder is nested 3 levels deep.

Output

Folder is nested 3 levels deep.

As shown, the ParentFolder property returns a Folder object that you can ma-nipulate. If you just want the name of the parent folder, use the GetParentFolderName method instead. This method returns a string containing the name of the parent folder and can be used as follows:

VBScript	JScript

```
Set fs = CreateObject
("Scripting.FileSystemObject")
par = f.GetParentFolderName
  folderpath
```

```
fs = new ActiveXObject
("Scripting.FileSystemObject");
par = f.GetParentFolderName
  (folderpath)
```

Here, if the folder path is C:\WinNT\System32, the par variable would be set to C:\WinNT. Note that if the folder path is a root folder, such as C:\, this method re-turns an empty string. The reason for this is that root folders don't have parent folders.

Checking for and Creating Folders

In the previous examples, we've assumed that the folder exists on the user's system. As this may not always be the case, you may want to test for a folder's existence before you try to work with it. To do this, you can use the `FolderExists` method of `FileSystemObject`. This method returns `True` if the folder exists and can be used as shown in Listing 10-3.

Listing 10-3: Using FolderExists

VBScript	JScript
checkfolder2.vbs	**checkfolder2.js**
```WScript.Echo (CheckFolder("C:\WinNT"))```	```WScript.Echo (CheckFolder("C:\\WinNT"))```
```Function CheckFolder(foldr)```	```function CheckFolder(foldr)```
```Dim fs, s```	```{```
``` Set fs = CreateObject```	```var fs, s = foldr;```
``` ("Scripting.FileSystemObject")```	```fs = new ActiveXObject```
``` If (fs.FolderExists(foldr)) Then```	``` ("Scripting.FileSystemObject");```
``` s = foldr & " is available."```	``` if (fs.FolderExists(foldr))```
``` Else```	``` s += " is available.";```
``` s = foldr & " doesn't exist."```	``` else```
``` End If```	``` s += " doesn't exist.";```
``` CheckFolder = s```	``` return(s);```
```End Function```	```}```
Output	**Output**
C:/WinNT is available.	C:/WinNT is available.

After checking for a folder's existence, one of the most common tasks you'll want to perform is to create a necessary folder. You can create folders with the `CreateFolder` method of the `FileSystemObject`. The main argument for this method is a string containing the path to the folder you want to create, such as

VBScript	JScript
```Set fs = CreateObject```	```var fs = new ActiveXObject```
``` ("Scripting.FileSystemObject")```	``` ("Scripting.FileSystemObject");```
```Set foldr = fs.CreateFolder```	```var foldr = fs.CreateFolder```
``` ("d:\working")```	``` ("d:\\working");```

Copying, Moving, and Deleting Folders

With Windows scripts, there are two different ways to copy, move, and delete files. You can use methods of `FileSystemObject` to work with multiple folders or you can use methods of the `Folder` object to work with individual folders.

MANIPULATING MULTIPLE FOLDERS

With `FileSystemObject`, the methods for copying, moving, and deleting folders are

- ◆ `DeleteFolder`
- ◆ `CopyFolder`
- ◆ `MoveFolder`

USING DELETEFOLDER   The `DeleteFolder` method is used to delete a folder and all its contents, which can include subfolders and files. When you use the method, you specify the path to the folder you want to delete and optionally force the method to delete read-only files. For example, you can delete a working directory in C:\working\temp as follows:

VBScript	JScript

`Set fs = CreateObject`
`  ("Scripting.FileSystemObject")`
`fs.DeleteFolder("C:\working\temp")`
	`var fs = new ActiveXObject`
	`  ("Scripting.FileSystemObject");`
	`fs.DeleteFolder("C:\\working\\temp");`

 The `DeleteFolder` method can be very dangerous. It'll let you specify the root folder for deletion, which will delete all contents on an entire drive.

If the directory contains read-only files that you wanted to delete, an error occurs and the delete operation is cancelled. To prevent this from happening, you must set the force flag to `True`. For example:

VBScript	JScript
`fs.DeleteFolder` `  "C:\working\temp",True`	`fs.DeleteFolder` `  ("C:\\working\\temp", "True");`

You can also use wildcards when deleting folders. To do this, specify the wildcard as the last element of the path. For example, you can delete the folders C:\working\test and C:\working\test2 as follows:

VBScript	JScript
`fs.DeleteFolder "C:\working\tes*"`	`fs.DeleteFolder("C:\\working\\tes*");`

USING COPYFOLDER   The `CopyFolder` method copies a folder and all its contents, which can include subfolders and files, to a new location. Using `CopyFolder`, you specify the source path of the folder you want to copy and the destination path for the folder. For example, you can copy C:\working to D:\working as follows:

VBScript	JScript

`Set fs = CreateObject`
`  ("Scripting.FileSystemObject")`
`fs.CopyFolder`
`  "C:\working", "D:\working"`
	`var fs = new ActiveXObject`
	`  ("Scripting.FileSystemObject");`
	`fs.CopyFolder`
	`  ("C:\\working", "D:\\working");`

You can also use `CopyFolder` to copy between existing folders. For example if both C:\working and D:\working exist, you can copy files and subfolders from C:\working to D:\working. However, you should follow several rules when you do this. If the destination directory already exists and any files are overwritten during the copy, an error occurs and the copy operation stops. To force the method to overwrite existing files, you must set the overwrite flag to `True`, such as:

VBScript	JScript
`fs.CopyFolder "C:\working",` `  "D:\working", True`	`fs.CopyFolder ("C:\\working",` `  "D:\\working", "True");`

If the destination directory already exists and you want to copy specific files and folders, use a wildcard as the final element of the source folder name. The following example would copy the C:\Working\test and C:\Working\test2 folders to D:\working\test and D:\working\test2:

VBScript	JScript
`fs.CopyFolder "C:\working\tes*",` `  "D:\working"`	`fs.CopyFolder("C:\\working\tes*",` `  "D:\\working");`

> **TIP**   Normally, you don't want to specify the last element of the destination path as a folder separator (\). If you do, the `CopyFolder` method assumes the destination folder exists and will not create it if necessary.

USING MOVEFOLDER   If you want to move a folder and all its contents to a new location, use `MoveFolder`. When you use the `MoveFolder` method, you specify the source path of the folder you want to move and the destination path. For example, you can move C:\data to D:\work\data as follows:

VBScript	JScript
| ```
Set fs = CreateObject
  ("Scripting.FileSystemObject")
fs.MoveFolder "C:\data",
  "D:\work\data"
``` | ```
var fs = new ActiveXObject
  ("Scripting.FileSystemObject");
fs.CopyFolder("C:\\data",
  "D:\\work\\data");
``` |

You can also use `MoveFolder` to move files and subfolders between existing folders. For example if both C:\working and D:\working exist, you can move files and subfolders from C:\working to D:\working. To do this, use wildcards to match subfolders and file contents, such as

VBScript	JScript
| ```
fs.MoveFolder "C:\working\tes*",
  "D:\working"
``` | ```
fs.MoveFolder("C:\\working\\tes*",
  "D:\\working");
``` |

 If you specify the last element of the destination path as a folder separator (\),the `MoveFolder` method assumes the destination folder exists and will not create it if necessary. Also, the move operation will not overwrite existing files or folders. In this case, the move fails the first time it tries to overwrite.

MANIPULATING INDIVIDUAL FOLDERS

With the `Folder` object, the methods for copying, moving, and deleting folders are

- ◆ Delete
- ◆ Copy
- ◆ Move

 You cannot use wildcards when copying, moving, or deleting individual folders.

USING DELETE   The `Delete` method of the `Folder` object works almost the same as the `DeleteFolder` method discussed previously. The method deletes a folder and all its contents, which can include subfolders and files, and can also force the deletion of read-only contents. The `Delete` method works with a specific `Folder` object reference and as a result, can delete a folder just by calling the method, such as:

VBScript	JScript

Set fs = CreateObject
var fs = new ActiveXObject
  ("Scripting.FileSystemObject")
  ("Scripting.FileSystemObject");
	Set f = fs.GetFolder("C:\working")
	var f = fs.GetFolder("C:\\working");
	f.Delete
	f.Delete()

If the folder contains read-only subfolders and files that you want to delete, you must set the force flag to `True`, such as

VBScript	JScript
f.Delete True	f.Delete("True")

USING COPY   The `Copy` method copies a folder and all its contents to a new location. With `Copy`, you obtain a `Folder` object and then set the destination path for the folder in the `Copy` method. For example, you can copy C:\working to D:\working as follows:

VBScript	JScript

Set fs = CreateObject
  ("Scripting.FileSystemObject")
Set f = fs.GetFolder("C:\working")
f.Copy "D:\working"
	var fs = new ActiveXObject
	  ("Scripting.FileSystemObject");
	var f = fs.GetFolder("C:\\working");
	f.Copy("D:\\working");

As with `CopyFolder`, you can also use the `Copy` method to copy between existing folders. For example if both C:\working and D:\working exist, you can copy files and subfolders from C:\working to D:\working. Here, you may want to force the method to overwrite existing files and you do this by setting the overwrite flag to `True`, such as

VBScript	JScript
f.Copy "D:\working", True	f.Copy("D:\\working", "True");

If you try to overwrite existing files and don't set the overwrite flag, an error occurs and the `Copy` operation stops.

USING MOVE   You use the `Move` method to move a folder and all its contents to a new location. Before you use `Move`, you must first obtain a `Folder` object and then you can set the destination path for the folder in the `Move` method. For example, you can move C:\data to D:\work\data as follows:

VBScript	JScript
| ```
Set fs = CreateObject
  ("Scripting.FileSystemObject")
Set f = fs.GetFolder("C:\data")
f.Move "D:\work\data"
``` | ```
var fs = new ActiveXObject
  ("Scripting.FileSystemObject");
var f = fs.GetFolder("C:\\data");
f.Move("D:\\work\\data");
``` |

You can also use `Move` to move files and subfolders between existing folders. For example if both C:\data and D:\backups\data exist, you can move files and subfolders from C:\data to D:\backups\data. However, the `Move` method will not overwrite existing files. If you try to do this, an error occurs and the operation stops.

Working with Special Folders

Although entering a specific value for folder paths works in many cases, there are times when you'll need to work with certain folders in a way that isn't specific to a particular system. For example, if you create a login script, users may log in from Windows 98, Windows NT, or another Windows operating system. These operating system files are installed in different locations by default and can be set to just about any directory name during installation.

So if you want to create a script that works with operating system files, you shouldn't really enter a precise path. Instead, you should work with environment variables that act as pointers to the location of the operating system files, such as `SystemRoot`. As discussed in Chapter 9, you can use the `ExpandEnvironment Strings` method of the `Shell` object to obtain a string representation of the `SystemRoot` environment variable. You can then assign this value to a method that uses the path information. An example is shown in Listing 10-4.

Listing 10-4: Working with paths and environment variables

VBScript	JScript
paths.vbs	**paths.js**
| ```
Set fs = CreateObject
  ("Scripting.FileSystemObject")
Set WshShell = WScript.CreateObject
  ("WScript.Shell")
osdir =
  WshShell.ExpandEnvironmentStrings
  ("%SystemRoot%")
Set f = fs.GetFolder(osdir)
``` | ```
var fs = new ActiveXObject
  ("Scripting.FileSystemObject");
var WshShell = WScript.CreateObject
  ("WScript.Shell")
osdir =
  WshShell.ExpandEnvironmentStrings
  ("%SystemRoot%")
var f = fs.GetFolder(osdir);
``` |

WScript.Echo f   WScript.Echo(f)

Output   **Output**

C:\WinNT   C:\WinNT

Accessing environment variables before working with folders requires a few extra steps that can be avoided by using the `GetSpecialFolder` method of `FileSystemObject`. With this method, you can directly obtain one of three folders: the Windows folder, the System folder, and the Temp folder. The method accepts a value that represents the folder you want to work with:

◆ 0 – For the Windows folder, such as C:\WinNT. Associated constant is `WindowsFolder`.

◆ 1 – For the System folder, such as C:\WinNT\System32. Associated constant is `SystemFolder`.

◆ 2 – For the Temp folder, such as C:\TEMP. Associated constant is `TemporaryFolder`.

An example using `GetSpecialFolder` is shown in Listing 10-5.

Listing 10-5: Working with special folders

VBScript	JScript
specfolder.vbs	**specfolder.js**

```
Set fs = CreateObject                var fs = CreateObject
  ("Scripting.FileSystemObject")       ("Scripting.FileSystemObject")
'Get the Windows folder              //Get the Windows folder
Set wfolder = fs.GetSpecialFolder(0) var wfolder = fs.GetSpecialFolder(0)
'Get the System folder               //Get the System folder
Set sfolder = fs.GetSpecialFolder(1) var sfolder = fs.GetSpecialFolder(1)
'Get the Temp folder                 //Get the Temp folder
Set tfolder = fs.GetSpecialFolder(2) var tfolder = fs.GetSpecialFolder(2)
```

File Administration

Many of the tasks you perform in Windows scripts will relate to files. You can use scripts to copy, move, and delete files. You can use scripts to create, read, and write text files as well. The types of text files you can work with include HTML, XML, scripts, and other types of files containing standard ASCII or Unicode text. The sections that follow examine key file administration tasks, including

◆ Examining and working with file properties

◆ Copying, moving, and deleting files

◆ Checking for and creating files

◆ Reading and writing files

Examining and Working with File Properties

Files have many different properties. Some of these properties can only be read. Others are read/write, which means you can change their values. A complete list of folder properties is shown as Table 10-4.

TABLE 10-4 PROPERTIES OF THE FILE OBJECT

Property	Description	Sample Return Value
Attributes	Sets or returns file properties.	32
DateCreated	Returns the file creation date and time.	6/6/99 11:07:14 AM
DateLastAccessed	Returns the date the file was last accessed.	9/10/99
DateLastModified	Returns the date and time the file was last modified.	9/10/99 5:21:45 PM
Drive	Returns the drive letter on which the file resides.	D:
Name	Returns the filename.	index.html
ParentFolder	Returns the Folder object of the parent folder.	C:\working
Path	Returns the path to the file.	C:\working\index.htm
ShortName	Returns the MS-DOS-compliant name of the file.	index.htm
ShortPath	Returns the MS-DOS-compliant path to the file.	C:\working\index.htm
Size	Returns the byte size of the file.	650
Type	Returns the file type.	Netscape Hypertext Document

Before you can examine file properties, you must reference the file through its related File object. You can then work with any of the file properties available. The following example shows how you can examine the size of a file:

VBScript	JScript

Set fs = CreateObject
  ("Scripting.FileSystemObject")
Set f = fs.GetFile("D:\index.htm")
fileSize = f.size
	fs = new ActiveXObject
	  ("Scripting.FileSystemObject");
	var f = fs.GetFile("D:\\index.htm")
	fileSize = f.size

One of the key properties you'll work with is Attributes. The value that is returned by the Attributes property is the combination of the related values for all the flags set for the file or folder. You can change file properties by setting Attributes to a new value or by adding and subtracting from its current value. With folders, however, you can only display attribute values.

Table 10-5 provides a complete list of Attribute values that can be used with files and folders. While read-only values cannot be changed, read/write values can be combined to set multiple attributes.

TABLE 10-5 ATTRIBUTE VALUES FOR FILES AND FOLDERS

Constant	Value	Description
Normal	0	A normal file with no attributes set.
ReadOnly	1	A read-only file. Attribute is read/write.
Hidden	2	A hidden file. Attribute is read/write.
System	4	A system file. Attribute is read/write.
Volume	8	A disk drive volume label. Attribute is read-only.
Directory	16	A folder or directory. Attribute is read-only.
Archive	32	A file with the archive bit set (meaning it has changed since last backup). Attribute is read/write.
Alias	64	A link or shortcut. Attribute is read-only.
Compressed	128	A compressed file. Attribute is read-only.

Changing read/write file attributes is easy. The following example sets the read-only flag for a file called logs.txt:

VBScript	JScript
`Set fs = CreateObject`	`fs = new ActiveXObject`
`  ("Scripting.FileSystemObject")`	`  ("Scripting.FileSystemObject");`
`Set f = fs.GetFile("D:\log.txt")`	`var f = fs.GetFile("D:\\log.txt")`
`f.Attributes = f.Attributes + 1`	`f.Attributes += 1`

Now you may be wondering what would happen if the file was read-only already and you added one to its value. The result is unpredictable but a hidden, read-only file (value 3) would become a system file (value 4). To ensure that you only set a particular flag, that is, if it's not set already, you can use an AND test. In Listing 10-6, the file is changed to read-only — only if this flag isn't already set:

Listing 10-6: Checking for attributes before making changes

VBScript	JScript
attribs.vbs	**attribs.js**
`Set f = fs.GetFile("D:\log.txt")`	`var f = fs.GetFile("D:\\log.txt")`
`If f.Attributes and 1 Then`	`if (f.Attributes && 1)`
	`{`
`f.Attributes = f.Attributes + 1`	`f.Attributes += 1`
`End If`	`}`

Checking for and Creating Files

So far, we've assumed that the file we want to work with exists on the user's system. However, this may not always be the case, and you may want to test for a file's existence before you try to work with it. To do this, use the `FileExists` method of `FileSystemObject`. This method returns `True` if the folder exists and False otherwise.

Listing 10-7 shows how you can test for a file's existence.

Listing 10-7: Using FileExists

VBScript	JScript
exists.vbs	**exists.js**
`WScript.Echo`	`WScript.Echo`
`  (CheckFile("C:\data.txt"))`	`  (CheckFile("C:\\data.txt"))`
`Function CheckFile(aFile)`	`function CheckFile(aFile)`
`Dim fs, s`	`{`
`  Set fs = CreateObject`	`var fs, s = aFile;`
`("Scripting.FileSystemObject")`	`fs = new ActiveXObject`
`  If (fs.FileExists(aFile)) Then`	`  ("Scripting.FileSystemObject");`
`    s = aFile & " is available."`	`  if (fs.FileExists(aFile))`

VBScript	JScript
exists.vbs	**exists.js**

```
  Else                                   s += " is available.";
    s = aFile & " doesn't exist."      else
  End If                                  s += " doesn't exist.";
CheckFile = s                           return(s);
End Function                            }
```

Output

C:/data.txt is available.

Output

C:\data.txt is available.

If a file you want to write to doesn't exist, you may want to create it. To do this, you can use the CreateTextFile method of the FileSystemObject. The main argument for this method is a string containing the path to the file you want to create, such as

VBScript	JScript

```
Set fs = CreateObject              var fs = new ActiveXObject
  ("Scripting.FileSystemObject")     ("Scripting.FileSystemObject");
Set aFile = fs.CreateTextFile      var aFile = fs.CreateTextFile
  ("d:\working\data.txt")            ("d:\\working\\data.txt");
```

The Folder object also has a CreateTextFile method. With the Folder object, you only specify the filename rather than a complete path, such as

VBScript	JScript

```
Set fs = CreateObject              var fs = new ActiveXObject
  ("Scripting.FileSystemObject")     ("Scripting.FileSystemObject");
Set f = fs.GetFolder("D:\working") var f = fs.GetFolder("D:\\working")
Set aFile =                        var aFile =
  f.CreateTextFile("data.txt")       f.CreateTextFile("data.txt");
```

The CreateTextFile method returns a TextStream object that you can use to work with the newly created file. If you try to create a file with the same name and path as an existing file, an error occurs. By default, CreateTextFile won't overwrite an existing file. You can change this behavior by setting the overwrite flag, such as

VBScript	JScript

```
Set aFile = f.CreateTextFile       var aFile = f.CreateTextFile
  ("data.txt", True)                 ("data.txt", "True");
```

Another default behavior is to create files in ASCII text mode. You can also set Unicode mode, and to do this, you need to set the Unicode flag to True, such as

VBScript	JScript

Set aFile = f.CreateTextFile
  ("data.txt", False, True)
	var aFile = f.CreateTextFile
	  ("data.txt", "False", "True");

 You cannot skip the overwrite flag when you set the Unicode flag. Instead, set the overwrite flag to True or False explicitly and then set the Unicode flag.

Copying, Moving, and Deleting Files

You can manage files using methods of `FileSystemObject` or methods of the `File` object. Use `FileSystemObject` methods when you want to work with multiple files. Use the `File` object when you want to work with individual files.

MANIPULATING MULTIPLE FILES

`FileSystemObject` methods for copying, moving, and deleting files are

♦ `DeleteFile`

♦ `CopyFile`

♦ `MoveFile`

USING DELETEFILE   You can use the `DeleteFile` method to delete one or more files. When you use this method, you specify the path to the file you want to delete and optionally force the method to delete read-only files. You delete one file by specifying an absolute path, such as C:\working\data.txt. You delete multiple files by using wildcards in the filename. For example, you can delete all .txt files in C:\working as follows:

VBScript	JScript

Set fs = CreateObject
  ("Scripting.FileSystemObject")
fs.DeleteFile("C:\working*.txt")
	var fs = new ActiveXObject
	  ("Scripting.FileSystemObject");
	fs.DeleteFile("C:\\working*.txt");

The `DeleteFile` method only deletes read-only files when you set the force flag to `True`, such as

VBScript	JScript

fs.DeleteFile
  "C:\working\data.txt",True
	fs.DeleteFile
	  ("C:\\working\\data.txt", "True");

If DeleteFile encounters a read-only file and you haven't set the force flag, the operation stops and no other files are deleted.

USING COPYFILE The CopyFile method copies one or more files to a new location. To copy a single file, specify the absolute path to the file you want to copy and then the destination path. For example, you can copy C:\working\data.txt to D:\backup\data.txt as follows:

VBScript	JScript
```Set fs = CreateObject ("Scripting.FileSystemObject") fs.CopyFile "C:\working\data.txt", "D:\backup\data.txt"```	```var fs = new ActiveXObject ("Scripting.FileSystemObject"); fs.CopyFile("C:\\working\\data.txt", "D:\\backup\\data.txt");```

You can copy multiple files by using wildcards in the file name as well. For example, to copy all .html files from C:\working to D:\webdata you can use

VBScript	JScript
```Set fs = CreateObject ("Scripting.FileSystemObject") fs.CopyFile "C:\working*.html", "D:\webdata"```	```var fs = new ActiveXObject ("Scripting.FileSystemObject"); fs.CopyFile("C:\\working*.html", "D:\\webdata");```

You can also use CopyFile to copy files between directories that already exist. For example if both C:\working and D:\working exist, you can copy files from C:\working to D:\working. However, you should follow several rules when you do this. If the files you are copying exist at the destination, an error occurs and the copy operation stops. To force the method to overwrite existing files, set the overwrite flag to True, such as

VBScript	JScript
```fs.CopyFile "C:\working*.txt", "D:\working", True```	```fs.CopyFile("C:\\working*.txt", "D:\\working", "True");```

CopyFile will not write into a read-only directory and it will not write over read-only files either. You cannot change this behavior with the overwrite flag.

USING MOVEFILE If you want to move one or more files to a new location, use MoveFile. To move a single file, specify the absolute path to the file as the source and then set the destination path. For example, you can move C:\data.txt to D:\work\data.txt as follows:

VBScript	JScript

`Set fs = CreateObject`
`  ("Scripting.FileSystemObject")`
`fs.MoveFile "C:\data.txt",`
`  "D:\work\data.txt"`
	`var fs = new ActiveXObject`
	`  ("Scripting.FileSystemObject");`
	`fs.CopyFile("C:\\data.txt",`
	`  "D:\\work\\data.txt");`

To move multiple files, you can use wildcards. For example, if you want to move all .txt files from C:\working to D:\backup, you can use

VBScript	JScript

`Set fs = CreateObject`
`  ("Scripting.FileSystemObject")`
`fs.MoveFile "C:\working\*.txt",`
`  "D:\backup"`
	`var fs = new ActiveXObject`
	`  ("Scripting.FileSystemObject");`
	`fs.CopyFile("C:\\working\\*.txt",`
	`  "D:\\backup");`

You can also use `MoveFile` to move files to an existing directory. For example if both C:\working and D:\working exist, you can move all .html files from C:\working to D:\working, such as

VBScript	JScript
`fs.MoveFile "C:\working\*.HTML",` `  "D:\working"`	`fs.MoveFile("C:\\working\\*.HTML",` `  "D:\\working");`

 If you specify the last element of the destination path as a folder separator (\), the `MoveFile` method assumes the destination folder exists and will not create it if necessary. Also, the move operation will not overwrite existing files. In this case, the move fails the first time it tries to overwrite.

MANIPULATING INDIVIDUAL FILES

With the `File` object, the methods for copying, moving, and deleting files are

◆ `Delete`

◆ `Copy`

◆ `Move`

You cannot use wildcards when copying, moving, or deleting individual files.

USING DELETE The Delete method of the File object deletes a file and can also force the deletion of a read-only file. This method works with a specific File object reference and as a result, you can delete a file just by calling the method, such as

VBScript	JScript
| ```
Set fs = CreateObject
  ("Scripting.FileSystemObject")
Set f = fs.GetFile
  ("C:\working\data.txt")
f.Delete
``` | ```
var fs = new ActiveXObject
  ("Scripting.FileSystemObject");
var f = fs.GetFile
  ("C:\\working\\data.txt");
f.Delete()
``` |

If the file is read-only, you must set the force flag to True, such as

VBScript	JScript
| ```
f.Delete True
``` | ```
f.Delete("True")
``` |

USING COPY The Copy method copies a file to a new location. With Copy, you must obtain a File object and then set the destination path for the file in the Copy method. For example, you can copy C:\data.txt to D:\working\data.txt as follows:

VBScript	JScript
| ```
Set fs = CreateObject
  ("Scripting.FileSystemObject")
Set f = fs.GetFile("C:\data.txt")
f.Copy "D:\working\data.txt"
``` | ```
var fs = new ActiveXObject
  ("Scripting.FileSystemObject");
var f = fs.GetFile("C:\\data.txt");
f.Copy("D:\\working\\data.txt");
``` |

As with CopyFile, you can also use the Copy method to copy over an existing file. To do this, you must set the overwrite flag to True, such as

VBScript	JScript
| ```
f.Copy "D:\working\data.txt", True
``` | ```
f.Copy("D:\\working\\data.txt",
  "True");
``` |

If you try to overwrite a file and don't set the overwrite flag to True, an error occurs and the copy operation fails.

USING MOVE   Use the Move method to move a file to a new location. Before you use Move, you must first obtain a File object and then you can set the destination path for the file in the Move method. You can move C:\data.txt to D:\work\data.txt as follows:

VBScript	JScript

`Set fs = CreateObject`
`  ("Scripting.FileSystemObject")`
`Set f = fs.GetFile("C:\data.txt")`
`f.Move "D:\work\data.txt "`
	`var fs = new ActiveXObject`
	`  ("Scripting.FileSystemObject");`
	`var f = fs.GetFile("C:\\data.txt");`
	`f.Move("D:\\work\\data.txt");`

You cannot use Move to overwrite an existing file.

Building the File System Administrator Script

The file system administrator script provides a utility library for working with files and folders. Through batch script (.WS) files you can access these utility functions in any of your scripts. The sections that follow show the source for the script as well as how the script can be used.

The File System Script

Listing 10-8 shows the file system administrator script. Because the script is written in JScript, be sure to pass path information in JScript format with double slashes as folder separators.

Listing 10-8: File system utility library

adminlib.js

```
// ************************
// Script: File System Utility Library
```

```
// Version: 0.9.2
// Creation Date: 6/15/99
// Last Modified: 9/1/99
// Author: William R. Stanek
// Email: winscripting@tvpress.com
// ************************
// Description: Provides a utility library for working
//              with files and folders. If called from
//              VBScript, be sure to pass path information
//              with double slashes.
// ************************

function GetSubFolders(folderPath, separator)
{
var fs, f, fc, s;
s = ""
fs = new ActiveXObject ("Scripting.FileSystemObject");
f = fs.GetFolder(folderPath);
  fc = new Enumerator(f.SubFolders);
  for (; !fc.atEnd(); fc.moveNext())
  {
    s += fc.item();
    s += separator
  }
 return(s);
}

function GetFiles(folderPath, separator)
{
var fs, f, fc, s;
s = ""
fs = new ActiveXObject ("Scripting.FileSystemObject");
f = fs.GetFolder(folderPath);
  fc = new Enumerator(f.Files);
  for (; !fc.atEnd(); fc.moveNext())
  {
    s += fc.item();
    s += separator
  }
 return(s);
}

function CheckExists(filePath)
{
```

Continued

```
    var fs, s;
    s = "False"
    fs = new ActiveXObject("Scripting.FileSystemObject");
    if (fs.FolderExists(filePath))
        s = "True";
    else if (fs.FileExists(filePath))
        s = "True";
    return(s);
    }

function GetInfo(filePath)
{
  var fs, f, s;
  fs = new ActiveXObject("Scripting.FileSystemObject");
  if (fs.FolderExists(filePath))
    f = fs.GetFolder(filePath);
  else if (fs.FileExists(filePath))
    f = fs.GetFile(filePath);

  s = "Name: " + f.Name + "\r\n";
  s += "Path: " + f.Path + "\r\n";
  s += "Date Created: " + f.DateCreated + "\r\n";
  s += "Date Last Accessed: " + f.DateLastAccessed + "\r\n";
  s += "Date Last Modified: " + f.DateLastModified;
  return(s);
}

function GetSize(filePath)
{
    var fs, f, s;
    fs = new ActiveXObject("Scripting.FileSystemObject");
    f = fs.GetFolder(filePath);
if (fs.FolderExists(filePath))
    f = fs.GetFolder(filePath);
  else if (fs.FileExists(filePath))
    f = fs.GetFile(filePath);
  s = f.size;
  return(s);
}

function GetType(filePath)
{
    var fs, f, s;
    fs = new ActiveXObject("Scripting.FileSystemObject");
    f = fs.GetFolder(filePath);
```

```
if (fs.FolderExists(filePath))
    f = fs.GetFolder(filePath);
  else if (fs.FileExists(filePath))
    f = fs.GetFile(filePath);
  s = f.type;
  return(s);
}

function CheckParentFolder(filePath)
{
 var fs, s = "";
 fs = new ActiveXObject("Scripting.FileSystemObject");
 s += fs.GetParentFolderName(filePath);
 return(s);
}

function SetArchiveAttribute(folderName)
{
  var fs, f, fc, s;
  fs = new ActiveXObject("Scripting.FileSystemObject");
  f = fs.GetFolder(folderName);
  fc = new Enumerator(f.Files);
  s = "";
  for (; !fc.atEnd(); fc.moveNext())
  {
    theFile = fs.GetFile(fc.item());

    if (!(theFile.attributes && 32))
    {
    theFile.attributes = theFile.attributes + 32;
    }


  }
  return("Finished!");
}

function ClearArchiveAttribute(folderName)
{
  var fs, f, fc, s;
  fs = new ActiveXObject("Scripting.FileSystemObject");
  f = fs.GetFolder(folderName);
  fc = new Enumerator(f.Files);
  s = "";
```

Continued

```
  for (; !fc.atEnd(); fc.moveNext())
  {
    theFile = fs.GetFile(fc.item());

    if (theFile.attributes && 32)
   {
    theFile.attributes = theFile.attributes - 32;
   }


  }
  return("Finished!");
}

function SetReadOnly(folderName)
{
  var fs, f, fc, s;
  fs = new ActiveXObject("Scripting.FileSystemObject");
  f = fs.GetFolder(folderName);
  fc = new Enumerator(f.Files);
  s = "";
  for (; !fc.atEnd(); fc.moveNext())
  {
    theFile = fs.GetFile(fc.item());

    if (!(theFile.attributes && 1))
   {
    theFile.attributes = theFile.attributes + 1;
   }


  }
  return("Finished!");
}


function ClearReadOnly(folderName)
{
  var fs, f, fc, s;
  fs = new ActiveXObject("Scripting.FileSystemObject");
  f = fs.GetFolder(folderName);
  fc = new Enumerator(f.Files);
  s = "";
  for (; !fc.atEnd(); fc.moveNext())
  {
```

```
   theFile = fs.GetFile(fc.item());
   if (theFile.attributes && 31)
  {
   theFile.attributes = theFile.attributes - 1;
  }


 }
 return("Finished!");
}

function CopyFile2Desktop(filePath)
{
  var fs, osdir, udir, dpath;
  fs = new ActiveXObject("Scripting.FileSystemObject");
  var WshShell = WScript.CreateObject("WScript.Shell");
  osdir = WshShell.ExpandEnvironmentStrings("%SystemRoot%");
  udir = WshShell.ExpandEnvironmentStrings("%UserName%");

  dpath = osdir + "\\Profiles\\" + udir + "\\Desktop\\"
  fs.CopyFile(filePath, dpath);
  return(dpath)
}

function MoveFile2Desktop(filePath)
{
  var fs, osdir, udir, dpath;
  fs = new ActiveXObject("Scripting.FileSystemObject");
  var WshShell = WScript.CreateObject("WScript.Shell");
  osdir = WshShell.ExpandEnvironmentStrings("%SystemRoot%");
  udir = WshShell.ExpandEnvironmentStrings("%UserName%");

  dpath = osdir + "\\Profiles\\" + udir + "\\Desktop\\"
  fs.MoveFile(filePath, dpath);
  return(dpath)
}

function DeleteFile(filePath)
{
  var fs;
  fs = new ActiveXObject("Scripting.FileSystemObject");
  fs.DeleteFile(filePath);
}

function DeleteFolder(folderPath)
```

Continued

```
{
  var fs;
  fs = new ActiveXObject("Scripting.FileSystemObject");
  fs.DeleteFolder(folderPath);
}
```

The file system utility library has many functions that you can call from other scripts. Most of the functions expect to be passed a folder path, such as

```
D:\\Working
```

or a file path, such as

```
D:\\working\\data.txt
```

A few exceptions, such as GetSubFolders and GetFiles, expect additional parameters.

Using GetSubFolders and GetFiles

The GetSubFolders and GetFiles functions return a list of subfolders or files in the referenced folder. These functions expect to be passed a folder path and a character to display as a separator. This separator can be a space, a comma, or special formatting character, such as \r\n for carriage return and line feed. Here's an example of how you can call GetFiles:

```
theList = GetFiles("C:\\WinnT", "\r\n")
```

If you use a .ws file, you don't have to place the GetFiles function in your script and can instead handle the function like a library call. With a .ws file you can use GetFiles as follows:

```
<Job ID="CreateFolders">
  <Script LANGUAGE="JScript" SRC="adminlib.js" />
  <Script LANGUAGE="JScript">
        theList = GetFiles("C:\\WinnT", "\r\n")
        WScript.Echo(theList)
  </Script>
</Job>
```

Using CheckExists

You can use the CheckExists function to determine if a resource you want to work exists. The function expects to be passed a file or folder path, and returns True if the resource exists and False otherwise. An interesting feature of this function is the `If ... Else If` construct that tests whether the path you've supplied references a folder of a file:

```
if (fs.FolderExists(filePath))
    s = "True";
else if (fs.FileExists(filePath))
    s = "True";
```

Here, you test for the existence of the file path as a folder and as a file. The `If ... Else If` construct allows a single function to work with files and folders, and it is used by many other functions in the system utility library, including `GetInfo`, `GetSize`, and `GetType`.

Using GetInfo, GetSize, and GetType

The `GetInfo` function expects to be passed a file or folder path and returns summary information for the file or folder. This information is placed on separate lines using \r\n and includes

◆ File or folder name

◆ File or folder path

◆ Date created

◆ Date last accessed

◆ Date last modified

The `GetSize` and `GetType` functions also return file or folder information. `GetSize` returns the byte size of the file or folder. `GetType` returns the file or folder type. A similar function is `CheckParentFolder`. This function returns the name of the parent folder for the specified resource.

Setting and Clearing File Attributes

The system utility library also has functions for working with file attributes. These functions are

◆ `SetReadOnly` — Sets the read-only attribute on all files in the folder.

◆ `ClearReadOnly` — Clears the read-only attribute on all files in the folder.

◆ `SetArchiveAttribute` — Sets the archive attribute on all files in the folder.

◆ `ClearArchiveAttribute` — Clears the archive attribute on all files in the folder.

These functions set the attributes on all files in a referenced folder but do not go through subfolders. Keep in mind that you can't change the archive attribute on read-only files. Because of this, you may want to call `ClearReadOnly` before calling `SetArchiveAttribute` or `ClearArchiveAttribute`.

You can set the read-only attribute on all files in the D:\working folder as follows:

```
SetReadOnly("D:\\Working")
```

If you use a .ws file, you don't have to place the `SetReadOnly` function in your script and can instead handle the function like a library call, such as

```
<Job ID="CreateFolders">
  <Script LANGUAGE="JScript" SRC="adminlib.js" />
  <Script LANGUAGE="JScript">
          ret = SetReadOnly("D:\\Working")
          WScript.Echo(ret)
  </Script>
</Job>
```

The set and clear functions use an `Enumerator` object to move through each file in the referenced folder. To obtain a file object, the function calls `GetFile` with the name of the current item in the enumerator list. The `file` object is then used to set or clear the appropriate attribute, such as

```
theFile = fs.GetFile(fc.item());
if (theFile.attributes && 32)
 {
    theFile.attributes = theFile.attributes - 32;
 }
```

Copying and Moving Files to the Desktop

Two other utility functions are `CopyFile2Desktop` and `MoveFile2Desktop` functions. These functions expect to be passed a file path and then either copy or move the file to the Windows desktop. The location of the desktop is determined using the environment variables `SystemRoot` and `UserName`, such as

```
osdir = WshShell.ExpandEnvironmentStrings("%SystemRoot%");
udir = WshShell.ExpandEnvironmentStrings("%UserName%");
```

The environment strings are then added to the `dpath` variable to build the complete path to the desktop:

```
dpath = osdir + "\\Profiles\\" + udir + "\\Desktop\\"
```

The result is a system- and user-specific desktop path, such as

```
D:\\WinNT\\Profiles\\WStanek\\Desktop\\
```

You can move a file to the desktop as follows:

```
MoveFile2Desktop("D:\\Working\\Data.txt")
```

 These functions are designed to work for Windows NT, and you'll need to tailor them for other Windows operating systems as necessary.

Using DeleteFile and DeleteFolder

The DeleteFile and DeleteFolder functions are used to delete files and folders respectively. You can use wildcards when calling these functions, such as

```
DeleteFile("D:\\working\\*.txt")
```

 Be careful when using the delete functions. Never pass a reference to a root folder, such as C:\.

Summary

As you've seen in this chapter, Windows scripts can work with folders and files in many different ways. You can create new files and folders. You can also move, copy, and delete files and folders. You can even view file and folder attributes. As you'll learn in the next chapter, you can build on these core administration techniques to perform more advanced file manipulation and management.

Chapter 11

Reading and Writing Files

IN THIS CHAPTER

◆ Opening text streams

◆ Reading text files

◆ Skipping lines in files

◆ Writing to files

◆ Building a file utility library

NOW THAT YOU KNOW the basics of file administration, you can move on to more advanced concepts, like reading and writing files. Windows scripts can read from and write to files provided the files are formatted with ASCII or Unicode text. ASCII formatted files include standard text, HTML, XML, and script files. You work with text files via the TextStream object, which you can obtain by creating a new file or opening an existing file. The TextStream object has many properties and methods for working with files. When you are finished with the file, closing it writes the end of file marker and closes the text stream.

Opening a Text Stream

Two methods are provided for opening files. You can use the OpenTextFile method of FileSystemObject or the OpenAsTextStream method of the File object. While both methods return a TextStream object, they are used in slightly different ways.

Working with OpenTextFile

The OpenTextFile method expects to be passed the full path to the file you want to open, such as

VBScript	JScript

Set fs = CreateObject
  ("Scripting.FileSystemObject")
Set ts = fs.OpenTextFile
  ("D:\working\data.txt")
	var fs = new ActiveXObject
	  ("Scripting.FileSystemObject");
	var ts = fs.OpenTextFile
	  ("D:\\working\\data.txt")

If you plan to work with the file, you should set the access mode as well. Three access modes are provided:

♦ 1 – Opens a file for reading. Associated constant is `ForReading`.

♦ 2 – Opens for writing to the beginning of the file. Associated constant is `ForWriting`.

♦ 8 – Opens for appending (writing to the end of the file). Associated constant is `ForAppending`.

As you can see, the access modes are designed for specific tasks, such as reading, writing, or appending. You must use the appropriate mode for the task you want to perform and then close the file before performing a different task. For example, if you want to write to a file, you must open it in `ForWriting` mode. Later if you want to read from the file, you must close the file and then open it in `ForReading` mode.

Beyond access modes, you can also specify that you want to create the referenced file if it doesn't already exist and set the file's format mode. To create a file if it doesn't already exist, set the create flag to `True`. Otherwise, the file isn't created and an error may occur. To set a file's format mode, use one of these values:

♦ -2 – Opens the file using the system default. Associated constant is `TristateUseDefault`.

♦ -1 – Opens the file as Unicode. Associated constant is `TristateTrue`.

♦ 0 – Opens the file as ASCII. Associated constant is `TristateFalse`.

Listing 11-1 opens a file in `ForWriting` mode. If the file doesn't exist, it is created automatically, which is handy, as you don't have to test for the file with `FileExists`. The file is also set to ASCII text mode, which is the default mode on most systems. The listing also creates an extensive set of constants for working with files. Use constants when you want your scripts to be easy to read.

Listing 11-1: Using OpenTextFile

VBScript	JScript
openfile.vbs	openfile.js
```Const ForReading = 1```	```ForReading = 1```
```Const ForWriting = 2```	```ForWriting = 2```
```Const ForAppending = 8```	```ForAppending = 8```
```Const TristateUseDefault = -2```	```TristateUseDefault = -2```
```Const TristateTrue = -1```	```TristateTrue = -1```
```Const TristateFalse = 0```	```TristateFalse = 0```

```
Set fs = CreateObject                  var fs = new ActiveXObject
  ("Scripting.FileSystemObject")         ("Scripting.FileSystemObject");
Set ts = fs.OpenTextFile               var ts = fs.OpenTextFile
  ("D:\working\data.txt", ForWriting,    ("D:\\working\\data.txt",
  True, TristateFalse)                   ForWriting, "True", TristateFalse)
```

Working with OpenAsTextStream

The OpenAsTextStream method is used much like OpenTextFile. The key differences are that you already have a file reference, so you don't have to set a file path, and you cannot set a create flag. Other than that, the methods are identical. Listing 11-2 shows how you can open an ASCII text file in ForReading mode.

Listing 11-2: Using OpenAsTextStream

VBScript	JScript
openstream.vbs	**openstream.js**

```
Const ForReading = 1                   ForReading = 1
Const TristateFalse = 0                TristateFalse = 0

Set fs = CreateObject                  var fs = new ActiveXObject
  ("Scripting.FileSystemObject")         ("Scripting.FileSystemObject");
Set f = fs.GetFile                     var f = fs.GetFile
  ("C:\working\data.txt")                ("C:\\working\\data.txt");
Set ts = f.OpenAsTextStream            var ts = f.OpenAsTextStream
  (ForReading, TristateFalse)            (ForReading, TristateFalse)
```

Reading Text Files

You can read from a text file only when you open it in the ForReading access mode. Once you open the file for reading, you can read information for the file in several different ways. You can read the entire contents of the file, character strings from the file, or you can read lines of information from the file.

Getting Ready to Read

Just because you can open a file doesn't mean it contains any information. Therefore, before you try to read the file, you should verify that it contains information. To do this, you can use the AtEndOfStream property of the TextStream object. The AtEndOfStream property returns True when you are at the end of a file and False otherwise. If the file exists but is empty, the AtEndOfStream property returns True immediately after you open the file.

You should also use the `AtEndOfStream` property to test for the end of file marker prior to reading additional information from a file. If you've reached the end of the file, you don't want to try to read. One way to test for an empty file and to check for the end of file marker prior to reading is to use a `Do While` loop as shown in Listing 11-3. Here, you check for the end of file prior to reading, which covers the case of an empty file and the case where the end of file marker has been reached.

Listing 11–3: Using AtEndOfStream

VBScript	JScript
eostest.vbs	**Eostest.js**

```
Const ForReading = 1
Const TristateFalse = 0

Set fs = CreateObject
  ("Scripting.FileSystemObject")
Set f = fs.GetFile
  ("C:\working\data.txt")
Set ts = f.OpenAsTextStream
  (ForReading, TristateFalse)
Do While theFile.AtEndOfStream <> True
'Read from the file
Loop
```

```
ForReading = 1
TristateFalse = 0

var fs = new ActiveXObject
  ("Scripting.FileSystemObject");
var f = fs.GetFile
  ("C:\\working\\data.txt");
var ts = f.OpenAsTextStream
  (ForReading, TristateFalse)
while (!f.AtEndOfStream) {
//Read from the file
}
```

Another helpful property is `AtEndOfLine`, which returns `True` if you reach an end of line marker. This property is useful if you are reading characters from files that have lines of variable length. Here, you read from the file until the end of line is reached, at which point you know you've reached the end of a field or record. An example using `AtEndOfLine` is shown here:

VBScript	JScript

```
Do While theFile.AtEndOfLine <> True
'Read characters from the file
Loop
```

```
while (!f.AtEndOfLine) {
//Read characters from the file
}
```

Your window into text files is gained through column and line pointers. The column pointer indicates the current column position within a file. The line pointer indicates the current line position within a file. To check the value of these pointers, use the `Column` and `Line` properties of the `TextStream` object respectively.

After opening a file, the column and line pointers are both set to 1. This means you are at column 1, line 1. If you then read in a line from the file, you are at column 1, line 2. If you read 10 characters from a file without advancing to the next line, you are at column 11, line 1. Being able to check the column and line position is very useful when you work with fixed-length records or want to examine specific lines of data.

Listing 11-4 shows how you can check the column and line position at various stages of reading a file. You'll find more pointers for using these properties later in the chapter.

Listing 11-4: Using the column and line properties

VBScript	JScript

fposition.vbs

```
Const ForReading = 1
Const TristateFalse = 0

Set fs = CreateObject
("Scripting.FileSystemObject")
Set f = fs.GetFile
("C:\working\data.txt")
Set ts = f.OpenAsTextStream
(ForReading, TristateFalse)
currColumn = f.Column
currLine = f.Line

WScript.Echo "Position is: Column " &
currColumn & " Line " & currLine
```

fposition.js

```
ForReading = 1
TristateFalse = 0

var fs = new ActiveXObject
("Scripting.FileSystemObject");
var f = fs.GetFile
("C:\\working\\data.txt");
var ts = f.OpenAsTextStream
(ForReading, TristateFalse)
currColumn = f.Column
currLine = f.Line

WScript.Echo("Position is: Column " +
currColumn + " Line " + currLine)
```

Reading from a File

You can read from a file using any of these methods:

- Read(*x*) — Reads *x* number of characters from a file.

- ReadLine — Reads a line of text from a file.

- ReadAll — Reads the entire contents of a file.

Whether you read a file all at once, a few characters at a time, or line by line depends on the type of information the file contains. If the file contains fixed-length records or is written as a single line of data, you may want to use Read or ReadAll. If the file contains lines of data and each line ends with an end-of-line marker, you may want to use ReadLine or ReadAll.

USING READ

Use the Read method to read a specific number of characters from a file. The read begins at the current column position and continues until the number of characters specified is reached. Because you want to maintain the information returned from Read, assign the return value to a variable. You can open a file and read 20 characters from it as shown in Listing 11-5.

Listing 11-5: Reading characters from a file

VBScript	JScript
readchar.vbs	**readchar.js**

```
Const ForReading = 1
Const TristateFalse = 0

Set fs = CreateObject
  ("Scripting.FileSystemObject")
Set f = fs.OpenTextFile
  ("C:\working\data.txt",
  ForReading, True)
returnValue = f.Read(20)
```

```
ForReading = 1
TristateFalse = 0

var fs = new ActiveXObject
  ("Scripting.FileSystemObject");
var f = fs.OpenTextFile
  ("C:\\working\\data.txt",
  ForReading, "True")
returnValue = f.Read(20)
```

The Read method doesn't stop at an end-of-line marker and instead reads the individual characters that make up this marker as 1 or 2 characters — either carriage return or carriage return and linefeed. To have the read stop when the end of line is reached, you should read one character at a time and test for the end of line before each successive read. For example:

VBScript	JScript

```
Do While theFile.AtEndOfLine <> True
val = val + theFile.Read(1)
Loop
```

```
while (!theFile.AtEndOfLine)  {
val += theFile.Read(1);
}
```

USING READLINE

For files written using lines, you can use the ReadLine method to read a line from the file. As with the Read method, you store the value returned by the ReadLine method in a variable so you can use the results. An example is shown as Listing 11-6.

When you read files written to with lines, you normally use ReadLine rather than Read. If, however, you read the first 20 characters in a line without reaching the end-of-line designator and then issue a ReadLine command, the ReadLine method will read from the current pointer position to the end of the current line.

Listing 11-6: Using ReadLine

VBScript	JScript
readln.vbs	**readln.js**

```
Const ForReading = 1
Const TristateFalse = 0


Set fs = CreateObject
("Scripting.FileSystemObject")
Set f = fs.OpenTextFile
 ("C:\working\data.txt",
 ForReading, True)
theLine = f.ReadLine
```

```
ForReading = 1
TristateFalse = 0


var fs = new ActiveXObject
("Scripting.FileSystemObject");
var f = fs.OpenTextFile
 ("C:\\working\\data.txt",
 ForReading, "True")
theLine = f.ReadLine()
```

Unless you know that each line of a file has a fixed-length, you probably won't use the `Column` pointer in conjunction with the `ReadLine` method. Instead, you'll use the individual lines of data to move around within the file. Let's say you want to extract data from a file five lines at a time. To do this, you can open the file for reading and then use a loop to advance through the file as shown in Listing 11-7.

Listing 11-7: Reading data sets with ReadLine

VBScript	JScript
readdata.vbs	**readdata.js**

```
Const TristateFalse = 0
count = 5
dataSet = 0

Set fs = CreateObject
  ("Scripting.FileSystemObject")
Set f = fs.OpenTextFile
  ("D:\data.txt", ForReading, True)
Do While f.AtEndOfStream <> True
  data = ""
  For a = 1 to count
   If f.AtEndOfStream <> True Then
    data = data + f.ReadLine
   End If
  Next
  dataSet = dataSet + 1
  WScript.Echo "Data Set " & dataSet
    & ": " & data
Loop
```

```
TristateFalse = 0
count = 5
dataSet = 0

var fs = new ActiveXObject
  ("Scripting.FileSystemObject");
var f = fs.OpenTextFile
  ("D:\\data.txt", ForReading, "True")
while (!f.AtEndOfStream) {
  var data = ""
  for (a = 0; a < count; a++) {
   if (!f.AtEndOfStream) {
    data += f.ReadLine()
   }
  }
  dataSet++
  WScript.Echo("Data Set " + dataSet
    + ": " + data)
}
```

USING READALL

The ReadAll method reads the entire contents of a file and is useful if you want to manipulate the file contents all at once or display the contents to a user. Listing 11-8 shows how you can read the contents of a file and display the results in a pop-up dialog box.

Listing 11-8: Using ReadAll

VBScript	JScript
readfile.vbs	**readfile.js**

```
Const ForReading = 1

Set fs = CreateObject
  ("Scripting.FileSystemObject")
Set f = fs.OpenTextFile
  ("D:\data.txt", ForReading, True)
fContents = f.ReadAll
f.Close

Set w = WScript.CreateObject
  ("WScript.Shell")
a = w.Popup (fContents,60,
  "Display File",1)
```

```
ForReading = 1

var fs = new ActiveXObject
  ("Scripting.FileSystemObject");
var f = fs.OpenTextFile
  ("D:\\data.txt", ForReading, "True")
fContents = f.ReadAll()
f.Close()

var w = WScript.CreateObject
  ("WScript.Shell");
a = w.Popup (fContents,60,
  "Display File",1)
```

Skipping Lines in a File

Skipping characters and lines are common tasks you'll want to perform when you read from a file. To do this, you can use these methods:

◆ Skip(x) – Skips *x* number of characters.

◆ SkipLine – Skips one line of text.

You cannot skip characters in a file you open for writing or appending. With the ForWriting mode, the file is initialized and any existing contents are deleted. With ForAppending mode, the file pointer is set to the end of the file, so no characters are skipped.

Using Skip

In a file you are reading, you set the number of characters to skip when you call the Skip method. In Listing 11-9, you skip the first 30 characters and then read the next 30 characters.

Listing 11-9: Working with Skip

VBScript	JScript
skipchar.vbs	**skipchar.js**

```
Const ForReading = 1
```

```
ForReading = 1
```

```
Set fs = CreateObject
  ("Scripting.FileSystemObject")
Set f = fs.OpenTextFile
  ("D:\data.txt", ForReading, True)
f.Skip(30)
record = f.Read(30)
```

```
var fs = new ActiveXObject
  ("Scripting.FileSystemObject");
var f = fs.OpenTextFile
  ("D:\\data.txt", ForReading, "True")
f.Skip(30)
record = f.Read(30)
```

Using SkipLine

The SkipLine method is also pretty straightforward. Each time you call the method, it skips one line in a file. It does this by looking for the next occurrence of the end-of-line designator. If you know the first three lines of a file have comments that you don't want to use in a data set, you can skip them as follows:

The SkipLine method looks for the end-of-line designator to determine when it has reached the end of a line. So if you call the method after reading part of a line with the Read method but before reaching the end of the line, SkipLine will find the end-of-line designator for the current line and then set the pointer to the beginning of the next line.

VBScript	JScript

```
For a = 1 to 3
  If f.AtEndOfStream <> True Then
    f.SkipLine
  End If
Next
```

```
for (a = 0; a < 3; a++) {
  if (!f.AtEndOfStream) {
    f.SkipLine()
  }
}
```

Writing to a File

You can write to text files using the ForWriting and the ForAppending modes. The access mode determines the initial position of the pointer within the file. With ForWriting mode, the file is initialized, erasing any existing data. The pointer is then set at the beginning of the file. With ForAppending mode, the pointer is set to the end of the file and any data you write adds to the existing data in the file.

Getting Ready to Write

While you may want to overwrite temporary data files, you probably don't want to inadvertently overwrite other types of files. If you have any doubts about whether a file exists, you should use the FileExists method to check for the file before trying to access it in write mode. The FileExists method returns True if the file exists and False if it does not exist. As shown in Listing 11-10, you can use the results of the FileExists test to determine whether you should open a file in ForWriting mode or ForAppending mode.

Listing 11-10: Setting mode based on FileExists

VBScript	JScript
fmode.vbs	**fmode.js**

```
Const ForWriting = 2
Const ForAppending = 8

aFile = "C:\data.txt"
Set fs = CreateObject
  ("Scripting.FileSystemObject")
If (fs.FileExists(aFile)) Then
  Set f = fs.OpenTextFile
    (aFile, ForAppending)
Else
  Set f = fs.OpenTextFile
    (aFile, ForWriting, True)
End If
```

```
ForWriting = 2
ForAppending = 8

aFile = "C:\\data.txt"
var fs = new ActiveXObject
  ("Scripting.FileSystemObject");
if (fs.FileExists(aFile))
  var f = fs.OpenTextFile
    (aFile, ForAppending)
else
  var f = fs.OpenTextFile
    (aFile, ForWriting, "True")
```

When you are finished writing to a file, you should close the file by calling the Close method. This writes the end-of-file marker to the file and releases the file. You are then free to open the file in a different mode, such as ForReading. You can close a file as follows:

VBScript	JScript
f.Close	f.Close()

Closing a file after a write is essential. If you forget to do this, the end-of-file marker may not be written to the file.

Writing to Files

Writing to a new file or appending data to the end of an existing file is fairly easy. You start by obtaining a `TextStream` object. Afterward, you open the file for writing or appending, then write to the file. Regardless of which write-related method you use, the write begins at the pointer position set when the file was opened (which is either the beginning or end of the file). You can write to a file using any of these methods:

- ◆ `Write(x)` – Writes *x* number of characters to a file.

- ◆ `WriteLine` – Writes a line of text to a file.

- ◆ `WriteBlankLines(n)` – Writes *n* blank lines to a file.

USING WRITE

The `Write` method writes strings to a file. You can set the string to write when you call the function, such as

VBScript	JScript
| ```
Set fs = CreateObject
  ("Scripting.FileSystemObject")
Set f = fs.OpenTextFile
  (aFile, ForAppending)
f.Write theData
f.Close
``` | ```
var fs = new ActiveXObject
  ("Scripting.FileSystemObject");
var f = fs.OpenTextFile
  (aFile, ForAppending)
f.Write(theData)
f.Close()
``` |

USING THE WRITELINE METHOD

The `WriteLine` method is used to write lines of data to a file. The run-time engine terminates lines with an end-of-line marker (the carriage return and line feed characters). You can use the `WriteLine` method as follows:

VBScript	JScript
| ```
Set fs = CreateObject
  ("Scripting.FileSystemObject")
Set f = fs.OpenTextFile
  (aFile, ForAppending)
f.WriteLine theLine
f.Close
``` | ```
var fs = new ActiveXObject
  ("Scripting.FileSystemObject");
var f = fs.OpenTextFile
  (aFile, ForAppending)
f.WriteLine(theLine)
f.Close()
``` |

USING THE WRITEBLANKLINES METHOD

The `WriteBlankLines` method is used to write empty lines to a file. The only contents on a blank line are end-of-line markers (the carriage return and line feed characters). When you call the `WriteBlankLines` method, you set the number of blank lines to add to the file, such as 3 or 5.

Normally, you'll use this method in conjunction with `WriteLine`, such as

VBScript	JScript
Set fs = CreateObject ("Scripting.FileSystemObject") Set f = fs.OpenTextFile (aFile, ForAppending) f.WriteLine theHeaderLine f.WriteBlankLines 1 f.WriteLine theDataLine f.WriteBlankLines 1 f.WriteLine theFooterLine	var fs = new ActiveXObject ("Scripting.FileSystemObject"); var f = fs.OpenTextFile (aFile, ForAppending) f.WriteLine(theHeaderLine) f.WriteBlankLines(1) f.WriteLine(theDataLine) f.WriteBlankLines(1) f.WriteLine(theFooterLine)

Building the File Utility Library

The file utility library provides essential functions for reading and writing text files. Through batch script (.WS) files you can access these utility functions in any of your scripts.

Listing 11-11: File System Utility Library

filelib.js

```
// ************************
// Script: File Utility Library
// Version: 0.9.3
// Creation Date: 6/20/99
// Last Modified: 9/1/99
// Author: William R. Stanek
// Email: winscripting@tvpress.com
// ************************
// Description: Provides a utility library for reading
//              and writing files. If called from
//              VBScript, be sure to pass path information
//              with double slashes.
// ************************


function ReadFile(theFile)
{
```

```
  var fs, f, r;
  var ForReading = 1;
  fs = new ActiveXObject("Scripting.FileSystemObject");
  f = fs.OpenTextFile(theFile, ForReading);
  r = f.ReadAll();
  return(r);
}

function ReadLineN(theFile,n)
{
  var fs, f, r;
  var ForReading = 1;
  n--
  fs = new ActiveXObject("Scripting.FileSystemObject");
  f = fs.OpenTextFile(theFile, ForReading);
  for (a = 0; a < n; a++) {
   if (!f.AtEndOfStream) {
    f.SkipLine()
    }
   }
  r =  f.ReadLine();
  return(r);
}

function ReadCharN(theFile,s,n)
{
  var fs, f, r;
  var ForReading = 1;
  fs = new ActiveXObject("Scripting.FileSystemObject");
  f = fs.OpenTextFile(theFile, ForReading);
  f.Skip(s);
  r =  f.Read(n);
  return(r);
}

function WriteLine(theFile,theLine)
{
  var fs, f;
  var ForWriting = 2, ForAppending = 8;
  fs = new ActiveXObject("Scripting.FileSystemObject")

  if (fs.FileExists(theFile))
   var f = fs.OpenTextFile (theFile, ForAppending)
```

```
                                                                    else
    var f = fs.OpenTextFile (theFile, ForWriting, "True")

    f.WriteLine(theLine);
    f.Close();
}

function WriteChar(theFile,theString)
{
  var fs, f;
  var ForWriting = 2, ForAppending = 8;
  fs = new ActiveXObject("Scripting.FileSystemObject")

  if (fs.FileExists(theFile))
   var f = fs.OpenTextFile (theFile, ForAppending)
  else
   var f = fs.OpenTextFile (theFile, ForWriting, "True")

  f.Write(theString);
  f.Close();
}
```

The file utility library provides functions for reading and writing text files. These text files are assumed to be in the default format for the system, which is normally ASCII text. Most of the functions expect to be passed a file path, such as

```
D:\\working\\data.txt
```

One of the most basic utility functions is `ReadFile`. This function reads an entire file and returns the contents for you to work with. You can use `ReadFile` to display the contents of a file in a pop-up dialog as follows:

```
var w = WScript.CreateObject("WScript.Shell");
w.Popup (ReadFile("D:\\data.txt"))
```

If you use a .ws file, you don't have to place the `ReadFile` function in your script and can instead handle the function like a library call. With a .ws file you can use `ReadFile` as follows:

```
<Job ID="CreateFolders">
  <Script LANGUAGE="JScript" SRC="filelib.js" />
  <Script LANGUAGE="JScript">
          theFile = ReadFile("D:\\data.txt")
          WScript.Echo(theFile)
```

```
</Script>
</Job>
```

Other functions in the library can be used in similar ways as well. You can use the ReadLineN function to read a specific line in a file, such as the eighth line. If you wanted to read the eighth line in the file, you pass in the file name and then the integer value 8, such as

```
theLine = ReadLineN("D:\\data.txt",8)
```

The ReadLineN function skips seven lines in the file and then reads the eighth line. The contents of this line are then returned. To read the first line in the file, you can pass in 1 as the line parameter, such as

```
theLine = ReadLineN("D:\\data.txt",1)
```

 Keep in mind that you cannot try to read a line that doesn't exist. For example, if the file contains 10 lines, you can't try to read the fifteenth line. If you do, no value is returned.

The ReadCharN function is used to read a specific group of characters in a file. For example, if you know that the file contains fixed-length records with each record having 80 characters, you can read in the third record by telling ReadCharN to skip 160 characters and then read 80 characters, such as

```
theRecord = ReadLineN("D:\\data.txt",160,80)
```

The file utility library also provides functions for writing to files. The WriteLine function writes a line to a file. The WriteChar function writes a block of characters to a file. You can use these functions to write to new files or to append to existing files. To ensure that existing files are appended rather then overwritten, the functions make use of the following If Else construct discussed in Chapter 10:

```
if (fs.FileExists(theFile))
    var f = fs.OpenTextFile (theFile, ForAppending)
else
    var f = fs.OpenTextFile (theFile, ForWriting, "True")
```

Again, this conditional test checks for a file's existence. If the file exists, the file is opened in ForAppending mode. Otherwise, the file is opened in ForWriting mode. You can use the WriteLine function as follows:

```
theFile = "D:\\data.txt"
theLine = "William Stanek, wrstane, wrs@tvpress.com, x7789"
WriteLine(theFile,theLine)
```

In a .ws file you can use WriteLine in much the same way:

```
<Job ID="CreateFolders">
  <Script LANGUAGE="JScript" SRC="filelib.js" />
  <Script LANGUAGE="JScript">
    theFile = "D:\\data.txt"
    theLine = "William Stanek, wrstane, wrs@tvpress.com, x7789"
    WriteLine(theFile,theLine)
  </Script>
</Job>
```

Summary

Windows scripts often need to read and write files, and you can use the techniques discussed in this chapter to help you accomplish just about any related task. ASCII formatted text files are the most common file format that you'll want to read and write. Many different types of files are formatted as ASCII text, including HTML files, XML, scripts files, and standard text files.

Chapter 12

Network and System Resource Management

IN THIS CHAPTER

◆ Working with drives

◆ Mapping network drives

◆ Managing network printers

◆ Configuring menus and startup applications

◆ Creating shortcuts

◆ Working with the Windows Registry

◆ Building a network resource administration library

IN THIS CHAPTER, YOU learn how to manage network and system resources. Network resource management involves working with shared resources, such as drives and printers. With drives, you can examine drive information and share network drives. With printers, you can set default printers and add or remove network printer connections. System resource management tasks include configuring menus, the desktop, and startup applications. The chapter also looks at working with the Windows Registry. Registry settings control system configuration options.

Managing Local and Network Drives

Two different ways of working with drives are available. You can work with a specific drive, such as the C: drive, or you can work with drive collections. Drive collections are containers for all the local and network drives on a particular system.

Working with Drives

Most functions that work with drives allow you to reference drive paths in any of the following ways:

♦ By drive letter, such as C or D

♦ By drive path, such as C:\ or D:\

♦ By network share path, such as \\ZETA\MYSHARE or \\OMEGA\DATA

Most network drives have a drive designator associated with them as well as a path. For example, the network drive \\ZETA\MYSHARE may be mapped on the system as the H: drive. You can obtain a drive designator for a network drive using the GetDriveName method of FileSystemObject. This method expects to be passed a drive path and can be used as follows:

VBScript	JScript
| ```
Set fs = CreateObject
  ("Scripting.FileSystemObject")
drv = fs.GetDriveName ("\\ZETA\DATA")
WScript.Echo drv
``` | ```
fs = new ActiveXObject
  ("Scripting.FileSystemObject");
drv = fs.GetDriveName("\\ZETA\\DATA")
WScript.Echo (drv)
``` |

Checking for a Drive

You'll usually want to test for a drive's existence before you try to work with it. To do this, you can use the DriveExists method of FileSystemObject. This method returns True if a drive exists and can be used as shown in Listing 12-1.

Listing 12-1: Checking for a drive

VBScript	JScript
checkdrive.vbs	**checkdrive.js**
| ```
WScript.Echo (CheckDrive("C"))
Function CheckDrive(drv)

Dim fs, s
  Set fs = CreateObject
    ("Scripting.FileSystemObject")
  If (fs.DriveExists(drv)) Then
    s = drv & " is available."
  Else
    s = drv & " doesn't exist."
  End If
 CheckDrive = s
End Function
``` | ```
WScript.Echo (CheckDrive("C"))
function CheckDrive(drv)
{
var fs, s = drv;
fs = new ActiveXObject
  ("Scripting.FileSystemObject");
  if (fs.DriveExists(drv))
    s += " is available.";
  else
    s += " doesn't exist.";

  return(s);
}
``` |
| **Output** | **Output** |
| C is available. | C is available. |

Using a Drive Object

After checking for a drive's existence, one of the most common tasks you'll want to perform is to obtain a Drive object. You can then use this object to check drive properties.

To obtain a Drive object, use the GetDrive method of FileSystemObject. The main argument for this method is a string containing the path to the drive you want to work with, such as

VBScript	JScript
Set fs = CreateObject ("Scripting.FileSystemObject") Set drv = fs.GetDrive("D")	var fs = new ActiveXObject ("Scripting.FileSystemObject"); var drv = fs.GetDrive("D")

Once you have a Drive object, you can examine its properties. To do this, you use the Drive object properties summarized in Table 12-1.

TABLE 12-1 PROPERTIES OF THE DRIVE OBJECT

Property	Description	Sample Value
AvailableSpace	Returns the amount of available space on the drive in bytes. This is a per-user value that can be affected by quotas.	54549493
DriveLetter	Returns the drive letter without a colon.	D
DriveType	Returns the drive type as an integer value. 0 for Unknown, 1 for Removable, 2 for Fixed, 3 for Network, 4 for CD-ROM, and 5 for RAM Disk.	2
FileSystem	Returns the file system type such as FAT, NFTS, and CDFS.	NTFS
FreeSpace	Returns the total amount of free space on the drive.	54549493
IsReady	For removable-media drives and CD-ROM drives, returns True if the drive is ready.	True
Path	Returns the drive path.	C:\
RootFolder	Returns a Folder object containing the root folder on the specified drive.	-

Continued

TABLE **12-1 PROPERTIES OF THE DRIVE OBJECT** (*Continued*)

Property	Description	Sample Value
SerialNumber	With removable media, returns the serial number of the media.	329941809
ShareName	With network drives, returns the network share name.	work
TotalSize	Returns the total size of the drive in bytes.	89766222212
VolumeName	Returns the volume name of the drive.	Primary

One of the most useful drive properties is FreeSpace. You can use this property to help you keep track of system resources throughout the network. For example, you can create a script that runs as a periodically scheduled job on your key servers, such as your e-mail and file servers. When the script runs, it can log the free space on key drives on the system. If any of the drives has less free space than is desirable, you can log a warning that the drive is getting low on space as well.

TIP Because the DriveInfo.js script may run through the AT scheduler, you'll need to map to the network drives you want to use. Mapping network drives is covered later in the chapter.

Listing 12-2 shows an example script for displaying drive information. You can use this script to obtain summary information for drives. If you extend the script to use a Drive collection, you can obtain a report for all drives on a system.

Listing 12-2: Obtaining drive information

driveinfo.js

```
drvpath = "C"
WScript.Echo(GetDriveInfo(drvpath))

function GetDriveInfo(drvpath)
{
  var fs, d, s, t, wnet, cname;

  wNet = WScript.CreateObject ("WScript.Network");
  cname = wNet.ComputerName;
```

```
fs = new ActiveXObject("Scripting.FileSystemObject");
d = fs.GetDrive(drvpath);
switch (d.DriveType)
{
  case 0: t = "Unknown"; break;
  case 1: t = "Removable"; break;
  case 2: t = "Fixed"; break;
  case 3: t = "Network"; break;
  case 4: t = "CD-ROM"; break;
  case 5: t = "RAM Disk"; break;
}
s = "=========================" + "\r\n";
s += cname + "\r\n";
s += "=========================" + "\r\n";
s += "Drive " + d.DriveLetter + ": - " + t;
s += " - " + d.FileSystem + "\r\n";
if (d.VolumeName)
 s += "Volume: " + d.VolumeName + "\r\n"
if (d.ShareName)
 s += " Share: " + d.ShareName + "\r\n"
s += "Total space " + Math.round(d.TotalSize/1048576)
s += " Mbytes" + "\r\n";
s += "Free Space: " + Math.round(d.FreeSpace/1048576)
s += " Mbytes" + "\r\n";
s += "=========================" + "\r\n";
return(s);
}
```

Output

```
=========================

ZETA

=========================

Drive C: - Fixed - FAT

Volume: Primary

Total space 2047 Mbytes

Free Space: 557 Mbytes

=========================
```

The drive information script uses a few new techniques. First of all, a Switch Case structure is used to convert the integer value returned by DriveType to a string:

```
switch (d.DriveType)
  {
```

```
case 0: t = "Unknown"; break;
case 1: t = "Removable"; break;
case 2: t = "Fixed"; break;
case 3: t = "Network"; break;
case 4: t = "CD-ROM"; break;
case 5: t = "RAM Disk"; break;
}
```

Next, the script builds the output by concatenating a series of strings. Tucked away in these strings is a function that converts the byte values returned by TotalSize and FreeSpace to a value in megabytes. The bytes to megabytes conversion is handled by dividing the return value by 1,048,576, which is the number of bytes in a megabyte. The result is then rounded to the nearest integer value using the Math.round() method. In the script, this comes together as

```
s += "Total space " + Math.round(d.TotalSize/1048576)
s += " Mbytes" + "\r\n";
s += "Free Space: " + Math.round(d.FreeSpace/1048576)
```

Examining All Drives on a System

The easiest way to examine all drives on a system is to use the Drives collection. You work with the Drives collection much like any other collection I've discussed in this book. In VBScript, you obtain the collection, then use a For Each loop to examine its contents. In JScript, you obtain the collection through an Enumerator object and then use the methods of the Enumerator object to examine each drive in turn.

Listing 12-3 shows a sample script that works with the Drives collection. The output provided is a partial listing of drives from my system. Note that the A: drive is a floppy drive. Because the drive didn't contain a disk when checked, the drive wasn't ready for certain tasks, such as reading the volume name or obtaining the amount of free space.

Listing 12-3: Working with the Drives collection

VBScript	JScript
dcol.vbs	**Dcol.js**
`WScript.Echo GetDriveList()`	`WScript.Echo(GetDriveList())`
`Function GetDriveList`	`Function GetDriveList()`
`'Initialize variables`	`{`
`Dim fs, d, dc, s, n, CRLF`	`\\Initialize variables`
`'Specify EOL designator`	`Var fs, s, n, e, d;`
`  CRLF = Chr(13) & Chr(10)`	

```
Set fs = CreateObject
  ("Scripting.FileSystemObject")
Set dc = fs.Drives

For Each d in dc

  n = ""
  s = s & d.DriveLetter & " - "
  If d.DriveType = Remote Then
    n = d.ShareName
  ElseIf d.IsReady Then
    n = d.VolumeName
  End If

  s = s & n & CRLF
Next
GetDriveList = s
End Function
```

Output

A -

C – PRIMARY

D – SECONDARY

E – MICRON

```
fs = new ActiveXObject
  ("Scripting.FileSystemObject");
e = new Enumerator(fs.Drives);
s = "";
for (; !e.atEnd(); e.moveNext())
{
  d = e.item();
  s = s + d.DriveLetter + " - " ;
  if (d.DriveType == 3)
    n = d.ShareName;
  else if (d.IsReady)
    n = d.VolumeName;
  else
    n = "(Drive not ready)";
  s += n + "\r\n";
}
return(s);
}
```

Output

A – (Drive Not Ready)

C – PRIMARY

D – SECONDARY

E – MICRON

Mapping Network Drives

Network drives allow users and scripts to access remote resources on the network. If you are using a script to configure network drives for a particular user, you should log in as this user and then run the script or have the user log in and then run the script. This ensures that the network drives are configured as necessary in the user's profile. On the other hand, if you are using a network drive in a script, such as a script that runs as a scheduled job, you should connect to the drive, use the drive, and then disconnect from the drive.

CONNECTING TO A NETWORK SHARE

Network shares aren't automatically available to users or to scripts. You must specifically map a network share to a network drive before it is available. In Windows scripts, you map network drives using the MapNetworkDrive method of the Network object. The basic structure for this method requires the drive letter to map the name of the network share to the local system, such as

VBScript	JScript
``Set wn = WScript.CreateObject
("WScript.Network")
wn.MapNetworkDrive "H:",
"\\Omega\data"```	```var wn = WScript.CreateObject
("WScript.Network")
wn.MapNetworkDrive("H:",
"\\\\Omega\\data")```

 The four backslashes used with JScript aren't a typo. Remember, in JScript you must escape each slash in a directory path with a slash.

When mapping a drive for a user, you can specify that the drive is persistent by setting the optional persistent flag to True. This updates the user profile to ensure the drive is automatically mapped in subsequent user sessions. You can set the persistent flag as follows:

VBScript	JScript
``Set wn = WScript.CreateObject
("WScript.Network")
wn.MapNetworkDrive "H:",
"\\Omega\data", True```	```var wn = WScript.CreateObject
("WScript.Network")
wn.MapNetworkDrive("H:",
"\\\\Omega\\data", "True")```

When mapping a network drive for use by scripts that run as scheduled jobs, you may need to set a user name and password in order to establish the connection. You do this by supplying the user name and password as the final parameters. In this example, scriptAdmin is the user name and gorilla is the password:

VBScript	JScript
``Set wn = WScript.CreateObject
("WScript.Network")
wn.MapNetworkDrive "H:",
"\\Omega\data", True,
"scriptAdmin", "gorilla"```	```var wn = WScript.CreateObject
("WScript.Network")
wn.MapNetworkDrive("H:",
"\\\\Omega\\data", "True",
"scriptAdmin", "gorilla")```

 Placing passwords in a script isn't a sound security practice. If you are going to set passwords in scripts, you should a) place the scripts in a directory with very limited access, and b) create a special account that is used only for scripts and has limited permissions.

DISCONNECTING FROM A NETWORK SHARE

When you are finished working with a network drive, you may want to disconnect the associated drive. To do this, you can use the `RemoveNetworkDrive` method of the `Network` object. Specify the designator of the network drive you want to disconnect, such as:

VBScript	JScript
| ```
Set wn = WScript.CreateObject
  ("WScript.Network")
wn.RemoveNetworkDrive "H:"
``` | ```
var wn = WScript.CreateObject
  ("WScript.Network")
wn.RemoveNetworkDrive("H:")
``` |

If a drive is still in use, it won't be disconnected. You can force the drive to disconnect by setting the optional force flag to `True`, such as

VBScript	Jscript
| ```
Set wn = WScript.CreateObject
  ("WScript.Network")
wn.RemoveNetworkDrive "H:", True
``` | ```
var wn = WScript.CreateObject
  ("WScript.Network")
wn.RemoveNetworkDrive("H:", "True")
``` |

The third and final parameter for `RemoveNetworkDrive` removes the persistent mapping for the drive. If you want to remove the persistent mapping for the drive in the user's profile, set this flag to `True`, such as

VBScript	JScript
| ```
Set wn = WScript.CreateObject
  ("WScript.Network")
wn.RemoveNetworkDrive
  "H:", True, True
``` | ```
var wn = WScript.CreateObject
  ("WScript.Network")
wn.RemoveNetworkDrive
  ("H:", "True", "True")
``` |

Managing Network Printers

Windows scripts can configure default printers, as well as add and remove network printers. A network printer is a shared printer that is accessible to other systems over the network. If you are using a script to configure printers for a particular user, you should log in as the user and run the script or have the user login and then run the script. This ensures that the printers are configured as necessary in the user's profile. If you are using a printer in a script, such as one that runs in a scheduled job, you should connect to the printer, use the printer, and then disconnect from the printer.

Setting a Default Printer

The default printer is the primary printer for a user. This printer is used whenever a user prints a document and doesn't select a specific destination printer. You can set a default printer using the SetDefaultPrinter method of the Network object. This method automatically updates the user's profile to use the default printer in the current session as well as subsequent sessions.

When you use SetDefaultPrinter, you must specify the network share for the printer to use as the default, such as \\NPSERVER\SW12. The network share path is the only parameter for SetDefaultPrinter. You can use the method in a script as follows:

VBScript	JScript
| ```
Set wn = WScript.CreateObject
  ("WScript.Network")
wn.SetDefaultPrinter
  "\\NPSERVER\SW12"
``` | ```
var wn = WScript.CreateObject
  ("WScript.Network")
wn.SetDefaultPrinter
  ("\\\\NPSERVER\\SW12")
``` |

Adding and Removing Printer Connections

Windows scripts manage connections to network printers much like they manage connections to network drives. You map printer connections using AddPrinterConnection. You remove printer connections using RemovePrinter Connection. Both methods accept similar parameters to the related network drive methods—MapNetworkDrive and RemoveNetworkDrive.

The basic structure for AddPrinterConnection requires a local resource name for the printer and the path to the network printer name. For example, if you work in an office building, you may want to map to the printer in the southwest corner of the twelfth floor. If the printer is shared as \\NPSERVER\SW12, you can map the printer to the local LPT1 port as follows:

VBScript	JScript
| ```
Set wn = WScript.CreateObject
  ("WScript.Network")
wn.AddPrinterConnection
  "LPT1", "\\NPSERVER\SW12"
``` | ```
var wn = WScript.CreateObject
  ("WScript.Network")
wn.AddPrinterConnection
  ("LPT1", "\\\\NPSERVER\\SW12")
``` |

The port is used with Windows 98 and ignored on Windows NT/2000.

If you just need to use the printer temporarily, you probably don't want to update the user's profile to maintain the printer connection in subsequent user sessions. On the other hand, if you are configuring printers that will be used regularly, you can set the optional persistent flag to True. This updates the user profile to ensure that the printer is automatically connected to in subsequent user sessions. You can set the persistent flag as follows:

VBScript	JScript
| ```
Set wn = WScript.CreateObject
  ("WScript.Network")
wn.AddPrinterConnection
  "LPT1", "\\NPSERVER\SW12",
  True
``` | ```
var wn = WScript.CreateObject
  ("WScript.Network")
wn.AddPrinterConnection
  ("LPT1", "\\\\NPSERVER\\SW12",
  "True")
``` |

When mapping a network printer for use by scripts that run as scheduled jobs, you may need to set a user name and password in order to establish the connection. You do this by supplying the user name and password as the final parameters. In this example, prUser is the user name and gorilla is the password:

VBScript	JScript
| ```
Set wn = WScript.CreateObject
  ("WScript.Network")
wn.AddPrinterConnection "LPT1",
  "\\NPSERVER\SW12", False,
  "prUser", "gorilla"
``` | ```
var wn = WScript.CreateObject
  ("WScript.Network")
wn.AddPrinterConnection("LPT1",
  "\\\\NPSERVER\\SW12", "False",
  "prUser", "gorilla")
``` |

> **TIP** An alternative to AddPrinterConnection is AddWindowsPrinter Connection. The method expects to be passed the path to the network printer and the name of the printer driver to use. An optional third parameter is the port to use, which defaults to LPT1 on Windows 98. Windows NT/2000 ignore the device driver and port information. Rather than using both methods, I recommend choosing the one that makes the most sense for your network and sticking with it, and AddPrinterConnection usually meets most needs.

When you are finished working with a network printer, you may want to remove the connection. To do this, you can use the RemovePrinterConnection method of the Network object. Specify the local designator of the printer you want to disconnect, such as

VBScript	JScript

Set wn = WScript.CreateObject
  ("WScript.Network")
wn.RemovePrinterConnection
  "PrinterSW12"
	var wn = WScript.CreateObject
	  ("WScript.Network")
	wn.RemovePrinterConnection
	  ("PrinterSW12")

You can force the printer to disconnect by setting the optional force flag to `True`, such as

VBScript	JScript

Set wn = WScript.CreateObject
  ("WScript.Network")
wn.RemovePrinterConnection
  "PrinterSW12", True
	var wn = WScript.CreateObject
	  ("WScript.Network")
	wn.RemovePrinterConnection
	  ("PrinterSW12", "True")

You can also remove the persistent mapping for a printer in the user's profile. To do this, set the third and final parameter to `True`, such as

VBScript	JScript

Set wn = WScript.CreateObject
  ("WScript.Network")
wn.RemovePrinterConnection
  "PrinterSW12", True, True
	var wn = WScript.CreateObject
	  ("WScript.Network")
	wn.RemovePrinterConnection
	  ("PrinterSW12", "True", "True")

Configuring Menus, the Desktop, and Startup Applications

Shortcuts provide quick access to application executables, local documents, and network resources. Shortcuts are also used to configure user menus and to set applications that start automatically when a user logs in. As an administrator, it is not very practical to run around creating desktop shortcuts, tailoring menus, and setting startup applications. Users can create their own shortcuts without that much difficulty and you probably don't want to get roped into micro-managing system administration. That said, there are times when you may want to be able to perform these tasks. For example, if you are installing a new system, you may want to have a standard set of menus, desktop shortcuts, and startup applications – and you can use Windows scripts to configure these settings.

Getting Started with Shortcuts

In the Windows operating system, menus, desktops, and startup applications are all configured with shortcuts, and it is the location of the shortcut that determines how the shortcut is used. For example, if you want to add a menu option for a user, you add a shortcut to the user's Programs or Start folder. These shortcuts then appear on the user's menu. If you want to configure startup applications for all users, you add shortcuts to the AllUsersStartup folder. These applications then automatically start when a user logs in to the system locally.

In Chapter 10, I talked about special folders that you may want to use when managing files and folders. There's also a set of special folders that you may want to use when configuring menus, the desktop, and startup applications, such as Programs, Start, and AllUsersStartup.

Table 12-2 provides a summary of special folders you can use with shortcuts. Keep in mind that these folders aren't available on all Windows systems. For example, Windows 95 systems can't use any of the global user folders. These folders are AllUsersDesktop, AllUsersPrograms, AllUsersStartMenu, and AllUsersStartup.

TABLE 12-2 SPECIAL FOLDERS FOR USE WITH SHORTCUTS

Special Folder	Usage
AllUsersDesktop	Desktop shortcuts for all users.
AllUsersPrograms	Programs menu options for all users.
AllUsersStartMenu	Start menu options for all users.
AllUsersStartup	Startup applications for all users.
Desktop	Desktop shortcuts for the current user.
Favorites	Favorites menu shortcuts for the current user.
Fonts	Fonts folder shortcuts for the current user.
MyDocuments	My Documents menu shortcuts for the current user.
NetHood	Network Neighborhood shortcuts for the current user.
Printers	Printers folder shortcuts for the current user.
Programs	Programs menu options for the current user.
Recent	Recently used document shortcuts for the current user.
SendTo	SendTo menu shortcuts for the current user.
StartMenu	Start menu shortcuts for the current user.
Startup	Startup applications for the current user.
Templates	Templates folder shortcuts for the current user.

Before you can work with a special folder, you need to obtain a `Folder` object that references the special folder. The easiest way to do this is to use the `SpecialFolders` method of the `Shell` object. This method expects a single parameter, which is a string containing the name of the special folder you want to work with. For example, if you want to add or remove desktop shortcuts, obtain the Desktop folder, such as

VBScript	JScript

`Set ws = WScript.CreateObject`
`  ("WScript.Shell")`
`dsktop = ws.SpecialFolders("Desktop")`
	`var ws = WScript.CreateObject`
	`  ("WScript.Shell")`
	`dsktop = ws.SpecialFolders("Desktop")`

Wondering why I didn't use the `SpecialFolders` method in Chapter 10's adminlib.js script? Well, I could have, but I was trying to demonstrate path-building techniques, and I also didn't want to confuse the issue by discussing shortcuts rather than folders.

Creating Shortcuts and Menu Options

Creating a shortcut is a very different process from most other administrative tasks we've looked at so far. In fact, you don't really *create* a shortcut — rather, you *build* shortcuts. The process goes like this:

1. Obtain a target folder for the shortcut.

2. Obtain a shortcut object.

3. Set properties for the shortcut.

4. Save the shortcut, which writes it to the target folder or menu.

Each of these steps is examined in the sections that follow.

OBTAINING A TARGET FOLDER FOR THE SHORTCUT

Previously, I covered how to obtain a special folder for a shortcut. You aren't limited to creating shortcuts for special folders, however. You can create shortcuts in any type of folder.

With a standard folder, you can obtain a pointer to the folder you want to use with the `GetFolder` method or any other method that returns a `Folder` object. If you want to create a shortcut in the D:\Working folder, you can do the following:

VBScript	JScript

Set fs = CreateObject
  ("Scripting.FileSystemObject")
Set f = fs.GetFolder("D:\Working")
	fs = new ActiveXObject
	  ("Scripting.FileSystemObject");
	var f = fs.GetFolder("D:\\Working");

OBTAINING A SHORTCUT OBJECT

Shortcuts can point to local and network files as well as remote Internet resources. With local or network files, the shortcut name must end with .lnk, which stands for link. With remote Internet resources, the shortcut must end with .url, which indicates a Universal Resource Locator. For brevity, I'll refer to these shortcuts as *link shortcuts* and *URL shortcuts*.

Regardless of type, you can obtain the necessary object for working with a shortcut via the CreateShortcut method of the Shell object. For link shortcuts, the method returns a WshShortcut object. For URL shortcuts, the method returns a WshUrlShortcut object. These objects have different sets of properties.

The name of the shortcut is the text that immediately precedes the file extension. For example, if you want to create a shortcut to Microsoft Word, you can name the shortcut MS Word using the following designator:

```
MS Word.lnk
```

Listing 12-4 shows how you can create a link shortcut named Yoyo. The shortcut is set to execute the Notepad text editor along the path %WINDIR%\notepad.exe, which is usually C:\WinNT\notepad.exe. Then the shortcut is saved to the Windows desktop with the Save method. Save is the only method for shortcut-related objects.

Listing 12-4: Creating a link shortcut

VBScript	JScript
lshortcut.vbs	**lshortcut.js**

Set ws = WScript.CreateObject
  ("WScript.Shell")
dsktop = ws.SpecialFolders("Desktop")
	var ws = WScript.CreateObject
	  ("WScript.Shell")
	dsktop = ws.SpecialFolders("Desktop")

Set scut = ws.CreateShortcut (dsktop
  & "\Yoyo.lnk")
scut.TargetPath =
  "%windir%\notepad.exe"
scut.Save
	var scut = ws.CreateShortcut (dsktop
	  + "\\Yoyo.lnk")
	scut.TargetPath =
	  "%windir%\\notepad.exe"
	scut.Save()

As you examine the previous listing, note how the folder path and the link path are concatenated. In VBScript, you add the paths together using

```
dsktop & "\Yoyo.lnk"
```

but in JScript, you use

```
dsktop + "\\Yoyo.lnk"
```

Listing 12-5 shows how you can create a URL shortcut named TVP. This shortcut is set to access the URL `http://www.tvpress.com/`. Then the shortcut is saved with the `Save` method. The shortcut is created without a folder path and as a result is created in the current working directory.

Listing 12-5: Creating a URL shortcut

VBScript	JScript
ushortcut.vbs	ushortcut.js

`Set ws = WScript.CreateObject`
`  ("WScript.Shell")`
`Set scut = ws.CreateShortcut`
`  ("TVP.URL")`
`scut.TargetPath =`
`  "http://www.tvpress.com/"`
`scut.Save`
	`var ws = WScript.CreateObject`
	`  ("WScript.Shell")`
	`var scut = ws.CreateShortcut`
	`  ("TVP.URL")`
	`scut.TargetPath =`
	`  "http://www.tvpress.com/"`
	`scut.Save()`

The forward slash is not a special character in JScript. Thus, the forward slash doesn't need to be escaped.

SETTING PROPERTIES FOR LINK SHORTCUTS

Link shortcuts are usually used to start applications or open documents rather than access a URL in a browser. Because of this, link shortcuts have different properties than URL shortcuts. The properties are summarized in Table 12-3. At first glance, it seems like a truckload of options but you can work through the properties one step at a time.

TABLE 12-3 PROPERTIES OF WSHSHORTCUT

Property	Description	Sample VBScript Value
Arguments	Arguments to pass to an application started through the shortcut.	"data.txt"
Description	Sets a description for the shortcut.	"Starts Internet Explorer"
Hotkey	Sets a hotkey sequence that activates the shortcut. Can only be used with desktop shortcuts and Start menu options.	"ALT+Z"
IconLocation	Sets the location of an icon for the shortcut. If not set, a default icon is used. The zero indicates the index position of the icon. Few applications have multiple icons indexed, so the index is almost always zero.	"netscape.exe, 0"
TargetPath	Sets the path of the file to execute.	"%windir%\netscape.exe"
WindowStyle	Sets the window style of the application started by the shortcut. The default style is 1. The available styles are the same as options 0-6 discussed in Chapter 9, Table 9-4.	1
WorkingDirectory	Sets the working directory of the application started by the shortcut.	"C:\data"

If you set any property incorrectly or set a property that isn't supported by a linked application, the shortcut may not be created. In this case, you'll need to correct the problem and try to create the shortcut again.

SETTING SHORTCUT ARGUMENTS   One of the most valuable options is the Arguments property. You can use this property to set arguments to pass in to an application you are starting. Using this property, you can create a shortcut that starts Microsoft Word and loads in a document at C:\Data\Todo.doc as shown in Listing 12-6.

Listing 12-6: Using Arguments with shortcuts

VBScript	JScript
args.vbs	**args.js**

```
Set ws = WScript.CreateObject
  ("WScript.Shell")
Set scut = ws.CreateShortcut
  ("To-do List.lnk")
scut.TargetPath = "C:\Program Files
  \Microsoft Office
  \OFFICE\WINWORD.EXE"
scut.Arguments = "C:\Data\Todo.doc"
scut.Save
```

```
var ws = WScript.CreateObject
  ("WScript.Shell")
var scut = ws.CreateShortcut
  ("To-do List.lnk")
scut.TargetPath = "C:\\Program Files
  \\Microsoft Office
  \\OFFICE\\WINWORD.EXE"
scut.Arguments = "C:\\Data\\Todo.doc"
scut.Save()
```

SETTING SHORTCUT HOTKEYS   When you add shortcuts to the Windows desktop or the Start menu, you can set a hotkey sequence that activates the shortcut. The hotkey sequence must be specified with at least one modifier key and a key designator. The following modifier keys are available:

- ◆ ALT – The Alt key
- ◆ CTRL – The Ctrl key
- ◆ SHIFT – The Shift key
- ◆ EXT – The Windows key

Modifier keys can be combined in any combination, such as ALT+CTRL or ALT+SHIFT+CTRL, but shouldn't duplicate existing key combinations used by other shortcuts. Key designators include alphabetic characters (A–Z) and numeric character (0–9) as well as Back, Clear, Delete, Escape, End, Home, Return, Space, and Tab.

Listing 12-7 creates a shortcut for the Start menu. The shortcut uses the hotkey ALT+SHIFT+C.

Listing 12-7: Using hotkeys with shortcuts

VBScript	JScript
hotkeys.vbs	**hotkeys.js**

```
Set ws = WScript.CreateObject
  ("WScript.Shell")
smenu = ws.SpecialFolders("StartMenu")


Set scut = ws.CreateShortcut
  (smenu & "\Internet Explorer.LNK")
scut.TargetPath = "C:\Program Files
```

```
var ws = WScript.CreateObject
  ("WScript.Shell")
smenu = ws.SpecialFolders("StartMenu")


var scut = ws.CreateShortcut
  (smenu + "\\Internet Explorer.LNK")
scut.TargetPath = "C:\\Program Files
```

VBScript	JScript

hotkeys.vbs

```
  \Plus!\Microsoft Internet
  \IEXPLORE.EXE"
scut.Hotkey = "ALT+SHIFT+C"
scut.Save
```

hotkeys.js

```
  \\Plus!\\Microsoft Internet
  \\IEXPLORE.EXE"
scut.Hotkey = "ALT+SHIFT+C"
scut.Save()
```

SETTING ICON LOCATION   When you create shortcuts for applications, the applications normally have a default icon that is displayed with the shortcut. For example, if you create a shortcut for Internet Explorer, the default icon is a large E. When you create shortcuts to document files, the Windows default icon is used in most cases.

If you want to use an icon other than the default, you can use the IconLocation property. This property expects to be passed an icon location and an icon index. Normally, the icon location equates to an application name, such as iexplore.exe or notepad.exe, and the icon index is set to 0. Listing 12-8 adds an option to the Programs menu for all users. The icon for this option is the Internet Explorer icon.

Listing 12-8: Specifying icons for shortcuts

VBScript	JScript

icons.vbs

```
Set ws = WScript.CreateObject
  ("WScript.Shell")
pmenu = ws.SpecialFolders
  ("AllUsersPrograms")

Set scut = ws.CreateShortcut
  (pmenu & "\Web Script.LNK")
scut.TargetPath =
  "%windir%\notepad.exe"
scut.Arguments =
  "D:\working\curr.vbs"
scut.IconLocation = "iexplore.exe, 0"
scut.Save
```

icons.js

```
var ws = WScript.CreateObject
  ("WScript.Shell")
pmenu = ws.SpecialFolders
  ("AllUsersPrograms")

var scut = ws.CreateShortcut
  (pmenu + "\\Web Script.LNK")
scut.TargetPath =
  "%windir%\\notepad.exe "
scut.Arguments =
  "D:\\working\\curr.vbs"
scut.IconLocation = "iexplore.exe, 0"
scut.Save()
```

Windows has to be able to find the executable. If the executable can't be found in the path, the icon can't be set. In this case, enter the full path to the executable, such as

```
scut.IconLocation = "C:\\Program
Files\\Plus!\\Microsoft Internet\\IEXPLORE.EXE, 0"
```

SETTING A WORKING DIRECTORY   The working directory sets the default directory for an application. This directory is used the first time you open or save files. Listing 12-9 creates a Start menu shortcut for Windows Notepad. The default directory is set to D:\working.

Listing 12-9: Using working directories

VBScript	JScript
wdir.vbs	**wdir.js**

```
Set ws = WScript.CreateObject
  ("WScript.Shell")
smenu = ws.SpecialFolders("StartMenu")


Set scut = ws.CreateShortcut
  (smenu & "\Notepad for Working.LNK")
scut.TargetPath =
  "%windir%\notepad.exe"
scut.WorkingDirectory = "D:\working"
scut.Save
```

```
var ws = WScript.CreateObject
  ("WScript.Shell")
smenu = ws.SpecialFolders("StartMenu")


var scut = ws.CreateShortcut
  (smenu + "\\Notepad for Working.LNK")
scut.TargetPath =
  "%windir%\\notepad.exe"
scut.WorkingDirectory = "D:\\working"
scut.Save()
```

SETTING PROPERTIES FOR URL SHORTCUTS

URL shortcuts open Internet documents in an appropriate application. For example Web pages are opened in the default browser, such as Internet Explorer. With URL shortcuts, the only property you can use is `TargetPath`, which sets the URL you want to use. Listing 12-10 creates a URL shortcut on the Start menu.

Listing 12-10: Creating an URL shortcut on the Start menu

VBScript	JScript
addsmenu.vbs	**addsmenu.js**

```
Set ws = WScript.CreateObject
  ("WScript.Shell")
smenu = ws.SpecialFolders("StartMenu")
Set scut = ws.CreateShortcut
  (smenu & "\Cool Web Site.URL")
scut.TargetPath =
  "http://www.centraldrive.com/"
scut.Save
```

```
var ws = WScript.CreateObject
  ("WScript.Shell")
smenu = ws.SpecialFolders("StartMenu")
var scut = ws.CreateShortcut
  (smenu + "\\Cool Web Site.URL")
scut.TargetPath =
  "http://www.centraldrive.com/"
scut.Save()
```

Creating Menus

Windows scripts can also create new menus. When you create menus, you add folders to existing special folders, such as Start or Programs. Start by obtaining a reference to the menu you want to add onto, such as

VBScript	JScript
| ```
Set ws = WScript.CreateObject
  ("WScript.Shell")
pmenu = ws.SpecialFolders ("Programs")
``` | ```
var ws = WScript.CreateObject
  ("WScript.Shell")
pmenu = ws.SpecialFolders ("Programs")
``` |

Then create a new menu by adding a folder to the special menu. The following example creates a submenu called Working under the Programs menu:

VBScript	JScript
| ```
Set fs = CreateObject
  ("Scripting.FileSystemObject")
Set foldr = fs.CreateFolder
  (pmenu & "\Working")
``` | ```
fs = new ActiveXObject
  ("Scripting.FileSystemObject");
var foldr = fs.CreateFolder
  (pmenu + "\\Working")
``` |

After you create the menu, you can add options to it. You do this by creating shortcuts that point to a location in the new menu. The following example creates a URL shortcut in the Working menu:

VBScript	JScript
| ```
Set ws = WScript.CreateObject
  ("WScript.Shell")
Set scut = ws.CreateShortcut (pmenu
  & "\Working\CentralDrive.URL")
scut.TargetPath =
  "http://www.centraldrive.com/"
scut.Save
``` | ```
var ws = WScript.CreateObject
  ("WScript.Shell")
var scut = ws.CreateShortcut (pmenu
  + "\\Working\\CentralDrive.URL")
scut.TargetPath =
  "http://www.centraldrive.com/"
scut.Save()
``` |

Updating Existing Shortcuts and Menu Options

Through Windows scripts, you can update the properties of any shortcut or menu option on the system. You do this by creating a new shortcut with the exact same name as the old shortcut. For example, if you created a Start menu shortcut named Notes.lnk, you can update its settings by creating a new shortcut named Notes.lnk.

In most cases, only the options you specifically set for the shortcut are overwritten. If necessary, you can clear an existing option by setting its value to an empty string. For example, Listing 12-8 created a shortcut for Notepad. This shortcut set an argument that opened a document called curr.vbs. If you delete curr.vbs and don't want to use it anymore, you can update the shortcut as shown in Listing 12-11.

Listing 12-11: Changing a shortcut

VBScript	JScript
change.vbs	**change.js**

```vbscript
Set ws = WScript.CreateObject
  ("WScript.Shell")
pmenu = ws.SpecialFolders
  ("AllUsersPrograms")

Set scut = ws.CreateShortcut
  (pmenu & "\Web Script.LNK")
scut.TargetPath =
  "%windir%\notepad.exe"
scut.Arguments = ""
scut.IconLocation = "iexplore.exe, 0"
scut.Save
```

```jscript
var ws = WScript.CreateObject
  ("WScript.Shell")
pmenu = ws.SpecialFolders
  ("AllUsersPrograms")

var scut = ws.CreateShortcut
  (pmenu + "\\Web Script.LNK")
scut.TargetPath =
  "%windir%\\notepad.exe "
scut.Arguments = ""
scut.IconLocation = "iexplore.exe, 0"
scut.Save()
```

Deleting Shortcuts and Menu Options

Shortcuts and menu options are specified in files. You can delete them as you would any system file. If a shortcut called Web.url is in the current working directory, you can delete it as follows:

VBScript	JScript

```vbscript
Dim fs
Set fs = CreateObject
  ("Scripting.FileSystemObject")
fs.DeleteFile "Web.URL"
```

```jscript
var fs
fs = new ActiveXObject
  ("Scripting.FileSystemObject");
fs.DeleteFile("Web.URL")
```

If a shortcut is in a special folder, such as the Start menu folder, you need to obtain the related folder object before trying to delete the shortcut. Use the path to the folder to retrieve the shortcut using the GetFile method of FileSystemObject. Afterward, call the Delete method of the File object. This removes the shortcut. Listing 12-12 shows an example of deleting a shortcut from the Start menu.

Listing 12-12: Deleting menu options

VBScript	JScript
deloption.vbs	**deloption.js**

```vbscript
Dim ws, fs, f, smenu
Set ws = WScript.CreateObject
  ("WScript.Shell")
Set smenu = ws.SpecialFolders
  ("StartMenu")
```

```jscript
var ws = WScript.CreateObject
  ("WScript.Shell")
smenu = ws.SpecialFolders
  ("StartMenu")
```

VBScript	JScript

deloption.vbs

```
Set fs = CreateObject
  ("Scripting.FileSystemObject")
Set f = fs.GetFile(smenu &
  "\Internet Explorer.LNK")
f.Delete
```

deloption.js

```
fs = new ActiveXObject
  ("Scripting.FileSystemObject");
f = fs.GetFile(smenu +
  "\\Cool Web Site.URL")
f.Delete();
```

Deleting Menus

Just as you can create menus, you can also delete them. Normally you delete submenus of special folders and not the special folders themselves. Start by obtaining a reference to the appropriate special folder, such as

VBScript	JScript

```
Set ws = WScript.CreateObject
  ("WScript.Shell")
pmenu = ws.SpecialFolders ("Programs")
```

```
var ws = WScript.CreateObject
  ("WScript.Shell")
pmenu = ws.SpecialFolders ("Programs")
```

Afterward, use the `GetFolder` method to delete the submenu. Listing 12-13 shows how you can delete a submenu called Working under the Programs menu.

Listing 12-13: Deleting a menu

VBScript	JScript

delmenu.vbs

```
Set ws = WScript.CreateObject
  ("WScript.Shell")
pmenu = ws.SpecialFolders ("Programs")
Set fs = CreateObject
  ("Scripting.FileSystemObject")
fs.DeleteFolder(pmenu & "\Working")
```

delmenu.js

```
var ws = WScript.CreateObject
  ("WScript.Shell")
pmenu = ws.SpecialFolders ("Programs")
fs = new ActiveXObject
  ("Scripting.FileSystemObject");
var foldr = fs.DeleteFolder
  (pmenu + "\\Working")
```

If you create a menu for all users, you must delete the menu via the related special folder. For example, if you create a submenu of `AllUsersStart Menu`, you must delete the submenu via the `AllUsersStartMenu` special folder.

Working with the Windows Registry

The Windows Registry stores system configuration settings. Through Windows scripts, you can read, write, and delete registry entries. Because the registry is essential to the proper operation of the operating system, you should only make changes to the registry when you know how these changes will affect the system.

 Improperly modifying the Windows Registry can cause serious problems and if the registry gets corrupted, you may have to reinstall the operating system. Always double check registry scripts before running them and ensure that they do exactly what you intend. Further, before you edit the registry in any way, you should create an up-to-date Emergency Repair Disk.

Understanding the Registry Structure

The registry stores configuration values for the operating system, applications, user settings, and more. Registry settings are stored as keys and values. These keys and values are placed under a specific root key, which controls when and how the keys and values are used.

The root keys are summarized in Table 12-4. This table also shows the short name by which you can reference the root key in a script. The three keys with short names are the ones you'll work with most often.

TABLE 12-4 REGISTRY ROOT KEYS

Short Name	Long Name	Description
HKCU	HKEY_CURRENT_USER	Controls configuration settings for the current user.
HKLM	HKEY_LOCAL_MACHINE	Controls system-level configuration settings.
HKCR	HKEY_CLASSES_ROOT	Configuration settings for applications and files. Ensures the correct application is opened when a file is started through Windows Explorer or OLE.
-	HKEY_USERS	Stores default user and other user settings by profile.
-	HKEY_CURRENT_CONFIG	Contains information about the hardware profile being used.

Under the root keys, you'll find the main keys that control system, user, and application settings. These keys are organized into a directory structure. For example, under HKEY_CURRENT_USER\Software\Microsoft you'll find folders for all Microsoft applications installed by the current user.

Through Windows scripts, you can assign values to new keys or you can change the values of existing keys. Values in the Registry appear as a string that consists of three components: the name of the value, the type of the value, and the actual value itself. In the following example, the key is HKEY_CURRENT_USER \Printers \ShowLogonDomain, the type is REG_DWORD and the value is 0x1:

```
HKEY_CURRENT_USER\Printers\ShowLogonDomain : REG_DWORD : 0x1
```

Key values are written by default as type REG_SZ but you can assign any of these data types:

- REG_BINARY — Identifies a binary value. Binary values must be entered using base-2 (0 or 1).

- REG_SZ — Identifies a string value containing a sequence of characters.

- REG_DWORD — Identifies a DWORD value, which is composed of hexadecimal data with a maximum length of 4 bytes.

- REG_MULTI_SZ — Identifies a multiple string value.

- REG_EXPAND_SZ — Identifies an expandable string value.

Reading Registry Values

You can read registry values by passing the name of the key or value you want to examine to the RegRead method of the Shell object. RegRead then returns the value associated with the key or value entry. For example, if you want to read the HKEY_CURRENT_USER\Printers\ShowLogonDomain key, use the following statements:

VBScript	JScript
Set ws = WScript.CreateObject ("WScript.Shell")	var ws = WScript.CreateObject ("WScript.Shell")
val = ws.RegRead ("HKCU\Printers\ShowLogonDomain")	val = ws.RegRead ("HKCU\\Printers\\ShowLogonDomain")

The RegRead method only supports the standard data types: REG_SZ, REG_EX-PAND_SZ, REG_MULTI_SZ, REG_DWORD and REG_BINARY. If the value contains another data type, the method returns DISP_E_TYPEMISMATCH.

Writing Registry Values

To write keys and value entries to the registry, use the `RegWrite` method. This method expects to be passed the key or value name as well as the value you want to set. You can also set an optional parameter that specifies the value type. If you don't set type parameter, the value is set as a string of type `REG_SZ`. If you set the value type, the type must be one of the following: `REG_SZ`, `REG_EXPAND_SZ`, `REG_DWORD`, or `REG_BINARY`.

Some value types are converted automatically to the appropriate format. With `REG_SZ` and `REG_EXPAND_SZ`, `RegWrite` automatically converts values to strings. With `REG_DWORD`, values are converted to integers in hexadecimal format. However, `REG_BINARY` must be set as integers. If you set an incorrect data type or an incorrect value, RegWrite returns `E_INVALIDARG`.

You can use `RegWrite` to update existing registry keys and values as well as to create new keys and values. If the path ends with a slash (or double slash for JScript), the entry is written as a key. Otherwise, the entry is written as a value entry. The following example changes the value entry for HKEY_CURRENT_USER \Printers\ShowLogonDomain:

VBScript	JScript
| ```
Set ws = WScript.CreateObject
  ("WScript.Shell")
val = ws.RegWrite
  ("HKCU\Printers\ShowLogonDomain",
  0, "REG_DWORD")
``` | ```
var ws = WScript.CreateObject
  ("WScript.Shell")
val = ws.RegWrite
  ("HKCU\\Printers\\ShowLogonDomain",
  0, "REG_DWORD")
``` |

With new keys, the registry automatically creates additional directory structures as necessary. Usually, you'll want to add new keys to the HKEY_CURRENT_USER root key. For example, you can create a new key for Windows scripts called HKEY_CURRENT_USER\WScriptingGuide and then add values to it. Because these values are stored in the current user's profile, they are persistent and aren't destroyed when the user logs out. This makes it possible to retain values across multiple user sessions.

Listing 12-14 shows an example of creating a registry key and a registry value for use with a script.

Listing 12-14: Creating registry keys and values

VBScript	JScript
createreg.vbs	**createreg.js**
| ```
Set ws = WScript.CreateObject
  ("WScript.Shell")
val = ws.RegWrite
  ("HKCU\WScriptingGuide\Author\",
``` | ```
var ws = WScript.CreateObject
  ("WScript.Shell")
val = ws.RegWrite
  ("HKCU\\WScriptingGuide\\Author\\",
``` |

VBScript	JScript

createreg.vbs
```
  "William Stanek")
val = ws.RegWrite
  ("HKCU\WScriptingGuide\Comments",
  "Gosh, I love that book!")
```

createreg.js
```
  "William Stanek")
val = ws.RegWrite
  ("HKCU\\WScriptingGuide\\Comments",
  "Gosh, I love that book!")
```

Network Resource Administration Script

The network resource library script provides utility functions for managing network resources. Use these functions as a starting point as you set out to manage the enterprise. The source for the library is shown in Listing 12-15.

Listing 12-15: Script for administering network resources

netreslib.js
```
// ************************
// Script: Network Resource Library
// Version: 0.9.7
// Creation Date: 6/30/99
// Last Modified: 9/15/99
// Author: William R. Stanek
// Email: winscripting@tvpress.com
// ************************
// Description: Provides a utility library for
//              managing network resources.
// ************************
function GetDriveInfo()
{
  var fs, d, e, s, t, wnet, cname;

  wNet = WScript.CreateObject("WScript.Network");
  cname = wNet.ComputerName;

  fs = new ActiveXObject ("Scripting.FileSystemObject");
  e = new Enumerator(fs.Drives);
  s = "";
  s += "=========================" + "\r\n";
  s += cname + "\r\n";
  s += "=========================" + "\r\n";
```

Continued

```
    for (; !e.atEnd(); e.moveNext())
    {

      d = e.item();
      switch (d.DriveType)
      {
      case 0: t = "Unknown"; break;
      case 1: t = "Removable"; break;
      case 2: t = "Fixed"; break;
      case 3: t = "Network"; break;
      case 4: t = "CD-ROM"; break;
      case 5: t = "RAM Disk"; break;
      }
      s += "Drive " + d.DriveLetter + ": - " + t + "\r\n";
      if (d.ShareName)
        s += " Share: " + d.ShareName + "\r\n"
      s += "Total space " + Math.round(d.TotalSize/1048576)
      s += " Mbytes" + "\r\n";
      s += "Free Space: " + Math.round(d.FreeSpace/1048576)
      s += " Mbytes" + "\r\n";
      s += "========================" + "\r\n";
    }
    return(s);
}

function GetDriveInfo2()
{
  var fs, d, e, s, t, wnet, cname;

  wNet = WScript.CreateObject("WScript.Network");
  cname = wNet.ComputerName;

  fs = new ActiveXObject ("Scripting.FileSystemObject");
  e = new Enumerator(fs.Drives);
  s = "";
  s += "========================" + "\r\n";
  s += cname + "\r\n";
  s += "========================" + "\r\n";

  for (; !e.atEnd(); e.moveNext())
  {

    d = e.item();
  if ((d.DriveType < 2) || (d.DriveType > 3))
```

```
  switch (d.DriveType)
  {
   case 0: t = "Unknown"; break;
   case 1: t = "Removable"; break;
   case 2: t = "Fixed"; break;
   case 3: t = "Network"; break;
   case 4: t = "CD-ROM"; break;
   case 5: t = "RAM Disk"; break;
  }
  s += "Drive " + d.DriveLetter + ": - " + t + "\r\n";
  if (d.ShareName)
   s += " Share: " + d.ShareName + "\r\n"
  s += "Total space " + Math.round(d.TotalSize/1048576)
  s += " Mbytes" + "\r\n";
  s += "Free Space: " + Math.round(d.FreeSpace/1048576)
  s += " Mbytes" + "\r\n";
  s += "=========================" + "\r\n";
 }
  return(s);
}

function CheckFreeSpace()
{
  var fs, d, e, s, tspace, fspace, wnet, cname;

  wnet = WScript.CreateObject("WScript.Network");
  cname = wnet.ComputerName;

  fs = new ActiveXObject ("Scripting.FileSystemObject");
  e = new Enumerator(fs.Drives);
  s = "";
  s += "=========================" + "\r\n";
  s += cname + "\r\n";
  s += "=========================" + "\r\n";

  for (; !e.atEnd(); e.moveNext())
  {

    d = e.item();
    if ((d.DriveType < 2) || (d.DriveType > 3))
      continue
    tspace = Math.round(d.TotalSize/1048576)
    fspace = Math.round(d.FreeSpace/1048576)
```

Continued

```
    if (fspace < (tspace*.1))
      {
       s += "Drive " + d.DriveLetter;
       if (d.VolumName)
        s += "Volume: " + d.VolumName
       if (d.ShareName)
        s += " Share: " + d.ShareName
       s += "\r\n!!!" + "\r\n";
       s += "Free Space: " + fspace
       s += " Mbytes" + "\r\n";
       s += "!!!" + "\r\n";
      }

  }
   return(s);
}

function MapDrive(drv, nshare)
{

  fs = new ActiveXObject("Scripting.FileSystemObject");
  if (fs.DriveExists(drv))
   {
    var wn = WScript.CreateObject ("WScript.Network")
    wn.RemoveNetworkDrive(drv)
   }
  else
   {
    var wn = WScript.CreateObject ("WScript.Network")
    wn.MapNetworkDrive(drv, nshare)
   }
}

function defPrinter(dp)
{
 var wn = WScript.CreateObject("WScript.Network")
 wn.SetDefaultPrinter (dp)
}

function AddPrinter(prntr, pshare)
{
 var wn = WScript.CreateObject("WScript.Network")
 wn.AddPrinterConnection(prntr, pshare)
```

```javascript
}


function RemPrinter(prntr)
{
 var wn = WScript.CreateObject("WScript.Network")
 wn.RemovePrinterConnection (prntr)
}

function AddDesktop(sname,trgt)
{

var ws = WScript.CreateObject ("WScript.Shell")
dsktop = ws.SpecialFolders("Desktop")
var scut = ws.CreateShortcut (dsktop + "\\" + sname + ".lnk")
scut.TargetPath = trgt
scut.Save()


}

function AddDesktopURL(sname,trgt)
{

var ws = WScript.CreateObject ("WScript.Shell")
dsktop = ws.SpecialFolders("Desktop")

var scut = ws.CreateShortcut (dsktop + "\\" + sname + ".URL")
scut.TargetPath = trgt
scut.Save()


}


function AddStartMenu(sname,trgt)
{

var ws = WScript.CreateObject ("WScript.Shell")
smenu = ws.SpecialFolders("StartMenu")
var scut = ws.CreateShortcut (smenu + "\\" + sname + ".lnk")
scut.TargetPath = trgt
scut.Save()


}
```

Continued

```
function AddStartMenuURL(sname,trgt)
{


var ws = WScript.CreateObject ("WScript.Shell")
smenu = ws.SpecialFolders("StartMenu")
var scut = ws.CreateShortcut (smenu + "\\" + sname + ".URL")
scut.TargetPath = trgt
scut.Save()


}


function CheckMenu(mname)
{
  var fs, f, fc, s;
  fs = new ActiveXObject("Scripting.FileSystemObject");
  var ws = WScript.CreateObject ("WScript.Shell")
  smenu = ws.SpecialFolders(mname)

  f = fs.GetFolder(smenu);
  fc = new Enumerator(f.Files);
  s = "";
  for (; !fc.atEnd(); fc.moveNext())
  {
    theFile = fs.GetFile(fc.item());
    s += theFile + "\r\n"
  }
  return (s)
}
```

Using GetDriveInfo

The `GetDriveInfo` function returns a summary of all drives on a system. If you want to run the script as a nightly AT job, you can log the information to a file using the .ws file shown in Listing 12-16. This script uses the file utility library (filelib.js) and the network resource library (netreslib.js).

The results of the script are stored in a file called logfile.txt. Sample output for this file is shown in the listing. Because the `WriteChar` function appends to existing files, information is added to the log file each time you run the script.

Listing 12-16: Logging drive information

logdriveinfo.ws

```
<Job ID="LogDriveInfo">
  <Script LANGUAGE="JScript" SRC="filelib.js" />
  <Script LANGUAGE="JScript" SRC="netreslib.js" />
```

```
<Script LANGUAGE="JScript">
        checkDrive = GetDriveInfo()
        WriteChar("logfile.txt",checkdrive)
</Script>
</Job>
```

Output into logfile.txt

=========================

ZETA

=========================

Drive C: - Fixed

Continued

Total space 2047 Mbytes

Free Space: 564 Mbytes

=========================

Drive G: - Removable

Total space 96 Mbytes

Free Space: 39 Mbytes

=========================

Drive H: - CD-ROM

Total space 584 Mbytes

Free Space: 0 Mbytes

=========================

The GetDriveInfo function as currently written checks all drives on the system, including removable drives. These drives must have media. If they don't, you may see a prompt asking you to check the drive. To get a report of fixed and network drives only, use the GetDriveInfo2 function. These statements within the For loop cause the function to skip checks for removable and CD-ROM drives:

```
if ((d.DriveType < 2) || (d.DriveType > 3))
    continue
```

Using CheckFreeSpace

Another useful function for tracking drive info is CheckFreeSpace. CheckFreeSpace returns a warning if a fixed or network drive has less than 10% free space available. The code that checks for free space is

```
tspace = Math.round(d.TotalSize/1048576)
fspace = Math.round(d.FreeSpace/1048576)
if (fspace < (tspace*.1))
```

Here, you take the total free space and multiply by .1 to come up with a value to compare to the amount of free space. The code that checks the free space percentage is easily updated. For example, if you want to report errors when there is 25% free space, you can update the function as follows:

```
tspace = Math.round(d.TotalSize/1048576)
fspace = Math.round(d.FreeSpace/1048576)
if (fspace < (tspace*.25))
```

The CheckFreeSpace function can also be run as a nightly AT job. Listing 12-17 shows a sample .ws file that maps a network share and then updates a central log file. Sample output for this log file is shown.

Listing 12-17: Checking free space on a drive

checkdriveinfo.ws

```
<Job ID="DriveInfo">
  <Script LANGUAGE="JScript" SRC="filelib.js" />
  <Script LANGUAGE="JScript" SRC="netreslib.js" />

  <Script LANGUAGE="JScript">
        checkDrive = CheckFreeSpace()
        MapDrive("X:", "\\\\Omega\\data")
        WriteChar("X:\\dspace.log",checkdrive)
        MapDrive("X:")
  </Script>
</Job>
```

Output into dspace.log

```
=========================

ZETA

=========================

Drive C

!!!

Free Space: 5 Mbytes

!!!


=========================
```

OMEGA

===========================

Drive C

!!!

Free Space: 27 Mbytes

!!!

Using MapDrive

MapDrive provides a single function for connecting and disconnecting drives. If the drive referenced in the first parameter exists, the drive is disconnected. Otherwise, the drive is connected to the network share passed in the second parameter. You can use MapDrive to connect a drive as follows:

```
MapDrive("Z:", "\\\\Zeta\\logs")
```

Later, you can disconnect the drive by calling

```
MapDrive("Z:")
```

Working with Printers

The network resource library also has functions for working with printers. These functions are defPrinter for setting a default printer, AddPrinter for adding a printer connection, and RemPrinter for removing a printer connection. The first parameter for all of these functions is the local name of the printer you are working with. AddPrinter expects a second parameter, which is the name of the network printer share you are connecting. You can call AddPrinter in a script as follows:

```
AddPrinter("MarketingPrinter", "\\\\Omega\\Prtrs\\Marketing")
```

Adding to the Desktop and Start Menu

To quickly add shortcuts to the desktop or Start menu for the current user, use the AddDesktop, AddDesktopURL, AddStartMenu, and AddStartMenuURL functions. While AddDesktop and AddStartMenu create link shortcuts, AddDesktopURL and AddStartMenuURL create URL shortcuts. These functions accept the same parameters: the name of the shortcut (without the .lnk or .url extension) and the target path of the shortcut.

Listing 12-18 shows how you can use these functions to add multiple desktop and menu shortcuts. The listing uses the file utility library as well as the network

resource library. The file options.txt contains the shortcuts being added to the desktop. The file adesktop.ws contains a batch script with the main script written in
VBScript.

Listing 12-18: Adding multiple shortcut

soptions.txt

```
WinScripting Home
http://www.tvpress.com/winscripting/
WinScripting Microsoft
http://msdn.microsoft.com/scripting/
WinScripting for IIS 5.0
http://msdn.microsoft.com/library/sdkdoc/iisref/aore2xpu.htm
adesktop.ws
<Job ID="AddShortcuts">
  <Script LANGUAGE="JScript" SRC="filelib.js" />
  <Script LANGUAGE="JScript" SRC="netreslib.js" />

  <Script LANGUAGE="VBScript">
  Dim numLines, theFile
  numLines = 6

  theFile = "D:\datatest.txt"

  For i = 1 to numLines Step 2

   theShortcut = ReadLineN(theFile, i)
   theTarget = ReadLineN(theFile, i+1)
   ret = AddDesktopURL(theShortcut, theTarget)

  Next
  </Script>
</Job>
```

```
Because this is the first time we've called JScript from VBScript via the util-
ity libraries, let's take a quick look at some key concepts. As the script
shows, when you call a JScript function that uses file paths, you don't need to
use the JScript syntax. File paths are automatically converted for you and this
is why you can set the file path as
D:\datatest.txt
However, you do have to use a slightly different syntax when calling functions
that don't return values. The script uses
ret = AddDesktopURL(theShortcut, theTarget)
rather than
AddDesktopURL(theShortcut, theTarget)
```

Even though the `AddDesktopURL` function doesn't return a value, you can call the function as though it does return a value. If you don't do this, VBScript thinks the function is a subroutine and you cannot use parentheses when calling a subroutine.

An interesting feature of the script is the use of a `For Next` loop to read lines from the file by two's. In the first iteration of the `For` loop, lines 1 and 2 are read from the options.txt file. The value of line 1 is assigned as the shortcut name. The value of line 2 is assigned as the target path. Then the `AddDesktopURL` function is called with these values. In the second iteration of the `For` loop, lines 3 and 4 are read from the options.txt file, and so on.

Managing Menu Options

The `CheckMenu` function is designed to help you track and manage menu options. You can pass the function the name of a special menu and the function returns a list of all options assigned through this menu. You can use the function in several different ways. If you are trying to determine whether a particular option is assigned to the current user or all users, you can call the function once with a current user menu and a second time with an all users menu, such as

```
WScript.Echo(CheckMenu(StartMenu))
WScript.Echo("================")
WScript.Echo(CheckMenu(AllUsersStartMenu))
```

Because the function returns the complete file path to the options, you can use the function to delete menu options as well. To see how, let's work through an example. Listing 12-19 obtains a list of options on the Programs menu for the current user and all users on the system. These options are written to a text file (poptions.txt). The script uses `WriteChar` from filelib.js and `CheckMenu` from netreslib.js.

Listing 12-19: Getting all menu options

```
getoptions.ws
<Job ID="GetOptions">
  <Script LANGUAGE="JScript" SRC="filelib.js" />
  <Script LANGUAGE="JScript" SRC="netreslib.js" />

  <Script LANGUAGE="VBScript">
    theOptions = CheckMenu("Programs")
    ret = WriteChar("d:\\poptions.txt", theOptions)
    theOptions = CheckMenu("AllUsersPrograms")
    ret = WriteChar("d:\\poptions.txt", theOptions)
</Script>
</Job>
poptions.txt
D:\WINNT\Profiles\All Users\Start Menu\Programs\Access.lnk
D:\WINNT\Profiles\All Users\Start Menu\Programs\Excel.lnk
D:\WINNT\Profiles\All Users\Start Menu\Programs\FrontPage.lnk
D:\WINNT\Profiles\All Users\Start Menu\Programs\PowerPoint.lnk
```

Continued

```
D:\WINNT\Profiles\All Users\Start Menu\Programs\Word.lnk
D:\WINNT\Profiles\All Users\Start Menu\Programs\PhotoDraw.lnk
D:\WINNT\Profiles\All Users\Start Menu\Programs\Web Script.LNK
D:\WINNT\Profiles\All Users\Start Menu\Programs\Web Script2.LNK
D:\WINNT\Profiles\All Users\Start Menu\Programs\Web Script3.LNK
```

You then edit the poptions.txt file and remove menu options that you don't want to keep. Afterward, you run listing 12-20 to remove the options from the menu. The script uses ReadLineN from filelib.js and DeleteFile from adminlib.js.

Listing 12-20: Deleting multiple menu options deloptions.ws

```
<Job ID="SystemInfo">
  <Script LANGUAGE="JScript" SRC="adminlib.js" />
  <Script LANGUAGE="JScript" SRC="filelib.js" />
  <Script LANGUAGE="VBScript">
  Dim numLines, theFile
  numLines = 4

  theFile = "d:\poptions.txt"

  For i = 1 to numLines Step 1

    theShortcut = ReadLineN(theFile, i)
    ret = DeleteFile(theShortcut)

  Next
  </Script>
</Job>
```

If you use this script, be sure to update the numLines variable to reflect the actual number of lines in the poptions.txt file.

Summary

As you learned in this chapter, Windows scripts simplify network and system administration. You can easily create scripts for managing free space on drives, updating menus, and a whole lot more. As you set out to work with resources, use the utility library developed in this chapter as a starting point and build on it until you perfect network and system administration through scripting.

Appendix A

Windows NT Command Shell Reference

APPENDIX A PROVIDES a reference resource for the Windows NT command shell. You'll find a quick reference for commands as well as detailed entries on command usage. Use this reference when you are searching for commands to perform core shell tasks. For a detailed reference on networking and account management commands, see Appendix B.

Once you find the command you want to work with, you shouldn't have any problems obtaining the information you need. Still, you'll be able to use the references more efficiently if you understand how the appendix is organized. The first command entry, titled Sample, explains the structure for entries. You should read this entry before moving forward.

append	debug	graftabl	rem
assoc	dir	graphics	ren
at	diskcomp	help	rename
attrib	diskcopy	if	replace
backup	diskcopy	label	restore
break	echo	md	rmdir
cacls	edit	mkdir	set
call	edlin	mode	setlocal
cd	endlocal	more	shift
chcp	erase	move	sort
chdir	exe2bin	ntbooks	start
chkdsk	exit	path	subst
cls	expand	pause	time
cmd	fc	pentnt	title
color	find	popd	tree
comp	findstr	print	type

compact	for	prompt	ver
convert	forcedos	pushd	verify
copy	format	qbasic	vol
date	ftype	rd	xcopy
del	goto	recover	

Sample

Working with reference entries

```
Syntax 1: sample [/a|/b] [message]
Syntax 2: sample [on|off]
```

/a   A switch you can pass to the command and how it is used.

/b   Another switch you can pass to the command and how it is used.

message   The text displayed in sample formatting. Syntax items in italics represent generic stand-ins for items you provide.

on|/off   Turns the sample on or off.

More Info:
An optional section for additional information on the command.
Examples:
An optional section with examples using the command, such as

```
sample /a "This is a test!"
sample off
```

append

Allows programs to open data files in designated directories as if they were in the current directory.

```
append [[drive:]path] [/x[:on|:off]] [/path:on|/path:off] [/e]
append ;
```

[*drive:*]*path*   Sets a drive and directory path to append.

/e	Stores a copy of the directories to append in the %APPEND% environment variable. /E may be used only the first time you use append after starting your system.
/path:off	Turns off path appending.
/path:on	Appends directory paths to file requests (even if a path is already specified).
/x:off	Appends directory paths only for requests to open files. /x:off is the default setting.
/x:on	Appends directory paths only to file searches and application execution.

More Info:
Append is useful when you want to be able to search a path for a file and is used in much the same way as path. To clear the appended directory list, enter a semicolon. To display the appended directory list, type **append** without parameters.

Examples:

```
append
append ;
append=C:\working;D:\mystuff\data;R:\network\users\wrstanek
```

assoc

Displays and modifies file extension associations.

```
assoc [.ext[=[fileType]]]
```

.ext	Sets the file extension to which the file type is associated
fileType	Sets the file type to associate with the file extension

More Info:
Display the current file associations by typing **assoc** without any parameters. Delete current file extensions by typing the file extension name with the command.

Examples:

```
assoc
assoc .pl=
assoc .pl=Perl
```

AT

Schedules commands and programs to execute at a specific date and time.

```
AT [\\computername] [ [id] [/delete] | /delete [/yes]]
AT [\\computername] time [/interactive]
AT [ /every:date[,...] | /next:date[,...]] "command"
```

"command"	Sets the command or script to run at the designated time.
/delete	Cancels a scheduled task. If *id* is omitted, all scheduled commands on the system are canceled.
/every:*date*[,...]	Runs the command on a recurring basis on each weekday or day of the month specified. Valid values are M, T, W, Th, F, S, Su, or 1 to 31. Separate consecutive days with dashes. Separate non-consecutive days with commas.
/interactive	Allows the job to interact with the desktop.
/next:*date*[,...]	Runs the task on a specific weekday or day of month. This is a non-recurring task.
/yes	Forces a confirmation prompt before deleting scheduled tasks.
computername	Sets a remote computer on which the task should run. If omitted, tasks are scheduled on the local computer.
id	The identification number assigned to a scheduled task.
time	Sets the time when command is to run in the format HH:MM. Time is set on a 24-hour clock (00:00 – 23:59).

More Info:

Tasks can be scheduled to run on a one-time or recurring basis. To list currently scheduled tasks, enter AT on a line by itself.

Examples:

```
AT 00:15 /every:M-Th "backup %systemroot%\profiles\%username% @@lb
f:\%username%"
AT 01:00 /next:Su "del c:\temp\*.tmp
AT 1 /delete
```

attrib

Displays and changes file attributes.

```
attrib [+r|-r] [+a|-a] [+s|-s] [+h|-h] @@1b
    [[drive:] [path] filename] [/s]
```

[[drive:] [path] filename]	Sets the drive, directory, or set of files to modify.
+r, -r	Sets or clears a read-only file attribute.
+a, -a	Sets or clears an archive file attribute.
+s, -s	Sets or clears a system file attribute.
+h, -h	Sets or clears a hidden file attribute.
/s	Processes matching files in the current directory and all subdirectories.

More Info:
You can use wildcards when specifying filenames.
Examples:

```
attrib +a c:\working\*.doc
attrib -r *.txt
```

backup

Performs file backups.

```
backup source destination-drive: [/s] [/m] [/a] [/f[:size]]@@1b
    [/d:date[/t:time]] [/l[:[drive:][path]logfile]]
```

source	Sets the drive, directory or files to back up.
destination-drive:	Sets the destination drive where backup copies onto.
/a	Adds the backup to an existing backup disk.
/d:date	Only backs up files changed on or after the specified date.

/f:[*size*]	Formats the destination disk with the default or specified size.
/l[:[*drive*:][*path*]*logfile*]	Creates a log file to record the backup operation. If the file exists, entries are appended. If /l is specified by itself, a log called BACKUP.LOG is created in the current directory.
/m	Only backup files with the archive attribute set.
/s	Includes all subdirectories in the backup.
/t:*time*	Only backup files that have changed at or after the specified time.

More Info:
The source and destination drives for the backup must be different. Backup destroys all information on the destination drive.
Examples:

```
backup c:\working z: /s
backup c: f: /l:c:\logs\backup.log
```

break

Turns Ctrl+C checking on and off on DOS systems or sets or clears breakpoints for the NT debugger.

```
break
```

cacls

Displays and modifies a file's access control list (ACL).

```
cacls filename [/t] [/e] [/c] [/g user:perm] [/r user [...]]@@1b
    [/p user:perm [...]] [/d user [...]]
```

filename	Displays ACLs for the specified files. You can use wildcards.
/c	Forces changes even if errors occur.

/d *user*	Denies specified user access.
/e	Edits ACL instead of replacing it.
/g *user:perm*	Grants specified user access rights. Rights can be R-Read, C-Change (write), or F-Full Control.
/p *user:perm*	Replaces specified user's access rights. Rights can be N-None, R-Read, C-Change (write), or F-Full Control.
/r *user*	Revokes specified user's access rights; can be used only with /e.
/t	Changes ACLs of specified files in the current directory and all subdirectories.

More Info:
You can use wildcards to specify more than one file. You can also specify more than one user if necessary.

Examples:

```
cacls c:\working\*.* /e /r guest
cacls c:\working\*.* /g wrstanek:f
```

call

Calls a script or script label as a procedure.

```
call [drive:][path]filename [batch-parameters]
call :label [args]
```

[*drive:*][*path*][*filename*]	Sets the name and location of the script to call.
batch-parameters	Sets any command-line information required by the script.
:*label* [*args*]	Sets a script label to call with optional arguments.

More Info:

When you call a script from within a script, the script executes and then control returns to the calling script. If you don't use `call` and reference a script name within a script, the second script executes and control isn't returned to the caller.

`call` can also be used with procedure labels. Here, the script goes to the specified label and executes its commands, and then control returns to the first line following `call`.

Examples:

call.bat

```
echo "Lets start!"
call :TASK1
call :TASK2

:TASK1
echo "Task 1 is executing"
goto :EOF

:TASK2
echo "Task 2 is executing"
goto :EOF
```

Output

```
Lets start!
Task 1 is executing
Task 2 is executing
```

cd

Displays the name of or changes the current directory.

```
chdir [/d] [drive:][path]
chdir [..]
cd [/d] [drive:][path]
cd [..]
```

`..`	Changes to the parent directory.
`[drive:]path`	Sets the drive and path to which you want to change.
`/d`	Changes current drive in addition to changing current directory.

More Info:

Enter **cd** on a line by itself to display the current working directory.

Examples:

```
cd
cd /d C:\working
```

chcp

Displays or sets the active code page number.

```
chcp [nnn]
```

nnn   Sets a code page number.

More Info:

Code pages are used to specify how character-based displays handle extended characters. Usually, the code page is 437 (U.S.) or 850 (Latin I). Changing the code page doesn't affect standard characters but does effect extended characters such as Cyrillic.

Enter **chcp** by itself to display the active code page number. Valid code page values include

437	United States
850	Latin I (multinational)
852	Latin II (slavic)
855	Cyrillic (Russian)
857	Turkish
860	Portuguese
869	Modern Greek

Examples:

```
chcp
chcp 437
```

chdir

Displays the name of or changes the current directory.

See cd.

chkdsk

Checks a disk for errors and displays a report.

```
chkdsk [drive:][[path]filename] [/f] [/v] [/r] [/l[:size]] [/C] [/I]
```

`[drive:]`	Sets the drive to check.
`[path]filename`	Sets the files and directories to check for fragmentation (FAT only).
`/c`	On NTFS, skips checking of cycles within the directory tree.
`/f`	Fixes errors on the disk.
`/I`	On NTFS, performs a less vigorous check of index entries.
`/l:size`	On NTFS, changes size of the check disk log (in KB). If size is not specified, the current size is displayed.
`/r`	Finds bad sectors and recovers readable information.
`/v`	On FAT, lists each file as it is checked.

Examples:

```
chkdsk /f /r c:
chkdsk c: d:
```

cls

Clears the console window.

```
cls
```

More Info:
Used at the command line or in a script to clear the console window.

cmd

Starts a new instance of the Windows NT command shell.

```
cmd [/x | /y] [/a | /u] [/q] [/t:fg] [[/c | /k] string]
```

string	A command file, script or program.
/a	Sets ANSI text for output (the default).
/c	Executes the command string and then terminates.
/k	Carries out the command string but remains active.
/q	Turns command echoing off
/t:*fg*	Sets the foreground/background colors.
/u	Sets output as Unicode character set.
/x	Enables command extensions (the default).
/y	Disables command extensions.

More Info:
Commands with extensions include: assoc, call, cd, chdir, color, del, endlocal, erase, for, ftype, goto, if, md, mkdir, popd, prompt, pushd, set, setlocal, shift, and start.
See color for a list of acceptable color values.

Examples:

```
cmd /k machinetest.bat
cmd /Q
```

color

Sets the foreground and background colors of the command shell window.

```
color [bf]
```

bf   Sets the background and foreground color of the command shell window.

More Info:
If no color value is specified, the command shell window colors are reset to the default value. The acceptable color values are

0 = Black   8 = Gray

1 = Blue   9 = Bright Blue

2 = Green   A = Bright Green

3 = Aqua   B = Bright Aqua

4 = Red   C = Bright Red

5 = Purple	D = Bright Purple
6 = Yellow	E = Bright Yellow
7 = White	F = Bright White

Examples:

```
color
color 07
```

comp

Compares the contents of two files or sets of files.

```
comp [data1] [data2] [/d] [/a] [/1] [/n=number] [/c]
```

data1	Sets location of first file(s) to compare.
data2	Sets location of second file(s) to compare.
/a	Displays differences in ASCII characters.
/c	Disregards case of ASCII letters when comparing files.
/d	Displays differences in decimal format. This is the default setting.
/1	Displays line numbers for differences.
/n=number	Compares only the first specified number of lines in each file.

More Info:
You can compare a group of files in one folder with a group of files in another folder using wildcard characters.
Examples:

```
comp D:\working\*.* E:\working\*.* /a
comp current.txt old.txt /n=500
```

compact

Displays or alters the compression of files on NTFS partitions.

```
compact [/c | /u] [/s[:dir]] [/a] [/i] [/f] [/q] [filename [...]]
```

filename	Sets the files or directories to compress.
/a	Displays or compresses files with the hidden or system attributes. These files are omitted by default.
/c	Compresses the specified files, directories, and/or drives. Directories will be marked so that files added afterward will be compressed.
/f	Forces the compression or uncompression on all specified files and directories, even those which are already flagged as compressed. Otherwise, flagged files and directories are skipped by default.
/i	Ignores errors. By default, compact stops when an error is encountered.
/q	Quiet mode so only essential information is reported.
/s	Includes subdirectories.
/u	Uncompresses the specified files, directories, and/or drives. Directories will be marked so that files added afterward will not be compressed.

More Info:

If you use compact without parameters, you can view the compression state of the current directory and any files it contains. You can use multiple filenames and wildcards.

Examples:

```
compact /i /c c:\working\scripts
compact /f /u d:\
```

convert

Converts FAT volumes to NTFS.

```
convert drive: /fs:NTFS [/v]
```

drive:	Sets the drive to convert to NTFS.
/fs:NTFS	Switch needed to convert the volume to NTFS.
/v	Run in verbose mode.

More Info:

If you try to convert the current drive or any drive being used by the operating system, you are prompted you to convert the drive on reboot. If you accept, a flag is set and the drive is converted the next time you reboot the system. If you decline, the operation is cancelled.

Examples:

```
convert d: /fs:NTFS
convert d: /fs:NTFS /v
```

copy

Copies or combines files.

```
copy [/a | /b] source [/a | /b] [+ source [/a | /b] [+ ...]]@@1b
     [destination [/a | /b]] [/v] [/n]
```

+	Indicates that files should be combined.
=	Combines a group of files specified with wildcards into a single destination file.
source	Sets the copy source.
destination	Sets the destination.
/a	Indicates an ASCII text file.
/b	Indicates a binary file.
/n	Uses short filename, if available, when copying a file.
/v	Verifies that new files are written correctly.
/z	Copies networked files in restartable mode, which reduces network write errors.

More Info:

When multiple files are copied or combined, copy lists the files being manipulated at the command line.

Examples:

```
copy *.txt d:\working\network\scripts
copy f1.txt + f2.txt + f3.txt /z combined.txt
copy *.rtf = combined.rtf
```

date

Displays or sets the date.

```
date [mm-dd-yy]
```

mm-dd-yy   Sets the date in MM-DD-YYYY format. MM can be 1-12. DD can
                  be 1-31. YY can be 80-99 or 1980-2079.

More Info:
Type in **date** and press Enter to set the date interactively.
Examples:

```
date
date 04-11-2002
```

del

Deletes one or more files.

```
del [/p] [/f] [/s] [/q] [/a[[:]attributes]]
    [drive:][path]filename
erase [/p] [/f] [/s] [/q] [/a[[:]attributes]]
    [[drive:][path]filename
```

[drive:][path]filename	Sets the file(s) to delete. Specify multiple files by using wildcards.
/a	Selects files to delete based on their attributes. These values are used:

/aa	Files ready for archive
/a-a	Files not ready for archive
/ah	Hidden files
/a-h	Not hidden files
/ar	Read-only files
/a-r	Not read-only files
/as	System files
/a-s	Not system files

/f	Forces deletion of read-only files.
/p	Prompts for a confirmation before deleting each file.
/q	Quiet mode, do not ask if okay to execute global delete (*.*).
/s	Deletes specified files from all subdirectories.

More Info:
Be careful when using the /s switch with wildcards. You can accidentally delete your entire drive.
Examples:

```
del *.xls /a-r
del s?????.doc
del *.* /q /f
```

debug

Starts the command-line debugger.

```
debug [[drive:][path]filename [testfile-parameters]]
```

[drive:][path]filename	Sets the executable file you want to debug.
testfile-parameters	Sets command-line information that is required by the executable you want to debug.
?	Displays a list of debugging commands once debug starts.

dir

Displays a list of files and subdirectories in a directory.

```
dir [drive:][path][filename] [/p] [/w] [/d] [/a[[:]attributes]]@@lb
    [/o[[:]sortorder]] [/t[[:]timefield]] [/s] [/b] [/l] [/n]@@lb
    [/x] [/c]
```

| [drive:][path][filename] | Sets drive, directory, and/or files to list. |

/a[[:]attributes]	Displays files and subdirectories with specified attributes. You can combine multiple attributes. Valid attributes are

d	Directories *and subdirectories (if applicable)
r	Read-only files
h	Hidden files
a	Files ready for archiving
s	System files
-	Prefix meaning not

/b	Don't add headings or summary information.
/c	Displays commas in file sizes. This is the default. Use /-c to disable display of commas.
/d	Same as wide but files are list sorted by column.
/l	Uses lowercase.
/n	Uses long list format with filenames on the far right.
/o[[:]sortorder]	Lists by files in sorted order. Sort order flags are

d	By date and time with oldest files first
-d	By date and time with most recently updated files first
e	By extension alphanumerically
-e	By extensions reverse alphanumerically
g	Group directories first
-g	Group directories last
n	By name alphanumerically
-n	By name, reverse alphanumeric
s	By size, smallest to largest
-s	By size, largest to smallest

/p	Pauses after each screen of information.

/s	Displays files in subdirectories as well.
/t[[:]timefield]	Controls which time field is displayed or used for sorting. Valid modifiers are

a	Last access date
c	Creation date
w	Last written date

/w	Uses wide list format.
/x	Displays the short file names as well as long file names. If no short name is present, blanks are displayed in its place.

More Info:

You can set directory listing preferences with the DIRCMD environment variable and then override presets if necessary by negating the default switch, such as /-x.

Examples:

```
dir /a:sh
dir /o:-d /x
```

diskcomp

Compares the contents of two floppy disks.

```
diskcomp [drive1: [drive2:]]
```

[drive1:]	Drive as source for comparison.
[drive2:]	Drive as target for comparison.

Example:

```
diskcomp a: b:
```

diskcopy

Copies the contents of one floppy disk to another.

```
diskcopy [drive1: [drive2:]] [/v]
```

[*drive1*:]	Source drive.
[*drive2*:]	Destination drive.
/v	Verifies that the information is copied correctly.

More Info:

To copy a disk on a system with only one floppy drive, you can specify the same drive for drive1 and drive2 (or just specify a single drive in the first place). When copying two disks, the disks must be the same type.

Examples:

```
diskcopy a: b: /v
diskcopy a:
```

doskey

Edits command lines, recalls Windows NT commands, and creates macros.

```
doskey [/reinstall] [/listsize=size] [/macros[:all | :exename]]
       [/history] [/insert | /overstrike] [/exename=exename]
       [/macrofile=filename] [macroname=[text]]
```

macroname	Sets a name for a macro you create.
text	Sets commands you want to record.
/exename=*exename*	Sets the executable to associate the macro with.
/history	Displays all commands stored in memory.
/insert	Turns on insert mode.
/listsize=*size*	Sets the size of command history buffer.
/macrofile=*filename*	Sets a file of macros to use in the current command shell.
/macros	Displays all macros for the current command shell.
/macros:all	Displays macros for all executables which have settings.
/macros:*exename*	Displays all macros for the specified executable.
/overstrike	Sets overwrite mode.
/reinstall	Installs a new copy of doskey.

More Info:

Use these techniques when working with the command history and macros:

◆ Use the up and down arrows to recall commands.

◆ ESC clears command line.

◆ F7 displays command history.

◆ ALT+F7 clears command history.

◆ F8 searches command history.

◆ F9 selects a command by number.

◆ ALT+F10 clears macro definitions.

Special codes you can use in macro definitions are

◆ $T   Command separator that allows multiple commands in a macro.

◆ $1-$9   Batch parameters that allow you to pass in arguments, %1, %2, %3, ..., and up to %9.

◆ $◆   Passes everything after the macro name to the specified command.

Examples:

```
doskey sdir=dir /s /o:e > dirlist.txt
doskey /macros /exename=ftp.exe
doskey /macrofile=mymacros.txt
```

echo

Displays messages, or turns command echoing on or off.

```
echo [on | off]
echo [message]
```

More Info:

Enter echo without parameters to display the current echo setting.

Examples:

```
echo on
echo "Hello, World!"
```

edit

Starts the MS-DOS editor.

```
edit [[drive:][path]filename] [/b] [/g] [/h] [/nohi]
```

`[drive:][path]filename`	Sets the path to the ASCII file to edit.
`/b`	Starts `edit` in black and white.
`/g`	Starts `edit` for use with CGA monitors.
`/h`	Displays `edit` in a larger window.
`/nohi`	Limits `edit` to 8 colors rather than 16 colors. Use if you see blinking text instead of bold.

Examples:

```
edit sample.txt /h
edit sample.txt /nohi
```

edlin

Starts `edlin`, a line-by-line text editor.

```
edlin [drive:][path]filename [/b]
```

`[drive:][path]filename`	Specifies the path to a file you want to edit (which is mandatory).
`/b`	Ignores EOF characters (Ctrl+Z).

Examples:

```
edlin autoexec.bat
edlin system.ini
```

endlocal

Ends localization of environment changes in a batch file.

```
endlocal
```

More Info:

Stops localization of variables started with setlocal. If you setlocal, all variables created with set var=value are deleted when endlocal is executed and all original variables are restored (if they were overwritten locally).

Example:

```
setlocal

rem work with local variables in here

endlocal
```

erase

Deletes one or more files.
See del.

exe2bin

Converts .exe files to binary format for use with debug.

```
exe2bin [drive1:][path1]input-file @@1b
    [[drive2:][path2]output-file]
```

[drive1:][path1]input-file	Sets the .exe file to be converted.
[drive2:][path2]output-file	Sets the binary file to be created with the .bin extension.

More Info:

If you don't specify an output file, the output file is named after the source. So the output for a file called hello.exe would be hello.bin.

Examples:

```
exe2bin help.exe
exe2bin help.exe D:\working\help-debug.bin
```

exit

Quits the cmd.exe program (command interpreter).

```
exit
```

More Info:
You can use this in scripts to exit the script and the command shell. If the command shell is in full-screen mode, `exit` returns you to NT.

expand

Uncompresses files compressed with the Microsoft distribution format.

```
expand [-r] source destination
expand -r source [destination]
```

`-r`	Rename expanded files.
`source`	Source files to be expanded.
`destination`	Destination file path.

More Info:
You can use wildcards when specifying the source files. Also, if you don't specify a destination path, the current directory is used.
Examples:

```
expand -r setup.ex_
expand *.ex_ d:\working\distro\
```

fc

Compares two files and displays the differences between them.

```
fc [/a] [/c] [/l] [/lbn] [/n] [/t] [/u] [/w] [/nnnn] @@lb
    [drive1:][path1]filename1 [drive2:][path2]filename2
fc /b [drive1:][path1]filename1 [drive2:][path2]filename2
```

`[drive1:][path1]filename1`	Source file for comparison.
`[drive2:][path2]filename2`	Target file to use in comparison.
`/nnnn`	When attempting to resync ASCII text files, this specifies the number of lines that must match before the command considers an area to be identical. By default, two lines must match

	before the command considers an area to be identical.
/a	Displays only the first and last lines for each set of differences.
/b	Performs a binary comparison.
/c	Disregards the case of letters in the comparison.
/l	Compares files as ASCII text.
/lb*n*	Sets the maximum consecutive mismatches before FC cancels the operation.
/n	Displays the line numbers on an ASCII comparison.
/t	FC compares tabs within files to spacing to detect differences. By default, FC converts tabs to spaces for comparisons. To turn this feature off, use this switch.
/u	Compares files as UNICODE rather than ASCII.
/w	Ignores white space (tabs and spaces) for comparison. Here, multiple spaces and tabs are converted to a single space for the comparison.

More Info:

In binary mode, fc displays all differences. In ASCII/Unicode mode, fc looks for differences area by area. The sizes of these areas are set with /*nnnn*, such as /0050.

Examples:

```
fc /a /1b50 /0004 attitude.txt changes.txt
fc /b cr.bin cr2.bin
```

find

Searches for a text string in files.

```
find [/v] [/c] [/n] [/i] "string" @@1b
    [[drive:][path]filename[ ...]]
```

[*drive:*][*path*]*filename*	Sets the file or files to search. You can use wildcards.
"*string*"	Sets the text string to find.

/v	Displays all lines NOT containing the specified string.
/c	Counts the number of lines containing the string.
/n	Displays line numbers with matching lines of text.
/i	Ignores case in search.

More Info:

Find can accept the output of other commands as input. If you do this, you don't need to specify a file to search.

Examples:

```
find /v "test" working.txt
dir | find /i " s"
```

findstr

Searches for strings in files using regular expressions.

```
findstr [/b] [/e] [/l] [/r] [/s] [/i] [/x] [/v] [/n] [/m] [/o]@@lb
    [/f:file] [/c:string] [/g:file] [strings]@@lb
    [[drive:][path]filename[ ...]]
```

strings	Sets the search text. If the text contains spaces, use quotation marks.
[drive:][path]filename	Sets the file or files to search.
/b	Matches pattern if at the beginning of a line.
/c:string	Performs search for the exact text specified in string (a literal search).
/e	Matches pattern if at the end of a line.
/f:file	Reads list of search files from the specified file (/ stands for console).
/g:file	Gets search strings from the specified file (/ stands for console).
/i	Ignores case.
/l	Uses search strings literally.

/m	Prints only the filename if a file contains a match.
/n	Prints line number before each line that matches.
/o	Prints character offset before each matching line to tell you where the match was found in the line.
/p	Skips files with nonprintable characters.
/r	Uses search strings as regular expressions (the default behavior).
/s	Searches subdirectories.
/v	Prints only lines that do not contain a match.
/x	Prints lines that match exactly. Requires the use of /c: or /l. Otherwise, no lines will match.

More Info:

When performing literal searches, multiple keywords are searched for individually. For example, if you enter **William Stanek**, findstr would search for lines with either William or Stanek by default. To change this behavior, use /l and not /r. With normal searches and /r searches, you can use regular expressions in the search text. Characters used in regular expressions are

.	Matches any single character. "TO" would match "TOY," "TON," and "TOP."
*	Matches zero or more occurrences. "TO*" would match "TOMORROW," "TODAY," and "TONIGHT."
^	Matches text only at the beginning of line. You could search for all lines beginning with TO: using "^TO:"
$	Matches text only at the end of the line. You could search for all lines ending with :RATED using ":RATED$"
[chars]	Matches a single character to any of the characters listed within the brackets, such as [abcABC]
[^chars]	Matches any single character except for the characters listed in the brackets, such as [^0123]
[x-y]	Matches a single character to any character in the specified range. For all uppercase letters use [A-Z]. For numerals use [0-9].

`[^x-y]`	Matches a single character to any character except if it is in the specified range. To exclude numerals from the matching, use [^0-9].
`\x`	Escapes a reserved character. For example, to match the backslash (\) in file paths in a search, you have to use \\, such as "C:\\working\\data".
`\<`	Matches the beginning of a word only.
`\>`	Matches the end of a word only.

Examples:

```
findstr /i "^TO: :RATED$" C:\working\temp\data*.txt
findstr /f:filelist.txt /g:searchstr.txt C:\*.txt
```

for

Runs a specified command for each file in a set of files.
   Command-line `for` looping:

```
for %variable in (set) do command
for /d %variable in (set) do command
for /r [[drive:]path] %variable in (set) do command
for /l %variable in (start,step,end) do command
for /f ["options"] %variable in (set) do command
```

   Script `for` looping:

```
for %%variable in (set) do command
for /d %%variable in (set) do command
for /r [[drive:]path] %%variable in (set) do command
for /l %%variable in (start,step,end) do command
for /f ["options"] %%variable in (set) do command
```

`%variable`	Represents a replaceable variable (used at the command-line).
`%%variable`	Represents a replaceable variable (used in scripts).
`(set)`	Sets a set of one or more files (or text strings to process).
`(start,step,end)`	Sets a sequence of numbers from start to end, by step amount. So (1,2,5) would generate the sequence 1 3 5 and (5,-2,1) would generate the sequence 5 3 1.

command	Sets the command to carry out for each file or text string. Parameters may be passed to the command.
`"options"`	Sets options for text searches of files. These options are

`eol=c`	Sets the end of line comment character, such as `eol=;`
`skip=n`	Sets the number of lines to skip at the beginning of files, such as `skip=5`
`delims=xxx`	Sets delimiters to use instead of space and tab, such as `delims=,:`.
`tokens=x,y,m-n`	Sets which tokens from each line are to be placed in variables for iteration, such as `tokens=1,3` or `tokens=2-5*`. You can specify up to 26 tokens (provided you don't try to set a variable higher than *z*).

More Info:

Note the different syntax used at the command line and in scripts. Basically, scripts use an additional % (so instead of `%var` you use `%%var`). For loops are covered in Chapter 5.

To examine `for` looping, consider the following example:

```
for /f "eol=; tokens=1,3* delims=,:" %i in (C:\working\*.txt) do
@echo %i %j %k
```

Here, the loop would parse each line in all text files found at C:\working. Line endings are designated with a semicolon and within lines the comma or colon are used to separate token parameters. The loop would pass the 1st token as `%i`, the 3rd token as `%j`, and all other token parameters are sent to `%k`.

You can also use commands or strings in `for` loops rather than files, such as

```
for /f "delims==" %i in ('set') do @echo %i
```

Here, you enumerate all environment variable names in the current environment. Notice that the delimiter for parameters is set as the equal sign (=).

Examples:

```
for /l %I in (1,1,8) do set ARRAY_%I=0
for /f "delims==" %i in ('set') do @echo "Variable :" %I
for /r in (*.bat) do copy %I C:\working\scripts
```

forcedos

Starts a program in MS-DOS (command.com) rather than in Windows NT Command Shell (cmd.exe).

```
forcedos [/d directory] filename [parameters]
```

/d directory	Sets the current directory for the specified program to use.
filename	Sets the program to start.
parameters	Sets parameters to pass to the program.

More Info:
Use this command if NT doesn't recognize your program as an MS-DOS application (or if it doesn't function at the NT command line).

Examples:

```
forcedos /D random.exe
forcedos random.exe
```

format

Formats a floppy disk or hard drive for use with Windows NT.

```
format drive: [/fs:file-system] [/v:label] [/q] [/a:size] [/c]
format drive: [/v:label] [/q] [/f:size]
format drive: [/v:label] [/q] [/t:tracks /n:sectors]
format drive: [/v:label] [/q] [/1] [/4]
format drive: [/q] [/1] [/4] [/8]
```

drive:	Specifies the drive to format.
/1	Formats a single side of a floppy disk.
/4	Formats a 5.25-inch, 360KB, floppy disk in a high-density drive.
/8	Formats a 5.25-inch disk with eight sectors per track.
/a:size	Overrides the default allocation unit size. NTFS supports 512, 1024, 2048, 4096, 8192, 16K, 32K, and 64K. FAT supports 8192, 16K, 32K, 64K, 128K, and 256K. NTFS compression is not supported for allocation unit sizes above 4096.

/c	Turns on file compression.
/f:*size*	Sets the size of the floppy disk to format. Common sizes are 360 or 1.2 for 5.25-inch disks and 1.44 or 2.88 for 3.5-inch disks.
/fs:*file-system*	Sets the type of the file system as FAT or NTFS.
/n:*sectors*	Sets the number of sectors per track. Used with /t and cannot be used with /f.
/q	Performs a quick format.
/t:*tracks*	Sets the number of tracks per disk side.
/v:*label*	Sets the volume label.

Examples:

```
format e: /FS:NTFS /C /V:Secondary
format a: /Q
```

ftype

Displays or modifies file types used in file extension associations.

```
ftype [fileType[=[command]]]
```

fileType	Sets the file type examine or change.
command	Sets the launch command to use when opening files of this type.

More Info:
To display the current file types, enter **ftype** without any parameters. To delete an existing file type, set its launch command to an empty string, such as

```
ftype perl=
```

If passing arguments, %0 or %1 are substituted with the file name being launched through the association. %* gets all the parameters and %2 gets the 1st parameter, %3 the second, etc. %~n gets all the remaining parameters starting with the *n*th parameter, where *n* may be between 2 and 9.

Examples:

```
assoc .pl=Perl
ftype Perl=C:\winnt\system32\perl.exe %1 %*
```

goto

Directs the Windows NT command interpreter to a labeled line in a script.

```
goto :label
goto :EOF
```

:label Sets a text string used in the scripts as a label.

More Info:
To create a label, enter a keyword on a line by itself, beginning with a colon, such as

```
:SUB1
```

You can use the target label of `:EOF` to transfer control to the end of the script. With `call`, this forces the caller to return.

Examples:

```
goto :SUB1

Insert commands here

:SUB1
```

graftable

Enables Windows NT to display an extended character set in full-screen mode.

```
graftabl [nnn]
graftabl /status
```

nnn	Sets a code page number.
/status	Displays the current code page selected for use with graftabl.

More Info:
Type **graftabl** on a line by itself to see the current code page setting. See `chcp` for more information on code pages.

Examples:

```
graftabl
```

```
graftabl 850
```

graphics

Prints the command shell window to a printer.

```
graphics [type] [[drive:][path]filename] [/r] [/b] [/lcd]@@lb
    [/printbox:std | /printbox:lcd]
```

`type`	Sets a printer type. Common printer types include	
	`hpdefault`	Any HP PCL (or compatible) printer
	`deskjet`	Any HP DeskJet (or compatible) printer
	`laserjet`	Any HP LaserJet (or compatible) printer
	`thinkjet`	IBM ThinkJet (or compatible) printer
`[drive:][path]filename`	Sets the path to a printer profile file.	
`/b`	Prints the background in color (if possible).	
`/lcd`	Prints using LCD aspect ratio.	
`/printbox:std`	Sets the print-box size as `std`.	
`/printbox:lcd`	Sets the print-box size as `lcd`.	
`/r`	Prints white on black as seen on the screen.	

Examples:

```
graphics laserjet
graphics deskjet /printbox:std /r
```

help

Provides Help information for Windows NT commands.

```
help [command]
```

command displays help information on that command.

More Info:

With some commands, you need to type the command name followed by the /? parameter to get help, such as

```
graphics /?
```

Example:

```
help cmd
```

if

Performs conditional processing in batch programs.

```
if [not] errorlevel number command
if [not] [/i] string1==string2 command
if [not] exist filename command
if [/i] string1 compare-op string2 command
if cmdextversion number command
if defined variable command
```

cmdextversion *number*	Sets a true condition if internal version number associated with the Command Extensions matches number. The first extension version is 1. cmdextversion conditional is never true when Command Extensions are disabled.
command	Sets the command to carry out if the condition is met.
compare-op	Performs comparison of *string1* and *string2* using the comparison operator provides. These operators are

equ	equal
geq	greater than or equal
gtr	greater than
leq	less than or equal
lss	less than
neq	not equal

`defined`	Sets a true condition if an environment variable is defined.
`errorlevel` *`number`*	Sets a true condition if the last program run returned an exit code equal to or greater than the number specified.
`exist` *`filename`*	Sets a true condition if the specified filename exists.
`/i`	Ignores case in string comparisons.
`not`	Executes the command only if the condition is false.
`string1==string2`	Sets a true condition if the specified text strings match. Strings can be variables passed as arguments, such as %1, or environment variables, such as %SystemRoot%.

More Info:

Two key environment variables are also available to `if` statements: %ERROR-LEVEL% and %CMDCMDLINE%. %ERRORLEVEL% represents the current value of `error-level` (as long as it wasn't set previously in the environment to something else). %CMDCMDLINE% represents the original command line passed to cmd.exe prior to any processing by cmd.exe (as long as it wasn't set previously in the environment to something else).

Examples:

```
if %ERRORLEVEL% gtr 1 goto fail
if exist c:\working goto SUB1
if "%OS%"=="Windows_NT" echo "OS is Windows NT"
```

label

Creates, changes, or deletes the volume label of a disk.

`label [drive:][label]`

`drive:`	The drive letter of the disk you want to name
`label`	The label for the drive

More Info:

Enter **label** without any arguments to change or delete the current volume's label.

Example:

```
label c: Primary
```

md

Creates a new directory or subdirectory.

```
mkdir [drive:]path
md [drive:]path
```

drive: Specifies the drive in which you want the new
                                directory created.

path   Specifies the path to the new directory or
                                subdirectory.

More Info:
As long as extensions are enabled in the command shell, md and mkdir can create multiple levels of directory structures. For example, you can create C:\work-
ing\scripts\fun when only the working folder previously existed.

Examples:

```
md C:\working\scripts\fun
mkdir C:\working\scripts\fun
```

mode

Configures a system device.
   serial port:

```
mode comm[:] [baud=b] [parity=p] [data=d]@@1b
    [stop=s] [to=on|off] [xon=on|off]@@1b
    [odsr=on|off] [octs=on|off] [dtr=on|off|hs]@@1b
    [rts=on|off|hs|tg] [idsr=on|off]
```

   device status:

```
mode [device] [/status]
```

redirect printing:

```
mode lptn[:]=comm[:]
```

select code page:

```
mode con[:] cp select=yyy
```

code page status:

```
mode con[:] cp [/status]
```

display mode:

```
mode con[:] [cols=c] [lines=n]
```

typematic rate:

```
mode con[:] [rate=r delay=d]
```

Examples:

```
mode LPT1=com3
mode con
```

more

Displays output one screen at a time.

```
more [/e [/c] [/p] [/s] [/tn] [+n]] < [drive:][path]filename
more /e [/c] [/p] [/s] [/tn] [+n] [files]

command-name | more [/e [/c] [/p] [/s] [/tn] [+n]]
```

[drive:][path]filename	Sets a file to display one screen at a time.
command-name	Sets a command whose output will be displayed.
/c	Clears screen before displaying page.
/e	Enables extended features.

/p	Expands form-feed characters.
/s	Reduces multiple blank lines to a single line.
/t*n*	Expands tabs to *n* spaces (default is 8).
+n	Starts displaying the first file at line *n*.
files	Specifies the list of files to be displayed. Files in the list are separated by blanks.

More Info:

If extended features are enabled, the following commands are accepted at the -- More -- prompt:

<Enter>	Display next line
<Space>	Display next page
?	Show help line
=	Show line number
f	Display next file
p *n*	Display next n lines
q	Quit
s *n*	Skip next n lines

Examples:

```
dir | more
more /c /e accounts.txt
```

move

Moves files from one directory to another directory on the same drive.

```
move [source] [target]
```

source	Sets the path and name of the files to move.
target	Sets the path and name where to move the files.

Examples:

```
move D:\*.bat D:\working\scripts\
move help.bat E:\help.bat
```

ntbooks

Runs the Windows NT online manuals.

```
ntbooks [/s] [/w] [/n:path]
```

/s	Accesses server manuals from a workstation.
/w	Accesses workstation manuals from a server.
/n:path	Specifies where to find the online manuals.

More Info:
By default, Windows NT looks for the online manuals on the distribution CD-ROM. If the CD-ROM isn't in the CD-ROM drive, you'll see a prompt asking you to specify where the online manuals are located. Either insert the CD or specify the drive path to the online manuals.

Examples:

```
ntbooks
ntbooks /s
```

path

Displays or sets a search path for executable files.

```
path [[drive:]path[;...][;%PATH%]
path ;
```

More Info:
The command path is set during logon using system and user environment variables, namely the %PATH% variable. To view current path setting, type **path** on a line by itself and press Enter. The directory order in the command path indicates the search order used by the command shell when looking for executables and scripts.

Update existing path information by appending a new path to the %PATH% environment variable, such as

```
path %PATH%;C:\scripts\networking
```

Clear the path by entering

```
path ;
```

Examples:

```
path
path C:\scripts\networking;%PATH%
```

pause

Suspends processing of a script and waits for keyboard input.

```
pause
```

More Info:
Suspends processing of a batch program and displays the message

```
Press any key to continue . . .
```

pentnt

Detects the floating-point division error in Pentium processors and turns floating-point emulation on or off.

```
pentnt [-c] [-f] [-o]
```

-c	Turns on conditional emulation. Here, floating point emulation is turned on only when the system detects the Pentium floating point division error at boot.
-f	Turns on emulation regardless of whether the error exists.
-o	Turns off forced emulation.

More Info:
The floating-point division error effects a limited number of PCs. If the error exists on your system, you can turn on emulation to correct the problem.
A reboot is required before changes take effect.

popd

Changes to the directory stored by `pushd`.

```
popd
```

More Info:
You can use this to return to a directory after changing to another directory. Once you pop the directory off the stack, the buffer is cleared.
Examples:

```
rem store current and change to c:\working\data
pushd C:\working\data

rem do some work here.

rem finished; restore previous working directory
popd
```

print

Prints a text file.

```
print [/d:device] [[drive:][path]filename[...]]
```

`/d:device`   Sets a print device.

`[drive:][path]filename`   Sets the files to print.

More Info:
Print devices you can use are parallel ports (LPT1, LPT2, LPT3) or serial ports (COM1, COM2, COM3, COM4). If you want to print multiple files separate file names with spaces.
Examples:

```
print /d:LPT1 stats.txt
print /d:COM1 net-test.txt working.txt
```

prompt

Changes the Windows NT command prompt.

```
prompt [text]
```

`text`	Sets the text for the new command prompt.

More Info:

Prompt can be made up of normal text and the following special codes:

`$a`	Ampersand character: &
`$b`	Pipe character: |
`$c`	Left parenthesis: (
`$d`	Displays current date, such as: Fri 09/10/1999.
`$e`	Escape code (ASCII character code 27)
`$f`	Right parenthesis:)
`$g`	Greater-than sign: >
`$h`	Backspace (used to erase previous character)
`$l`	Less-than sign: <
`$n`	Current working drive, such as: C:\
`$p`	Current drive and path, such as: C:\ or C:\working if you are in the working directory.
`$q`	Equal sign: =
`$s`	Inserts a space.
`$t`	Displays current time down to the millisecond, such as 09:10:35.70.
`$v`	Displays the Windows NT version, such as Windows NT version 4.0.
`$_`	Inserts a carriage return and linefeed.
`$$`	Dollar sign character: $
`$+`	Displays a series of plus sign (+) characters that correspond to the number of directories on the `pushd` stack. You can use `pushd` to store the current working directory before changing to a different directory.
`$m`	Displays the remote UNC name associated with the current drive letter in the form \\servername\share, such as \\ZETA\HOME. If current drive is not a network drive an empty string is displayed.

Examples:

```
prompt $T$$
prompt $V$$
```

pushd

Saves the current directory then changes to a new directory.

```
pushd [path | ..]
```

path   Sets the directory to make the current directory.

More Info:
If a network path is specified, `pushd` creates a temporary drive letter that points to that specified network resource and then changes the current drive and directory, using the newly defined drive letter. Temporary drive letters are allocated in reverse alphabetical order, starting at Z: and using the first unused drive letter found. See also `popd`.

Examples:

```
rem store current and change to \\Omega\working\data
pushd \\Omega\working\data

rem do some work here.

rem finished; restore previous working directory
```

popdQBASIC

Starts the Qbasic interpreter.

```
qbasic [/b] [/editor] [/g] [/h] [/mbf] [/nohi] [[/run] @@1b
    [drive:][path]filename]
```

[[*drive:*][*path*]*filename*]	Sets the program file to load or run.
/b	Runs Qbasic in black and white mode (even if you have a color graphics card).
/editor	Starts the MS-DOS Editor.
/g	Sets mode for CGA screen.

/h	Increases the size of the interpreter window if possible.
/mbf	Converts the built-in functions mks$, mkd$, cvs, and cvd to mksmbf$, mkdmbf$, cvsmbf, and cvdmbf, respectively.
/nohi	Sets 8-color palette instead of 16-color palette.
/run	Runs the specified Basic program before displaying it.

rd

Removes a directory.

```
rmdir [/s] [/q] [drive:]path
rd [/s] [/q] [drive:]path
```

[drive:]path	Sets a drive and directory to remove.
/q	Sets quiet mode so you aren't prompt to confirm removal of subdirectories.
/s	Removes all subdirectories as well.

More Info:
Be careful when using wildcards with rd, especially if you use the /s switch.
Examples:

```
rd c:\working\data\*.bat
rmdir c:\working\data\*.bat
```

recover

Recovers readable information from a bad or defective disk.

```
recover [drive:][path]filename
```

[drive:][path]filename	Sets the drive, directory, or file to recover.

Example:

```
recover a:
```

rem

Adds comments to scripts.

```
rem [comment]
```

comment   The text of the comment
More Info:
Lines that begin with rem aren't interpreted.
Examples:

```
rem **************************
rem * Author: William R. Stanek
rem **************************
```

ren

Renames a file.

```
rename [drive:][path]filename1 filename2.
ren [drive:][path]filename1 filename2.
```

[drive:]path   Sets the drive and directory path to use.

filename1   The file you want to rename.

filename2   The new name for the file.

More Info:
You cannot specify a new drive or path for the destination file. Because of this, the renamed file is always located in the same directory as the original file. If the filename contains spaces, use double quotation marks.

Examples:

```
rename D:\working\scripts\network\dat.bat netb-test.bat
ren D:\working\scripts\network\dat.bat netb-test.bat
```

rename

Renames a file or files.
See ren.

replace

Replaces files from one directory with files from another.

```
replace [drive1:][path1]filename [drive2:][path2] [/a] [/p]@@1b
    [/r] [/w]
replace [drive1:][path1]filename [drive2:][path2] [/p] [/r]@@1b
    [/s] [/w] [/u]
```

`[drive1:][path1]filename`	Sets the source files. You can use wildcards to specify multiple files.
`[drive2:][path2]`	Sets the directory where files are to be replaced.
`/a`	Adds new files to destination directory. This option cannot be used with the /s or /u switches.
`/p`	Prompts for confirmation before replacing or adding files.
`/r`	Replaces read-only files and unprotected files.
`/s`	Replaces files in all subdirectories of the destination directory. This option cannot be used with the /a switch.
`/u`	Replaces files only when they are older than source files. This option cannot be used with the /a switch.
`/w`	Waits for you to insert a disk before beginning.

Examples:

```
replace A:\*.bat C:\working\data\ /a
replace C:\data\*.doc D:\data\current\ /u
```

restore

Restores files that were backed up with the backup command.

```
restore drive1: drive2:[path[filename]] [/s] [/p] [/b:date]@@1b
```

```
[/a:date] [/e:time] [/1:time] [/m] [/n] [/d]
```

drive1:	Sets the drive on which the backup files are stored.
drive2:[*path*[*filename*]]	Sets the destination drive to which the backed up files will be restored. Can include the complete path and with individual files, a filename.
/a:*date*	Restores only those files that have changed on or after the specified date.
/b:*date*	Restores only those files that have changed on or before the specified date.
/d	Displays files on the backup disk without performing the restore operation.
/e:*time*	Restores only those files that have changed at or earlier than the specified time.
/1:*time*	Restores only those files that have changed at or later than the specified time.
/m	Restores only files that have been modified since the last backup.
/n	Restores only files that no longer exist on the destination disk.
/p	Prompts before restoring read-only files or files that changed since the last backup.
/s	Restores all subdirectories under path.

More Info:

Restore can only be used with backup. If another backup tool was used to create the backup, you shouldn't use restore.

Examples:

```
restore e: c:\data\ /s
restore f: /d
```

rmdir

Removes a directory.
See rd.

set

Displays or modifies Windows NT environment variables.

```
set [variable=[string]]
set /a expression
```

`expression`	The numerical expression to evaluate.
`string`	Sets a series of characters to assign to the variable.
`variable`	Sets the environment-variable name.
`/a`	Specifies that you are evaluating a numerical expression.

More Info:

Enter set without parameters to display the current environment variables. You can also view the value of a specific variable or all variables whose names begin with the letter you enter after a set, such as

```
set u
```

To remove a variable set it to an empty value, such as

```
set temp=
```

When evaluating expressions, the order of precedence from highest to lowest is

`( )`	For grouping.
`* / %`	For multiplication, division, and modulus.
`+ -`	For addition and subtraction.
`<< >`	For logical shifts.
`&`	For bitwise and.
`^`	For bitwise exclusive or.
`|`	For bitwise or.
`= *= /= %= += -=`	For assignment operators.
`&= ^= |= <<= >=`	For expression separators.

Examples:

```
set TEMP=D:\working\temp
set /a sum= X*Y
set /a sum+=1
```

setlocal

Begins localization of environment changes in a batch file.

```
setlocal
setlocal enableextensions | disableextensions
```

enableextensions   Turns on command extensions within the localized
                          environment.

enableextensions   Turns off command extensions within the localized
                          environment.

More Info:
All variables created with set var=value are valid only within the localized environment. When endlocal is executed and all original variables are restored (if they were overwritten locally) and the localized variables are deleted.

Examples:

```
setlocal

rem work with local variables in here

endlocal
```

shift

Shifts the position of replaceable parameters in scripts.

```
shift [/n]
```

/n   Tells the command to start shifting at the nth argument, where n may be
       between zero and eight.

More Info:
Shifting is useful if you need to access arguments beyond the first nine passed in to the script. If you call shift without arguments, all parameters are shifted by 1. Here, %0 is discarded and replaced with %1, %1 becomes %0, %2 becomes %1, and so on. Rearrange parameters passed in to a script.

Use /*n* to specify where shifting begins so you can retain previous parameters if necessary. For example, if you use

```
shift /2
```

then %3 becomes %2, %4 becomes %3, and so on, but %0 and %1 are unaffected. **Examples:**

```
shift
shift 4
```

sort

Sorts input.

```
sort [/r] [/+n] < [drive1:][path1]filename1 [>@@lb
    [drive2:][path2]filename2]
```

```
[command |] sort [/r] [/+n] [> [drive2:][path2]filename2]
```

[drive1:][path1]filename1	Sets a source file to be sorted.
[drive2:][path2]filename2	Sets a destination file where the sorted input is to be stored.
command	Sets a command whose output is to be sorted.
/+n	Sorts the file according beginning with column n.
/r	Reverses the sort order (Z to A, then 9 to 0).

More Info:
Sort used alphanumeric sorting by default and can accept input from commands.
Examples:

```
dir | sort > sorted_dir.txt
sort /+25 < users.txt > sorted_users.txt
```

start

Starts a new command shell window to run a specified program or command.

```
start ["title"] [/dpath] [/i] [/min] [/max] [/separate|/shared]@@1b
    [/low | /normal | /high | /realtime] [/wait] [/b]@@1b
    [command/program] [parameters]
```

"title"	Sets title to display in the command shell window's title bar.
/b	Starts application without creating a new window.
/dpath	Sets the starting directory for the application.
/high	Starts application with a high system priority.
/i	Passes the current environment to the new window.
/low	Starts application with a low system priority.
/max	Starts window maximized.
/min	Starts window minimized.
/normal	Starts application with a normal system priority.
/realtime	Starts application with a realtime system priority.
/separate	Starts a 16-bit Windows program in separate memory space.
/shared	Starts a 16-bit Windows program in shared memory space.
/wait	Starts an application and waits for it to terminate.

More Info:

System priority sets a relative value for how much processor time the application gets. You should rarely use the realtime priority.

Examples:

```
start "Testing..." "dir | sort"
start "Housekeeping Tasks" /low /min cmd /c htasks.bat
```

subst

Maps a path to a drive letter.

```
subst [drive1: [drive2:]path]
subst drive1: /d
```

drive1:	Sets a virtual drive to which you want to assign a path.
[*drive2:]path*	Sets a physical drive and path you want to assign to a virtual drive.
/d	Deletes a virtual drive.

More Info:
Enter **subst** with no parameters to display a list of current virtual drives.
Examples:

```
subst k: d:\working\scripts
subst k: /d
```

time

Displays or sets the system time.

```
time [time]
time [/T]
```

time   Sets the time in [HH:[MM:[SS.[hh]]]][A|P] format.

/t   Displays the current time without a prompt.

More Info:
Time is normally set on a 24-hour clock. You can also set an A.M. or P.M. value if you use the A or P modifiers. Valid values are

Hours: 0 to 23

Minutes: 0 to 59

Seconds: 0 to 59

Hundredths: 0 to 99

Examples:

```
time /t
time 22:50
```

title

Sets the title for the command shell window.

```
title [string]
```

string The title for the command prompt window.

Example:

```
title Testing...
```

tree

Graphically displays the directory structure of a drive or path.

```
tree [drive:][path] [/f] [/a]
```

/a   Use ASCII instead of extended characters to draw the directory structure.

/f   Display the names of the files in each directory.

Examples:

```
tree c:\winnt
tree c:\ /a > fs-struct.txt
```

type

Displays the contents of a text file.

```
type [drive:][path]filename
```

[drive:][path]filename   Sets the file you want to view at the command line.
     Examples:

```
type stats.txt
type stats.txt | more
```

ver

Displays the Windows NT version.

```
ver
```

More Info:
Use in scripts to determine the current OS version.

verify

Tells Windows NT whether to verify that your files are written correctly to a disk.

```
verify [on | off]
```

on   Turns verification on.

off   Turns verification off.

More Info:
Enter **verify** without a parameter to display the current `verify` setting. Verify is normally turned off as it is not needed with most drive and file system types.
Examples:

```
verify
verify off
```

vol

Displays a disk volume label and serial number.

```
vol [drive:]
```

drive: The drive letter of the disk for which you want to see volume info.

More Info:
Enter **vol** without a parameter to display information for the current drive.
Examples:

```
vol
vol H:
```

xcopy

Copies files and directory trees.

```
xcopy source [destination] [/a | /m] [/d[:date]] [/p] [/s [/e]]@@lb
    [/v] [/w] [/c] [/i] [/q] [/f] [/l] [/h] [/r] [/t] [/u]@@lb
    [/k] [/n] [/z]
```

source	Sets the source file or files to copy, which must include a drive or path.
destination	Sets the destination location for the copy.
/a	Copies only files with the archive attribute set. The command doesn't change the attribute setting.
/c	Continues to copy even if errors occur.
/d:*date*	Copies files changed on or after the specified date. The date format is MM-DD-YY. If no date is specified, copies only those files whose source time is newer than the timestamp on the destination file(s).
/e	Performs an extended copy which includes subdirectories (even if those subdirectories are empty). Same as using both /s and /e. The switch may be used to modify /t.
/f	Displays both source and destination file names while copying.
/h	Copies hidden and system files also.
/i	Creates directories and subdirectories at the destination if they don't exist.
/k	Keeps the read-only attribute for files. Normally, this is removed.
/l	Lists files that would be copied instead of actually copying them.
/m	Copies files with the archive attribute set and then turns off the archive attribute.
/n	Copies using short names. Use this option when copying from NTFS to FAT.
/p	Prompts user to confirm before creating each destination file.
/q	Quiet mode; does not display file names while copying.
/r	Overwrites read-only files at the destination.
/s	Copies directories and subdirectories under source. Option will not copy empty directories or subdirectories.
/t	Creates directory tree based on the source, but does not copy files. Does not include empty directories or subdirectories. Use /t with /e to include empty directories and subdirectories.
/u	Updates by copying only files that already exist in destination.
/v	Verifies the copy (which Windows NT already does by default).

/w   Prompts user to press a key before copying.

/z   Copies files to remote locations in restartable mode to reduce copy errors. Here, if an error occurs during file copy the copy procedure for the file is restarted.

More Info:

You can use wildcard characters when copying files. If you aren't sure what a particular xcopy command will do, use the /l option first.

Examples:

```
xcopy C:\working\data\*.txt D:\data\current\ /u
xcopy D:\*.* E:\info\ /l
xcopy C:\data D:\data /t /e
```

Appendix B

Reference for Shell Networking Commands

APPENDIX B PROVIDES A reference resource for Windows NT command shell networking commands. These commands provide the core utilities you'll use to create networking scripts and to implement enterprise-wide solutions. You'll find a quick reference for commands as well as detailed entries on command usage and syntax.

Once you find the command you want to work with, you shouldn't have any problems obtaining the information you need. Still, you'll be able to use the references more efficiently if you understand how the appendix is organized. The first command entry, titled Networking Sample, explains the structure for entries. You should read this entry before moving forward.

arp	net config workstation	net time
finger	net continue	net use
ftp	net name	net view
hostname	net pause	netstat
ipconfig	net send	nslookup
nbtstat	net session	ping
net	net share	rcp
net computer	net start	rexec
net config	net statistics	route
net config server	net stop	tracert

Networking Sample

Working with reference entries

```
Syntax 1: sample [/a|/b] [message]
Syntax 2: sample [on|off]
```

/a	A switch you can pass to the command and how it is used.
/b	Another switch you can pass to the command and how it is used.
message	The text to display in sample formatting. Syntax items in italics represent generic stand-ins for items you provide.
on|off	Turns the sample on or off.

More Info:
An optional section for additional information on the command.
Examples:
An optional section with examples using the command, such as

```
sample /a "This is a test!"
sample off
```

arp

Displays and modifies the IP-to-Physical address translation tables used by the address resolution protocol (ARP).

```
arp -a [inet_addr] [-n if_addr]
arp -d inet_addr [if_addr]
arp -s inet_addr eth_addr [if_addr]
```

eth_addr	Sets the physical MAC address in hexadecimal format, such as HH-HH-HH-HH-HH-HH where H is a hexadecimal value from 0 to F. Each network adapter card has a built-in MAC address.
if_addr	Sets the network address of the network interface adapter to modify. If you don't specify an address, the first available interface is used.
inet_addr	Sets an internet address.
-a	Displays current ARP entries.
-d	Deletes the specified entry.
-g	Same as -a.
-N if_addr	Displays the ARP entries for the network interface specified by *if_addr*.
-s	Adds the host and associates the Internet address *inet_addr* with the Physical address *eth_addr*. The Physical address is given as 6 hexadecimal bytes separated by hyphens. The entry is permanent.

More Info:

Address Resolution Protocol (ARP) cache is maintained by Windows NT workstations and servers. Use the `arp` command to view and manage this cache.

Use `ipconfig` to get a list of MAC addresses for a system's network adapter cards. If you `ping` an IP address on the LAN, the address is automatically added to the ARP cache.

Examples:

```
arp -a
arp -d 192.168.15.25
```

finger

Displays information about users and systems via a system providing appropriate server services.

```
finger [-l] [user]@host [...]
```

`-l`   Appends information in long list format (if available).

`user`   Specifies the user you want information about.

`@host`   Specifies the server name or domain.

More Info:

Once a popular way to find more information on a user, `finger` has largely fallen into disuse. Using `finger` Requires TCP/IP and access to the Internet. If you omit the user name, the host server displays information about all users on the host.

Example:

```
finger -l william@tvpress.com
```

ftp

Transfers files using FTP (File Transfer Protocol).

```
ftp [-v] [-d] [-i] [-n] [-g] [-s:filename] [-a]@@lb
    [-w:windowsize] [host]
```

`host`   Sets the host name or IP address of the remote host to
                          which you want to connect.

-a	Uses any available local interface to bind data connection. Can sometimes resolve connectivity problems.
-d	Sets debug mode, which displays all messages sent between the client and the server.
-g	Allows you to use wildcards when setting file and path names.
-i	Turns off interactive mode when you are transferring multiple file. Used to perform unattended transfers.
-n	Turns off auto-login during the initial connection.
-s:*filename*	Designates a text file containing FTP commands; the commands will automatically run after FTP starts.
-v	Turns off display of remote server responses.
-w:*buffersize*	Sets a new transfer buffer size, overriding the default buffer size of 4096 bytes.

More Info:

When you transfer files in scripts using FTP, be sure to use a transfer file which can contain any available FTP commands and to turn off interactive prompts for transferring multiple file. Be sure to set the transfer mode as either text or binary based on the type of files you are transferring. The following FTP commands are available once you start the utility:

!	Exits to the command shell.
?	Gets command help.
append	Starts a download in the current directory and appends to an existing file (if available) rather than overwriting the file.
ascii	Sets transfers mode to ASCII text. Use this with text file transfers to preserve end of line designators.
bell	Turns beep on/off for confirmation of command completion. Default is off.
binary	Sets transfer mode to binary. Use with executables and other binary file types.
bye	Exits to the command shell.
cd	Change remote working directory.
close	Closes FTP session but doesn't exit the FTP utility.
debug	Turns debug mode on/off. Default is off.

delete	Deletes a file on the system you are connected to for transfers.
dir	Lists contents of directory on the system you are connected to for transfers.
disconnect	Closes the connection to the remote system.
get	Downloads a file from the remote system.
glob	Allows you to use wildcards when naming files and directories.
hash	Turns hash mark printing on/off. If this property is set, the # character prints each time the buffer is transferred, provided a visual cue for progress.
lcd	Changes the working directory on the local system, such as lcd c:\winnt\system32.
literal	Sends arbitrary FTP command.
ls	Lists contents of remote directory. Because the command is designed after the Unix ls, all normal ls flags are available, such as ls –l or ls –lsa.
mdelete	Deletes multiple files on the remote system.
mdir	Lists contents of multiple remote directories.
mget	Downloads multiple files from the remote system.
mkdir	Creates a directory on the remote system.
mls	Lists contents of multiple remote directories.
mput	Sends multiple files to the remote system.
open	Opens a connection to a remote system specified following the command, such as open idg.com.
prompt	Turns prompt mode on/off for mget, mput, and mdelete. Default mode is off.
put	Sends a file to the remote system.
pwd	Prints working directory on remote machine.
quit	Quits FTP sessions and exits to the command shell.
quote	Sends arbitrary FTP command.
recv	Downloads a file from the remote system.
remotehelp	Gets help from remote server.
rename	Renames a file on the remote system.

`rmdir`	Removes a directory on the remote system.
`send`	Sends a file to the remote system.
`trace`	Traces the IP route of the file transfer.
`type`	Sets the transfer type and toggles between ASCII and binary.
`user`	Starts logon procedure or to change users while connected to a remote host.
`verbose`	Turns verbose mode on/off. Default is off.

Example:

```
ftp -i -g -s:tranf.txt idg.com
ftp -i idg.com
```

hostname

Displays the hostname of the computer.

```
hostname
```

More Info:
Command is only available if TCP/IP is installed.
Example:

```
hostname
```

ipconfig

Displays TCP/IP configuration values and allows you to interact with DHCP.

```
ipconfig [/all | /release [adapter] | /renew [adapter]]
```

`/all`	Displays full configuration information.
`/release`	Releases the IP address for the specified adapter.
`/renew`	Renews the IP address for the specified adapter.

More Info:
The `/release` and `/renew` switches are useful when your network uses DHCP.
`Renew` forces the computer to request new address information from the DHCP

server. Release forces the computer to release the dynamic IP address assigned by the DHCP server.

Examples:

```
ipconfig /renew
ipconfig /release
```

nbtstat

Displays status of NetBIOS over TCP/IP.

```
nbtstat [-a RemoteName] [-A IP_address] [-c] [-n]@@lb
    [-r] [-R] [-s] [-S] [interval] ]
```

interval	Redisplays selected statistics, pausing interval seconds between each display. Press Ctrl+C to stop redisplaying statistics.
-A IP_address	Displays a remote computer's statistics by IP address
-a RemoteName	Displays a remote computer's statistics by NetBIOS name.
-c	Displays the local computer's name cache including IP addresses.
-n	Displays local NetBIOS names.
-R	Reloads LMHOSTS after deleting the names from the NetBIOS name cache.
-r	Displays statistics for names resolved by broadcast and via WINS.
-S	Displays all client and server sessions by IP addresses.
-s	Displays all client and server sessions, converting destination IP addresses to host names via the local HOSTS file.

More Info:
Useful for obtaining local and remote system NetBIOS information.
Examples:

```
nbtstat -a mars1
```

```
nbtstat -A 192.152.16.8
nbtstat -c
```

net

Accesses networking utilities

```
net [accounts|computer|config|continue|file|group|help|@@1b
    helpmsg|localgroup|name|pause|print|send|session|@@1b
    share|start|statistics|stop|time|use|user|view]
```

More Info:
Many networking commands begin with net. Look for specific descriptions in this appendix.

net accounts

Manages user account and password policies:

```
net accounts [/forcelogoff:{minutes | no}] [/minpwlen:length]@@1b
    [/maxpwage:{days | unlimited}] [/minpwage:days]@@1b
    [/uniquepw:number] [/domain]
net accounts [/sync]
```

/domain	Specifies that the operation should be performed on the primary domain controller of the current domain. Otherwise, the operation is performed on the local computer. (Applies only to Windows NT workstations that are members of an NT domain. By default, Windows NT servers perform operations on the primary domain controller.)
/forcelogoff:{minutes	no}	Sets the time in minutes before a user is forced to log off when the account expires or valid logon hours expire. Users receive a warning prior to being logged off. By default, the option is set to no, which prevents forced logoff.

`/maxpwage:{days	unlimited}`	Sets the number of days that a password is valid. The default is 90 days and the range is 1-49,710 days.
`/minpwage:days`	Sets the minimum number of days before a user can change a password. The default is 0, which sets no minimum time. The range is 0-49710.
`/minpwlen:length`	Sets the minimum number of characters for a password. The default is 6 characters and the range is 0-14.
`/sync`	Used on a primary domain controller to synchronize all backup domain controllers with the primary. On backup, the option only synchronizes that backup with the primary.
`/uniquepw:number`	Specifies the number of unique passwords a user must use before being able to reuse a password. The default is 5 and the range is 0-24.

More Info:

Use `net accounts` to manage user and password policies. To manage the accounts themselves, use `net user`, `net group`, or `net localgroup`. If you enter `net accounts` by itself and press Enter, you get a summary of current user and password policies.

Examples:

```
net accounts /domain /minpwlen:8 /maxpwage:45 /minpwage:10
net accounts /sync
```

net computer

Adds or removes computers from the network.

```
net computer \\computername {/add | /del}
```

`\\computername`	Sets the computer to add or delete from the domain.
`/add`	Adds the specified computer to the domain.
`/del`	Removes the specified computer from the domain.

More Info:

Net computer adds or removes computers from a domain. The command is available only on Windows NT servers and is only applicable to the default domain.

Examples:

```
net computer \\pluto8 /del
net computer \\saturn /add
```

net config

Displays or modifies configuration information for the workstation or server service.

```
net config [[server | workstation] [options]]
```

server	Accesses the server service.
workstation	Access the workstation services.
[options]	Options to use in configuring the service.

More Info:

See net config server and net config workstation for details.

net config server

Displays or modifies configuration information for the server service.

```
net config server [/autodisconnect:time] [/srvcomment:"text"]@@1b
    [/hidden:{yes | no}]
```

/autodisconnect:time	Sets the number of minutes a user's session can be inactive before it is disconnected. The default is 15 minutes. The range is –1 to 65535 minutes. Use –1 to have the service never disconnect user sessions.
/srvcomment:"text"	Adds a comment for the server that is displayed in browse lists such as in Server Manager or net view. Enclose the comments in quotation marks and use up to 48 characters.

/hidden:{yes | no}   Allows you to prevent the server from being
                                displayed in browser lists. The default is no.
                                Although a server is hidden from view, it is still
                                accessible.

More Info:
Enter **net config server** on a line by itself to see the current configuration of the
server service.
Examples:

```
net config server
net config server /autodisconnect:10 /hidden:yes
```

net config workstation

Displays or modifies configuration information for the workstation service.

```
net config workstation [/charcount:bytes]@@1b
    [/chartime:msec]@@1b
    [/charwait:sec]
```

/charcount:bytes   Sets the number of bytes Windows NT collects before
                                sending the data to a communication device. The default
                                is 16 bytes and the range is 0-65535 bytes. If
                                /chartime:msec is also set, Windows NT acts on
                                whichever condition is satisfied first.

/chartime:msec   Sets the amount of time in milliseconds that Windows
                                NT collects data before sending the data to a
                                communication device. The default is 250 milliseconds
                                and the range is 0-65535000 milliseconds. If
                                /charcount:bytes is also set, Windows NT acts on
                                whichever condition is satisfied first.

/charwait:sec   Sets the number of seconds that Windows NT waits for a
                                communication device to become available. The default
                                is 3600 seconds and the range is 0-65535 seconds.

More Info:
Enter **net config workstation** on a line by itself to see the current configuration
of the Workstation service.

Examples:

```
net config workstation
net config workstation /charcount:32
```

net continue

Resumes a paused service.

```
net continue service
```

service   Specifies the service to resume.

More Info:

Use net continue to resume a paused service. Services that can be paused and resumed include File Server For Macintosh, Ftp Server, Lpdsvc, Net Logon, Network DDE, Network DDE DSDM, NT LM Security Support Provider, Remoteboot, Remote Access, Server, Schedule, Server, Simple TCP/IP Services, and Workstation.

Example:

```
net continue "file server for macintosh"
```

net file

Manages open files on a server.

```
net file [id [/close]]
```

id   The open file's identification number.

/close   Closes an open file and releases locked records.

More Info:

Enter **net file** by itself to display a complete listing of open files, which includes the name of the user who has the file open and locks (if applicable).

Examples:

```
net file
net file 0001 /close
```

net group

Manages global groups.

```
net group [groupname [/comment:"text"]] [/domain]
net group groupname {/add [/comment:"text"] | /delete}@@lb
   [/domain]
net group groupname username [...] {/add | /delete} [/domain]
```

groupname	Sets the name of the global group to work with. When you specify only the group name, to view a list of users in the global group.
username[...]	Lists one or more usernames to add to or remove from a global group. Use spaces to separate multiple usernames.
/add	Creates a global group, or adds a username to an existing global group.
/comment:"*text*"	Adds an optional description for the global group. The comment can have up to 48 characters and must be enclosed in quotation marks.
/delete	Removes a global group, or removes a username from a global group.
/domain	Specifies that the operation should be performed on the primary domain controller of the current domain. Otherwise, the operation is performed on the local computer. (Applies only to Windows NT workstations that are members of an NT domain. By default, Windows NT servers perform operations on the primary domain controller.)

More Info:

Enter **net group** by itself to see a list of all global groups. Be sure to use quotation marks in group or user names that have spaces.

Examples:

```
net group "domain admins"
net group "domain admins" wrstanek /add
```

net helpmsg

Displays information about Windows NT network messages.

```
net helpmsg message#
```

message#   The 4-digit number of the Windows NT message you need help
                    with.

   Example:

```
net helpmsg 3871
```

net localgroup

Manages local groups.

```
net localgroup [groupname [/comment:"text"]] [/domain]
net localgroup groupname {/add [/comment:"text"] | /delete}@@1b
    [/domain]
net localgroup groupname username [...] {/add | /delete} [/domain]
```

groupname	Sets the name of the local group to work with. When you specify only the group name, to view a list of users in the local group.
username[...]	Lists one or more usernames to add to or remove from a local group. Use spaces to separate multiple usernames.
/add	Creates a local group, or adds a username to an existing local group.
/comment:"*text*"	Adds an optional description for the local group. The comment can have up to 48 characters and must be enclosed in quotation marks.
/delete	Removes a local group, or removes a username from a local group.
/domain	Specifies that the operation should be performed on the primary domain controller of the current domain. Otherwise, the operation is performed on the local computer. (Applies only to Windows NT workstations that are members of an NT domain. By default, Windows NT servers perform operations on the primary domain controller.)

More Info:

Use `net localgroup` by itself to see a list of all local groups. Be sure to use quotation marks in group or user names that have spaces.

Examples:

```
net localgroup "account operators"
net localgroup "account operators" wrstanek /add
```

net name

Controls the list of recipients for messenger service messages.

```
net name [name [/add | /delete]]
```

name	The message name designated to receive messages. You can use up to 15 characters.
/add	Adds a messaging name alias to a computer. Typing **net name** *name* also works.
/delete	Removes a messaging name from a computer.

More Info:

Use this command to set names of users who should receive messages for the computer. Enter **net name** by itself to display the current list of names. You cannot delete the current computer's name or the currently logged on user from the list. These name entries are set to receive messages by default. See `net send` for details on sending messages.

Examples:

```
net name wrstanek
net name wrstanek /delete
```

net pause

Suspends a service and puts it on hold.

```
net pause service
```

service	The service to put on hold.

More Info:

When you use `net pause` to pause a service, you can use `net continue` to resume it. Services that can be paused and resumed include File Server For Macintosh, Ftp

Server, Lpdsvc, Net Logon, Network DDE, Network DDE DSDM, NT LM Security
Support Provider, Remoteboot, Remote Access, Server, Schedule, Server, Simple
TCP/IP Services, and Workstation.

Example:

```
net pause "remote access"
```

net print

Displays print jobs and shared queues.

```
net print \\computername\sharename
net print [\computername] job# [/hold | /release | /delete]
```

`\\computername`	The name of the computer sharing the printer queue.
`sharename`	The name of the shared printer queue.
`job#`	The number assigned to the print job in the print queue.
`/delete`	Removes a job from a queue.
`/hold`	Pauses the print job.
`/release`	Releases a print job that is held.

More Info:

Use `net print` to manage shared printer queues and display queue status. To
manage the shared printers themselves, use `net share`.

Examples:

```
net print \\zeta\eng1
net print 0043 /delete
```

net send

Sends a messenger service message.

```
net send {name | * | /domain[:name] | /users} message
```

name	The username, computer name, or messaging name to send a message to. If a name has spaces, enclose it in quotation marks.

*	Sends the message to all the names in your workgroup or domain.
message	The message to send. Quotation marks aren't needed.
/domain[:*name*]	Sends the message to all the names in the current domain. Use name to set an alternative domain or workgroup name.
/users	Sends the message to all users connected to the server.

More Info:
Use net send to send messages to other users, computers, or messaging names on the network. The Messenger service must be running on the user's computer to receive messages. If you send a message to a specific user, the user must be logged on and running the Messenger service to receive the message.

Examples:

```
net send wrstanek "What are you working on?"
net send /domain "Please log off Opus. System maintenance."
```

net session

Manages connections to a server.

```
net session [\\computername] [/delete]
```

computername	The name of the Windows NT server you want to examine.
/delete	Disconnects the local computer and the designated workstation or server, closing all open files for the session. If you don't specify a computer name, all sessions are ended.

More Info:
Net session lists or disconnects sessions between the local computer and other computers on the network. Enter net session to examine the local computers sessions. Enter net session *computername* to examine sessions on another computer. The command only works on servers.

Examples:

```
net session \\pluto
net session \\jupiter /delete
```

net share

Manages shared printers and directories.

```
net share sharename
net share sharename=drive:path [/users:number | /unlimited]@@lb
    [/remark:"text"]
net share sharename [/users:number | /unlimited]@@lb
    [/remark:"text"]
net share {sharename | devicename | drive:path} /delete
```

devicename	Sets one or more printers shared by *sharename*. You can use LPT1: through LPT9:.
drive:path	Sets the complete path of the directory to be shared.
sharename	Sets the network name of the shared resource.
/delete	Stops sharing the specified resource.
/remark:"text"	Adds an optional comment about the shared resource. Quotation marks are mandatory.
/unlimited	Specifies that an unlimited number of users can simultaneously access the shared resource
/users:number	Sets the maximum number of users who can simultaneously access the shared resource.

More Info:

Enter **net share** with a sharename only to display information about the specified share.

Examples:

```
net share netdata="r:\network\data\" /unlimited
net share netdata /delete
```

net start

Starts network services or lists network services that are running.

```
net start [service]
```

service	The service to start. Enclose service names with spaces in quotation marks.

More Info:

Enter **net start** by itself to list running services. Services you can start on workstations and servers include but are not limited to Alerter, Client Service For Netware, Clipbook Server, Computer Browser, DHCP Client, Directory Replicator, Eventlog, FTP Server, LPDSVC, Messenger, Net Logon, Network DDE, Network DDE DSDM, Network Monitoring Agent, NT LM Security Support Provider, Remote Access Connection Manager, Remote Access ISNSAP Service, Remote Access Server, Remote Procedure Call (RPC) Locator, Remote Procedure Call (RPC) Service, Schedule, Server, Simple TCP/IP Services, SNMP, Spooler, TCPIP NetBIOS Helper, Ups, and Workstation.

These additional services are available only on Windows NT servers: File Server For Macintosh, Gateway Service For Netware, Microsoft DHCP Server, Print Server For Macintosh, Remoteboot, and Windows Internet Name Service.

Net start can also start network services not provided with the Windows NT operating system.

Examples:

```
net start "Microsoft DHCP Server"
net start "Windows Internet Name Service"
```

net statistics

Displays workstation and server statistics.

```
net statistics [workstation | server]
```

server   Displays Server service statistics.

workstation   Displays Workstation service statistics.

More Info:

Enter **net statistics** by itself to list the services for which statistics are currently available.

Examples:

```
net statistics workstation
net statistics server
```

net stop

Stops network services.

```
net stop service
```

service   The service to stop. Enclose service names with spaces in quotation marks.

More Info:

Stopping a service cancels any network connections the services are running. You must have administrator privileges to stop services. The EventLog service cannot be stopped.

Services you can stop on workstations and servers include but are not limited to Alerter, Client Service For Netware, Clipbook Server, Computer Browser, DHCP Client, Directory Replicator, FTP Server, LPDSVC, Messenger, Net Logon, Network DDE, Network DDE DSDM, Network Monitoring Agent, NT LM Security Support Provider, Remote Access Connection Manager, Remote Access ISNSAP Service, Remote Access Server, Remote Procedure Call (RPC) Locator, Remote Procedure Call (RPC) Service, Schedule, Server, Simple TCP/IP Services, SNMP, Spooler, TCPIP NetBIOS Helper, Ups, and Workstation.

These additional services are available only on Windows NT servers: File Server For Macintosh, Gateway Service For Netware, Microsoft DHCP Server, Print Server For Macintosh, Remoteboot, and Windows Internet Name Service.

Net stop can also start network services not provided with Windows NT.

Examples:

```
net stop "Microsoft DHCP Server"
net stop "Windows Internet Name Service"
```

net time

Displays time and synchronizes time with remote computers.

```
net time [\\computername | /domain[:domainname]] [/set]
```

\\computername   The name of a server you want to check for time.

/domain[:domainname] Sets the domain (rather than a computer) with which to synchronize time.

/set   Synchronizes the computer's time with the time on the specified server or domain.

More Info:

Enter **net time** by itself to display the current date and time on the network's time server (which is normally the primary domain controller).

Examples:

```
net time \\pluto /set
net time /domain:infotech /set
```

net use

Manages remote connections.

```
net use [devicename | *] [\\computername\sharename[\volume]@@lb
    [password | *]] [/user:[domainname\]username]@@lb
    [[/delete] | [/persistent:{yes | no}]]
net use [devicename | *] [password | *]] [/home]
net use [/persistent:{yes | no}]
```

*	Prompts for a required password.
\\computername	Specifies the UNC name of the server to connect to. If the computer name contains blank characters, enclose the double backslash (\\) and the computer name, the share in quotation marks, such as "\\PLUTO\NETDATA"
devicename	Assigns a device to connect to or disconnect from. A device name is either a disk drive (lettered D: through Z:) or a printer (LPT1: through LPT9:). Type an asterisk instead of a specific device name to assign the next available device name.
domainname	Sets a domain. Otherwise, the current domain is used.
password	The password needed to access the shared resource.
username	The username with which to log on.
/delete	Disconnects the specified connection.
/home	Connects users to their home directory.
/persistent	Determines whether the connection is persistent. The default is the last setting used.
\sharename	The network name of the shared resource.
/user	Used to set the user name for the connection (if it is different than the currently logged-in user's name).

\volume	Sets a NetWare volume on the server. Client Services for Netware or Gateway Service for Netware must be running.
yes	Makes connections persistent, which saves connections as they are made and restores them at next logon.
no	Does not make a connection persistent.

More Info:
Enter **net use** by itself to display a list of network connections.
Examples:

```
net use \\pluto\netdata * /persistent
net use \\pluto\netdata /delete
```

net user

Manages user accounts.

```
net user [username [password | *] [options]] [/domain]
net user username {password | *} /add [options] [/domain]
net user username [/delete] [/domain]
```

*	Prompts for the password.
password	Assigns or changes a password for a user account.
username	Sets the name of the user account to create, view, or modify.
/add	Adds a user account.
/delete	Removes a user account.
/domain	Specifies that the operation should be performed on the primary domain controller of the current domain. Otherwise, the operation is performed on the local computer. (Applies only to Windows NT workstations that are members of an NT domain. By default, Windows NT servers perform operations on the primary domain controller.)

Options:

/active:{yes | no}	Enables or disables a user account. If the account is not active, the user cannot log on. The default is yes.
/comment:"text"	Sets a description of up to 48 characters for the account. Enclose the text in quotation marks.

/countrycode:*nnn*	Sets the operating system country code for the user's help and error messages. A value of 0 is the default.
/expires:{*date* | never}	Determines whether the user's account expires. The default is never. Expiration dates can be in mm/dd/yy or dd/mm/yy, depending on the country code.
/fullname:"*name*"	Sets the user's full name. Enclose the name in quotation marks.
/homedir:*pathname*	Sets the path of the user's home directory. The path must exist before you can use it.
/passwordchg:{yes | no}	Determines whether users can change their own password. The default is YES.
/passwordreq:{yes | no}	Determines whether a user account must have a password. The default is YES.
/profilepath[:*path*]	Sets a path for the user's logon profile.
/scriptpath:*pathname*	Sets the location of the user's logon script.
/times:{*times* | all}	Specifies the times and days a user is allowed to logon. Times are expressed as day[-day][,day[-day]],time[-time][,time [-time]] and limited to 1-hour increments. Days can be spelled out or abbreviated (M, T, W, Th, F, Sa, Su). Hours can be 12- or 24-hour notation. For 12-hour notation, use AM or PM. The value all means a user can always log on. A null value (blank) means a user can never log on. Separate day and time entries with commas and units of time with semicolons.
/usercomment:"*text*"	Allows a user comment to be added or changed.
/workstations: {*computername*[,...] | *}	Lists as many as eight workstations from which a user can log on to the network. If /workstations has no list or if the list is *, the user can log on from any computer.

More Info:

Enter **net user** by itself to list the user accounts for the server. The command works only on servers.

When you want to create or modify domain accounts, be sure to enter **/domain**.

Examples:

```
net user wrstanek happydayz /ADD
net user wrstanek /DELETE
```

net view

Displays available network resources.

```
net view [\\computername | /domain[:domainname]]
net view /network:nw [\\computername]
```

\\computername	Specifies the computer whose shared resources you want to view.
/domain:domainname	Sets the domain for which you want to view computers that have resources available. If the domain name is omitted, all domains on the network are listed.
/network:nw	Displays all the servers on a NetWare network. If a computer name is specified, only the resources available on that computer are displayed.

More Info:
Enter **net view** without options to display a list of computers in the current domain or network.
Examples:

```
net view \\delta
net view /domain:engineering
```

netstat

Displays status of network connections as well as protocol statistics.

```
netstat [-a] [-e] [-n] [-s] [-p protocol] [-r] [interval]
```

interval	Redisplays selected statistics, pausing between each display. Press CTRL+C to stop redisplaying statistics. If this option is omitted, information is only displayed once.
-a	Displays connections and listening ports.

-e	Displays Ethernet statistics. This may be combined with –s to obtain additional details.
-n	Displays IP addresses and port numbers rather than computer names.
-p *protocol*	Shows connections for the specified protocol (TCP or UDP). If the –s option is used with –p, you can view protocol information for TCP, UDP, ICMP, or IP.
-r	Displays the contents of the routing table.
-s	Displays per-protocol statistics. By default, statistics are shown for TCP, UDP, ICMP, and IP. Use with –p to examine a specific protocol.

More Info:

Unlike most other commands, most options provide completely different types of information. TCP/IP networking must be installed.

Examples:

```
netstat -a
netstat -s -p TCP
```

nslookup

Shows the status of Domain Name System (DNS) for servers and workstations with DNS resolution.

```
nslookup [-option] [computer | server]
```

-option An option to perform a query with; in the form -command=value or -command. The most commonly used command is querytype, which set the type of record you want to examine. Record types include A, CNAME, MX, NS, PTR, and SOA.

computer	The host name or IP address you want to look up in DNS.
server	The DNS server to use for the lookup. If you don't specify a server, the default name server is used.

More Info:

To use this command, TCP/IP networking must be configured. DNS lookup can be performed interactively or non-interactively. DNS lookups are most useful if you need to look up the IP address of a known host or examine DNS entries. If you want to see if a particular Internet host is available, PING is a better command to use.

Examples:

```
nslookup www.tvpress.com
nslookup -querytype=mx tvpress.com
```

ping

Sends data to a computer to determine if a network connection can be established.

```
ping [-t] [-a] [-n count] [-l size] [-f] [-i TTL] [-v TOS]@@lb
    [-r count] [-s count] [[-j host-list] | [-k host-list]]@@lb
    [-w timeout] destination-list
```

destination-list	A list of computers to ping; specified by hostname or IP address. If NetBIOS resolution is enabled for the computer/domain, you can also use NetBIOS names (the computer name is an NT domain).
-a	Resolve IP addresses to hostnames when pinging.
-f	Specifies that the ping packet shouldn't be fragmented when it goes through gateways.
-i *TTL*	Sets Time To Live value.
-j *host-list*	Sets the packet route using the host list. The route doesn't have to include all potential gateways. Use spaces to separate host names.
-k *host-list*	Sets a strict packet route using the host list. The route must be inclusive of all gateways. Use spaces to separate host names.
-l *size*	The number of bytes to send in the ping. The default is 64 and the maximum is 8192.
-n *count*	Number of times to ping the specified computer. The default is 4.
-r *count*	Displays the route taken by the ping packets. Count determines the number of hops to count from 1 to 9.
-s *count*	The timestamp for the number of hops set by count.
-t	Ping repeatedly until interrupted.
-v *TOS*	Sets the Type Of Service.
-w *timeout*	A timeout set in milliseconds.

More Info:

TCP/IP networking must be configured. Ping is a good command to use before trying to work with an Internet resource. If the ping returns bad IP address or host unreachable, you know the computer you want to work with isn't available.

Examples:

```
ping -t www.idg.com
ping -n 50 www.idg.com
```

rcp

Copy files from Windows NT to a Unix system running RCP services.

```
rcp [-a | -b] [-h] [-r] [host][.user:]source [host][.user:]@@1b
    path\destination
rcp [-a | -b] [-h] [-r] source1 source2 ... sourceN destination
```

`host.user:source`	Sets the source of the copy. If host is specified as an IP address, you must specify the user. In Windows NT, directory names are separated with backslashes ("\").
`host.user:destination`	Sets the destination path relative to the logon directory on the remote host. In Unix, directory names are separated with forward slashes ("/").
`-a`	Sets ASCII transfer mode. In this mode, the normal Windows NT end of line characters are converted to Unix end of line characters. This is the default transfer mode.
`-b`	Sets binary file transfer mode.
`-h`	Transfers hidden files.
`-r`	Sets recursive copy mode. The contents of all subdirectories at the source are copied to the destination. Destination must be a directory if you use this option.

More Info:

Use `rcp` to copy files to Unix systems. The Unix system must be running the appropriate services.

Examples:

```
rcp -r pluto.wrstanek:c:\data\ armites.wrstane:/usr/home/wrs/
rcp -b c:\data\*.* armites:/usr/home/wrs/data/
```

rexec

Executes commands on remote hosts running the REXEC service.

```
rexec host [-l username] [-n] command
```

`command`	Sets the command to run on the remote host.
`host`	The remote host on which to run the command.
`-l username`	The user name on the remote host. If used, you'll be prompted for a password.
`-n`	Redirects the output of the command to NULL.

More Info:

Requires TCP/IP networking and the remote host must be running the REXEC service. The username is authenticated before the command is executed.

Example:

```
rexec delta -lwrstane -n batchrun.bat
```

route

Manages network routing tables

```
route [-f] [command [destination] [mask netmask] [gateway]@@lb
    [metric costmetric]]
```

`-f`	Clears the routing tables of gateway entries. This option is executed before running any of the available route commands.
`-p`	When used with the ADD command, makes the route persistent so it continues to exist when the system is restarted. When used with the PRINT command, prints a list of persistent routes.

command	Allows you to specify one of these route commands:

print	Prints a route
add	Adds a route
delete	Deletes a route
change	Modifies a route

destination	Sets the route destination host.
mask *netmask*	A subnet mask to associate with the route entry. The default network mask is 255.255.255.255.
gateway	The gateway for the route.
metric *costmetric*	Sets a numeric cost metric for the route. Valid values are from 1 to 9999.

More Info:

If you use a host name for the destination rather than an IP address, route looks in the NETWORKS file to resolve the destination to an IP address. If you use a host name for a gateway, route looks in the HOSTS file to resolve the host to an IP address. If the command is print or delete, you can use wildcards for the destination and gateway.

The cost metric is useful in determining which route the local computer attempts to use first. Routes with a metric of 1 are always attempted before routes with higher cost metrics.

Examples:

```
route -p add mail.idg.com 255.255.255.0 214.15.8.2 1
route delete mail.idg.com 214.*
```

tracert

Displays the path between the local computer and a remote computer.

```
tracert [-d] [-h maximum_hops] [-j host-list]@@lb
    [-w timeout] target_name
```

target_name	The remote computer to locate.
-d	Does not convert IP addresses for hops.
-h *maximum_hops*	The maximum number of hops between the local computer and the target.

-j *host-list*	Sets the trace route using the host list. The route doesn't have to include all potential gateways. Use spaces to separate host names.
-w *timeout*	Waits the specified number of milliseconds before timing out.

More Info:

Tracing the route between two computers is extremely helpful in troubleshooting network routing problems.

Examples:

```
tracert tvpress.com
tracert -d tvpress.com
```

Index

Special Characters

@ command, shell scripts, 23, 25–26

<> (angle brackets), VBScript inequality, 216

! (exclamation), JScript logical Not, 240

!= (exclamation equal), JScript inequality, 238

: (colon), shell script labels, 112

; (semicolon), shell script path names, 34

,, (commas), VBScript null parameters, 229

' (single quotes), VBScript comments, 209

^ (caret)
    JScript bitwise Or, 242
    shell script escape character, 51–52
    shell script logical exclusive OR, 96
    VBScript exponents, 215

~ (tilde), JScript bitwise Not, 242

() (parentheses)
    in command prompt, 27
    shell script grouping commands, 70, 72–74
    simulating in shell scripts, 98–99

$ (dollar), dollar sign in command prompt, 28

$_ (dollar underscore), line feed in command prompt, 28

$+ (dollar plus), PUSHD stack directories in command prompt, 28

$* (dollar asterisk), shell script macro arguments, 58

$a (dollar a), ampersand in command prompt, 27

$b (dollar b), pipe character in command prompt, 27

$c (dollar c), parentheses in command prompt, 27

$d (dollar d), date in command prompt, 27

$f (dollar f), parentheses in command prompt, 27

$g (dollar g), greater than in command prompt, 27

$h (dollar h), backspace in command prompt, 27

$l (dollar l), less than in command prompt, 28

$m (dollar m), UNC name in command prompt, 28

$n (dollar n), working drive in command prompt, 28

A

continued

continued

Notes

Notes

Notes

Notes

Notes

my2cents.idgbooks.com

Register This Book — And Win!

Visit **http://my2cents.idgbooks.com** to register this book and we'll automatically enter you in our fantastic monthly prize giveaway. It's also your opportunity to give us feedback: let us know what you thought of this book and how you would like to see other topics covered.

Discover IDG Books Online!

The IDG Books Online Web site is your online resource for tackling technology — at home and at the office. Frequently updated, the IDG Books Online Web site features exclusive software, insider information, online books, and live events!

10 Productive & Career-Enhancing Things You Can Do at www.idgbooks.com

- Nab source code for your own programming projects.

- Download software.

- Read Web exclusives: special articles and book excerpts by IDG Books Worldwide authors.

- Take advantage of resources to help you advance your career as a Novell or Microsoft professional.

- Buy IDG Books Worldwide titles or find a convenient bookstore that carries them.

- Register your book and win a prize.

- Chat live online with authors.

- Sign up for regular e-mail updates about our latest books.

- Suggest a book you'd like to read or write.

- Give us your 2¢ about our books and about our Web site.

You say you're not on the Web yet? It's easy to get started with IDG Books' *Discover the Internet,* available at local retailers everywhere.